A LAND FIT FOR CRIMINALS

A LAND FIT FOR CRIMINALS

*An Insider's View of Crime, Punishment
and Justice in England and Wales*

David Fraser

THE CHOIR PRESS

First published in the United Kingdom in 2006 by
The Book Guild Ltd

This edition published by
The Choir Press 2022

ISBN 978-1-78963-312-2

To Martyn Samuel, a lifelong friend

'We do not need psychologists to tell us the simple truth that if you reward bad behaviour you will get more of it... We should not be surprised that we are now engulfed in crime. The offenders have taken their cue from us.'

Contents

Foreword

Social scientists, civil servants and Ministers of the Crown have conspired for decades to deceive the public about the state of law and order. They have consistently underestimated the level and severity of crime. They have insisted on the efficacy of methods of crime prevention and control which patently do not work. They have stubbornly persisted with utopian theories of crime, criminality and punishment which fail entirely to take account of human nature and social reality. They have routinely belittled the everyday concerns about crime of the man and woman in the street. They have condescendingly denigrated the genuine understanding of criminality provided by commonsensical experience. They have rubbished the real expertise about law and order – based on daily involvement with the destructive effects of crime – of police officers, magistrates, probation officers and local councillors. Modern criminology constitutes a tissue of pseudo-liberal prejudice and counter-productive phoney knowledge. Contemporary penal policy comprises a vast body of misconceived and nonsensical doctrine which has the effect of exculpating criminals, punishing victims and escalating social collapse.

David Fraser's book *A Land Fit for Criminals* provides a welcome and overdue antidote. Based on many years of experience in the Probation Service, on careful analysis of statistics and documentation, and on thoughtful, intelligent appraisal of all the relevant facts, it reveals the appalling state of law and order in modern Britain. More than this, it proposes a way forward for improving the situation and getting crime back under control.

I strongly commend *A Land Fit for Criminals*: to all those who work in the criminal justice system; to students – currently force-fed with lies and propaganda about crime; to journalists – commonly deceived by highly spun statistics; to our elected representatives at local and parliamentary level – who should all have to hand this truthful and realistic account of the state of lawlessness and disorder on our streets; and not least to the general reader – who will find here a rational vindication of his or her concerns and anxieties, and support for popular determination to punish and control criminals effectively.

In a recent letter to the press (*London Evening Standard*, 29 July 2004), PC Norman Brennan of the Victims of Crime Trust wrote as follows: 'I believe the situation on law and order is so bad that, to borrow a medical term, it is on a life-support machine. In my personal and professional opinion, the criminal justice system is in crisis.' *A Land Fit for Criminals* makes a powerful contribution to addressing this crisis. I hope that it is widely read, that the validity of its analysis is acknowledged and that the policy proposals it suggests are put into effect urgently.

We must not wait for action until the domestic equivalent of the 9/11 Attacks – generalised community decay, widespread riot and everyday resort to vigilante justice – is upon us. Before this happens – and it may be quite soon, as suddenly and unpredictably as 9/11 – we must start to trust and support the police, clean up the courts and strengthen them, and catch criminals and punish them hard.

Professor David Marsland, MA, Ph.D, FRSH
September 2004

Preface

Every year in the UK at least 30 million people are victimised by criminals allowed to roam free in the community. Yet, on 5 December 2004, despite the often harmful consequences for the individuals and families involved, the government's feeble response to this national scandal was to propose improved conditions in court for victims and witnesses to 'reduce their stress'. This is the equivalent of providing slightly more comfortable seats in hospital waiting rooms for patients made ill in the first place by the quack medicines still being prescribed for them. This book is therefore written for the thousands of people who are involved with, or work in, the criminal justice system, be they ministers of state, government advisors, MPs, administrators or policy makers in the civil service, senior and front-line personnel in police, probation, and prison departments, students, youth justice workers, judges, magistrates, clerks and others associated with the courts, as well as all drug and rehabilitation workers who work with offenders. It is an appeal to them to become aware of the immense harm caused to the public by current criminal justice policies. It is also aimed at the general public, to help them understand how and why our justice system disrupts and disadvantages them rather than the criminals.

It therefore presents an analysis of crime, punishment and justice from the point of view of the crime-beleaguered public, rather than from the closed world inhabited by many criminologists, who frequently view crime from the offender's perspective.

It is not, therefore, a calm, dispassionate review of this subject – the sort that academic criminologists write for other academics to read. It is, as I have indicated, a passionate cry for the public to be aware of the gross deceptions that are worked on them by government and criminal-justice propaganda, which presents an entirely false analysis of the causes and cures for crime. I believe this book will galvanise the interests of wide sections of the community because it identifies the justice system's preoccupation with the offender, the pseudo social and psychological explanations for his behaviour, and the failed sentencing policies it has inflicted upon a vulnerable public. No criticisms are intended against individual front-line workers in the justice system – for example police, probation, prison and other rehabilitation staff in various settings. They have no choice but to follow the policies set for them by their organisations, whether they agree with them or not.

Vast numbers of individuals and families have been victimised by offenders who should have been locked up for their previous offence. As a result, it has become increasingly apparent to the public that the government's reliance on 'community efforts' and 'agency partnerships to tackle the crime problem' are empty words that offer them no protection. There are increasing signs that the public are hungry for a more realistic analysis of crime and its causes, and want an approach to law and order which, whilst not inhumane, puts their safety first and considerations for the offender second. This book puts forward a powerful argument for these changes and fills a gap in criminal justice literature which has long been ignored. It is therefore highly controversial and contradicts much of the current thinking about crime and how to deal with it. It is highly critical of current sentencing policies and provides unassailable evidence that they are driven by ideology and cost saving and are no longer concerned with the protection of the public. This book lays down a challenge to every professional in the criminal justice system who reads it and who is involved in creating, promoting or otherwise supporting current sentencing policies, to square their conscience against what they find here. Those that reject the arguments in these pages are free to publish a rejoinder which explains why present practices put offenders centre stage and not the public.

I frequently listen to or read the views of MPs and others via the radio, TV and press, as they express their opinions about crime, its causes, and how criminals should be sentenced. Through such broadcasts, the public is constantly told that persistent offenders are best dealt with in the community and that prisons do not work. Yet the hard evidence concerning these issues contradicts these assertions. So why are our sentencing practices based on these falsehoods?

Why are they constantly argued for in public debates? Would the same contributors mislead the public by arguing that bridges should be built with wood and Plasticine? Of course not. Yet for reasons which I explore in this book the public is constantly misled about crime, its causes and what types of sentence protect them from crime and those that do not.

Accordingly this book is not a rant based on opinion, but argued from evidence gathered over thirty-four years of working in the Probation Service, prisons and the National Criminal Intelligence Service and on twenty years of research. It draws on over 1,500 references and charts the disintegration of our criminal justice system since the 1950s, the collapse in local law and order, and the harmful consequences this has had for the public.

What I discovered during my work in the Probation Service and in the National Criminal Intelligence Service is that placing persistent offenders back in the community as an alternative to prison does not work, either as a means of reform or of protecting the community. Twenty years' research of government archives and other sources has confirmed this and has demonstrated beyond argument that our criminal justice system fails to protect the public from crime. I also discovered that those in government and others in the field of criminal justice go out of their way to cover up this failure with untruths, misleading propaganda, and false claims of success based on the manipulation of statistics and the use of meaningless jargon. This book decodes much of the obfuscation used by officials and criminal justice policy makers and translates into plain English some of the jargon and 'statistical speak' used by the Home Office and the National Probation Service to maintain their pretence of success.

I have described many instances of this government 'double-think'. For example, early in 2004 criminal justice officials were faced with the incontrovertible evidence of the failure of community offender supervision methods, recently imported from Canada, to exert any influence on the offending behaviour of the thousands of criminals referred to these programmes. The response of the Home Office to this embarrassing debacle has been to publish a coloured brochure called 'Targets for Offender Management 2004–05'. Its objectives avoid any reference to reconvictions and instead are couched in meaningless 'department speak'.

As another example, the government has been telling the public since the mid 1990s that crime is falling. This assertion is based on the figures obtained from the British Crime Survey (BCS), which measures crime by asking how many individuals, in chosen samples of the community, have been victims of crime. Whilst these results have always exceeded the number of crimes recorded by the police, the BCS has reported a fall in crime from 18 million crimes a year in the late 1990s to 12 million in July 2004. The Home Secretary (at the time of writing) has stated that 'these are the most accurate crime figures', yet this is a gross deception as his own department produced a report in 2002, not generally known to the public, which showed that the more accurate figure was nearer 60 million crimes a year. In addition, their claims that crime is falling is contradicted by their own separate reconviction figures for the 155,000 offenders under supervision to the Probation Service. These have not shown any decrease over the years in which BCS crime is supposed to have fallen. The latest figures available in Home Office Bulletin 15/04 published in December 2004 show that the reconviction rate for all males was 61 per cent, whilst for those with one or more previous convictions when given a community sentence it was 67 per cent. It must be remembered that these figures are based on just those who are convicted, and with a 5 per cent detection rate for all crimes their true failure rate will be far worse. The State now blatantly tells the public what it wants them to hear; that is, that crime is generally decreasing, even though the public's experience tells them that this is not true. Many communities are so besieged by criminals unchallenged by a police force hampered by demands beyond their resources that they have banded together to hire private patrols to protect them from criminals.

This book explains how all governments since the 1950s have, in addition, misled the public about the so-called success of all forms of community supervision of persistent offenders and describes in detail how they have created the myths that prison 'does not work' and that 'too many offenders' are sent to jail by our courts. This book counters these deceptions by bringing to light the evidence, hitherto hidden by anti-prison propaganda, which shows how few persistent offenders are jailed and the successful record of our prisons, not only in protecting the public but also in reforming offenders.

It further explains *why* the crime rate has been allowed to rise to its present level, explains *how* this has come about, and uncovers, for the first time, the deliberate and prolonged propaganda campaign used to persuade the public to accept sentencing policies which undermine their safety. It sets out to counteract this brainwashing by presenting the facts relating to crime, criminals and prisons and reveals the deception techniques used by past and present governments to hide their true sentencing agenda, which has been to substitute the fight against crime with a war against prison.

It highlights the harmful effect of crimes on its victims and the lack of recognition by Parliament, civil servants and criminal justice practitioners of its corrosive effect on the standard of life and general well-being of millions of people.

The book deals with a number of highly controversial developments, many not generally known to the public, such as the politicisation of the police force and its withdrawal from crime fighting in some areas. It asks whether police 'political correctness' was an unnamed factor in the chain of events which led to the Soham murders by Ian Huntley.

As previously mentioned, I have presented an analysis of crime, sentencing and justice from the perspective of the public, and it is intended to fuel a new and different debate about crime and justice which is long overdue. It is not a text book with topics organised in watertight compartments under separate chapter headings. This book tells a story and therefore at certain points some themes reappear to lend their colour to different parts of the narrative. It is intended to be controversial, as the evidence it presents contradicts the common assumptions about crime, criminals and sentencing presented on a daily basis in the media, and demonstrates that offenders are not corrupted by prison but by the unchallenged success of their criminality. In particular, it highlights the problems caused by the attitude of many judges and magistrates and argues they should be held to account for the harm caused to the public by offenders they have released into the community, bringing them into line with the monitoring now carried out of doctors, hospitals and schools.

It points to the growing and dangerous alienation of the public from the police and the judicial system in general, owing to the collapse of local law and order in many areas of the country, and the failure to provide justice and retribution for victims in particular and the public in general. It describes how the criminal justice system, faced with the evidence of its failure to protect the public, has retreated more and more into 'pseudo activity' and the publication of coloured brochures and reports listing their achievements related to increasingly meaningless targets. For example, in July 2004 one police service announced its intentions to circulate over 600,000 copies of its expensively produced annual report to every household in its catchment area. Despite the fact that the police from this force are hardly ever in evidence and frequently fail to respond to calls for help, this report boasted of its success in reducing crime based on 'partnership' work with the public.

Whilst writing this book I was contacted by a number of people from different parts of the country who had become desperate in their search for protection from criminals. Some reported they were living in isolated farmhouses plagued by burglars and unprotected by the police, and who closely identified themselves with the plight of Tony Martin. Others spoke of living in streets occupied by hostels or houses run by organisations such as the National Association for the Care and Resettlement of Offenders (NACRO). They spoke of a living nightmare brought about by the non-stop crime, intimidation, vandalism and harassment inflicted on them by their criminal residents. All spoke of their total failure to get local politicians, MPs, criminal justice officials, police, or indeed anyone to take any notice of their desperate situation.

The book predicts an increase in the social unrest already seen in some cities, in which police have clashed violently with vigilantes attempting to take the law into their own hands, and argues such developments threaten the stability of our political system.

It also reveals the depth of anti-prison ideology to be found amongst those responsible for framing our sentencing laws, and the financial strictures of the Treasury, whose influences have played a large part in bringing about the now massive problems of crime and disorder now experienced throughout Britain. It reveals the misrepresentation of these issues by politicians, criminal justice officials, many academics and the anti-prison lobby organisations and provides the reader with the key to understanding the hidden agenda followed by those in our justice system whose decisions leave crime victims and the public in general bewildered, frustrated and angry.

The government frequently presents the public with some new crime initiative, often in response to public criticism of court proceedings or other loopholes in the justice system, and the analysis offered in this book will help the public see through the falseness of the remedies offered and brings to notice the enormous injustices inflicted on millions of people by persistent criminals and a criminal justice system corrupted by foolish ideology, and organised almost entirely around the so-called needs of offenders.

Finally this book explains why the 20 to 30 million people victimised by crime every year in the UK (based on British Crime Survey figures only) have no influence over those whose decisions concerning sentencing policy ruthlessly backfire on them. It offers a strategy for change which will answer many of the anxieties of those who have been victimised by crime and others who are fearful they may become so. It presents the urgent case for the adoption of sensible sentencing laws to protect the public from the persistent offender unmotivated to change.

Acknowledgements

I am indebted to Professor David Marsland for writing the Foreword and for his support during the writing of this book.

Thanks are due to the following for their time and help with the early drafts: Maureen Woolley, Mike Jeffries, Mike Allen, Malcolm Rigby, Constance Rigby and Ron McKewan.

I am indebted to Geoffrey Parmiter for his review of the manuscript and his helpful suggestions.

I must also thank Anne Jewell for her help with the references.

Posthumous thanks are due to Martyn Samuel for his review of chapter three.

Thanks are due to Clare Fraser, whose research identified pivotal material for the early chapters and to Adam Fraser for his help with the graphical display of the data.

I must also thank those prison officers, court workers, probation officers, police officers and magistrates from different parts of the country, as well as members of the public who provided me with much valuable information and help, and particularly Mike Jeffries for his informed insights into the work of the court-based victim support volunteers.

I am grateful to Rosemarie Fraser and Dr Sybil Eysenck for their editing of the final script and their helpful suggestions concerning some of the chapters.

I am also indebted to the generosity and help from the directors of the Criminal Justice Association, Peter Coad and Brian Lawrence, and also to Ronald Lewis; their informed and ground-breaking papers on a variety of criminal justice issues have been a constant source of inspiration.

Likewise, I must acknowledge the assistance of those government officials who were prepared to talk to me and provide written information; the helpful material provided by CIVITAS on their web site; and the expert technical assistance from Adam Stevens and Michael Burgun, which they provided at various times throughout this project.

Finally, thanks are due to my wife for enabling it all to happen.

Author's Note

Criminal statistics and legislation are constantly being updated. Unless otherwise stated, the legislative and statistical information in this book generally covers the period up to 2002. Some references are made to developments after this time, but, for example, this book does not include the 2003 Criminal Justice Act, most sections of which did not come into force until 4 April 2005. (Some of its provisions are dealt with in the discussion of the Auld Report which preceded it.)

However, the import of the 2003 CJ Act, and the publication by the Home Office of more recent crime figures (e.g. Home Office Bulletin 11/05, *Crime in England and Wales, 2004/5*), in no way detract from the main thrust of the argument central to this book.

Similarly, more recent crime figures for Britain, 2003 - 2022, especially those for violent crime, reinforce the urgent case for sentencing policies which will protect the public from persistent offenders.

Explanation of Terms Used

(A) UK

In most cases the use of the term 'UK' means England and Wales as the crime statistics used in this book refer to Home Office figures which are based on those countries.

(B) Britain, British

Unless otherwise indicated in the text, the term 'Britain' refers to England and Wales, and the term 'British' to the people of those two countries.

(C) British Crime Survey (BCS)

This is a measurement of crimes against people living in private households in England and Wales.

(D) Parliament

This term refers to the Houses of Parliament at Westminster.

(E) Government

Unless otherwise stated this term refers to the general machinery of government, not simply the ministers in post at the time. Also, unless otherwise stated, the term refers to all governments since the Second World War of whatever political persuasion.

(F) Probation, Community Supervision

For the sake of clarity, I have used the terms 'probation' or the more general description 'community supervision' to describe court orders which direct the probation service to supervise offenders in the community.

Prior to 2001 there were three main types of offender supervision:

Probation Orders:

These could have various conditions attached to them and generally lasted for two years (previously provided for by Subsections 2 and 3 and Schedule 1A of the Powers of Criminal Courts Act 1973, and Subsections 41 to 45 and Schedules 2 and 3 of the Powers of Criminal Courts (Sentencing) Act 2000).

Community Service Orders:

These required the offenders to carry out up to 240 hours of work at the direction of the Probation Service (previously provided for by Section 14 of the Powers of Criminal Courts (Sentencing) Act 1973, and Subsections 46 to 50 and Schedule 3 of the Powers of Criminal Courts (Sentencing) Act 2000).

Combination Orders:

These combined elements of the above two orders (previously provided for by Section 11 of the Criminal Justice Act 1991, and Section 51 and Schedule 3 of the Powers of Criminal Courts (Sentencing) Act 2000).

Change of names brought about by the Criminal Justice and Court Services Act 2000:

Probation Orders became 'Community Rehabilitation Orders'.

Community Service Orders became 'Community Punishment Orders'.

Combination Orders became 'Community Punishment and Rehabilitation Orders'.

Offenders can also be supervised under Curfew Orders, Action Plan Orders, Attendance Centre Orders, Drug Testing and Treatment Orders, Reparation Orders and Supervision Orders (for those under 17 years), and where appropriate these have been described in the text.

(G) The Safety of the Public

Frequent reference is made to the extent to which community sentences for offenders threaten the safety of the public. This means, unless otherwise stated, they are exposed to the risk of offences being committed against them by offenders being supervised in the community.

(H) Parole

I have used the term 'parole' to describe arrangements whereby prisoners are released before the end of their prison sentence under supervision to the Probation Service.

However, the 1991 Criminal Justice Act introduced new early-release arrangements for serving prisoners. It stated that prisoners serving up to four years were to be automatically released at the halfway stage of their sentence and those serving between one and up to four years would be released on 'automatic conditional release' (ACR) and supervised on licence until the three-quarter stage of their sentence.

Those serving four years and over could be considered for release on parole licence at the half way stage, but otherwise would be automatically released at the two-thirds point in their sentence; both types of release would be subject to supervision on licence until the three-quarter stage of their sentence.

All prisoners released under these arrangements can be recalled to prison for further offences committed up to the sentence expiry date.

Introduction:
Under Crime's Lengthening Shadow

The author hopes that this book will be of interest to all of those who are concerned about the serious breakdown in law and order now occurring in the United Kingdom, and that it will be of some help to those who have become the victims of crime, and to those who are fearful they might be.

I recognise that this book cannot restore the loss of confidence or undo the physical and/or emotional damage which is the frequent legacy of these experiences; nor can it take away the nagging anxiety or remove the devastating loss of privacy and sense of safety endured by many who fall victim to criminals.

It does, however, set out to offer hope to those living in the shadow of crime that things can be different. It will argue that we do not have to go on being helpless in the face of continued victimisation by persistent criminals. It stresses that sentencing policies can, without recourse to extreme measures, be changed in order to protect us, rather than threaten our safety as they do now.

It argues that for this change to come about, the public must be told the truth concerning the injustices inflicted upon them by a criminal justice system that has become focused almost exclusively on the so-called 'rights' of the offender. The dissemination of accurate information about crime and sentencing will enable the public, and victims of crime in particular, to lobby their parliamentary representatives for change, if they so wish, in an informed way. It is imperative that they are listened to by all those who wield influence over the sentencing laws of this country. It is their decisions which all too frequently backfire mercilessly upon the vulnerable public, and this book offers an analysis of why the vast army of the victims

1

of crime, which increases by millions each year, has no influence on those who are involved in the making or carrying out of sentencing policy.

The official records show that, each year, the courts in the United Kingdom sentence thousands of persistent criminals to a period of supervision in the community. Incredibly, this is despite the fact that the judge or magistrate knew, at the time of sentence, of their frequently long record of previous convictions and their complete lack of motivation to reform. The evidence shows that having gained their freedom they continue to commit horrendous numbers of crimes. This has had an effect on the quality of the lives of their victims, and the public in general, unequalled by any other recent phenomenon. Important questions present themselves:

Why do the courts deliberately inflict persistent offenders on the community when it is in their power to protect society by sending them to prison?

Why have judges been allowed to subvert the will of Parliament by frequently not passing the mandatory sentences provided for by legislation?

Why have we ignored the obvious success of prisons in the United States in reducing crime?

Why is the focus of sentencing policy the interest and well-being of the criminal and not that of his victim?

Why do the Home Office and the Probation Service make false claims of success for offender community supervision programmes based on highly questionable research methods and so put the public at risk?

Why has the Human Rights Act been interpreted so as to protect the rights of criminals and totally ignore the rights of the victims of crime?

Why has the criminal justice establishment turned its back on zero-tolerance policy when it has been such a success in those areas where it has been used?

Why does Home Office crime prevention strategy rely on restricting the public's freedom of movement by advising them to lock themselves away behind ever more intrusive security measures, whilst leaving ever-larger numbers of criminals the freedom to roam?

Why does the Crown Prosecution Service thwart the police in their attempts to bring criminals to justice?

This book sets out to answer these questions by drawing on facts

2

and a body of objective evidence not generally known to the majority of the public. It could not be more at variance with the propaganda and misleading information concerning crime, criminals and prisons which has been fed to the British public by the anti-prison lobby over the last three decades.

There may well be those who will find some of the things they read in this book difficult to believe, but its arguments rest on more than thirty-four years experience of working and research in the criminal justice system. It presents the facts which show beyond doubt that the sentencing policy followed by the courts in this country is an unmitigated disaster, offering the public no protection from persistent criminals. Furthermore, it reveals how official propaganda and deceit have kept the truth of this failure from the public and have tricked us into supporting sentencing policies which have, paradoxically, played a significant part in undermining our safety and general sense of security.

This book is devoid of ideology. The author has no professional, ideological or organisational position to defend. The case it puts forward is not based on opinion but on the facts, which are offered without spin or slant. The motivation to write this book has been to bring to notice the enormous injustices inflicted on the innocent public by persistent criminals and a criminal justice system corrupted by foolish ideology, and to present the urgent case for change.

I believe that the information presented here represents the official scandal, not just of the decade, but of the century; its implications for every member of the public cannot be overestimated. However, it will be for the readers to judge this conclusion for themselves and the arguments that underpin it.

Chapter 1

A Lost World

Criminals, particularly persistent property offenders, are never far away from us. We may not see them but they are close by, watching what we do and where we go. They patrol our streets, probing our houses with experienced criminal eyes, on the lookout for an easy target, constantly searching for the telltale sign that would make a particular house vulnerable to a quick break in. We may not notice them, but they shadow us, waiting for their opportunity to strike. When they do, they do so quietly and efficiently, frequently stealing our property from under our very noses.

A friend of mine recently attended his son's graduation ceremony held in a large cathedral in the south-west of England. To him, the congregation, consisting of hundreds of parents and friends all enjoying an important family occasion, appeared normal and void of threat. He stood up to speak to a group of friends; he did no more than turn his back on his chair where he had placed his digital camera, but in the space of only fifteen seconds his camera was stolen. The criminal must have been no more than a hand's reach away from him, watching and waiting for an opportunity to steal.

A neighbour moved into our street a few months ago. He works from home, so for the majority of the time his house is occupied. He works in the front room, and he and his laptop computers can be seen clearly from the street. On one occasion he left his house for forty-five minutes to visit the local shop and forgot to lock one of the windows. During that brief interlude a burglar climbed in through the unsecured window and stole both of his two expensive laptop computers. It seems clear that the criminal had been watching him, unnoticed.

Recently I helped my daughter move flat. We carried her possessions down the stairs and parked them by the front door, as a prelude to loading them into the car. We managed to stagger our visits to the door, so one of us was always watching the growing pile of household items. But we got our timing wrong on just one occasion. For no more than a half a minute neither of us was overseeing my daughter's possessions. In that briefest of interludes, which could be counted in seconds, her large framed mirror was stolen from among the items piled in the doorway. Neither of us saw or heard the thief, but he had clearly seen us and, with a jackal-like instinct, had targeted us as his next victims.

Some time ago I attended a meeting on Christmas Eve in a hotel close to where I live. In the foyer of the hotel was a distraught family of two parents and two small children. They had arrived moments before after a long journey. They had just parked their car and within minutes it was broken into and all of their luggage, including Christmas presents and other property, had been stolen. The children were sobbing, and the parents, shocked and angry, were trying to get their heads around the immense problems which faced them at being away from home and having lost all of their property including money and credit cards.

Tragically, we all know of similar incidents, because it has happened to us and/or to people we know. I could easily fill the whole of this book with examples which illustrate the devastating and intrusive effect of crimes on their victims. Those who rule us have lost their grip on law and order (as the following chapters of this book will make clear), and as a result our communities are now awash with crime in a way that they were not even thirty years ago.

Criminal justice officials become very defensive when faced with statements about rising crime and are quick to rebuff the notion that crime 'is as bad as the British public think'. Many claim that crime hasn't risen and argue it is simply that more crimes are reported to the police. But we know that this is not true because the British Crime Surveys have been tracking the incidence of crime through large surveys of the population, which are quite separate from the figures of crime recorded by the police. These surveys have shown for example that in 1981 66 per cent of burglaries were reported, exactly the same percentage as in 1995. In 1981, 40 per cent of woundings were reported, and in 1995 it was almost the same at 39 per cent. Overall, between 1981 and 1995, the total incidence of crime as measured by the British Crime Survey (BCS) increased by 83 per cent, whilst reported crime increased by 91 per cent.

The argument that rising crime has been a statistical illusion falls down because many people are alive who remember how relatively rare crime was in the 1950s. Because of this, people then were more likely to report crime than they are now and so unreported crime would have been lower than now.[1]

However, Home Office statisticians like to claim, as they did in 1998, that the public was grossly overestimating the extent of crime and underestimating the severity of sentencing, leading to an 'unjustified contempt for the courts based on ignorance'.[2] All this says is that the researchers did not agree with the level of severity of sentencing expected by the public. But whether the public overestimate crime or underestimate sentencing severity is irrelevant.

The Home Office preoccupation with the public's *perception* of crime and sentencing is a red herring. The fact that they have gone to the trouble to publish research findings on this subject[3] indicates, I believe, that they see it as a way of distracting the public's attention from their actual *experience* of crime, which is that millions of them are victimised every year by criminals. This dreadful reality is unaltered by whatever *their* perceptions of crime might be.

For example, over the last three decades there has been a dramatic increase in the chances of us being victimised by criminals. For example, the risk of our becoming a victim of car crime in 1979 was one in eleven. By 1995, it was one in five, and now today, only seven years later, almost everyone is, with three out of four drivers falling victim to car crime.[4] In 1979, we had a one in thirty-two chance of being burgled. By 1995, it was one in eleven.[5] Although BCS figures suggest that burglary rates have fallen since then, many hundreds of thousands are still victimised by this crime every year and so remains a major problem for the UK public.

In addition, other offences such as the theft of bicycles, woundings, robberies, theft from persons, common assaults and vandalism all now occur in large numbers.[6] Yet even this is not the whole story, as the Home Office admits that large numbers of crimes are not reported.[7]

By the late 1990s the English crime rate had overtaken the crime rate of the United States.[8] An official report shook the British establishment by providing evidence that, contrary to popular conception, British people were more likely to be assaulted or mugged than Americans. It showed that the rates for most types of serious offence – burglary, assault, robbery and motor vehicle theft – were higher in England and Wales than in the United States.

One way to understand the enormity of the crime explosion is to take note of the increase in the numbers of people (per 100,000 of the population) found guilty of indictable offences. In 1957 this was 340.[9] By 1991 this figure had soared to 1,400 (see Note 1).[10] What makes this even more dramatic is the fact that during this period the detection rate for crimes went down. In other words, despite the fact that fewer crimes were being cleared up each year (relative to all crimes being committed), more and more people were being found guilty because of escalating crime.

Jack Straw's response, whilst making his debut speech as British Home Secretary to the European Council of Ministers in Brussels in 1997, was to say that the 'UK crime rate was the result of the incompetence of the previous Tory government'.[11] However, whilst their record in office in protecting the public from crime was nothing less than appalling, it was Roy Jenkins, an earlier Labour Party Home Secretary, who had first introduced the idea of the more liberal sentencing policies.

This dire picture received independent support from an International Crime Victimisation Survey, which in 1997 reported the UK's high incidence of serious crime compared to several other industrial nations.[12] In July of that year it was recorded that thirteen crimes a minute were committed by young offenders, costing victims and the government billions of pounds a year.[13]

It is difficult to escape the shadow of the persistent criminal. In July 2002 a report was published which revealed the utter despair of shopkeepers in the north of England, who were faced with unrelenting theft, robberies, burglaries and crimes of violence. One shop alone had suffered twenty-three attacks in eighteen months. These included assaults by a gang armed with baseball bats and canisters of ammonia-based oil.[14] Apart from the financial loss, the fear and stress for the victims is incalculable.

It is their (and our) unalienable right to go about their lawful business without fear of attack or molestation; it is the first duty of government to protect its citizens from internal and external threats. Yet, incredibly, the limp response from the government was to invite these shopkeepers to *bid* for Home Office money to be used to increase their safety, as if protection from criminals was a condition to be auctioned.

Over the last four years, BCS estimates for the number of crimes committed every year have ranged between 16 million and the more recent figure of 12 million crimes committed against individuals and their property.[15] To make matters worse, the vast majority of these offences are never cleared up,[16] and the rotting influence of this ever-growing mountain of crimes which are never dealt with from any psychological, legal or justice standpoint is fast undermining our faith in law and order and our belief in the justice system. (Sceptics will point to the drop in BCS figures as evidence that current crime policies are working, but the inherent problems with the BCS estimates, to be discussed in Chapter Nine, prevent any such conclusion.)

But it was not always like this. I grew up in a world where it was possible to put things down without fear of them being taken; where it was possible to leave one's bicycle outside a shop without fear of it being stolen. When I was at school in the 1950s, we kept all of our books and possessions in desks which had no locks. Yet nothing was ever stolen. By the 1980s my children had to carry all of their books around with them in huge, ungainly bags because if they left them anywhere the thieves would strike.

When I was a child, the operation of leaving the house was simple and straightforward. You simply went out and closed the door behind you. It was a manoeuvre accomplished without thought or anxiety. But today it is dogged by fears of predatory burglars who roam through our towns and villages and who commit hundreds of thousands of burglaries every year. As a result, for many, the once simple act of leaving their house has become a nightmare of anxiety and complicated security routines. Have all the windows and doors been locked? Does the house seem vulnerable in any way? Has the alarm been set? Will anyone leave anything on the doorstep and give away the fact that there is no one in? Because of the prevalence of crime we have lost the ability to be spontaneous, relaxed and carefree in carrying out normal day-to-day routines.

In a village in south-west France recently I watched local people arrive by car at the small square in front of the local shops. They left their cars unlocked and walked away with the keys still in the ignition. Many did not even bother to close the car door properly. In the UK this world has been lost to us. Not only would we almost certainly have our car stolen if we dared behave in such a relaxed way, but as victims we would be castigated by the police and others and told it was our fault.

However, the evidence shows that fifty years ago we were able to live much freer and more spontaneous lives and that the world was in many respects a safer place. Whilst our communities were not crime-free, the levels of offending were a fraction of what they are today as demonstrated in Figure 1.1.

Figure 1.1: Numbers of crimes (in thousands) per 100,000 UK population

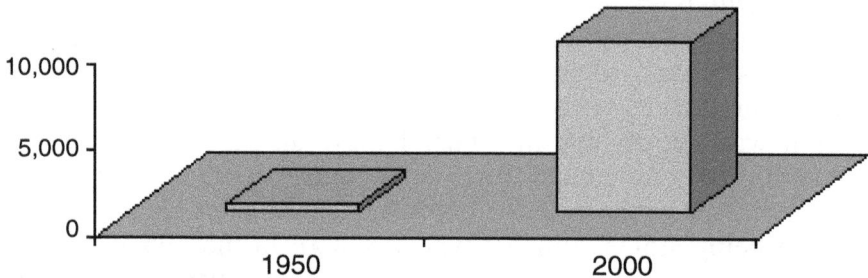

Source: UK Government, *Intelligence and Security Committee Annual Report, 1999–2000*

Even allowing for the effect of changes in the method used to record crime, the figures in Figure 1.1 are a devastating indictment of the failure of all governments since the 1950s to protect the public from crime.

In those days preventative detention – 'PD' – kept many persistent property offenders, as well as child molesters, in prison for very long periods of time. As a very young child I was allowed to play in the street out of sight of adults in a way that would now be unthinkable in many communities.

In the world in which I grew up we were properly constrained by a fear of authority and respect for private property. I remember that neighbours frequently left their front and back doors open, untroubled by fear of burglars. Private possessions were left out in public places, safe in the knowledge that they would not be stolen; for example, tradesmen left parcels and other possessions at garden gates or on doorsteps without fear of their disappearing.

But today our possessions are not safe even in the privacy of our own homes. Whilst writing this chapter I have received a

Neighbourhood Watch telephone message from the police, warning me to hide my car keys even when they are *inside* my own house and not leave them lying around. Burglars are currently breaking into houses and stealing the car keys in order to take their stolen items away in the car parked at the front of the house.

Yet when I was a child Yale locks were thought to be sufficient for the main door of the house, and few people felt the need for heavier, more expensive locks and door chains. Windows were rarely locked.

Today the police and Neighbourhood Watch organisations bombard us with advice on how to keep ourselves and our possessions safe from criminals. Pamphlets and newsletters provide us with detailed security strategies for our houses, flats and garden sheds; they warn us not to open the door to people we do not know and advise us how to keep our bicycles and other possessions safe; they offer guidance on how women should carry their handbags in the street to minimise opportunities for robbers; they tell us how to secure our cars and not to leave anything inside the car, and offer advice on how to mark all our possessions with special pens.[17] The very fact that such advice now has to be repeatedly issued to the public is a barometer indicating the extent of the courts' failure to protect us from crime.

Magazines and newspapers are now full of advertisements for security items, encouraging householders to turn their homes into fortresses. The increasing prevalence of heavy locks and chains, metal roller blinds for windows, private security patrols, alarm systems and security lights has given many of our neighbourhoods the appearance of defended camps surrounded by a hostile army.[18] This is an accurate description because persistent criminals are engaged in an undeclared war on the public.

When I was a child there was no need for the high street of the town where I lived to be festooned with CCTV cameras, had they existed. Churches were not locked because theft from them was extremely rare. 'Stealing by finding' was a criminal offence, and from this there flowed a natural and general expectation that money and other items found in the street would be handed in to the police station. Garden furniture and ornaments did not have to be cemented to the ground for fear of thieves.

Whilst walking out we did not have to hide our money and wallets inside our clothing, or carry our possessions in such a way

11

as to cut down the chance of a sneak attack from thieves. Those who were fortunate enough to own boats or caravans were not systematically targeted by thieves as they are now.

Nothing, it seems, is safe from persistent criminals. Computer chips, cars and car badges, slate tiles, period fireplaces, books, church reliquaries, mobile telephones, horses, paintings, watches, antiques, cars, wallets, cheque books, handbags, cash, jewellery, TVs, music systems, car hi-fi systems, cameras, laptops, clothing, oak-veneered coffins,[19] hunting dogs and even skulls from a village church are but a few of the items I have recently seen identified in the press as having been stolen by criminals. But it is the loss of personal items, sometimes of little monetary value, which can be so devastating to the victims involved; their deep sense of hurt and loss never appears on a crime sheet.

In just one regional TV news item in July 2002, lasting two minutes, it was reported that during that day a local woman had been violently robbed in the street, that ram-raiders had completely destroyed a shop they were trying to rob and that several churches in the region had been robbed. It also announced that a high-rise block of flats was going to be pulled down 'because of the high incidence of crime in and around this building'.[20] (Why not deal with the criminals instead?)

In that lost world where I grew up the police seemed to be everywhere. On one occasion, when I was sixteen, I set out to cycle home as dusk was falling and discovered my back light was not working. I took a chance and rode off anyway. Within five minutes a police car cruised by and waved me down. The two policemen got out and gave me a dressing down I shall never forget. They reinforced the fact that I was breaking the law because I was riding my bicycle without proper lights and told me to walk home. I set off somewhat shaken, my guilt suitably aroused. They returned a few minutes later to make sure I was still walking. Not a serious matter one might think, but the determined policing of minor infringements created an atmosphere where more serious crime was discouraged. We now call it zero tolerance.

Today, of course, one frequently sees cyclists riding without lights and almost as frequently the police ignore them. This contributes to the corruption of respect for the law. Millions of more serious crimes go undetected, and irrespective of the reasons for this the effect on the criminal is equally corrupting. From the criminal's viewpoint his offending has been ignored, and he is encouraged to think he can do it again. We are now a society engulfed in crime. The continued depredations of the persistent offender have undermined the quality of our lives to a degree unequalled by any other phenomenon.

At the same time as our increasingly liberal society has seen its crime rates go through the roof, it has been fashionable for our liberal press and other commentators to denigrate more authoritative foreign governments and in particular to sneer at countries such as Singapore with high levels of social control and low crime rates. It may not be widely known that, just after the war, Singapore's then leader-to-be Lee Kuan Yew paid a visit to London. In a recent interview on the radio he told how he travelled to Piccadilly Circus by tube train, and as he emerged onto the pavement he stood and watched an unsupervised newspaper stall.[21] He saw people stop and take a newspaper and then put their money in an old cardboard box next to the stall. He even saw people put in money notes and take out exactly the right change. Otherwise, no one interfered with or touched the money left uncovered and open to the world. He said to himself, 'This is a well-ordered and disciplined society.'

Lee Kuan Yew witnessed many other examples of the UK population's law-abiding behaviour and he returned to Singapore determined that his country would be run on the principles he saw in operation in this country. Inspired by the level of social order and respect for private property he had witnessed during his visit to the UK, he not only changed Singapore from a war-ravaged and desperately poor country into one of the wealthiest of nations, but he also made it one of the safest; it now has one of the lowest crime rates of any modern developed country.

During his radio interview Lee Kuan Yew lamented with some irony that the United Kingdom, which had inspired him so much, had since lost its grip on law and order, and from that point of view was now a very different country from the one he had first visited over forty years ago.

But what has brought this about? What has happened since Lee Kuan Yew's visit to cause Britain to become the lawless place it has become?

In August 1998 the then Home Secretary, Jack Straw, commented that we now have more cars, TVs and other personal possessions worth stealing than we had, for example, in the 1950s.[22] This idea that it is inevitable that in modern societies crime goes up as we become wealthier is a myth. From a logical point of view, crime is likely to be more prevalent in societies where people are poorer and short of the basic necessities of life, because there is more reason for them to steal.

Also, during the last half of the nineteenth century, England went through a great social, agricultural and urban upheaval, as we changed from an agricultural to an industrial based nation.[23] Yet the crime rate in London, the centre of this upheaval, went down during this period.

In reflecting on the changes in the UK since Lee Kuan Yew's visit it is worth noting that in 2001 the crime rate per 100,000 of the population in Singapore was 693. In the UK it was over 10,000.[24]

The difference in these crime rates, as illustrated in Figure 1.2, is so breathtaking it may be hard to take in. But the story it tells is eloquent in its simplicity. Lee Kuan Yew went out of his way to make sure that anyone who decided on a life of persistent crime

Figure 1.2: Comparison of UK & Singapore crime rates (per 100,000 population)

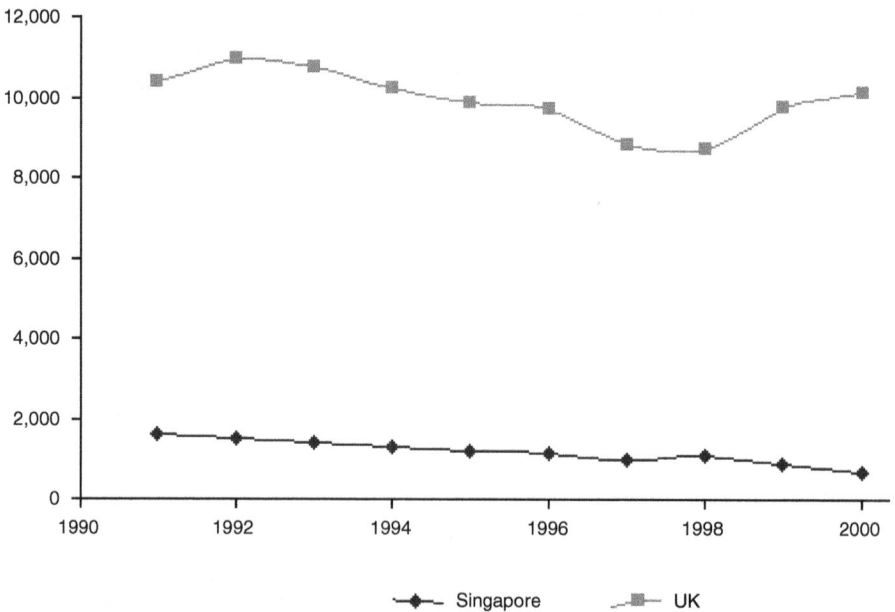

Source: Singapore Government Crime Statistics, 2002; UK Government, *Intelligence and Security Committee Annual Report, 1999–2000*

14

would be discouraged, unrewarded and, in most cases, imprisoned. We, on the other hand, have done the opposite and the reason for our dramatic increase in crime is that we have gone out of our way to make life easier, safer and more rewarding for persistent criminals.

Had we, like the Singapore government, spared no expense in making the pursuit of a criminal life unbearably hard, full of risk and totally without reward, we would not be facing the crime problem we are today. As it is, in the short space of forty years, we have turned our country into a land fit for criminals. In the next chapters, we will look at how and why this extraordinary state of affairs has come about.

Chapter 2

The Retreat from Reality

'[They] have never had it so good'

The record of all governments in the UK since the late 1960s in relation to crime prevention has been disastrous. Incredibly, as the following chapters will show, this has been largely self-inflicted. Our present-day crime problem is not a 'natural phenomenon' of our modern urban society, as some academics would have us believe. The bizarre fact is that all governments since the 1960s have gone out of their way to introduce policies that have encouraged criminals to become more criminal. Numerous obstacles have been put in the way of finding, arresting and convicting them. As a result the way has been paved for criminals to carry out their offending at will with almost no fear of being caught.

Figure 2.1: Few crimes end in prison sentences

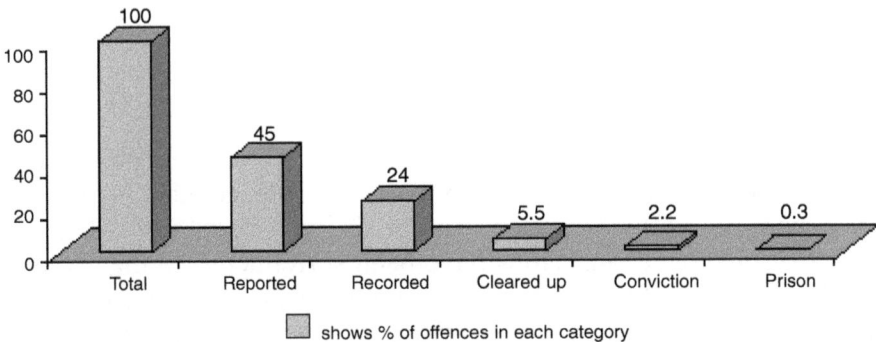

shows % of offences in each category

Source: Home Office Research & Statistics Department Digest 4, *Information on the Criminal Justice System in England & Wales, 1999*

A criminal also has little to fear should he be in the tiny minority who are put before a court, as there are now numerous obstacles to him losing his liberty. The evidence for this could not be clearer. Over the last six years, British Crime Survey estimates for the number of crimes committed every year have ranged between 18 and 13 million. Yet, as shown in Figure 2.1, only 5.5 per cent are detected, and of those, only 2 per cent are ever processed in court. Only a mere 0.3 per cent of crimes ever result in a prison sentence.

In January 1996 a photograph was published on the front page of a national newspaper. It showed a woman PC in hospital with horrendous head and face injuries. She had gone to investigate a burglary and had been hit over the head with an iron bar by the offender.[1] The very fact that the offender felt able to mete out such savage violence to a policewoman indicated that he had no concern for the injuries he inflicted on his victim, nor did he fear the law's retribution for such savagery.

We do not need psychologists to tell us the simple truth that if you reward bad behaviour you will get more of it. Instead of sparing no expense, and leaving no stone unturned in order to protect the public from crime, our criminal justice system rewards criminals for committing crime in the community; it rewards them when they get to court (if they are ever apprehended), and should they be in the tiny minority who are sent to prison, they are rewarded with early release. To quote Harold Macmillan, '[They] have never had it so good.' The streets of our towns and villages are now theirs for them to do with as they wish. We should not be surprised that we are now engulfed in crime. The offenders have taken their cue from us.

Obstacles to Detection

We have far too few police to effectively protect the public from crime. Every time a criminal commits an offence and is not seen or is unopposed by a policeman, he is, in effect, rewarded. The streets of our towns and cities have been surrendered to the criminal, and it is a gift he has accepted with both hands, as the crime figures show. How can a police force, whose size was allowed to fall from 128,290 in 1993 to 124,800 in 2000, cope with millions of offences every year? No matter how resourceful, how clever, how determined

18

the police are, they will not win the war against crime because they are too thin on the ground.

Every time our police force shrinks, it is a gift to criminals because their chances of being deterred, chased or captured diminishes, which encourages them to commit more crimes against us. Jack Straw admitted that between Labour coming to power in May 1997 and March 2000 the number of police officers had fallen by 1,400.[2] In 1998 the Home Office produced a report which rejected the idea of 'random and unfocused policing'.[3] This was its excuse for saving money by cutting back drastically on the numbers of patrolling police officers, who by then had all but disappeared from our streets. A quarter of all police authorities in England no longer have a police station open for twenty-four hours. Some do not have a police station at all.[4]

It is rare to see a policeman patrolling our streets. Community bobbies have been withdrawn from many towns and villages. This has caused at least one town council in the south-east, so desperate were they to find some protection from the criminals who were victimising them, to approach the police about paying for a beat bobby.[5]

I have heard it argued that there is no clear correlation between the number of police and the crime rate. That is because police numbers have not been increased anywhere near enough. Common sense tells us that if there are lots of policemen in our communities, visible to all – on foot, on horseback, in cars, standing on street corners, supervising busy areas, patrolling shopping areas, watching our houses – thieves and burglars are going to find it more difficult to carry out their crimes, with a greater chance of being caught when they do so.[6]

But we do not have to rely on common sense to carry this point. When crime in New York had reached crisis proportions, the city authorities recruited an additional 15,000 police officers. As a result of this massive increase the number of offences fell by a staggering 54 per cent, and there was also a 70 per cent fall in murders and manslaughters.[7] What is more, the crime rate has stayed down. In October 2003, New York crime figures were again reported to be lower than the previous year and their murder rate had fallen to its 1963 level.[8] In contrast, in May 2001, the Police Federation reported that in London a 10 per cent reduction in police numbers had been accompanied by a 12 per cent increase in overall crime.[9] This

Figure 2.2: UK street robberies per 100,000 population

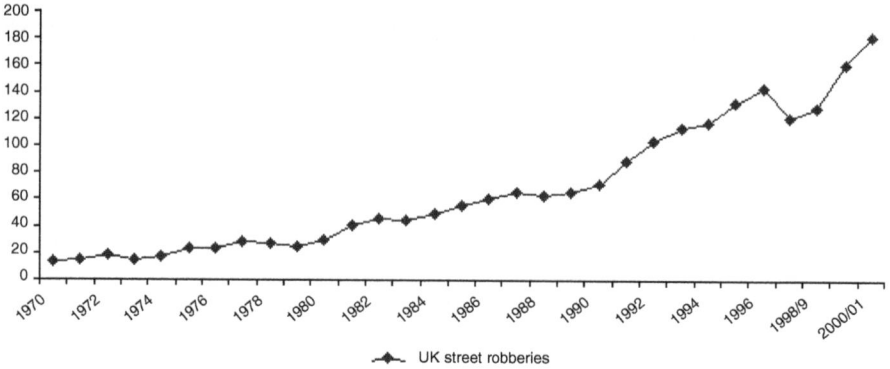

Source: *Street Robberies in the UK*, UK Government Crime Statistics 2004

included a devastating increase in street robberies, as shown by Figure 2.2. This crime in particular reflects the falling numbers of police officers on the beat. If we leave street criminals unopposed, we should not be surprised when they take full advantage of it.

This point is illustrated by the success of the police in some areas, during 2002, in combating street robberies by specifically targeting this problem using 'high visibility' patrols. But because of the critical shortage of police, this has frequently been accompanied by a rise in the offending of other criminals such as burglars, who make hay while the attention of the police is diverted away from them.[10] Nothing could more clearly illustrate how ridiculously threadbare our police force has become.

Another influential factor in this increase was the 1982 Criminal Justice Act which placed severe restrictions on the use of imprisonment for young offenders. This provision has remained despite the fact that it has been known for some time that the peak age for offending remains at or around eighteen years. The consequence was that those muggers (the majority of whom are young offenders) who were among the tiny minority to be caught had even less chance of going to prison and therefore even less reason not to rob victims in the street. It should have been no surprise, therefore, that the Home Office figures for 2000 reported that the numbers of offences committed by males under the age of eighteen years increased to 80,600.[11]

There was also a general retreat by the police from 'stop and

20

search' activity following the severe impositions of the 1984 Police and Criminal Evidence Act and again, several years later, the criticisms of police racism in the wake of the Stephen Lawrence inquiry. In January 2000, for example, street crime had soared to its highest level for over five years, with significant increases in muggings, burglary and car crimes. During the same period the number of people being stopped and searched by the Metropolitan Police fell by about 50 per cent.[12]

The formula is straightforward. If we make it unsafe for criminals to carry out crime, we get less of it. If, on the other hand, we capitulate to criminals and reward them by giving them the run of the streets, making it safer and easier to offend, we will get an avalanche of crime. New York, which has amazed the world over the last five years with its dramatic cuts in the crime rate, has more than 45,000 officers, whereas London, with a similar population, has only 24,000. Berlin, which has only half the population of London, has far more police officers.[13]

It has always surprised me that police morale in our country has stood up as well as it has, given the enormity of their uphill struggle. Between 1989 and 2001, for example, the numbers of police in the UK never rose much above 128,000. Table 2.1 shows how inadequate

Table 2.1: Police numbers and the crime rate

Year	Total numbers of police	Crime rate (in millions)
1989	125,631	14.8
1990	126,777	14.9
1991	127,495	15.0
1992	127,627	17.5
1993	128,290	18.0
1994	127,897	18.4
1995	127,222	18.7
1996	126,901	17.3
1997	127,158	16.4
1998	126,814	15.0
1999	126,096	14.6
2000	124,800	14.0
2001	126,000	13.4

Source: Home Office Digest 2, *Information on the Criminal Justice System in England & Wales*, 1993; Home Office Statistical Bulletin Issue 21/98, *The 1998 British Crime Survey, England & Wales*; 'Labour leaves the thin blue line 1,400 thinner', *Metro*, 28 March 2000; Home Office Digest 4, *Information on the Criminal Justice System in England & Wales*, 1999; *The Times*, 28 June 2001, 'Blunkett pledges biggest rise in police numbers'

these numbers are compared to the crime rate as measured by the British Crime Survey. As hopeless as these odds are for the police to deal with, in reality it is far worse, because these figures do not take into account that a murder or other major incident will divert large numbers of police from other crime duties. In March 2004, for example, eight terrorist suspects were arrested on the back of an operation which involved seven hundred police officers.[14] Also, as reported by Metropolitan Police commissioner Sir John Stevens, sometimes hundreds of police have to be taken off the streets to do office duties and telephone work.[15]

It must have been a marvellous experience for a New York policeman at the outset of mayor Rudolph Giuliani's zero-tolerance crime campaign. Until then he was a member of an outnumbered, underfunded and undervalued force, often humiliated by the mountain and diversity of crime frequently carried out under his very nose. The landscape of parts of this city were contoured by the pimps, beggars, thieves, drug dealers, drunks, muggers and murderers. Then, under the zero-tolerance regime, the city authorities decided to take the policing of crime seriously. Funding was released, police numbers were increased by a huge factor, and – just as importantly – the police were valued and recognised for the important job they had to do. The New York crime problem could not have been solved, irrespective of their numbers, without a police force whose morale and determination were high. As a result, they took back the streets of their city from the criminals on behalf of the public they served.[16]

It is generally accepted that the success of the extremist Jean-Marie Le Pen in the French elections in early 2002 was due in no small part to the country's concern about rising crime. Putting Le Pen in second place in preference to the more moderate socialist Lionel Jospin was a clear shot across the bows of the French government from their electorate for whom crime was a major concern. In the run-offs Le Pen was defeated, and France as well as Europe breathed a sigh of relief.

But the new administration in France had heard the message from the voters, and it lost no time in deciding to increase its force of gendarmes by 18,000.[17] The French government, it seems, has begun to realise what it will take if they are to be serious about dealing with crime. On the other hand, the UK government's response to its crime problem of epidemic proportions is to allocate small amounts of money to establish teams of 'street wardens' to help in the fight against crime.[18] Meanwhile, it goes on thinking of ways to release early those few persistent offenders who are in gaol, and inventing ways of avoiding others still criminally active in the community being sent there in the first place.

Barriers to Being Arrested

Police inactivity when faced with crimes is another way in which criminals are rewarded and encouraged. A growing number of such instances have come to my attention; it is, I believe, an indication that the police are showing signs of burn-out. This well-researched condition is described as a form of emotional exhaustion, which comes about when we are overexposed to demands and expectations which cannot be met.[19] Faced with the constant stress resulting from impossible demands, the motivation of the individual and the organisation drains away.

Some of these demands come from excessive paperwork. For example, in 1999 it was reported that a police constable had spent an entire shift processing 249 pieces of paper to deal with one simple arrest over a bottle of whisky.[20] These insatiable bureaucratic demands can only act as a brake on the determination of the police to apprehend criminals.

In another example of police inactivity a local butcher used film taken on his CCTV camera to show the police who it was who had stolen large amounts of meat from his shop. The film clearly identified the thieves. Despite being told where they lived, the police took no action and instead advised the victim to take civil action. Needless to say, the butcher had not the time or money to do this and so once more the offenders escaped, despite clear evidence of their guilt.

Neither do the police reserve this tactic just for property crime. For example, in 2002, in north-west London, an elderly Jamaican was attacked and robbed by a gang of black youths. The incident affected him badly and he has been in frail health ever since. Yet the only response the police could muster was to advise the elderly victim to bring out a private prosecution.[21] In another recent incident, a student's room was robbed by his landlady while he was out. Another student member of the household witnessed this. They both gave their evidence to the police constable who called to see them shortly after the theft had taken place. To their astonishment, he told them there was nothing he could do because he 'would not get the case past his sergeant', who, he was sure, would reject it. Again, nothing was done.[22] In any case, by not arresting the suspect (which he had every right to do under Section 24 of the Police and Criminal Evidence Act 1984), he was saving himself the tedium of filling out *at least* seventeen forms. The constable knew that even if he did make the effort to get the case past his sergeant and the more formidable obstacle of the Crown Prosecution Service, there was a high chance that, if the landlady pleaded not guilty, she would get away with it and that even if she were found guilty she would receive a derisory sentence. So why bother? The question of justice, the need to uphold the law, and the loss sustained by the victim were not even considered.

The police are crushed between an avalanche of crime on the one hand and enormous obstacles which prevent them from catching and convicting criminals on the other. We should not, therefore, be surprised at any sign of erosion of police morale and determination. In January 2003 a police force in the north of the country provided a clear example of this mindset. They refused to prosecute an offender who had been caught red-handed burgling his victim's garden shed. To the amazement of the victim, who had apprehended the burglar and handed him over to the police, they decided they did not have enough evidence to proceed. The burglar claimed that he and his associates (who escaped) were sheltering from the rain!

The police ignored the fact that the intruders had been apprehended on the victim's property and had attacked him with bricks, and that it was not even raining on the day of the incident. Surely common sense and the normal demands of natural justice dictated that, at the very least, the intruder's word should have been tested against that of the victim and the other witnesses by taking the matter to court. But this was not to be. Two years later, owing to the determination of the victim, the offender was found guilty of this burglary in a civil court and the judge declared that the original police decision not to prosecute had been 'regrettable'.[23]

What is even more regrettable is that examples such as this can be replicated probably in their thousands, yet no one is prepared to see them as symptoms of a deep and worrying malaise which is undermining our criminal justice system.

The problems faced by the police in terms of stress and overload, and the effect these have on their abilities to protect the public, will be taken up again in more detail in Chapter Nine, but suffice it to say here that Parliament votes large sums of money for a police force whose job is to protect society by apprehending and arresting suspect offenders. Yet police decisions to take no action when faced with criminal acts, usually made informally and at low level, subvert the will of Parliament by diverting offenders away from the judicial system that is put there to deal with them. Thus offenders are frequently rewarded and protected by the very service whose job it is to bring them to book. This must not be misunderstood. This is not a wilful response on the part of the police; it is because, I believe, their motivational batteries have run flat. Whilst racism has been identified as a problem in our police force, it is burn-out which is institutionalised.

Obstacles Between Arrest and a Court Appearance

One of the best ways to reward offenders is to caution them, rather than put them before a court and charge them with the offences they have committed. Cautions are administered after an arrest where the offender admits the offence. The police have long assumed the right to caution,[24] and since the 1980s a number of Home Office circulars have been produced to offer guidelines on its use and to extend the practice.[25]

There is no way of knowing accurately how many offences offenders commit after a caution, but it is known that thousands have been given repeated cautions due to continued offending and then have gone on to receive criminal convictions. Despite this, in 1992 the Young Offenders Committee of the National Association for the Care and Resettlement of Offenders (NACRO) argued that cautioning should be extended in view of its 'success',[26] a description which those victimised by the offenders concerned would hardly agree with. The only tangible 'success' is for the offender in escaping punishment for the offences he has committed, an aim which NACRO unashamedly supports. In doing so it does the persistent offender no favours because nothing could encourage him more to go on with his life of crime.

Cautions are not just used for minor infractions of the law but also for thousands of serious crimes, as shown in Table 2.2.

Table 2.2: The use of cautions (2000)

Offence	Dealt with by cautions	Offence	Dealt with by cautions
Violence	19,900	Burglary	6,600
Robbery	600	Theft & handling stolen goods	67,600
Fraud & forgery	6,200	Criminal damage	3,200
Drug offences	41,100	Assault	15,500
Public order offences	13,400	Theft of cars	4,300
Other summary offences (non-motoring)	35,200		

Source: Home Office 20/01, *Cautions, Court Proceedings and Sentencing, England & Wales*, 2000

Yet in its statistical bulletin the Home Office actually describes cautioning as 'giving a range of *less serious offenders* a chance to reform without obtaining a criminal record' – hardly a statement which fits the dangerous and serious crimes actually dealt with in this way.[27]

But why was cautioning introduced? Was it to improve the low clear-up rates for offences? The promise of a caution is a powerful incentive for the offenders to own up, rather than plead not guilty and risk a court appearance. One thing is certain, it has nothing to do with the protection of the public. It is a cynical device to keep offenders out of the courts in order to ease the pressure on the judiciary and avoid the possibility not only of a prison sentence, but of any sentence. As early as 1991, for example, some of the highest cautioning rates were to be found in the parts of the country with the highest crime rates.[28]

This almost desperate drive to keep offenders out of the courts can be illustrated by the Audit Commission's criticism of the police for not using the 'caution plus schemes' for young offenders, involving them in compensation or programmes to deter substance and alcohol abuse.[29] Normally such programmes are targeted at offenders who have been convicted and sentenced to a period of community supervision. What the Audit Commission criticism reveals is the utter determination of the criminal justice system to deal with as many offenders as possible without recourse to the courts. In other words, to save money they are quite prepared to ignore that the law has been broken.

26

A further demonstration is provided by the example of the Home Office directive to the West Midlands Police Force in 1991 to *increase* their use of cautions in order to 'ease pressure on the jails and over-clogged court system'. This order came about in a report which identified that 18 per cent of adult offenders were cautioned in the West Midlands, compared with the national average of 27 per cent.[30] That a police force should be taken to task because 'too many' offenders have been put before the court beggars belief.

What message does this give to the burglars, robbers, violent criminals and others who are dealt with in this way? At the very least, it tells them that it does not matter if they break the law. What does it say to their victims? Surely no practice could more undermine the authority of the law in the eye of the offender and diminish the victims' and public's confidence in our justice system.

How are we to describe a criminal justice system which thinks so little about defending its citizens from crime that it orders more cautioning of offenders rather than ensure their crimes are dealt with properly before the law? The answer is that it has become a system whose purpose is to put as much distance as possible between the offender and an eventual prison sentence. The reason? Because it is erroneously believed that this will save money, and this has become a more important objective than protecting the public.

Although the Home Office, in March 1994, felt forced to issue a warning against the over-use of cautioning by the police,[31] this was, I believe, no more than a public-relations exercise in response to the growing disquiet about the number of offenders being dealt with in this way. In reality, it was delighted with this trend because it served its purpose in keeping offenders out of court and away from prison. This was demonstrated by their proliferation of the cautioning idea in order to widen its use. For example, cautions now apply only to adults. Offenders aged between 10 and 17 are issued with 'reprimands', and, if caught again for more offences, they are issued with 'final warnings'. Thus the shelf life of the reprimand/warning/caution concept as a means to keep the offender out of court and out of prison, has been considerably extended. The criminals, of course, gain a great deal from the perverted logic of repeated warnings. They gain yet more time to go on victimising yet more members of the public. For example, Home Office research has demonstrated that offenders who had previously committed offences were over three times as likely to commit crime again than those without any past criminal history.[32] Likewise, the reconviction rate of offenders who receive repeat cautions is more than twice that of those who are cautioned for the first time.[33]

Incredibly, in a grotesque attempt to justify cautioning, especially for juvenile offenders, a number of officials claimed that during the twelve years up to 1998, the recorded rate of offending by juveniles aged 10–17 years fell by 27 per cent. Other Home Office data suggested that the number of boys aged 10–14 found guilty or cautioned has dropped noticeably since 1990. Such claims are meaningless because between 1990 and 2000 the number of *informal* warnings given to juveniles by the police increased and large numbers of others have been 'diverted' away from the judicial system altogether and no formal action taken against them.[34] This point was emphasised by recent independent research by the Joseph Rowntree Foundation, which found evidence of disturbingly high levels of criminality among teenagers.[35]

The reward element attached to cautions was increased in February 2001, when Jack Straw announced that offenders cautioned for cannabis use need no longer declare their previous cautions to prospective employers. This was to avoid the 'stigma' attached to such a record, and the possibility of their job applications being turned down because of it.[36] Such measures further blur the distinction between right and wrong, and between law-abiding and law-breaking. There would be no cannabis dealers and importers if there were no users. Yet dealers and importers are prosecuted and sometimes sent to prison.

Without a doubt, one of the biggest strokes of fortune enjoyed by criminals in recent years was the creation of the Crown Prosecution Service (CPS) in October 1986. No organisation could have done more to make the lives of criminals easier, safer and more rewarding.

Before the inception of the CPS, the police were responsible for prosecuting the offenders they had arrested. The test they used to decide whether or not to prosecute was simple: was there enough evidence to give a realistic prospect of a conviction? They were advised by solicitors, and while no system is perfect, it worked well. Their motive was to protect the public by ensuring the guilty were brought to justice. Not so the CPS. It is said that its purpose was to restore public confidence in the criminal justice system; it was argued that as a prosecuting authority independent of the police, it would avoid miscarriages of justice and weed out (or discontinue) 'hopeless' cases at an early stage and therefore avoid futile and expensive trials.

What has happened since suggests its real purpose was to cut down the number of offenders appearing in court, and so save costs. This is the driving force behind the CPS – not to bring offenders to justice. One CPS lawyer has stated that, 'the Home Office is leaning on us left, right and centre. We should discontinue more and more cases. Everything is driven by budgetary considerations. Things have gone completely to pot. When I started as a police prosecutor everyone wanted to prosecute. The police wanted to prosecute, the courts wanted to deal with cases, and the magistrates wanted to sentence. Now, no one wants to do any of these things'.

As described by Brian Lawrence in his book *They Call It Justice*, 'poor performance' in CPS terms means too many offenders going before the courts. 'Improvement' is brought about by an increase in the numbers of cases discontinued.[37] The response of the thousands of criminals who have got away with their crimes, thanks to the CPS, must be a mixture of pleasurable bewilderment and contempt. Lawrence goes on to explain that the *Code for Crown Prosecutors* says prosecutors must always think carefully about the interests of the victims of a crime when deciding whether or not to prosecute an offender. However, in practice the grounds on which they have to make this decision revolves so much around costs and the need to save money that the victims are rarely given a thought.

In his book, Lawrence revealed, for example, that it is known from lawyers who had attended Crown Prosecution meetings that during these discussions not one word was said about improving justice for the victims. Usually the entire meeting was given over to discussions about the need to reduce costs regardless of the consequences. If it was thought that the cost of the court procedure was such that it would be 'against the public interest' to proceed, then the case was to be dropped. Pressure from the Home Office to discontinue more and more cases is so great that this was to be held to even when there was clear evidence that the offender had committed the crime.

Where it was not possible to avoid taking the offender to court, they were instructed to 'downgrade' the charges for wholly inappropriate reasons. Rather than holding trials for offences that the defendant had committed, it was thought better to save money by letting them plead guilty to minor offences. In 1993, for example, some barristers were making known their concerns about the application of this practice to crimes of violence. In large numbers of cases, charges of actual bodily harm were being reduced to the lesser crime of common assault, and charges of affray were being changed to the lesser offence of 'threatening words'.

In one case known to me, the CPS lawyer was so keen to 'plea bargain' an offence down to a lesser charge that the offender was unaware until he got to court that he faced a charge of handling stolen goods and not burglary. The lawyers concerned had not even bothered to talk to him about it.

In addition, CPS lawyers were directed that where trials were inevitable, they should, wherever possible, only be on charges that could be dealt with in a magistrate's court. This was to prevent the defendant exercising his right to be tried by a judge and jury at the Crown Court, where the costs would be far greater.

CPS lawyers are not just under immense pressure to discontinue winnable cases, they are praised for doing so at the earliest possible stage. If the statistics show that a prosecutor has discontinued cases early it improves his image and his chances of promotion. If he makes the decision to discontinue later on in the process – that is, only when it is clear it is appropriate – it is seen as poor judgement.

Many CPS lawyers who have sent files back to the police with the request for more information so a decision could be made have been criticised for being 'too thorough'. They were told that if the police file did not provide an excellent case first time, it should be discontinued. The police were not to have a second chance to put things right or rectify understandable human errors. The reasons for this, of course, were that it was cheaper and easier and distorted the figures in favour of the CPS, because it not only recorded a satisfactorily completed case but additional weighting was given for doing it speedily.[38]

Common sense indicates that it must have been obvious from the start that these ruthless cost-saving practices would result in fewer convictions. As early as 1992, the CPS threw out a staggering 193,000 cases presented to them by the police.[39] In one glaring example, in the same year, the CPS closed the file on two armed robbers who robbed a minicab driver of his money and his car. There were no fewer than eleven strands of evidence which linked them to the crime, including their fingerprints, and in the case of one of them, actually being seen abandoning the stolen vehicle.

Although it is well known that forensic-type evidence is much more reliable than evidence based on human memory, when the cab driver failed to pick out the offenders in an ID parade, the CPS used this as an excuse to drop the case.[40]

So the government's response of 'surprise' to the news in 1997 that there had been a dramatic drop in convictions of *one-third*, despite a massive increase in crime, had a definite hollow ring to it.[41] What did it expect? This surely was exactly what they wanted.

It is difficult to avoid the conclusion that the enquiry the government launched to investigate this dramatic downturn in convictions since the CPS came into being was no more than a public-relations exercise aimed at quelling the growing disquiet among the police, many lawyers and the public in general about the massive injustices perpetrated by the CPS by allowing so many criminals to get away with crimes they had committed.

I also believe that the savage press criticism of Barbara Mills,[42] the then head of the CPS, was a convenient distraction from the real cause of the malaise, which was Home Office pressure to cut costs by reducing the number of offenders dealt with in court. If, as argued by one newspaper, the CPS leadership 'was not pulling out all the stops to fight the tidal wave of rising crime, or targeting those offences that closely affect individuals, or encouraging prosecutors to be bold on the public behalf', was this not because it was following out its orders?[43]

This may have been true in more ways than one. The fact that Barbara Mills denied the obvious and said that a criticism aired on BBC2 that she 'was soft on crime to save trouble and money' was wrong,[44] suggests, I believe, that she was loyally following a script given to her by others. What is beyond doubt is that the only section of society to benefit from the work of the CPS is the criminal fraternity. They would not disagree with the alternative title given to the CPS by the police – 'Criminal Protection Society' – because this is exactly what it is.

Barriers to Being Convicted

Only a tiny minority of offenders ever get to court. But those that do have little to fear. The court system in England and Wales has largely become organised around the needs and protection of criminals.

Our very strict rules of evidence, the frequent intimidation of witnesses, sharp practices by lawyers, and the illegal and delaying tactics of the accused are all allowed to operate in his favour. As a result, many guilty criminals are not convicted and walk away from the court free to carry on their life of crime. The problem is widespread and well known. In a speech made at the 1995 Conservative Party Conference Michael Howard remarked, with considerable understatement, that 'lawyers are masters of using procedure to win their case'.[45] I recently met a barrister who was triumphant that the client she had defended that day had been found not guilty. I asked her, 'But did he commit the crime?' 'Oh yes, of course,' she said.

There are too many instances where judges keep to the letter of the law, but not its spirit, by an over-strict application of the rules of evidence, thus allowing the accused person, who is frequently a persistent criminal, to walk free. For example, in 2001 a crown court in the south of England heard a case in which an elderly woman (well into her eighties) was ruthlessly hoaxed by a group of men to whom she needlessly paid £20,000. They targeted her because she lived alone, and having frightened her into believing her front drive needed to be tarmacked, they then intimidated her into paying them this outrageous sum in advance. She gave them the money and they disappeared without any work being done. During the trial the judge allowed the defence counsel to question the elderly victim in an aggressive manner. Put under pressure from the defence barrister, she could not remember, when asked, whether she had paid the men by cheque or with cash. At this point the judge intervened and said that in view of the victim's inability to provide this important information he was going to stop the trial. He then threw the case out. The effect on the victim of this incredible decision cannot be imagined, but we can have no doubt about its euphoric effect on the defence barrister and his clients.[46]

In another example a group of young men were arrested and put on trial for a dreadful attack on a local youth, which caused him to lose his sight and which left him semi-crippled. The thugs who beat him were clearly identified by no fewer than six witnesses who were present at the scene when the attack took place. There was no dispute about their evidence. The police (and the CPS) were sloppy in their presentation of the case and said there were twelve witnesses to the assault. It emerged during the trial that six of these were just repeating what the other six genuine witnesses had told them. On hearing this the judge stopped the trial on the grounds that the evidence 'was contaminated'. It would be difficult to find a clearer example of how courts can become organised around the protection of the defendant to the exclusion of justice for the victim.[47]

In yet another example it was reported that the Customs and Excise had made a series of blunders in the way they presented their evidence to the court when prosecuting a group of defendants accused of illegally importing millions of pounds worth of alcohol. They had failed to tell the court that the evidence against the accused was instigated by a sting operation. Despite this error, it was clear that the defendants were guilty, and indeed, one of them had already pleaded guilty. Yet the judge threw the case out because he knew that any decision to allow the case to continue was vulnerable to appeal by the defendants, even in the case of the guilty plea. Once again, all of the accused got away with their crimes. All had been previously convicted for other offences.[48]

In April 2002 the parents of the murdered child Damilola Taylor were dealt a devastating blow when the trial of the accused collapsed. It did so because the judge decided that one of the main witnesses, a fourteen-year-old girl, was a 'phantasist'. It was true that she changed her story and that she did not present well. However, she was an unsophisticated teenager who was left to the mercy of ruthless and aggressive questioning by the defence which caused her to become angry and confused. Her vulnerability should have been recognised and steps taken to protect her from such tactics,[49] but once again the very worst aspects of our adversarial system were allowed to prevail and in the opinion of many, justice for the victim and his family was denied.

I have been told by court staff that the intimidation of witnesses and victims is common in the court environment and that it frequently causes them to give up, so the case against the criminal collapses. These reports are backed up by figures held in the Lord Chancellor's Office (2002 data), which reveal that no fewer than 30,000 criminal cases collapse each year because witnesses are frightened by intimidation. This is a staggering indictment of our so-called justice system.[50] The problem has reached such epidemic proportions that in January 2003 a crown court judge took the unusual step of speaking out about the problem.[51]

Yet if there were sufficient police at crown courts, and procedures which allowed them to arrest those responsible, and the courts were compelled to remand them in custody, the problem would be largely solved. But for a long time now our thrombosis-like criminal justice system has been quite unable to offer obvious, common sense solutions such as these to defend the public against the continued onslaught from criminals.

However, intimidation could be reduced if the accused person was restricted to a designated area within the court, in order to keep him away from the witnesses and/or victims. But they are free to roam. In fact, I know of one crown court where a barrister often elects to meet the defendants in the same part of the building where the witnesses and victims are encouraged to wait. This increases the chances and opportunities for direct intimidation. One court worker said that over a five-year period they had never known a judge take any action against intimidation, whether during or before the trial, inside or outside the court. The reason for this was that if the act of intimidation is denied, the court cannot act on the word of the victim alone. Therefore cumbersome evidence-taking machinery has to be invoked. This takes so long that everyone, including the victim, is put off by the process.

If he ever makes it to the dock, the defendant is allowed to indulge in practices which border on the dishonest, and which greatly improve his chance of getting away with his crimes. It may not be widely known that the defendant is allowed to sack his lawyers twice at any stage of his trial. This means a new trial date is set, new jurors have to be found and a new judge appointed. All of this causes huge delays, allowing for the victims' and witnesses' memory to fade, much to the detriment of the prosecution case.

The system also allows lawyers to instigate delays for a variety of reasons (for example, the defendant can become 'ill'); it also allows the defendant to raise unlimited objections to the evidence, to object to a juror on the grounds that he or she was asleep, and also to object to people chosen for an ID parade, as well as delaying the ID parade by claiming he is unwell or for other reasons. These tactics are formidable obstacles to gaining a conviction, as they frequently contribute to the collapse of the victims' and witnesses' morale and undermine their motivation to proceed.

I once spent twelve months tracking down a dangerous sex attacker who was eventually arrested, having been identified by no fewer than six adult witnesses as the perpetrator of serious offences against three girls in a public swimming pool. They all agreed to attend an ID parade. It looked like an open-and-shut case. The defendant, a known persistent criminal, was allowed to delay one ID parade after the other. He did this repeatedly over a course of months, with various excuses ranging from 'a broken arm' to being ill.

The witnesses fell by the wayside one by one, either because they could no longer remember with confidence what he looked like, or because they simply became fed up and withdrew their support. The case against him, which could have resulted in a long prison sentence, collapsed, and he walked away from the court free to carry on with his obsessive and dangerous crimes. This man did eventually go to prison, but only because he went abroad and committed his crimes in another country. They caught and sentenced him to a long period of imprisonment within months of his arrival, whereas he had been allowed to evade justice in this country for years.

Barriers to Being Imprisoned

Should an offender be one of the tiny minority who are convicted for their offences there is no need for him, in the vast majority of cases, to be alarmed. At this point a series of sentencing tactics are brought into play designed to downgrade the seriousness of what he has done and thus to justify a lenient sentence.

If he had any doubt before the criminal will certainly know at this point that the criminal justice system is not only on his side but will go to extraordinary lengths to protect him from the consequences of his offending. Nothing could have made this clearer, for example, than the provisions of the Criminal Justice Act 1991 which stated that further offending no longer leads to an automatic breach of a current community sentence.[52] Likewise, the 1992 version of the Home Office National Standards for the Probation Service laid down that an offender would be allowed to breach his community order three times (by failing to comply with the order) before any formal action be taken against him.[53]

Persistent offenders are rarely charged with a single offence. In my twenty-six years in the Probation Service I cannot remember one. It is common for them to be charged with multiple offences. At the point of sentence, it is also common for the court to be asked to 'take into account' large numbers of other offences –

so-called TICs – that the offender has admitted *in addition* to those that have appeared on the charge sheet.

In practice, what it means is that if the offender admits to the TICs – and I recall from my days as a probation officer that as many as fifty TICs was not uncommon – he effectively receives no punishment for them. No matter that he has profited enormously from these offences; no matter that he has caused enormous stress, fear and anxiety for countless people; no matter that he has broken the law even. With one stroke of the pen he is literally given those for nothing.

It therefore pays the offender to ask for other offences to be taken into account. One prolific teenage burglar, for example, admitted that he always 'owned up to everything' because he had quickly discovered that no matter how many other burglaries he asked to have taken into consideration, his sentence was always light and only ever referred to those on the charge sheet. This was despite the fact that on one occasion he asked to have a staggering 175 other burglaries taken into account.[54]

In addition, the sentence for the offences for which he is charged almost never reflects all of those offences. It is common practice for the court to pass a sentence for the first offence and deal with additional offences by means of concurrent sentences. A concurrent sentence runs parallel to the first. For example, in the summer of 2000 a crown court judge in the south of England passed a sentence on a persistent and prolific burglar, saying: 'On your own admission you are a prolific and persistent burglar. This offence is so serious that only a custodial sentence can be justified. Burglary is an offence that causes untold distress to people and the sum total of distress you have caused in your life is untold. The sentence is four years' imprisonment – *concurrent* to the sentence you are at present serving' (my italics).[55] This meant that, despite the severity of the judge's statement, he made a present of the second charge of burglary to the offender, and all that he gained from it. The burglar served just one four-year sentence because the second sentence of four years was to run parallel with the first. The icing on the cake for this offender would be that with parole he would be released after having served only just over two and a half years.

In a further example a criminal was convicted of two separate charges of robbery and was sentenced as follows: robbery first count – six years' imprisonment; robbery second count – six years' imprisonment *concurrent* to the first sentence. With parole he could be out in less than three years, despite the dangerousness and severity of his offences. Even appalling crimes against children are dealt with in this way. In 2001 a defendant was convicted of two counts of rape against his thirteen-year-old daughter. He was sentenced to twelve years on each count, *concurrently*, which meant in effect he was only punished for one offence. To make matters worse from the point of view of justice for the victim, his sentence was reduced to ten years on appeal. In other words, despite a theoretical sentence of twenty-four years, he would serve no more than between five and six years in prison.[56]

The courts often use concurrent sentences even when dealing with multiple offending committed by the offender whilst on the run. For example, in February 1996 a persistent offender was arrested for burglary and bailed to another date. He failed to appear. Whilst at large, he committed yet more crimes. He was arrested again in September 1997 and charged with more burglary offences. Incredibly, he was bailed once more and yet again he failed to appear. He remained on the run until January 1999, when he was finally sentenced to six months' imprisonment for the first charge of burglary and six months concurrent for the second charge.[57] Thus the offender was given a powerful message – that the court did not regard the second burglary, committed whilst he was on the run, as important. We should not be surprised that the effect was to encourage him to continue with his life of crime.

During my work in the Probation Service I saw countless examples of multiple offences being dealt with in this way. It is as if the court cannot bring itself to realistically sentence the offender for all of the crimes he has committed. I believe that this inhibition stems from the realisation that, if they did, they would invariably have to sentence the offender to a substantial period in prison. Just as we have seen that the driving force for cautions and other 'diversion' tactics is to keep criminals out of the courts, so the driving force for this sentencing tactic is to limit the amount of time the offender spends in gaol.

A Licence to Offend

In addition, the trend, since the late 1960s, for courts generally to pass increasingly lenient non-custodial sentences has acted as an effective obstacle to imprisonment. For example, Home Office figures for 1998 showed that there were 1,468,900 sentences passed in England and Wales, but only 6.8 per cent of these involved imprisonment.[58] Table 2.3 shows the overall percentages for different types of sentencing in the magistrates' courts for England and Wales, where almost 95 per cent of all offenders are dealt with. From this we can see that the courts impose fines on large numbers of offenders despite the fact that thousands of them ignore this sanction and refuse to pay. For example, in November 2002 it was reported that tens of millions of pounds of unpaid fines had been written off as being too difficult to enforce.[59] The evidence of their sentencing record shows beyond doubt that the courts have lost sight of their primary duty to protect the public from persistent and serious offenders. This issue will be dealt with in more detail in a later chapter, but Table 2.4 gives an idea of the extent to which the courts will go to protect the persistent criminal from prison, including those who have committed serious offences which are particularly known to cause enormous physical and emotional harm to their victims.

What is extraordinary is that at the time of passing these community-based sentences, the courts would have known about the offenders' past history of persistent offending and would have been in no doubt of the risk they posed to the public if given their freedom. The reconviction rates for the majority of those under the supervision of the probation service is over 60 per cent,[60] but what is worse is that these represent just those offenders who have been caught. The

Table 2.3: Percentages for different types of sentencing

Type of sentence	Percentage of total
Discharges	24
Fines	36
Community sentence	29
Prison	7
Other	3

Source: Home Office Research & Statistics Department Digest 4, *Information on the Criminal Justice System in England and Wales*

Table 2.4: Persons sentenced to probation supervision by offence (1998)

Offence		Offence	
Violence against the person	5,337	Sexual offences	863
Burglary	4,310	Robbery	274
Theft & handling stolen goods	14,011	Fraud & forgery	2,630
Criminal damage	1,209	Other indictable offences	7,300
Summary offences	18,978		
All offences	54,912		

Source: Home Office, Probation Statistics England & Wales, 1998

low detection rate of 5.5 per cent[61] means that their reoffending rate is nearer 100 per cent. Table 2.4, therefore, is chilling evidence of the courts' willingness to issue offenders with *a licence to offend*.

I could fill this book with examples of sentences whose leniency has rewarded the offender and denied justice to the victims, but one or two will serve for illustrative purposes.

In 2001 a sentenced prisoner broke out of goal. Whilst on the run he burgled a house. He was caught and the usual plea-bargaining tactics were employed and the prosecution accepted a lesser charge of handling stolen goods. The judge kept putting off his decision about sentencing the offender; only when the release date of his prison sentence had been passed (the one from which he had escaped), did the judge give him a derisory fine for the offence of handling stolen goods.[62] In effect, the criminal got away with the serious crime of burglary, and his offence of breaking out of gaol was ignored. The effect on the criminal must have been similar to that experienced at a passing-out parade. He stood before the authorities, who, having judged his performance, publicly rewarded him, leaving him encouraged and motivated to pursue his life of crime.

In another example, a teenager crashed a car he had stolen into two elderly women. They both suffered horrific injuries. As a result one is now confined to a wheelchair and the other cannot walk without the support of a frame. The youth court merely passed a three-month curfew order on the offender, placed him under supervision for one year and ordered him to pay £250 in compensation to each victim.[63] Such lenient sentencing is an ugly distortion of justice and an insult to the victims.

Sentencing travesties such as these are common. Courts frequently appear mesmerised by concerns for the offender and willing to seize on any excuse to pass a light sentence and avoid sending the offender to goal. A recent illustration of this was provided by the defendant who was linked to two burglaries by DNA evidence. He also pleaded guilty to possessing an offensive weapon, two further burglaries and criminal damage. He had attempted to use a CS gas spray against a policeman, and had thrown bricks at one particular victim who had disturbed him during one of the burglaries. The crown court judge was told by the defence barrister that since his arrest the defendant had 'attended an anger management course and that his former partner was going to take him back'. On hearing this preposterous line of mitigation, the judge sentenced him to two years' probation with a condition that he attend courses as required.[64]

What, I wonder, went through the mind of the judge at that moment? Did he really believe that this offender's persistent burgling was something to do with being 'angry'? Was it not obvious that the offender burgled for easy gain, and his use of bricks and CS gas spray to avoid being caught meant that he was dangerous? Even in the unlikely event that his 'anger' was part of his motivation for offending – so what? Surely the public needed to be protected from him, whatever his reasons for offending. It is difficult to know whether the judge was genuinely naive, or, with his career in mind, was simply glad to be presented with an excuse to pass a lenient sentence so as to avoid any possibility of an appeal. Either way, justice was again perverted and the court system further exposed to ridicule.

Lenient sentencing is now widespread and used for every type and grade of criminal offence. During a recent trial of company executives the court learned that they had ruthlessly swindled 17,000 couples out of a total of £31 million in the world's largest timeshare fraud. This represents £6 million for each offender. Far from passing sentences which matched their crimes, the judge leaned over backwards to keep their sentences as low as possible. Each was only gaoled for between fourteen and eighteen months. If we divide the £6 million each of them earned from the crime by the length of their sentence it can be computed that the price paid by each criminal for every £428,571 gained was only one month's imprisonment. This represents excellent value for the criminals and made their crime a good business risk.[65]

Soft sentencing is now the norm. The following were taken from a regional newspaper for just one day in 2000:[66]

Case 1 – Assault on a female	2-year probation order
Case 2 – Burglary	Conditional discharge for 1 year
Case 3 – Assault	Conditional discharge for 6 months
Case 4 – Assault	1-year probation order
Case 5 – (i) Theft; (ii) Receiving stolen goods; (iii) Attempted deception; (iv) not surrendering to custody	6-month probation order
Case 6 – Burglary & assault	Conditional discharge for 1 year
Case 7 – Theft	Conditional discharge for 1 year
Case 8 – Criminal Damage	Conditional discharge for 1 year

Other examples of leniency shown towards offenders are so bizarre and so devoid of any consideration for justice and the victims' plight that they are difficult to believe. In one such case in 1993 a persistent young offender deliberately set light to a woman in a shop in an unprovoked attack upon her. It was only the quick reactions of those standing by that saved her from the most horrendous injuries. Within three weeks, the victim learned that her attacker had been sent to an adventure camp run by social services and he was enjoying a wide range of sports activities including mountain biking and forest walks.[67] It would be difficult to think of a more effective way of rewarding the offender for his callous and dangerous assault.

Home Office statistics reveal that thousands of offences of theft and burglary are dealt with by means of an absolute or conditional discharge, sometimes with a fine.[68] The large amounts of money made by persistent criminals will be discussed in Chapter Eight, but, given their huge profits from offending, these derisory sentences are tantamount to giving the criminals an official seal of approval, encouraging them to continue with their life of crime.

Judges and magistrates, in addition to criminals, are largely responsible for our high crime rates. No matter how large or effective our police force is, their hard work in detecting and catching criminals is largely wasted whilst judges and magistrates continue to pass lenient sentences and allow persistent offenders back into the community to carry on victimising the public.

Rewarding Those Sent to Prison

It must now be clear, even to a newcomer to this subject, that the seasoned and persistent criminal knows he has little to fear from the courts. Persistent offenders also know that if they are among the tiny fraction who are sent to prison, the machinery of the criminal justice system is almost entirely devoted to ensuring that almost all of them get out long before they have served all of the (often) short sentences. One cog in this machinery is the Sentencing Advisory Panel. The government established the Sentencing Advisory Panel under the auspices of the Crime and Disorder Act 1998[69] as a supposedly independent advisory body that provides objective advice and information to the Court of Appeal to assist the court when it formulates or revises sentencing guidelines. Yet, in a private interview, one of the board members admitted that after only two or three meetings it became apparent that the panel's remit to 'propose to the Court of Appeal that it frame or revise guidelines for a particular category of offence' was simply jargon for its real but undisclosed purpose, which was to increase pressure for sentences to be reduced.

Prior to Michael Howard becoming Home Secretary, the provision for allowing sentenced prisoners out on temporary licence for a few days, for either domestic or job finding reasons, had become seriously abused.

During a speech to the House of Commons on 18 November 1994, he referred to the high number of prisoners who absconded whilst on home leave, and announced changes to tighten up these arrangements.[70] Thus he brought to an end one of the many unofficial rewards that prisoners had enjoyed for many years.

During my seven years of working in a prison, for example, it was common for these licences to be demanded by the prisoners 'as of right'; they became adept at targeting those prison staff they felt they could intimidate the most in order to get their way with an application (often bogus) for temporary release. I can even recall an occasion when a prisoner, using the telephone on the prison wing where he was situated, rang the outside female probation officer and frightened her into writing a letter to the governor, which contained statements that she knew were not true, but which strongly supported the prisoner's application for a temporary release licence.

As a result of malpractices of this sort, I am certain that, over the years, hundreds if not thousands of prisoners have been allowed time out of prison on entirely false pretences. However, this practice was, as indicated, rightly clamped down on by Michael Howard, one of the few home secretaries prepared to see beyond the advice of his officials, and with the courage to put such things right.

Despite the loss of this illegal perk, gaoled prisoners still had lots to be thankful for. They knew for example, that whatever length of prison sentence the judge or magistrate had given them they would serve only part of it. For example, all those sentenced to less than four years are automatically given 50 per cent remission.[71] Thus the impact of the sentence is seriously reduced.

No doubt the offenders were originally bemused by the 'double-speak' of the Criminal Justice Act 1991 – the implications of which, for example, meant that a 'three-year sentence meant eighteen months', but its implications would have soon dawned on them. With what must have been a great sense of relief and satisfaction, the offender now knew, with absolute certainty, that the authorities were against keeping him in prison except for the shortest possible time; so he had little to fear and his future career as a criminal was as secure as it could be.

This early-release scheme was, as indicated, laid down by the Criminal Justice Act 1991,[72] which said that prisoners serving up to four years should be released automatically after serving only half of their sentence, under the terms of an Automatic Conditional Release (ACR). What is more, the recall aspect of the 'conditional release' period was not activated until 1998.[73] As a result, during that seven-year gap, thousands of offenders who broke the terms of their early release by committing more offences, or in other ways, got away with it.

Prisoners given four years or more are eligible, if thought suitable, for Discretionary Conditional Release after serving only half of their sentence. If not released earlier, they get released automatically when they have served two-thirds of their sentence.

On top of all this, the Crime and Disorder Act 1998 introduced Home Detention Curfews (to be discussed more fully in Chapter Seven) that allowed selected prisoners to be released even earlier (at that stage this was approximately two months before their normal release date, although it has been extended since).[74] They are fitted with an electronic tag, which many will be surprised to know, only monitors them for between nine and twelve hours in the twenty-four-hour cycle.

Sentencing has become a farcical game that can no longer be taken seriously. Letting offenders out of prison as fast as possible has become one of the major preoccupations of the Home Office; it means that the money, time and trouble spent in catching, prosecuting and sentencing criminals, many of them dangerous and persistent, are frequently wasted. As already noted, we should not be surprised if such practices seriously erode police morale and cause them to question the point of all their efforts in catching the criminals in the first place.

Thus the protection of the public and the provision of justice are objectives that have lost their importance, and is illustrated by the fact that thousands of persistent, dangerous and professional criminals are released after serving only part of their sentence. I can recall a criminal who had shot and killed a bank clerk whilst carrying out an armed robbery. At the time his previous record showed him to be an established and dangerous career criminal. He was given thirteen years in prison, but he was out before he had served eight years. This appalling example can be replicated many times over.

In another example, an offender (now gaoled for life as a result of a murder) had been previously sentenced at the Old Bailey to twelve years for armed robbery, but he was released from that sentence after having served only four years.[75] In November 1999 the widow of a murdered policeman learnt that one of the gang of post office robbers involved in the killing of her husband was likely to be freed after serving only six years in prison. What is more, this parole review was made long before her case with the Criminal Injuries Compensation Board had even started. When interviewed, she struggled to find the words to express her feelings of anger and sense of betrayal.[76]

Persistent burglars, car thieves and many other property offenders, who undermine the quality of life of millions of people, no longer have any reason to care if they become part of the tiny minority who are sent to prison. They know the authorities are on their side and will make it their business to see they are released as quickly as possible.

As a further example, despite all the government's announcements concerning its determination to get tough on burglars, the average prison sentence given by magistrates for this crime for each year between 1997 and 1999 was a mere 3.5 months; this increased slightly in 2000 to 5.1 months.[77] This is based, it must be remembered, on the sentence given by the court. Early release on Home Detention Curfew will reduce this even further. These lenient sentences for burglary stand out as all the more extraordinary when compared with the maximum prison sentence allowed for this offence, which is fourteen years.

Bail: A Shield for More Crime

Yet another way in which we offer rewards and encouragement to persistent offenders is to remand them on bail, rather than in custody, whilst they wait for the charge against them to be dealt with.

One of the arguments put forward for bailing defendants is that it is against natural justice to place them in custody before they have been tried, particularly so for those eventually found not guilty. Such an argument is understandable for defendants who are genuinely not guilty and who pose no threat to the community.

However, the way the government has allowed the Bail Act of 1976 to be applied makes it clear that its real purpose is, yet again, to keep down the prison population, no matter what the cost or consequences for the general public. The evidence for this is that since the imposition of the Bail Act, the government has sat back and watched the courts bail thousands of persistent offenders, sometimes repeatedly, who very clearly posed a threat to the public. The result has been an orgy of re-offending by the offenders concerned.

By the early 1990s the amount of crime committed by those on bail had reached epidemic proportions. In 1991, for example, Northumbria police released a survey showing that 38 per cent of the crime in their area was committed by 'bail bandits';[78] at the other end of the country the Avon and Somerset police revealed that a third of all crime in its area was committed by offenders on bail for other offences. As one example, they reported that one man charged with stealing £3,500 from a building society carried out a further £8,500-raid while on bail, and, in another example, a burglar committed a hundred other crimes whilst he was on bail.[79] He told police that having been caught once he felt 'he had nothing to lose'.[80]

Faced with a high percentage of crime committed by those on bail, chief constables called for a change in the law to allow them to remand persistent offenders in custody and so protect the public.[81] In one police area in 1991, for example, an average of thirty-four homes were burgled every day, and fourteen of those were committed by criminals already charged with other offences and bailed by the police.

However, it is not just property offenders who are bailed. In November 2001 a twenty-year-old man made an unprovoked attack on a man outside a shop situated in a town on the south coast. The shop owner gave a witness statement to the police. The attacker later returned and smashed the shop's windows, fruit machine and counter with a metal bar. The attacker, who was on bail at the time of these offences, had committed no fewer than forty-five previous crimes – many of them assaults on police.[82]

What is even harder to understand is that persistent offenders unmotivated to reform are frequently bailed again and again, even when it is known that they have continued to offend whilst on bail. For example, cases cited by the police include one of a man who was arrested by a police officer who saw him commit a street robbery. Despite police objections, the court granted him bail and he went on to commit more offences of robbery and violence. Charged with these offences, the court, almost unbelievably, bailed him *again*.[83]

In a second example, a twenty-three-year-old man was arrested for a shop burglary and granted bail. He was rearrested for burgling the same shop premises and bailed yet again. He burgled the shop a third time and, following arrest, was bailed once more. In a third example an eighteen-year-old was bailed following offences of burglary and stealing cars. Whilst this case was pending, he was arrested for being in possession of property stolen in a burglary. It was only after a fourth arrest that the police made a successful application in a magistrates' court for him to be remanded in custody.[84]

The *Justice of the Peace* reported that of a total of 165 offenders placed before one particular magistrates' court for breach of bail conditions, 108 were rebailed. Furthermore, out of a total of 134 offenders who had appeared more than once before the same magistrates' court during 1990, 72 had re-offended twice whilst on bail, 26 offenders three times, 16 of them four times, and 7 five times, and in one case an offender had re-offended eleven times whilst on bail.[85]

The criminal knows that, as is frequently the case, the additional crimes committed on bail will make little or no difference to his subsequent sentence. He is aware that the courts will go to any lengths to avoid passing a prison sentence or, if one is passed, it will be short or concurrent; from his point of view there is no reason to stop offending.

Faced with growing unease in the country about the prolific offending of 'bail bandits', the government set about giving the appearance of doing something about the problem, albeit, in reality, it left the problem largely unsolved. For example, it enacted the Criminal Justice and Public Order Act of November 1994, which said there should be 'no right' to bail for persons accused or convicted of committing an offence whilst on bail, with effect from 10 April 1995.[86]

Notice the use of the phrase 'no right'; this is conspicuously different from telling the courts they cannot use bail in these circumstances. This added legal obfuscation still allows the courts to bail prolific offenders; thus the government kept the bail door open, whilst at the same time, giving the impression that they were doing the opposite.

Despite the measures taken in the Criminal Justice and Public Order Act of November 1994, which included giving the police added powers, in some circumstances, to refuse bail, the issue of offenders committing crime whilst on bail continued to be a problem.[87] Again, the government's response fell short of using its powers to intervene and unambiguously stop courts from bailing persistent offenders (which it could have done at any time). Instead, in 1996, it created a further diversion by setting up the Bail Issues Steering Group, made up of government departments, professional bodies and criminal justice agencies, in order to give the public the impression that it was still determined to confront the problem.

The supposed purpose of this 'talking shop' was to review findings from a number of bail studies and make an appropriate response. Predictably, it decided it needed yet more information before it could do so (as if the crime figures for those on bail were not enough) and instigated yet more research.

From the point of view of the safety of the public, the results published by the Home Office in 1998 were catastrophic. Despite claims by the Home Office that adult offending on bail had been reduced since the imposition of the 1994 Criminal Justice and Public Order Act,[88] the 1998 research results showed that as many as one in four adult defendants committed crimes whilst on bail, and one in three juveniles,[89] totalling at least 50,000 crimes each year.[90] This was despite Jack Straw's statement a year before (in 1997) that he would give magistrates the power to remand in custody male juvenile persistent offenders under the age of fourteen years, and female offenders under the age of sixteen years.[91] However, five years later, as at August 2002, there has been no change in the law regarding the bailing of juveniles; the courts still did not have the powers promised by Jack Straw. His statement was simply a well-rehearsed tactic to placate public opinion at the time.[92]

In response to the catastrophic state of affairs identified by the 1998 Home Office research results, the then Home Office minister Alun Michael made a statement remarkably similar in tone to the empty promise made by Jack Straw only twelve months previously. He also announced that 'the government was determined to confront the problem of bail abuse', and said that proposals in the forthcoming Crime and Disorder Bill would 'address the situation'.[93]

He either did not mean it or he did not know what the bill was going to say, or possibly his advisors, in a bid to placate those who were still restive at the continued problem posed by bail bandits, simply misled him. Either way, when the Bill became the Crime and Disorder Act 1998,[94] it did nothing to stop courts remanding persistent offenders on bail. Its only two bail clauses, Sections 54 and 55, referred to the imposition of bail conditions and strengthening the use of sureties. In fact, Section 54 potentially *increased* the powers of the police to grant bail (see Note 1). Once again, the minister's statement had been nothing more than a smokescreen to hide the fact that the bail arrangements were going to be left substantially unchanged, allowing prolific offenders to go on victimising thousands of members of the public.

Thus the government's apparent show of concern, its instigation of research, its changes in the law, and the commission of working parties to examine the issue of offending on bail, were all meant to give the impression that they were making every effort to deal with the problem. But this was pseudo activity to hide their real purpose, which was to do nothing to encourage or enable the courts to remand more persistent offenders in custody, and thus further highlight the acute shortage of prison places.

The government was afraid that, if the courts were given real powers to protect the public and remand in custody all of the offenders who posed a risk of further offending, the prisons would be swamped. One source of their anxiety was that by 2001 they knew that an earlier Home Office estimate, made in August 1992, that 'most crime was committed by a small number of hard-core offenders'[95] was either inaccurate or by then simply out of date. Their up-to-date intelligence now told them that there were at least '100,000 persistent offenders responsible for half of crime'.[96]

The existence of such large numbers of offenders unmotivated to change is the devastating result of sentencing policies which have so lavishly rewarded their criminal behaviour. Criminals who would have been deterred early on in their offending careers by a tough zero-tolerance-style response have voted in increasing numbers in favour of sticking unwaveringly to a life of crime because it has been made risk-free, easy and highly profitable by the inept and weak response shown to them by all governments since the Second World War.

The government's own financial and ideological objections to embarking on a substantial prison-building programme would ensure that there were never going to be enough prison places for anything like this number; therefore it had to stick tenaciously to its covert aim of keeping down the number of remands in custody at all costs.

Whilst the consequences of this policy for the thousands victimised by those on bail are dreadful, they are made worse by knowing that, for some of them, their victimisation was to a certain extent avoidable. If the courts had seized their opportunity and properly exercised the powers given to them by the 1976 Bail Act they could have remanded in custody at least some offenders who threatened the safety of the public. The government might then have faced awkward demands to fund the required increase in prison places. This would not have been as difficult as has been made out. If the Home Office can find temporary holding places to house illegal immigrants, they can do so with regard to offenders, until more permanent prison places become available.

One of the clauses of the 1976 Bail Act clearly states that if the magistrates have reason to believe that the offender would continue to offend if given bail, they can, in certain circumstances, remand him in custody. Despite the fact that such offenders are easy to identify, the courts frequently do not use this power. On the other hand, as far as the police are concerned, the Police and Criminal Evidence Act 1984 did not specifically provide for the detention of an offender in custody on the grounds that further offences are likely.[97] That is in itself quite an extraordinary omission, and there may well have been a reason for it. I strongly suspect that the government was not going to give the police powers to remand offenders in custody unless it could possibly help it, because it knew they would use them. But why have the courts generally failed to use even their limited powers to remand at least some offenders in custody?

Intimidating the Courts

The answer is that for the last thirty years the courts have been put under immense pressure from a number of different directions not to send offenders to gaol, either on remand or as a sentence; their sentencing record shows how effective this pressure has been.

During the 1970s and 1980s, some of this pressure came from a number of well-known anti-prison organisations who regularly published what were known at the time as 'ball and chain' lists. These were 'league tables' showing the number of prison sentences passed by magistrates' courts in different parts of the country. Their undisguised purpose was to intimidate lay magistrates into ideologically 'outlawing' the use of prison, by exposing those who topped the league tables to ridicule, criticism and hostility. During these years, I had frequent and close contact with a number of lay justices and I can testify to the fact that this vicious form of barracking had a powerfully draining effect on their confidence.

Intimidation of magistrates sometimes took on more direct and sinister forms. A clerk of the court in the West Midlands told me that he once watched in horror as a probation officer performed an ugly parody of the Nazi-style goose step march in the court, in full view of the magistrates, to demonstrate his disagreement with the sentence they had just passed on an offender. That the confidence of the magistrates and other court officials was already in decline can be judged by the fact that no action was taken against the probation officer concerned.

Magistrates' willingness to use prison as a means of protecting the public was further undermined by the unchallenged propaganda fed to them by the Probation Service in their regular 'liaison' meetings with their local magistrates. In the 1960s, these meetings had been used by the magistrates to check on the progress of offenders and also to find out if probation officers were carrying out the magistrates' intentions as far as the supervision of the offender was concerned. Many in the Probation Service did not like being held to account by the justices in this way; they argued that was the job of their own management structure. Therefore, during the 1970s, the format of these meetings was changed to one which kept the magistrates informed about the work of the service and briefed them on the latest offender supervision methods. In reality, it gave the Probation Service unbridled opportunity to brainwash the lay justices with their anti-prison ideology, and their false claims of success for the community supervision of offenders.

In the absence of any other, more objective information, more and more magistrates succumbed to this torrent of misinformation, and incredibly they, too, began to adopt anti-prison rhetoric and to believe the lie that to supervise persistent offenders in the community was a more effective way of protecting the public from crime than prison. In addition, their major journal, *The Magistrate*, refused to publish articles that opposed anti-prison ideology, even when they were backed up by all the available evidence.

A third and equally potent form of anti-prison propaganda aimed at undermining the will of both judges and magistrates to sentence persistent offenders to prison came in the form of reports on offenders presented to the courts by probation officers. Ostensibly intended to help the court decide on a suitable sentence for the offender, they became, from the early 1970s onwards, the vehicles for the Probation Service's anti-prison policy. During the 1980s, the determination by the Probation Service to divert as many offenders as possible from prison reached such an intensity that some chief probation officers issued instructions to their staff to avoid any language that might make the magistrate even think about the possibility of a prison sentence. A 'commissar' system was even established whereby each report was checked by a colleague to make sure these rules were followed. Whilst the style of probation reports has recently changed and some are now more realistic, this has occurred too late to reverse the anti-prison indoctrination of

51

many magistrates and judges brought about by their reading of tens of thousands of probation reports over a period of more than two decades.

The results of this stranglehold on free debate have been dramatic. It was not, as has been suggested, that magistrates were failing to remand many offenders in custody because they *misunderstood* the Bail Act,[98] it was because of the relentless pressure on them from their own hierarchies, as well as the propaganda, intimidation and bullying by the anti-prison factions, aimed at discouraging them from sending offenders to prison, either at the remand stage or for sentence.

This pressure has been so undermining that, as already indicated, many magistrates (and judges) have adopted the thinking and rhetoric of those who so ruthlessly set out to influence them. The evidence for this is that the courts go out of their way not to send the majority of prolific and persistent offenders to prison. Instead they allow most of them to return to the community where they continue to victimise the public with often calamitous results for people's well-being and peace of mind. The anti-prison propagandists can be well satisfied. They have done their job well.

Chapter 3

The Undeclared Propaganda War

The previous chapter has described in some detail *how* the criminal justice system in the United Kingdom has gone about making life easier and more rewarding for criminals. However, just as important and equally compelling is to ask *why* these extraordinary developments have come about. What has motivated those in positions of influence to decide that this is how our criminal justice system should operate?

The Influence of the Treasury

The influence of the Treasury in the general governance of the country in the modern post-war period has been pivotal. Its philosophy leads it to a natural suspicion that government spending, unless checked and managed, has an inherent tendency to get out of control.[1]

From the 1950s onwards, one particular source of anxiety for the Treasury in this respect has been the prison budget. The long-term projections of expenditure on prisons no doubt led Treasury, Home Office officials and others in the criminal justice system to believe that this was unlikely to decline, and in all probability would continue to rise. The problem which therefore faced them was this: how could they control the prison budget when they could do nothing about the criminal behaviour that gave rise to the demand for prison places?

Their solution was to find a way of persuading the British people to support sentencing policies that allowed the majority of persistent offenders to remain in the community. Such policies would enable them to restrict the demand for prison places, as far as was possible, and so exert some measure of control on prison costs. But how were they to do this? What could they possibly do or say to persuade the public that the majority of persistent criminals who continually robbed them, burgled their homes and stole their property should not go to prison, but stay living in the community, shoulder to shoulder, as it were, with their victims? How could they do this without seeming to rub salt into the wounds of millions of those who had been victimised by criminals?

Techniques of Persuasion

To understand the solution they hit upon, we must turn to the influence of two men whose ideas provided exactly the sort of template that was required. One is almost unknown to the general public; the other, however, is related to arguably one of the most famous persons of the twentieth century.

The first is Professor Leslie Wilkins. Although he has received little official recognition, it has been said of him that he was one of the most scientifically distinguished criminologists of his generation.[2] He was born in 1915, and in the lead-up to the Second World War he joined the aircraft industry. He had a deep interest in statistics, and during the war he applied these skills to the analysis of aircraft accidents. He later joined the government's Social Survey team, and displayed impressive predictive statistical skills. As a result, he was asked to work in the field of criminal justice.

Wilkins' study of a sample of wartime infants concluded they were 'exceptionally delinquent' and led him to hypothesise that this was associated with the stressful social and family conditions which prevailed during the war years.[3] This was seized upon by criminal-justice policy makers who saw the propaganda opportunity to promote the idea that criminals in general were victims of society's strains and stresses and should not carry the sole blame for their offending. Instead, so their argument went, we should focus on the many social factors associated with crime such as poverty, family influences, unemployment, education and so on, even though no such causal links had ever (or have ever) been established. The idea that society and its associated problems were to blame for crime, and not the criminal, was exactly the sort of message that the government needed the public to accept in order to be able to control expenditure on prisons.

Whilst Professor Wilkins hypothesised that the high levels of delinquency exhibited by children in his study were associated with the absence of a father figure owing to the war, it must be said that none of his work took the simple-minded view that social problems 'caused' crime. What fell into the lap of the post-1950s government officials, who were more than ready to misuse the results of Wilkins' research, was the *idea* that crime could be presented to the public as being attributable to social causes, whose remedy could be sought in community strategies, and not by imprisoning the offender.

In addition, applying statistical analysis to information collected by research on these 'social problems' would give this notion a level of respectability and mystique that would fall neatly in line with the government's propaganda purposes. The ring fencing of these supposed 'crime related social problems' with the academic language of research and analysis would make them less accessible to argument and dissent by the lay public, who increasingly would have to yield to the supposed expertise of the social scientists.

The fact that this so-called 'scientific' analysis would be bogus was irrelevant to the government's cause. Although the spectacle of researchers looking for data to fit their unfounded theories about the causes of crime was pseudo-science, it would nevertheless form the backbone of a new university-based social-science industry. Its 'research' results would help promote the government's propaganda message; anyone arguing against their conclusions that crime was the result of social problems could be labelled as ignorant and reactionary. Between the late 1950s and the 1970s, these theories were further developed by a number of left-wing criminologists in such books as *The New Criminology: For a Social Theory of Deviance*.[4] In this publication, for example, the authors argued that 'we are confronted once again with the central question of man's relationship to structures of power, domination and authority – and the ability of men to confront these structures in acts of *crime, deviance and dissent*' (my italics). Thus, their social theories promoted criminals as 'revolutionaries', struggling against an oppressive State. Indeed, such ideas had already been disseminated at regular conferences of left-wing criminologists that had met during the 1950s and 1960s, under the title of the 'New Deviancy Symposium', and there is little doubt that many criminal justice policy makers and practitioners were more than willing to be influenced by them.

If, in addition, the myth that the causes of crime were 'complex' and only comprehensible to 'experts' could be successfully projected onto the public, they would then, under the illusion that the 'experts' knew best, be more likely to accept the propaganda message that 'prison does more harm than good'. This would ensure some measure of acceptance from the public that criminals should be allowed to stay in the community, despite the immense harm and distress they were causing because of their continued criminality.

The government officials in the Treasury and the Home Office now had the propaganda message they needed. The British people were to be told that the causes of crime were 'social'; crime was to be seen as the result of pressures emanating from our communities, rather than the fault of the offender. The belief that sufficient numbers of the public would be susceptible to such a campaign was founded on powerful and convincing demonstrations by market researchers that propaganda could be used very effectively to influence the thinking and behaviour of large numbers of people. One particularly influential member of this new and growing industry was Edward Bernays. He was the nephew of Sigmund Freud, and he was very interested in his uncle's ideas that the behaviour of individual people could be influenced, at least in part, by unconscious forces within themselves. In the decades before and after the Second World War, Bernays applied these ideas to the advertising of products on behalf of large corporations in the United States. He had stunning success, as indicated by the following example.

In the 1930s the American tobacco corporations wanted to increase their sales by persuading women to smoke. At that time, there was a powerful social taboo against this practice. They hired Bernays to create an advertising concept to achieve this. He arranged for a group of glamorous women to be photographed and filmed smoking cigarettes, which they were seen to carry strapped to their thighs by means of a black garter. They all gave the impression of being relaxed, happy and successful, smiling into the cameras under the slogan 'The Torch of Freedom'. These images were broadcast all over America in newspapers, on advertising hoardings, and in magazines and cinemas. The sales of cigarettes to women rocketed throughout the country. Bernays reasoned that a suitably worded, well-presented slogan could exert influence on the thinking of large groups of people, especially if the slogan made connection with the unconscious wishes or fears of the target group. He argued that in this case, the slogan, supported by the powerful imagery, had linked with the unconscious wishes of women to be as 'powerful as men' and free of the social taboos which subjugated them.

Even those sceptical of the role of the 'unconscious' in these matters could not deny his incredible success, which Bernays repeated using a wide variety of propaganda scenarios for many different products. Whatever the dynamics of his propaganda formula were, they worked. Thus by the late 1950s, there was widespread knowledge about the effectiveness of propaganda and its potential as an instrument of social coercion. Indeed, Vance Packard's now legendary book, *The Hidden Persuaders*, warned of the increasingly powerful psychological techniques being used by big business in advertising their products.[5]

There was therefore every good reason for those in power to believe that suitable slogans delivered in the right way could engineer the consent of the British people to a sentencing policy which allowed the majority of persistent offenders to stay in the community. These 'hidden persuaders' could also anticipate such policies would cause the public great harm; therefore the propaganda message would have to be well managed and continually reinforced.

The message that crime is the fault of 'society' is doubly powerful because in effect it suggests that individual members of the public must share the blame for offenders being forced into a life of crime. Thus the propaganda engages the community's guilt, known by psychiatrists and therapists to be a powerful driver of human behaviour. For example, Ben Sheppard's recent review of the psychiatric treatment of shell-shocked soldiers identified guilt to be a common theme in the illness of these patients.[6] In addition, those who, in the 1930s, pioneered the application of psychoanalytic techniques to market research, such as Edward Bernays and Ernest Dichter[7] had discovered that guilt offered powerful opportunities for advertisers to manipulate public opinion and behaviour.

This was clearly demonstrated in the advice given by Bernays to a large US food manufacturer in the 1940s. The company had pioneered a packet of ready-made cake mix. They were convinced it would sell well to increasingly busy American housewives, as it would allow them to make cakes in half the time. They were puzzled by the poor sales and took the problem to Bernays. He eventually told them to add one sentence to the instructions on the packet. That sentence was 'add an egg'. The sales of the pre-made cake mix rocketed. Bernays' analysis was that the housewives rejected the cake mix because it made them feel guilty about 'being lazy' and 'not being a good provider' for their family. Including the instruction 'add an egg' to the cake mix allowed housewives to feel they were providing properly for their family, a response greatly assisted by the powerful symbolic nature which 'eggs' represented for them.

Thus, engaging society's guilt about criminals enabled the additional slogan 'prison makes people worse' to be even more effective. Once the community had been persuaded that criminals were 'victims' of its own acquisitiveness and unfairness, it would feel reluctant to advocate prison for the persistent offender because that would be tantamount to victimising him again, and so be doubly unfair.

The Propaganda War Gets Under Way

By the 1950s, the results of earlier experiments in psychoanalytic based and motivational market research by public-relations and advertising companies had coalesced into well-established advertising strategies. By 1951, for example, advertising agencies were being urged to see themselves as 'one of the most advanced laboratories in psychology'.[8] Confidence in these techniques was such that, later in the decade, professional advertising journals claimed that 'psychology not only held the key to understand people, but the method to control their behaviour'.

I believe it was therefore no accident that it was in the late 1950s that the government officials in the United Kingdom unleashed their undeclared anti-prison propaganda war on an unsuspecting public, with a report entitled *Penal Practice in a Changing Society*.[9] Ostensibly, this report set out to discuss the changing role of prisons and the problems of rising crime and ways and means of coping with it. The report even acknowledged that more prisons would probably have to be built as resources became available. However, there was much in it to indicate that its major purpose was to prepare the British people for significant changes in sentencing practice and that these in the long run would place less emphasis on prison and more on community penalties as a way of confronting what the report referred to as the 'environmental' dimensions of crime. It spoke, for example, of the need for research into the 'varied and complex causes' of crime. However, nowhere did it explain the evidence trail which showed how it reached these assumptions concerning the existence of such 'causes'. The report also encouraged universities to take part in this research. The officials involved recognised that research by academics on this subject would lend a powerful respectability to their arguments in the eyes of the vulnerable public. What was important for their purposes was to encourage the public to keep alive in their minds the idea that persistent offenders committed crime because of the influence of pressing social or psychological forces beyond their control; a theory all the more to be believed because 'social scientists' and other 'experts' were saying so on the basis of their 'research'.

In the 1960s social scientists and sociologists answered the government's call and a flood of books on crime and its 'causes' were published by such authors as Fyvel, Jones, Miller, Wilson, Cohen, West, Gibbens, Cloward and Ohlin, and Mays to name but a few.[10] Between them they discussed, as potential factors influencing crime and delinquency, physical and psychological problems, the 'inner conflicts' of adolescence, the environmental pressures of school, neighbourhood and poor housing estates, the influence of peers and gangs, anti-authority youth culture, lack of job training, the effects of 'rapid social change', personal insecurity, broken homes and early problems in childhood.

Social-science students in the 1960s were given many of these as standard study texts. They were all redolent with unproven ideas, but nevertheless they quickly gained ground in the minds of increasing numbers of people with specialist interests as well as the general public. For example, in Fyvel's book *The Insecure Offenders*, he posed the question: 'What is the shape of society that is producing increased numbers of offenders?'[11] Thus not only did he automatically assume that society was 'producing' crime, but furthermore he presented it as if it was something that 'everyone knew' and was beyond being questioned. Such ideas, it seems, had already become established as tablets of truth, which few dared question.

Likewise, Howard Jones, in *Crime in a Changing Society*, spoke of the need for our penal system to 'become an effective agency of treatment'. He argued that better *diagnosis* (my italics) of the offender's problem was required and that the sentencing function of the court should be handed to a treatment authority.[12] Thus he promoted the idea that the criminal was not so much responsible for his actions, but more the victim of a malaise not of his making but which must be identified and 'treated', as with an illness. Indeed, Fyvel even suggested that criminals might be seen as 'victims' of society and its various pressures.[13]

Nothing could suit the cause of the anti-prison propagandists more than the popularisation of such ideas. Their acceptance as general currency would encourage the public to support the idea that increasing numbers of criminals should be 'treated' in the community and not sent to prison. It is for this reason, I believe, that at no time has the public been exposed to a proper debate on these ideas. For example, even though crime may be believed by many to be influenced by psychological and social factors, they are irrelevant to the problems posed to us by the persistent offender. By the time an offender has become 'persistent', it is far too late for any insights into his background or other problems to be of any use. I shall return to this theme later in the book, but for the present suffice it to say that methods of working with offenders based on such 'understanding' have blatantly failed to stop them offending.

So whether or not such 'causes' of crime become established with any certainty in the future, they are redundant in the face of well-established, persistent, hard-core offenders who have typically already been offered all sorts of help with their 'problems'. As the official records show, the vast majority of them have been given a string of non-custodial sentences by long-suffering courts. During this time, armies of social workers and probation officers have made numerous 'interventions' into the lives of these offenders based on insights into the pressing social and psychological factors assumed to be associated with their offending behaviour; yet they have failed to reform. The priority is for the public to be protected from them, and the only sure way of doing that is for the persistent offenders concerned to lose their freedom, irrespective of their age.

The timing of the 1959 report *Penal Practice in a Changing Society*, was highly significant, following closely in the wake of heightened Treasury anxieties about rising prison costs and the failure of the prison-building programme to meet the demand for places. It was therefore not surprising that it introduced the idea that preventive detention (the system of imprisoning persistent and dangerous offenders for long periods of time) would have to be 'reviewed' – a clear signal that, at a certain point in the future, it was to be phased out, as indeed proved to be the case.

Thus from the late 1950s all governments, whatever their political persuasion, have fed the British people with a diet of anti-prison propaganda. The level of sincerity with which this propaganda has been disseminated has been varied. Some ministers and their government officials appear, for ideological reasons, to believe in their own anti-prison rhetoric, as opposed to others, not driven by ideology, who have set out to manipulate public opinion for reasons of government policy. Others have supported an anti-prison policy for career reasons, and, rather than rock the boat, they have kept any misgivings they may have had to themselves.

There have also been ministers who simply lacked knowledge or any strong sense of commitment to these issues and were prepared to follow the anti-prison philosophy of their more zealous officials. For example, in 1992 an experienced judge expressed his concern that John Patten's officials (he was then an under minister at the Home Office) 'may have preyed on his lack of legal experience to get through some cranky ideas by which they appear to be obsessed, but which might not appeal to the majority of Members of Parliament if they took the trouble to study them, and will certainly not appeal to the victims of crime'.[14] The cranky ideas he was referring to were those contained in the 1991 Criminal Justice Act, which as we shall see in a moment, absurdly tried to rule out prison as a sentencing option for the majority of offenders.

Fuelled by these and other sources, this anti-prison rhetoric has over the years increased in tempo, as the fight against crime has been substituted by a war against prisons. Government ministers, civil servants, MPs, prison-reform groups, as well as many in the media, have targeted the British people with non-stop propaganda to persuade them that, for example, 'prisons are more expensive than supervising offenders in the community'; 'there are too many people in prison'; 'the United Kingdom sends more people to prison than most other European countries'; 'prisons are colleges of crime'; prisons make people worse'; 'offenders can be more effectively supervised in the community'; 'the methods used by the Probation Service in supervising offenders in the community are effective in reducing crime'.

Such slogans are designed to excite the public's anxieties about the possible threat of increased taxation to meet the ever-rising costs of prison as well as their sense of shame and guilt at the prospect of imprisoning offenders who are 'victims' of society and less fortunate than themselves. However, what the public has never been told is that there exists a reliable body of evidence which, as I shall discuss later, overwhelmingly contradicts every one of these slogans.

The War Against Prison

By the late 1960s, the public were thought to have been sufficiently prepared to ensure their acceptance of a softer approach to sentencing. From 1967 onwards, numerous criminal justice acts were passed, each of which made it easier for the courts to avoid using prison as a sentencing option. As already mentioned, the enthusiasm of some home secretaries for these increasingly liberal sentencing policies emanated from their own ideologically based anti-prison beliefs, as well as for reasons of government policy. Others were carried along by the advice of their officials, which they were unable to counter due to their lack of knowledge in these matters.

Roy Jenkins was an example of one Home Secretary who appeared to believe in the anti-prison ideology espoused by Home Office civil servants. He spoke passionately in support of a liberal approach towards sentencing, and towards the end of his time in office the Criminal Justice Act of 1967 was passed, which for the first time, allowed judges to suspend prison sentences. Two years later, when James Callaghan was Home Secretary, the Children and Young Persons Act 1969 was passed. This introduced the absurd idea of 'intermediate treatment', which in effect meant that young offenders who had committed offences such as burglary or other forms of theft were to be rewarded with holidays and other activities such as sailing and horse-riding lessons. The message aimed at the public was clear. It was society's fault that these youngsters had turned to crime; therefore society had to make it up to them.[15]

The public's compliant response to these innovations no doubt encouraged the government to believe it could further open the liberal floodgates with yet more anti-prison legislation. As a result the Criminal Justice Act 1972 gave the courts still more non-custodial options to use when sentencing offenders. This act brought in 'community service', which allowed the offender to remain free and the court to sentence him to so many hours work in the community. This provision sounded punitive, which reassured the sceptics that the government was being 'tough' on crime. Nothing, of course, could have been further from the truth. The same Act also introduced 'Day Training Centres' for offenders, to be used as an alternative to a prison sentence. These provided three-month programmes, run on a daily basis, aimed at dealing with some of the supposed causes of crime, such as a lack of education and employment. These centres were situated in the community allowing the offenders to return to their homes at the end of the day. They were monumental failures and had no impact on the reconviction rates of the offenders concerned, who continued to victimise the public with their continued offending.

Yet government officials ignored this evidence and some centres were kept going for years afterwards. This is because their real purpose was to keep alive in the minds of the public the *idea* that crime is caused by problems associated with, for example, unemployment, lack of job skills and education – all of which, it is often argued, can be made worse by sending the offender to prison.

The courts had now been given several non-custodial sentencing options. But the anti-prison legislators had not yet finished; they were to dream up yet more ways of avoiding the offender being sent to prison. Their next innovation, made available in the Criminal Justice Act 1973, allowed the courts to pass a prison sentence and then 'defer' it for a period of time. The offender was allowed his freedom and, if he avoided further convictions during the period of deferment, he was no longer subject to the threat of the custodial sentence. (This provision, like a number of others, was to backfire on the intentions of the legislators, and so in time it fell out of favour.)

Government officials were encouraged by the quiet response of the public to this anti-prison legislation and took it as a signal that their propaganda campaign had been successful. Flushed with this success they decided to open the liberal sentencing floodgates wider than ever before; the Criminal Justice Act 1982 placed severe restrictions on the use of prison for offenders under twenty-one years, and in 1991 a Criminal Justice Act was passed which attempted to close off prison as a sentencing option for almost all persistent property offenders; as a result it contained some of the most absurd and unworkable clauses ever seen in the history of sentencing legislation in the United Kingdom.

The Emperor's New Clothes

Three particular clauses of this Act amounted to a 'criminals' charter', as they unambiguously set out to make life easier, safer and more rewarding for criminals. The first said that no matter how many offences an offender had committed, the court could sentence him only for one and, in some special circumstances, for two of them. The criminal who stood before the courts charged with, for example, fifty offences, must have thought he was dreaming when he learned that the courts were going to ignore forty-nine of them.

The second of these clauses said that, when sentencing an offender, the court could not take into account his previous convictions or his failure to comply with previous sentencing arrangements. Thus, offenders who by their continued criminality had shown their contempt for the leniency previously shown to them by the courts, in an attempt to encourage them to reform, were to be sentenced as if for the first time.

The third clause ordered that fines should be set by means of a formula which reflected the offender's (so-called) ability to pay and a system of fixed points (or units) allocated to each offence indicating its seriousness.[16] This resulted in bizarre and totally unjust sentences: persistent burglars who claimed they had no money (because they were 'unemployed') escaped with derisory and meaningless fines, while first-time motoring offenders who earned good salaries were fined at draconian levels.

In addition, the requirements not to take into account previous convictions when sentencing, and to only pass sentence for one offence when several had been committed, were so absurd that they deeply fractured the court's understanding of basic justice and common sense. These ridiculous clauses, therefore, soon proved unworkable, even to a judicial system brainwashed with anti-prison propaganda, and after only seven months they were all abolished. Never before in our modern legal history had sections of an Act of Parliament been abolished so quickly after their inception; never had parts of an Act been found to be so inept and out of touch with reality.

Yet despite these extraordinary events, there was hardly a ripple in the press or the community at large. There were predictable protests from the anti-prison groups such as the Howard League, the Prison Reform Trust and the Probation Service,[17] but Parliament kept its head down over the issue. Kenneth Clarke, the new Home Secretary, whose clear-sightedness had brought an end to these legal sentencing aberrations, was hardly challenged and the press gave minimal coverage to a legal scandal that should have rocked Fleet Street. It was as if a collective sense of shame and bewilderment prevented any proper re-examination in Parliament of what had happened.

This sense of shame and unease experienced by many MPs (and others) was no doubt increased by the fact that they knew that these clauses had been discussed and ruminated upon for months during the committee stages of this bill. Yet few MPs, if any, spoke out against them. How could so many intelligent and resourceful individuals have not seen their sheer lunacy? A few parliamentarians have since had the courage to say that in retrospect they cannot understand why they supported those parts of the bill. It was as if they were in a dream (or perhaps a nightmare) induced, I would argue, by the ceaseless mantra of the anti-prison lobby.

There is no doubt that many MPs surrendered their critical faculties during the debate on these particular clauses of the 1991 Act, partly as a result of their being exposed to anti-prison propaganda for so long, and partly because they were blinded by the pseudo-science of those who argued in favour of it. This led many of them to assume that their natural instinct to want to reject these particular parts of the Act was based on their ignorance of this subject. They allowed themselves to be gulled into believing that others must know better than they did – and rather than reveal their supposed ignorance and risk intimidation by the vociferous anti-prison zealots, they decided to go along with their arguments and so voted in favour of the now infamous three requirements described above.

Their chief architect was David Faulkner, previously a senior Home Office civil servant, who later became a Fellow of St John's College, Oxford. He has gone on record as saying that there are too many people in prison (how does he know?), and has resorted to mental gymnastics in his attempt to justify the thinking behind the Criminal Justice Act 1991, describing it as 'a common sense view of punishment'.[18] He also complained that Kenneth Clarke had abolished the relevant parts of the Act 'without consultation', and argued that the Criminal Justice Act 1991 was an attempt to 'create a reformed and effective justice system which recognised the capacity and will of the offender to change and to improve if they are given guidance.[19]

Such statements show him to be a naive armchair spokesman on these issues with no real understanding of what it is that motivates persistent criminals. It is precisely because persistent offenders have continued to commit crime, despite being given guidance and countless opportunities to reform, that they have demonstrated they have no will to change. Crime pays too well, and the risks are far too small for there to be any incentive for them to give up. For Faulkner and others to project persistent criminals as those who 'need help, guidance and encouragement' is as removed from reality as it is possible to be.[20] Also there is nothing remotely reformative about laws which only allow the courts to sentence an offender for one offence when he has committed numerous crimes, which stops them taking into account the offender's previous conviction history, and which forces the court to impose fines based on lies from the offender concerning his means to pay. It should be obvious to all that such insanity encourages offenders to go on committing crime.

From a common-sense standpoint, it seems incredible that these baseless and dangerous ideas, which were no more than the pet theories of certain government officials, should ever have been taken seriously, let alone be translated into official sentencing policy. However, when viewed through the eyes of the anti-prison propagandists, such notions are seen as central to their purpose. However, on this occasion, they had gone too far; these clauses of the 1991 Act had proved to be so out of touch with reality that even a government basically sympathetic to them had to give way and abolish them. For the first time since the 1960s, the anti-prison ideologists, both inside and outside of Whitehall, had suffered a setback. But they were not to be denied. Their tactic was to lie low and wait for the next opportunity to revive these further extreme anti-prison measures.

A Second Bite of the Apple

Such an opportunity arrived ten years later in 2001 with the publication of the Auld Report, which was commissioned by Tony Blair's government to make radical proposals for the reform of the criminal justice system.[21] The anti-prison civil servants and their fellow ideologues were determined to seize this opportunity to engineer yet more powerful restraints on the court's use of prison; but this time they were more careful and in the Auld Report they used all their arts of deception to disguise their intentions with spin and obfuscation.

The report, published in 2001, was so worded that it gave the initial impression that it recommended putting the victim and the protection of the public centre stage of a reformed criminal justice system. However, on closer examination it is found that nothing could be further from the truth. Instead, as shall be discussed in Chapter Six, it is a powerful invocation of much of the spirit and intentions of the discredited 1991 Act.

The 'Apparatchiks'

The public should be in no doubt that the Auld Report reflects the anti-prison ideology still being followed by powerful government officials. The career structure of these civil servants has ensured that few of them will break ranks and fail to support the party line that prisons 'fail and are overused'. I have met with a number of civil servants and have presented them with compelling evidence which showed that prisons protect the public from crime and that community supervision of persistent offenders puts the public at risk. They have always been implacably polite, giving the appearance of listening most attentively, but this is a mask. They pull down steel shutters in their mind and block out any evidence which demonstrates that their sentencing policies are wrong.

They are reminiscent of the Russian apparatchiks described in Gail Sheehy's book *Gorbachev*.[22] She describes them as an army of full-time paid professional functionaries who were employed to maintain the Soviet communist state system and its propaganda machine. Thousands of these bureaucrats were employed to fill out false returns in order to support the claims of their factory bosses that target output levels had been reached. These returns, which everyone involved knew were false, were then submitted to their Kremlin masters. The motivation to do so for the thousands of officials involved was that it kept them in paid work, held the promise of some sort of future, and it kept them safe from the censure of their leaders whose sanctions they had cause to fear.

In the case of our civil servants, few of them if any would risk telling their superiors that they had evidence which showed that the policy advice they have given to ministers on the question of sentencing of offenders was seriously flawed. The need to guard and promote their careers keeps them quiet and the concern not to blot their copybook results in many becoming preoccupied with looking over their shoulders, constantly on guard against being controversial.[23] Thus, the evidence of the failure of our criminal justice system is never acted upon, with disastrous results for the public.

Sometimes this process is reversed and officials find themselves under pressure from ministers to provide information to support a departmental decision already decided upon. For example, toward the end of 1999, I was told by a senior civil servant that when 'New Labour' came to power in 1997, his department received instructions to provide the government with data it could use to back up its already made policy decision to put North American style offenders' programmes at the centre of its community-sentencing strategy. Almost three years later, Michael Brown, writing in the *Independent*, pointed out that evidence was mounting generally to show that ministers were no longer interested in weighing up objective advice dealing with all aspects of a particular policy. The results of the UK experiments styled on American community offender programmes were a failure but this was ignored. Instead, the government preferred to take individual snippets of information, often out of context, to justify a policy they had already fixed upon.[24]

Nicholas Jones has pointed out in his book *Control Freaks*, that as soon as New Labour came to power they set about politicising the Central Office of Information and the Civil Service generally,[25] but many officials had already been following their own agenda in relation to sentencing policy for years. However, according to one newspaper report, the process of politicisation of the Civil Service was widened when the Prime Minister, Tony Blair, instructed the then Permanent Secretary, Sir Robin Mounsfield, to carry out a review of the work done by Civil Service information officers in order to 'raise their game'.[26] This resulted in former Prime Minister John Major delivering a sweeping indictment of the Blair government, and accusing it of eroding the trust of the people by undermining Parliament and politicising the Civil Service.[27]

The Hypnotic Effect of the Cinema

However, ministers and officials have not had to conduct their anti-prison propaganda campaign alone. Hundreds of films have been screened in the United Kingdom since the 1950s with plots involving brutal behaviour by prison guards, prison escapes, wrongful imprisonment, harsh and unjust sentences, as well as vulnerable prisoners being subjected to intimidation, violence and corruption at the hands of other inmates. For example, *Weak and the Wicked* (1954), *The Defiant Ones* (1958), *The Chase* (1966), *Papillon* (1973), *Midnight Express* (1978), *Escape from Alcatraz* (1979), *The Shawshank Redemption* (1994).[28]

Whether intended or not, the mesmeric effects of such repeated and often powerful images have played a significant role in influencing our ideas about prisons. The notion that prisons are wrong, bad and corrupting has been driven deep into the unconscious mind of the public, increasing their vulnerability to the spurious arguments from so called 'experts' in the criminal justice system, as well as various prison-reform groups, and many academics and some journalists, that 'prison does not work' and that persistent offenders should be dealt with in the community.

The Fifth Columnists

The prison-reform groups in the United Kingdom such as the Howard League for Penal Reform, the Prison Reform Trust and the National Association for the Care and Resettlement of Offenders (NACRO) are no longer just prison-reform movements promoting better conditions for inmates. They have become vociferous, ideological pressure groups hungry for any opportunity to brainwash the judiciary and the public with their message that prisons fail and that most offenders can be dealt with more effectively by being left in the community.

The ruthlessness of their campaign to achieve these ends should not be underestimated. For example, in 1993 an article appeared in *The Magistrate* in which NACRO claimed that '88 per cent of adult ex-offenders and 80 per cent of young ex-offenders on their training schemes did not reoffend',[29] a statement which is unsupported by all known facts as well as by common sense. Had this ridiculous statement been anywhere near the truth we would largely have

69

solved the problem of crime in this country, and other nations would have imported the NACRO system to solve their problems. The prison-reform groups refuse to acknowledge the simple but powerful truth that whilst persistent offenders are locked up they are not free to predate on the public, and they deny the immense value of prison as a way of providing tangible protection to countless potential victims of crime.

The Howard League, for example, openly argues against the use of prison for all persistent property offenders, including burglars and robbers. Material on its web site states: 'Prisons are overused and imprisonment should only be used as a last resort for violent offenders who pose a threat to society'.[30] Such a policy would ensure that persistent burglars, car thieves and other property offenders would always be free to commit crime where and when they liked, and this denies that the effects of such crimes can be as damaging as those of crimes of violence. The prison-reform groups have become ideological fifth columnists whose objectives threaten the safety of the public whose support they covet. They unashamedly own no accountability to millions of those who each year fall victim to the criminals they campaign to keep out of gaol.[31]

Their anti-prison propaganda is music to the Treasury's ears. For example, all of them claim that prisons fail. The Prison Reform Trust was responsible for the propaganda slogan 'Prison makes bad people worse'. NACRO argued against minimum prison sentences for burglars, which were intended to give the public a measure of protection,[33] and the Howard League describes prison as a 'brutal experience'.[33] These erroneous ideas, however, serve the government's propaganda purposes in more ways than one. Whilst the propaganda has persuaded sufficient numbers of the public to allow anti-prison and other liberal sentencing measures to be passed without protest and unrest, many remain sceptical. However, on occasions, even the placid majority, as well as the sceptics, have become restive in the face of the growing and chronic crime problem. At such times, as we have already seen, the government has frequently used public-relations-type 'spin' to manage the moment of crisis and placate public feelings about crime and disorder by announcing policies 'to get tough on crime'. It never does, of course, but the predictable protests from the anti-prison lobby about the promised new 'tough' measures to protect the public from criminals provides the government with excellent propaganda. The effect is that the public see the government as on their side in taking a firm line against offenders, when, in fact, nothing could be further from the truth.

In fact, since 1991, the government has benefited generally from the illusion that it has been tough on crime. For example, it has been criticised for reverting to a more punitive and prison-based sentencing policy. The prison reform groups have cited the rise in the prison population and other measures, such as the introduction of mandatory sentences for burglars, as evidence for this. The reality, as we shall see later, is very different. The rise in the prison population has been wrongly interpreted, and mandatory sentences, much criticised for being too severe, are in fact incredibly lenient.

The prison reform groups do not represent the public, and as already stated they are not accountable to those who fall victim to the criminals they campaign to keep out of gaol. They appear to wield considerable influence on our criminal justice policies because their anti-prison philosophy fits in with the government's own objectives, and Home Office and Treasury civil servants are happy on occasions to let them do their talking for them. One reason why the prison-reform groups can do this so effectively is that they have captured the attention of many in the media who are ever ready to give them a platform.

The Media's Blind Spot

Many radio, TV and newspaper journalists wittingly or unwittingly, have allied themselves with the powerful anti-prison factions both inside and outside of the government. As a result, they regularly mislead the public with articles which argue that prison does not work, that it makes people worse, and that supervising offenders in the community is both cheaper and more effective at protecting the public from crime. But the evidence overwhelmingly undermines all of these arguments; many appear not to know these facts; while others appear willing to ignore them if they do not fit with their own ideological beliefs.

It is unthinkable that the facts referring to the correct method of wiring a plug, treating a disease or mending the brakes on a car would be misrepresented or ignored when information on these subjects was transmitted to the public. Those responsible would be only too aware of their overriding duty of care and would go to

71

great lengths not to mislead or misinform. Such subjects are underpinned by basic knowledge and facts obtained as a result of serious research, experimentation and years of accumulated experience. Those who write and speak about them ensure that what they communicate is rooted in the evidence. Why, therefore, are the same standards of care and sense of professional responsibility not exercised in the dissemination of information about crime and sentencing? This subject, no less than others, is rooted in factual evidence. Yet many newspapers and current-affairs programmes disseminate anti-prison arguments either in ignorance of, or in defiance of, the facts.

Media hosted discussions about crime and sentencing are often carried out by those who know nothing about these matters. Ill-informed MPs and ministers for example frequently feel free to trip out their pet ideas on crime and its related matters in a way that they would not dream of doing with other subjects. As a result, the public is dangerously misinformed about the ability of community sentences to protect them from crime and are encouraged to support sentencing policies which directly undermine their safety.[34]

For example, during the late 1980s I can remember listening to BBC Radio 4's *Today* programme whilst driving to the prison where I had worked for seven years. A well-known presenter introduced his question to a minister with the statement, 'We all know that we send too many people to prison in this country...' This introductory remark was made with great assurance and confidence; it conveyed the belief that this statement was something 'everyone knew' and was beyond question. Yet as I listened, I knew I was driving to a prison which, despite its huge catchment area (it served magistrates' courts districts from several parts of the country) was only half-full. What is more this institution took the seventeen to twenty-year-old offender age group, known to be highly prolific offenders. If any prison was going to be full, it should have been ours. Yet for some years it had only ever been half-full at the most, and was often far less occupied than that. At the very time that the *Today* programme was confidently misleading the public over the numbers of offenders being given custodial sentences, the Home Office were drawing up plans to close our prison and many more besides.[35] The reality, that courts were not (and are not) sending 'too many offenders to prison', is lost in a stream of misinformation and other propaganda, long before it can reach the public's ears.

Newspaper stories frequently major on the problem of prison overcrowding. Some have emotively called it a 'cancer'.[36] The reason for this overcrowding, they argue, is that the courts are too eager to send offenders to prison,[37] and then frequently go on to make the case that the United Kingdom sends more people to prison than many other countries.[38] Rarely do they argue the other way – that the reason for overcrowding is simply that we do not have enough prisons. Many in the press also promote the idea that offenders are victims of the system and make use of every opportunity to print stories about miscarriages of justice.[39] Few argue the case for the thousands of victims robbed of justice by guilty criminals who get away with their crimes.

The general effect of much of the press reporting on sentencing is to show prisons in a negative light. For example, headlines such as 'When punishment becomes a crime'[40] and 'When to punish is to betray'[41] encourage the community to feel guilty about sending offenders to prison. Likewise, headlines such as 'Children behind bars' stir up visions of young 'innocents' being sent to prison by a cruel and repressive regime.[42] The journalists concerned often fail to report that the juveniles who are sent to prison have all been given several chances to reform, and that over a long period of time they have been given practical help, support and counselling, but that despite these efforts they have continued to commit crime. For example, the fourteen to seventeen-year-olds with whom I worked in prison were all persistent hard-core offenders; years of supervision by various agencies in the community had failed to reform them. The sum total of the misery they had caused their victims was incalculable.

Many in the media misinterpret the rise in prison numbers, apply the wrong analysis to prison overcrowding, fail to understand the motivation which drives the persistent offender, wrongly promote him as a 'victim', misrepresent incidents of suicide in prison, and generally reveal either a lack of understanding of the positive role that prisons play in our sentencing framework or choose not to acknowledge it. Thus, this constant stream of misreporting has done much to leave many of the public dangerously misinformed and with a negative mindset towards prison. Knowingly or unknowingly, the press has made a major contribution to the anti-prison propaganda war engineered by officials and others in the criminal justice system, which has helped bring our so-called 'justice' system almost to its knees.

Chapter 4

A Review of a Dysfunctional System

Let's take stock about what I have said so far. The purpose of the criminal justice system is to protect the public from crime and provide justice for those victimised by criminals. However, the first three chapters of this book have demonstrated that the sentencing tactics followed by successive governments and the courts since the 1950s ensures it does none of these things. The ruthless pursuit of liberal sentencing policies, determined, to the exclusion of all other considerations, by the demand to limit spending on prisons, has resulted in a dysfunctional system that, far from protecting the public from crime, needlessly exposes it to victimisation from thousands of offenders.

I have described, for example, the development of administrative and judicial practices whose highly contradictory purpose has been not only to *downgrade* the offences committed by criminals in order to *minimise* their sentence, but to steer offenders away from the courts altogether. Far from being tough on crime, as successive governments have claimed to be, there has been, for almost forty years, a relentless drive to keep more and more persistent offenders in the community.

I have also suggested that post-war long-term predictions of rising prison costs would have convinced the government that it was imperative to find ways of bringing these under their control. Their sensitivities about this would have been heightened by the results of the prison-building programme carried out between 1952 and 1959.[1] At the end of that period, the level of overcrowding remained unchanged, confirming, no doubt the Treasury's anxieties that the prison budget, unless something was done, would be potentially beyond their power to control. For here was an aspect of government

75

concerned with financing a demand not susceptible to the normal levels of influence.

Whereas, for example, the State's educational needs can be defined and planned for, and therefore related to a measure of budgetary control, the criminal behaviour of offenders leading to the demand for prison places is beyond such influence. As described by Anthony Sampson in *The Changing Anatomy of Britain*, the influence of the Treasury on setting budgetary limits for each government department is pivotal,[2] and it is likely it was first and foremost the threat to their *power* to control events in relation to prison demand, just as much as the wish to control expenditure, that caused the Treasury such anxiety.[3]

Cost-saving has not been the only motive for keeping prison building to a minimum. As argued by Professor David Marsland, there were, in the first post-war generation of government administrators, many of whose ideas had been shaped by 'reconstructionist socialism'.[4] They were instinctively anti-authoritative in their attitude towards prisons, which they perceived as repressive organs of a capitalist state; their ideology shaped criminals as the victims of society. Over fifty years later, at the beginning of the twenty-first century, many of those in positions of influence in the criminal justice system continue to reflect many aspects of this philosophy.

The Treasury's attitude towards the allocation of money for prison places has been and remains one of draconian control. Building new prison places has been entertained only when the government's back was forced to the wall, and even then far too few places have been provided. The government's white paper in 1959 announcing an expansion in prison places for young offenders was forced on them by the sheer weight of necessity, and their grudging response meant that the number planned for fell far short of what was required.

Almost thirty years later, the story was the same. In the ten-year period between 1992 and 2002 the Treasury agreed money for less than two new prisons each year,[5] and in 2003 the Chancellor reinforced this resistance by stating that he was 'unconvinced that building more jails is good value for money' despite the fact that between 1993 and 1997 increased prison numbers were accompanied by a fall in the crime rate, with all of its attendant financial and personal benefits to individuals and the community generally.[6] This is to be compared to the Treasury's willingness to go on funding expensive community programmes for offenders years after they had been officially recognised as having failed.[7]

Likewise, it was the Treasury's refusal to pay for sufficient new prison places which, in 1997, caused Jack Straw, the new Home Secretary, to announce that he was considering abandoning the recently enacted 'get tough' sentencing laws for burglars. The previous government had introduced the 'three strikes and you're out' clause for these offenders in response to growing public alarm and unrest over the horrendous burglary rate. It was therefore expected that as he had supported these measures during the election campaign, Jack Straw would swiftly bring this legislation, designed to imprison more burglars, into effect. However, whatever his intentions, he was stopped dead in his tracks by Treasury reluctance to finance this measure, that they claimed could cost up to £1 billion for jailing the estimated extra 7,000 criminals.[8]

There can be little doubt that serious discussions took place behind closed doors, about how to manage this problem. The news release to the press in July 1997 that the Home Secretary was considering abandoning these clauses was no doubt a 'flyer' – a device to test public opinion on the issue. What followed provides a fascinating insight into how power is sometimes brokered between elected representatives and government officials. In the event, the 'three strikes' clause was not removed from the statute book. There is, circumstantially, a strong case to suggest that the new Labour government was advised it would face serious political fallout if it got rid of these clauses and that it would be better to do nothing. Such a conclusion would have been based on the assessment that the courts were unlikely to cooperate with these mandatory sentencing arrangements, and on the expectation (or hope?) that therefore, very few, if any, burglars would be sent to prison for the mandatory sentence of three years.

This is exactly what happened. A Home Office civil servant accidentally let slip that between 1998 and 2002, only *six* mandatory sentences were passed for burglary, despite the thousands of burglars brought before the courts during the same period. The instruction issued by the Home Secretary in the autumn of 2002 to his civil servants that this information should be kept secret highlights the government's sensitivity over this issue and its guilty involvement in this outcome.

Thus the Treasury's resistance to funding the 'three strikes' clause remained in place and no one challenged their obstruction of parliamentary legislation. However, the government was, in any case, already faced with a shortage of prison places. Therefore, as a sop to public opinion, the Treasury agreed to an immediate injection of £43 million pounds, announced as an 'emergency measure to create more prison places'. Nevertheless, it was nowhere near the sum required to meet the needs of the projected shortfall.[9] Its willingness to spend millions of pounds in emergency handouts is the price the Treasury is prepared to pay in order to avoid spending the billions of pounds it knows is required to offer the public proper protection from criminals.

It was surely more than a coincidence that in the same year (1997) it was reported that ministers had become alarmed by the problem caused by the courts 'sending more people to jail than the Home Office expected'.[10] But how could they possibly have any expectations about the numbers of people being sentenced to prison when it is not their job to decide on sentencing? Such admissions serve only to confirm the interest the executive has in influencing sentencing decisions, arising from their obsessive preoccupation with controlling the prison budget. So much for the 'separation of powers' supposedly being one of the key pillars of our constitution.

By 1998 the naive and largely untutored enthusiasm of Labour ministers to tackle the crime problem was foundering on the rocks of this obsession. The Labour government, whilst trying to make it look as if it was still pushing ahead with its much trumpeted 'zero-tolerance' crime policy, had in reality abandoned it. By then they knew that a real zero-tolerance crime initiative would result in the demand for many more prisons. The undercurrents of financial and ideological objection to prisons within the criminal justice establishment both inside and outside of the government were so deep and pervasive that such policies could not survive. Therefore it was no surprise that its Crime and Disorder Bill carefully avoided any specific reference to 'zero-tolerance', though it held to the pretence that some of its measures were 'in a similar spirit'.[11]

I have also suggested that the government's solution to the problem of how to keep the brakes on the prison budget has been to convince the public that the majority of persistent offenders, particularly property offenders, should be dealt with in the community rather than in prison; to this end, I have argued that they have engineered the public's (at least) passive consent to a system which has kept the use of prison to a minimum for most persistent offenders. The public's (sometimes bewildered) acquiescence to these bizarre sentencing arrangements has been achieved by a propaganda campaign which has, for the last forty years, increasingly misled them over the so-called social, psychological and environmental causes of crime, and misinformed the public over the alleged advantages of community-based interventions for offenders over that of prison.

This message has been regularly reinforced with powerful slogans identified in a previous chapter: for example 'prison does not work'; prison makes people worse; prisons are colleges of crime; prisons are more expensive than community penalties for offenders; 'overcrowding is the AIDS virus of prisons'. These ideas have been drummed into the psyche of the British people so successfully that many now believe they are unquestionable truths, and this success has been due, in no small measure, to the ability of anti-prison ideologists both inside and outside of the government to divert the public's attention away from the powerful body of evidence which blatantly contradicts their arguments.

Whilst new prisons have had to be built, and home secretaries sometimes have to be seen demanding more money for prison programmes, as evidenced for example in September 2002, by the well-publicised row between the Treasury and the Home Secretary over this issue,[12] the brakes have been kept firmly on the provision of new prison places. This has been the objective of repeated claims by Home Office ministers that 'only sex and violent offenders should be sent to prison', rather than any concerns about how best to protect the public from crime.

Likewise, appeals made in 1988 by the then Home Secretary, Douglas Hurd, for the courts to pass 'fewer jail sentences',[13] and more recently in 2002, from prison governors for 'the government to avert the looming crisis in prison overcrowding',[14] are examples of the rhetoric that has for decades helped maintain the sense of crisis in our prisons. This has provided the government with the rationale for diverting large numbers of offenders away from the judicial process, freeing thousands of others into the community before they have finished their sentence,[15] and creating more non-custodial sentences, instead of locking up for longer and longer periods the thousands of persistent offenders who continue to predate upon the public.

It follows, therefore, that the constant shortfall in prison provision is not an accident. Neither is it due to the courts sending too many offenders to jail. It is the result of policy. This may sound perverse, but keeping the prisons in a near state of crisis as far as accommodation is concerned serves the purpose of the anti-prison cliques perfectly; it creates the illusion that the prisons are full because they are being 'over-used' by the courts who are seen to be taking a hard line with offenders. This line of argument is not new, as long ago as 1987 the Home Office was blaming the courts for the prison population reaching its then all-time high of 48,181.[16]

Overcrowded prisons then give rise to newspaper headlines such as 'Courts are jailing more villains'[17] and 'Sentencing policy means jails will be full in the new year'[18] and 'Prison riots warning due to overcrowding';[19] such alarmist talk is exactly what the government wants the public to hear – because it leaves the entirely false impression that the courts are fulfilling their duty to protect the public by being tough on offenders, in stark contrast to the reality which is that only a tiny minority of offenders are sent to prison.

Crowded prisons provoke criticisms not just from the press but also from prison-reform groups, and sometimes even from some liberal senior law lords, who predictably press the government to introduce more measures to bring down prison numbers. In February 2001, it was reported that the then Chief Inspector of Prisons 'was at odds with the Home Office' over his claim that 'prisons contained at least 20,000 people who should not be there'.[20] While they may pretend to be on their back foot in the face of such criticisms this is again exactly the response the government officials want. They can then argue that they are bowing to pressure when they introduce measures to reduce the prison population when in fact they had intended them all along.

In October 2002 the following headline appeared in a national newspaper: 'Jail sentences must be cut to ease overcrowding, says Lord Chief Justice Woolf'.[21] In the same newspaper and on the same day there appeared another article headed 'Hundreds of offenders to be freed early'.[22] The government's timing of this announcement, of yet another early-release scheme for prisoners, was surely more than a coincidence. Lord Woolf's remarks, intended to excite fears about prison overcrowding, gave the government a good moment to release to the public the difficult news that hundreds of more criminals were about to be let loose into the community before they had completed their prison sentence. Thus the public were once

80

again duped into believing the necessity for yet more early-release schemes for criminals in prison.

Liberal sentencing policies to divert offenders from prison are not, as we are encouraged to see, the results of prison overcrowding due to excessive zeal by the courts; the 'overcrowding', which has been deliberately engineered by the failure to build enough prison places, is used as an excuse for anti-prison policies which the government were determined to bring in anyway.

To some it may at first seem implausible that government officials should have been playing a double hand and deceiving the public both over the extent to which prison is used as a sentencing option and their objective of diverting as many offenders as possible, not just from prison, but from being charged with their offences in the first place. But such a scenario offers, perhaps, the only explanation for the presence in our criminal justice system of so many bizarre and contradictory features, and explains why it is prey to foolish and unproven ideas. For example, despite all the government's public promises about getting tough on crime and protecting the public (the present Labour government's manifesto pledge in 2001, for example, was to increase by 100,000 the numbers of offenders brought to court), why is it that this number actually fell by 9 per cent between March 1999 and March 2002? This effect was widespread with thirty-three out of the forty-two police force areas in the United Kingdom recording this decline.[23]

This alarming picture was confirmed by a report from the Audit Commission published in 2002 which showed that, based on the 5.2 million *recorded* crimes, criminals have only a one in sixteen chance of being caught.[24] However, the detection rate for *all* crimes is far worse, with over 90 per cent of offences going unpunished.[25] These figures could not provide a clearer demonstration of the government's determination to 'filter out' as many offenders as possible from the judicial system, by whatever means, in order to control expenditure, rather than bring them to justice.

One of the chief organs of this 'filtering' policy is the Crown Prosecution Service. Reference has already been made to the fact that it closes the files on hundreds of thousands of offences brought to it by the police, even when there is sufficient evidence to gain a conviction. In 1993, a report issued by the union representing Crown Prosecution lawyers, gave a devastating picture of the low morale, red tape and inefficiency of the service.[26] Nine years later it was still being reported on as cumbersome and inefficient.[27]

I have also provided clear evidence that for those few offenders who do reach court soft sentencing is now the norm, particularly for those committing multiple offences, no matter how serious they are. For example, as I write this chapter a dangerous drug dealer has just been sentenced for carrying class A drugs and a loaded firearm. He received three years for the firearms offence and thirty months for two separate drug offences, but once again, the judge made the sentences concurrent.[28] With 50 per cent automatic remission, the offender will be left with just eighteen months. Considering the threat this offender posed to the public and to the police who chased him through the streets whilst he was armed, such a sentence is a farce.

Lenient sentencing by the courts goes a long way to explain the police attitude which says that there is no point in making arrests because nothing is going to happen to the offenders; it also explains the increasing bravado and contempt which offenders show for the law. Likewise, no one has seriously considered the undermining effects on our justice system, of cautioning over half a million offenders between 1998 and 2000, many, as we have seen, for very serious crimes.[29] I have pointed out that cautioning has increased as a result of pressure by the Home Office on the police to use it as the routine method for dealing with juvenile offenders. In 1954, 5 per cent of indictable offences cleared up by the police were dealt with by means of a caution; in 1994 it was 16 per cent.[30]

Despite the lip service from the criminal justice establishment that they recognise the harmful effects of such crimes as burglary, significantly fewer of these offenders are now jailed than in the past. For example, between 1981 and 1995 the number of burglars sentenced to prison in the United Kingdom fell from 7.8 per 1,000 offenders to 2.2 per 1,000 offenders. Yet over the same period the burglary rates more than doubled from 40.9 per 1000 homes to 82.9 per 1000 homes. In the 1960s a burglar was five times more likely to be jailed than today.[31]

This reduction in the use of prison is consistent with the arguments put forward by many liberal social-science academics who have claimed that crime is associated with 'social causes' and that imprisoning offenders exacerbates these problems. Some have compared jails to hospitals, making the point that it would be foolish to put everyone who was ill into a hospital, an observation which ignores that criminals threaten the public whereas those who are ill do not.[32] Some have even argued that imprisoning large numbers of offenders is 'unethical' and would result in a 'prisonised, fear-dominated society'.[33] The fact that only the criminals would be 'fear dominated' by such a policy seems to have escaped them.

However, social science is a branch of learning widely recognised to be low in scholarship. It has been the subject of several critical papers by highly respected academics, many of them distinguished sociologists, such as Stanislav Andreski, Julius Gould, Anthony Flew, David Marsland, Allan Bloom, to name but a few.[34] Yet in 2002, we were treated to the spectacle of the Shadow Home Secretary making a major policy speech in which he confidently claimed that 'society creates criminals',[35] despite the lack of any evidence for this association.

Home Office research however, claims to have identified those societal 'risk factors' which can result in criminal behaviour; for example poverty, poor housing, poor parenting, the influence of delinquent family members and friends, low IQ and poor school attainment, to name but a few.[36] Yet common sense shouts out that if this were the case we would have largely solved the crime problem years ago. It must be as well known to the Home Office, as well as to others, that not everyone associated with these so-called 'risk factors' commits crime, and that during decades of effort using social work interventions based on these assumptions, social workers and probation officers have consistently failed to reform persistent offenders. The journalist Leo McKinstry previously worked as constituency assistant for Harriet Harman MP in Inner London. He admitted that as a result of the horrific catalogue of muggings and vandalism he faced, he realised that it was absurd to see criminals as society's 'victims'. He came to the view that offenders were motivated entirely by greed and brutal self-gratification and the real victims were their innocent targets.[37]

In Chapter Two I argued that some academics have endeavoured to mislead the public into believing that crime is so complex that it is beyond their capacity to understand it, a criticism echoed by Theodore Dalrymple in a major newspaper article in 2000.[38] Jock Young in his book *The Exclusive Society* has gone further and has admitted that the hidden agenda of many liberal sociologists is to minimise police intervention in matters of crime.[39]

The background to this disturbing admission has been the massive increase in almost all categories of crime since the 1950s. When it became known in 2002 that serious crime committed by young people had doubled over the previous seven years, the response from the liberal establishment was to say that 'this was society's problem' and that society should ask of itself 'why would a fourteen-year-old mug an old lady?'[40] Yet the pertinent question is why has it become impossible for many to see that the reason young offenders (or any other offender) mug members of the public is because it pays them to do so. It brings them easy money; they know the chances of being caught are almost nil; and if their luck runs out and they are apprehended, they know nothing will happen to them. In short, a persistent offender has no reason, from his point of view, for *not* committing offences. He has no reason to fear of the law.

But the government does not want this logical and more realistic view to gain general currency in the debate about crime because it would lead to the demand for an increase in the use of prison and this is contrary to its aims, even though it is loath to admit it. For example, it was obvious to all that a number of the more bizarre clauses of the Criminal Justice Act 1991 tried to rule out the use of prison for almost all persistent property offenders, yet, incredibly, the then Home Office Minister publicly stated that 'he would not like anybody to presume that this Act is a measure designed to empty our prisons'.[41] This classic political statement can be taken to mean exactly the opposite. The long-term consequences of the determination to control prison spending has meant that almost all sentencing measures, no matter how much the government tries to dress them up with pseudo-rehabilitative aims, have as their motive either the diversion of offenders from prison or the early release of those who are there.

Likewise, in September 1999, the government sought to deflect attention from their own anti-prison agenda by launching a withering attack on 'liberal left-wing academics' and accused them of obstructing the government's fight against crime.[42] But they were cynically playing to the public gallery; in reality, their sentencing policies had a great deal in common with the liberal views of those same academics it suited them to publicly criticise.

Similarly, a year later the Home Secretary tried to distance the government from the effect of the bail laws by criticising magistrates for bailing too many criminals, and by so doing, he argued, 'undermine the efforts of the police who had worked hard to catch the offenders and bring them to justice'.[43] Such hypocrisy was, however, too much even for a brow-beaten magistracy, who pointed out that the government knew well enough that it was their legislation that provided for a presumption in favour of bail. This collision of purpose between the police, who work hard to find and arrest offenders in order to protect the public, and the presumption of bail practised in our courts, has done much to undermine the forces of law and order.

Likewise, although the need for substantial increases in police numbers could not be more obvious from the point of view of the protection of the public, they are kept short of manpower. In Chapter Two I referred to the results of a survey, carried out in 2001, of thirty-seven police forces, which showed that a significant minority no longer had a police station open all of the time, whilst others only had their station open for one hour a day.[44] During the last half-decade the crime-beleaguered public has watched helplessly while nearly a thousand police stations have been closed. Within four years of the Labour government coming to power in 1997, thirty were shut in the metropolitan area of London alone.

In numerous other police forces throughout the country it is no longer possible for a member of the public to find a police officer at the police-station desk around the clock. In 2000, to quote one example, the Gloucestershire Police Force decided to close all of its stations at night, and even put a notice on the front door of one of them telling the public to use a telephone box to report crime. The North York Police, on the other hand, reported that its main station in York was open twenty-four hours a day, but that the public had to knock hard on the door to be let in.[45]

I have also discussed the lamentable fact that over the last decade patrolling police officers have become a rarity in our towns and all but disappeared in rural districts. This followed questionable Home Office research which made the absurd suggestion that the presence of police on the streets is of limited value in combating crime and that allowing them to walk the streets for hours on end is an expensive luxury.[46]

But this was no more than a shallow device to save money and an affront to the general public's common sense and experience.[47] Less than two years later the Home Office was offering £13 million to community groups to establish foot patrols of local wardens to deter burglars and other criminals.[48] Yet on other occasions the Home Office has argued that such uniformed street patrols reduce

85

only the fear of crime, but this is contradicted by numerous examples of street patrols by the police resulting in a significant reduction of crime. This was acknowledged by the Prime Minister in 2003 when he said 'uniformed policing has reduced crime; we need to deny the criminal their habitat. The way to do that is by having a uniformed presence.'[49]

Despite what Home Office researchers may say, it is unarguable that increased police numbers in New York and other places have significantly contributed to them becoming safer. Victims of robbery and muggings in London were in no doubt that there had been a massive increase in street crime following a fall in police street stop-and-search activity whilst on street patrol.[50] In addition, many locally adopted schemes to fight crime, in such diverse locations as Great Yarmouth, Manchester, South Yorkshire and West Yorkshire, to name but a few, have frequently relied on increased street patrols for their success.[51] And in contradiction of their own departmental research, home secretaries have often promised 'more bobbies on the beat' when faced with demands to do something about rising crime, as well as donating grants for 'street warden' schemes to increase foot patrols in certain crime hot spots.[52]

The effect of an overstretched police force is to limit the number of offenders who are arrested and eventually sentenced, which is entirely consistent with the sentencing strategy of limiting not only the use of prison but the numbers of criminals being processed by the judicial system. Not only are the police assailed by an impossible workload, but morale has been dealt a near-mortal blow by the Crown Prosecution Service who have targeted them rather than the criminals by perversely seeking every opportunity to reject the cases the police present to them. Considering the key role of the police force in the fight against crime, it is difficult to think of an outcome more alien to the objectives of maintaining law and order.

The contradictions that have invaded our criminal justice system over the last forty years have been profound in their effects. It has become distrusted and associated with injustice in the mind of the public, who have, until now, given it tacit acceptance. There are signs public tolerance is wearing thin. For example, as we have already seen, the criminal justice system now ensures that the majority of persistent offenders, unmotivated to reform, are placed back into the community, and it is the public who pay a heavy price by being repeatedly victimised as a result. Far from protecting the public from crime, the criminal justice apparatus is used to release increasing numbers of prisoners into the community before they have finished their prison sentence, and also allows persistent offenders to go on offending whilst they are on bail.

A criminal justice system that genuinely set out to protect the public would contain none of these features, as all of them clearly threaten the safety of the public. If none of these outcomes were intended, why are they tolerated? The fact that they are indicates that none of these quirky and plainly dysfunctional features of our criminal justice system are accidents; they are the results of a criminal justice policy that has, in the interests of saving money and false ideology, deliberately substituted the fight against crime with a war against prison. As a result, the millions of crimes committed every year by the 155,000 offenders in the community under the supervision of the Probation Service,[53] have significantly undermined the quality of life of millions of victims. Nevertheless, they have had to accept that the vast majority of the criminals concerned escape any form of justice.

That this state of affairs has been brought about in the main without public protest or unrest is due largely to the effects of anti-prison propaganda which, as previously discussed, has for years powerfully misled and misinformed the public about crime, criminals and prisons. Not only has this choked off the natural instinct of the public to protest about the government's catastrophic failure to protect them from crime, but it has also robbed them of their inalienable right to live in peace and enjoy their possessions without molestation. Not only has the public been duped into accepting harmful liberal sentencing policies without protest, but some seem so programmed by anti-prison propaganda that, given the relevant prompt, their reflex is to defend the very sentencing practices which have caused them and their neighbours untold misery and grief.

Chapter 5

Prisons: British Errors and American Enlightenment

Almost all of the information disseminated to the British public about prisons is highly misleading and frequently incorrect. The media often publishes the propaganda of the well-organised and vociferous anti-prison lobby. This claims that there are too many people in prison, that the UK sends more people to prison than many other countries, that prisons fail and are colleges of crime, that prisons are 'human dustbins' with entirely negative regimes, and that prisons are more expensive than the alternative of placing the offender on some form of community supervision.

All of these are contradicted by the facts. Data held in government archives and elsewhere shows overwhelmingly that prisons are more effective than community penalties in their ability to protect the public and to reform criminals. But this is evidence that many officials in the criminal justice system would prefer to ignore.

I frequently hear many private individuals, as well as public officials argue vehemently against the use of prison. This lack of normal caution in discussing a subject about which most of them know very little indicates, I believe, that their response is a reflex, a conditioned response brought about by years of exposure to unrelenting anti-prison brainwashing. This unwillingness to give up long held ideas, even in the face of evidence which overwhelmingly contradicts them, is well known to psychologists and to historians. In the sixteenth century, for example, Copernicus produced a mathematical model which demonstrated that the sun, and not the earth was the centre of our universe. But for a long time after this, individuals and organisations with vested ideological and career interests in preserving the old ideas about the cosmos resisted this evidence.

Similarly today, I believe, many in the criminal justice system ignore the evidence which undermines their anti-prison ideology, often to protect their careers and reputations. The criminal justice establishment has hitched its wagon firmly to an anti-prison agenda, and I know that at least one official has admitted that even those who may have known, or suspected that they were in error, simply cannot lose face and turn back.

'Too many people are sent to prison'

We are frequently told that the UK imprisons far too many of its offenders and sends more people to prison than most other European countries. Neither statement is true. But even if it were, we should remember that communities are despoiled and blighted by crime and not by the proportion of its population in prison. In fact, only 2.2 per cent of all offences ever result in a conviction and only 0.3 per cent of offences results in a custodial sentence.[1] Thus the statement that we have too many offenders in prison is shown to be meaningless.

The analysis, in Figure 5.1, of a sample of just over 10 million crimes taken from the 16.4 million crimes reported by the 1998 British Crime Survey could not make this clearer. A further breakdown of how these 10.2 million crimes were dealt with is also highly

Figure 5.1: Analysis of a sample 10.2 million crimes (1998)

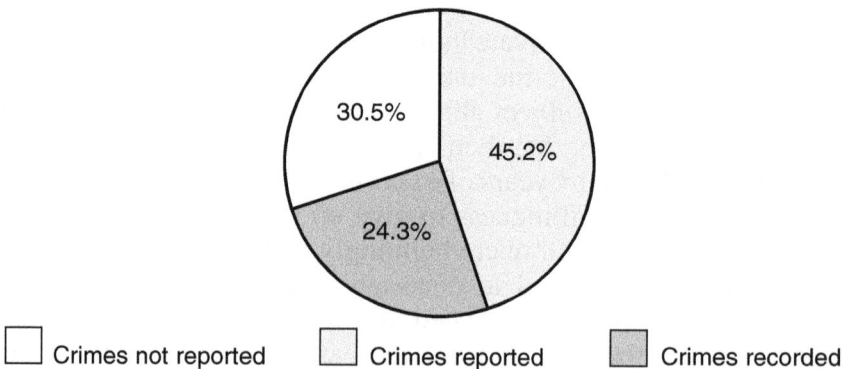

☐ Crimes not reported   ☐ Crimes reported   ▨ Crimes recorded

Source: Home Office Research & Statistics Department, *Digest 4: Information on the Criminal Justice System in England & Wales*, 1999; Home Office Statistical Bulletin, Issue 21/98, *The British Crime Survey, England & Wales*

Table 5.1: Breakdown of outcomes from a sample 10.2 million crimes (1998)

Offences	Committed	Cleared up	Found guilty	Cautioned	Sentenced to custody
Vandalism	2,917,000 (100%)	84,550 (2.9%)	58,475 (0.2%)	31,455 (1.1%)	1,594 (0.1%)
Domestic burglary	1,639,000 (100%)	129,830 (7.9%)	32,706 (0.2%)	3,475 (0.2%)	10,113 (0.6%)
Car theft	375,000 (100%)	62,980 (16.8%)	22,417 (6.0%)	6,113 (1.6%)	4,541 (1.2%)
Bicycle theft	549,000 (100%)	12,060 (2.2%)	2,584 (0.5%)	1,411 (0.3%)	113 (0.02%)
Wounding	714,000 (100%)	158,890 (22.3%)	80,639 (11.3%)	31,714 (4.4%)	11,085 (1.6%)
Robbery	897,000 (100%)	3,541 (2.6%)	16,366 (1.8%)	1,315 (0.2%)	5,828 (0.7%)
Totals of Offences	**10,198,000 (100%)**	**563,241 (5.5%)**	**223,056 (2.1%)**	**79,915 (0.78%)**	**33,956 (0.3%)**

Source: Home Office Research & Statistics Department, *Digest 4: Information on the Criminal Justice System in England & Wales*, 1999; Home Office Statistical Bulletin, Issue 21/98, *The 1998 British Crime Survey, England & Wales*

revealing (see Table 5.1). On the basis of this table a bookmaker would offer lucrative odds against the chances of an offender ever being caught, let alone being found guilty and sent to prison. What this analysis powerfully demonstrates is that criminals have a clear field of fire as far as committing crime is concerned. The fact that only a tiny fraction of offences are cleared up means that, from the criminal's point of view, the time and energy spent in committing crime is a safe and worthwhile investment. The inescapable conclusion is that they can, for all intents and purposes, commit crime with impunity. When offenders read in the newspapers that the criminal justice establishment thinks that too many of them are in prison, they must find it hard to believe their luck.

Yet, despite these facts, in November 2002, and on the same day that a newspaper reported that crime had reached such dreadful levels that it was driving businesses away from some city centres,[2] the Home Secretary, the Lord Chief Justice, the Attorney-General and the Lord Chancellor joined forces in an unprecedented appeal to the courts to send *fewer* offenders to prison.[3]

Is it likely that the most senior leaders of our criminal justice system are unaware of the evidence which shows that, despite the recent increase in prison numbers, only a tiny minority of offenders are sent to prison, that community based sentences fail utterly to stop the tide of crime which engulfs our communities, and that prison overcrowding is due entirely to a shortage of places? This seems improbable, but if they are aware of these facts, then we can only deduce they choose to ignore them for their own ideological reasons; alternatively, they have been misled by their officials into believing that the courts use jail as a sentencing option far too frequently.

Either way, this almost frantic appeal denies the fact that magistrates' courts, who sentence 95 per cent of all offenders, already allow 86 per cent of all those convicted of a criminal offence to go straight back into the community, many under supervision to the Probation Service.[4] It is a matter of public record that they are frequently persuaded by defence lawyers and probation officers to put the freedom of persistent offenders before the protection of the public. As previously pointed out, official statistics make it clear that alternative sentences are already used far more frequently than prison for the majority of offenders.[5] The record of previous convictions of those receiving their first prison sentence shows that the leniency of the courts has allowed these persistent offenders to go round the alternative sentencing tariff several times before a prison sentence is passed. This pattern of sentencing often takes place over a long period of time during which the persistent offender victimises countless innocent members of the public. Thus, the paradox is that prisons, as a sentencing option, are not an overused resource, but underused, and that very few offenders are jailed. This is despite the recent increase in the prison population which has been grossly misinterpreted.

For example, in 2002 the breakdown of the prison population of England and Wales was as follows: there were 5,587 foreigners, 13,081 remand prisoners, 4,210 women prisoners, 831 civil prisoners and 5,060 prisoners serving life sentences. Subtracting these from the 71,218 total prison population, we are left with only 42,449 convicted UK-domiciled male persistent offenders behind bars.[6] By 2003, the numbers of foreign prisoners had increased dramatically and made up 13 per cent of the total prison population of 74,000.[7] Taking this figure into account, the numbers of jailed convicted UK-domiciled male persistent offenders – those who cause most harm to the public and from whom they need the maximum protection

– was only 39,629. This small minority should be compared with the 155,000 persistent offenders who are allowed to roam free in the community under the supervision of the Probation Service,[8] where they are known to victimise the public at will – a massive 78 per cent of the total. The further significance of this comparison is the enormous harm they cause to the public, which leaves many victims emotionally and physically scarred, with a much-reduced standard of life and peace of mind.

Those who claim we have too many in prison conveniently forget that the prison population consists of groups of offenders for whom no other sentence is possible. As shown above, the 74,000 in our jails (2003 figure) consists of thousands of remand prisoners, life-sentenced prisoners and foreign nationals, who together make up almost a third of those in prison. It must also be remembered that those remanded in custody have been judged to pose too great a risk to the public to be allowed their freedom, even in the eyes of a judiciary that is compelled by legislation to allow bail in all but the most extreme circumstances. It cannot be said, therefore, that we have too many remand prisoners in jail.

The UK Parliament suspended the death penalty for murder in 1965 and abolished it permanently in 1969, substituting a life sentence. Since then, the homicide rate in the UK has significantly increased, and in 1999 it was almost three times what it was in 1962.[9] As a result, large numbers of people have been jailed for life; between 1987 and 2001, for example, there was a 93 per cent increase in this category of prisoner received into the prison system.[10] But for them there is no alternative, so whatever their numbers it cannot be argued that we have 'too many' life-sentenced prisoners in jail. This is particularly so when we remember that large numbers of them only serve a short tariff before they are released into the community.

Thousands of foreign nationals, who have swelled our prison population, often serving long sentences, will all go home on release and therefore they cannot be included in the calculations of prison numbers of concern to the British public. These concern only those who will live here when they have completed their sentence.

The focus of our attention should be, therefore, on the numbers of UK-domiciled male persistent offenders in our prisons. This is the group which has caused enormous harm to the public by their callous and persistent offending, leaving even our liberal courts no alternative but to jail them. Yet there are less than 45,000 of them (including convicted female offenders) in our prisons. This startlingly small number shows how false the present so-called 'crisis' is concerning our prison population. We do have a crisis, but it is brought about by the government's willingness to let more than 155,000 persistent offenders stay in the community where they commit millions of offences each year, not the relatively insignificant number in our prisons.[11]

The anti-prison ideologists have also criticised the numbers of female offenders in prison, which in 2000 was 3,400, an 8 per cent increase over the previous year. In 2002, it was 4,210, representing an 18 per cent increase over the previous twelve months.[12] Critics have fostered the belief that many of them have been put behind bars for what they claim are trivial offences such as non-payment of fines or TV licences. Nothing could be further from the truth. Large numbers of these sentences relate to very serious offences such as burglary and drug-related crimes.[13] A woman is as capable as a man in knowing right from wrong. Being a mother of young children or being pregnant has not stopped many from committing crime; neither should it stop a female offender from paying the penalty for wrongdoing.

International Comparisons

It is often claimed that the UK sends more of its population to prison than most other European countries. This calculation is based, for each country, on the numbers in prison compared with its overall population. But this is a trap to lead the unwary into believing that we send more of our criminals to prison than other European countries.

In order to establish how lenient or severe it is in its use of prison, it is necessary, for each country, to compare that country's prison population with its crime rate. On that basis the use of imprisonment in the UK is found to be much lower than many other countries as demonstrated in Figure 5.2.

More recent comparative data also indicates that prison in the UK is underused, as shown in Figure 5.3. These comparisons show that the UK sends *fewer* of its offenders to jail than the other countries, but has the highest numbers in jail compared with its overall population, which reflects its high crime rate.

94

Figure 5.2: International comparisons in use of imprisonment (1996)

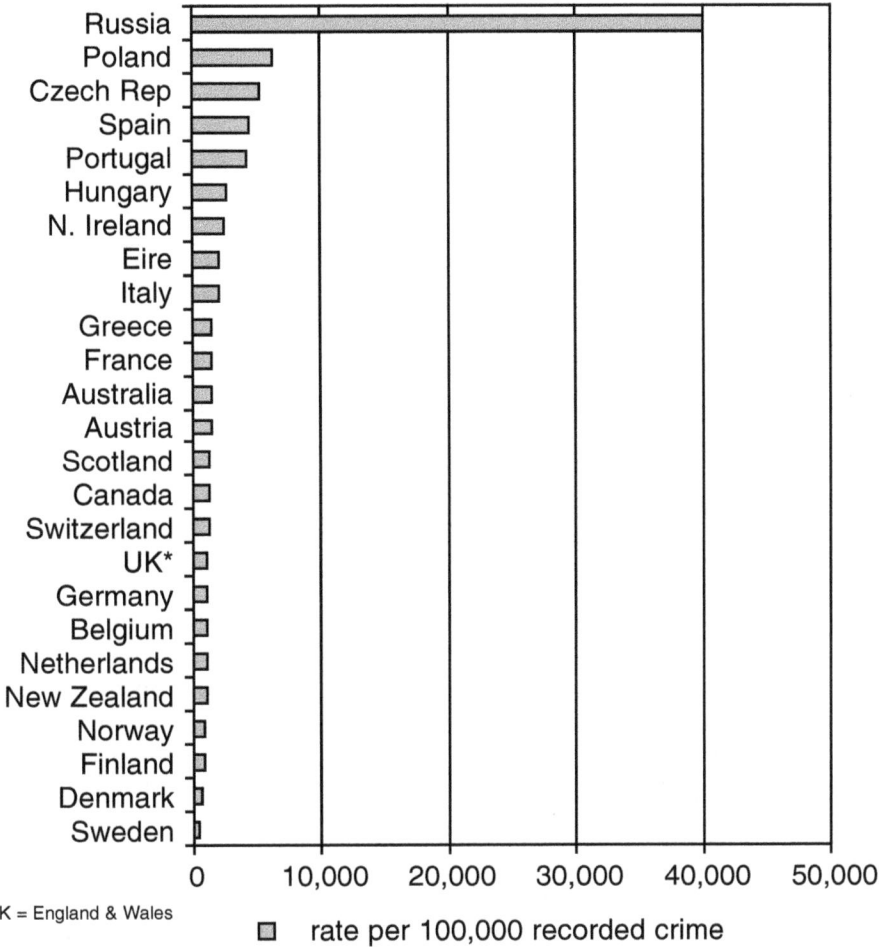

Source: Home Office, *Criminal Statistics England & Wales*, 1996

Research has also shown that the United Kingdom is one of the most lenient sentencers in relation to most individual crime categories.[14] For example, out of fifteen countries, the UK is the fifth most lenient in relation to rape, the most lenient in relation to assault and the fourth most lenient in relation to robbery. The only reason why the UK is the third most *severe* sentencer for homicide compared with thirteen other countries is that we have a mandatory life sentence for this offence, and therefore the courts

Figure 5.3: International comparison of prison populations (1999)

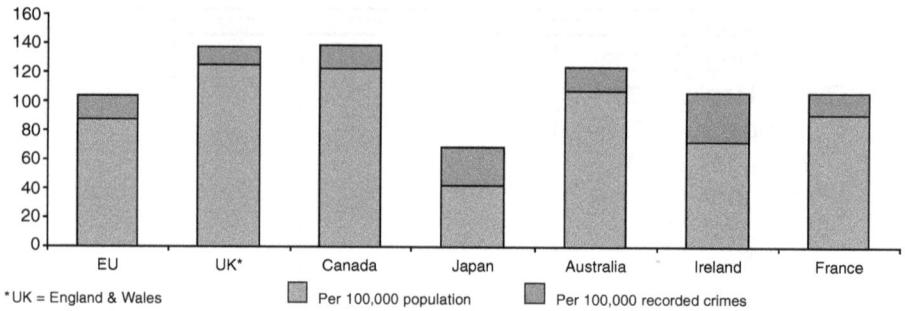

Source: Civitas, *Crime Rates in the UK*, 2003

have no alternative but to pass a life sentence once guilt has been established.

'Prisons Fail'

The public are frequently told by the anti-prison lobby that 'prisons are a failure'. It is an absurd statement. Prisons can never fail because whilst an offender is locked up he cannot commit any more offences. What is more, it is the only sentence at our disposal which can give the public this gilt-edged guarantee. Incapacitation of the offender can only be said to fail because an offender is imprisoned too late or let loose too soon, or because not enough criminals are imprisoned.

Charles Murray, an American criminologist, has untied many of the knots created by the obtuse arguments of anti-prison academics and he has demonstrated that, far from failing, prisons are a reliable bulwark against crime and that, as the United Kingdom has used prison less, so crime has gone through the roof.[15] For example, as shown in Figure 5.4, between 1955 and 1993 there was a sustained decline in the use of imprisonment in the UK. During this period, the number of reported crimes increased twelve-fold while the numbers of prisoners only doubled. During this period the risk of going to jail if you committed a crime was cut by no less than 80 per cent.

Thus, this period saw the unfolding of a golden age for criminals in the UK, as crime became much less risky. In 1954, for example,

Figure 5.4: The decline in imprisonment and the rise in crime in the UK

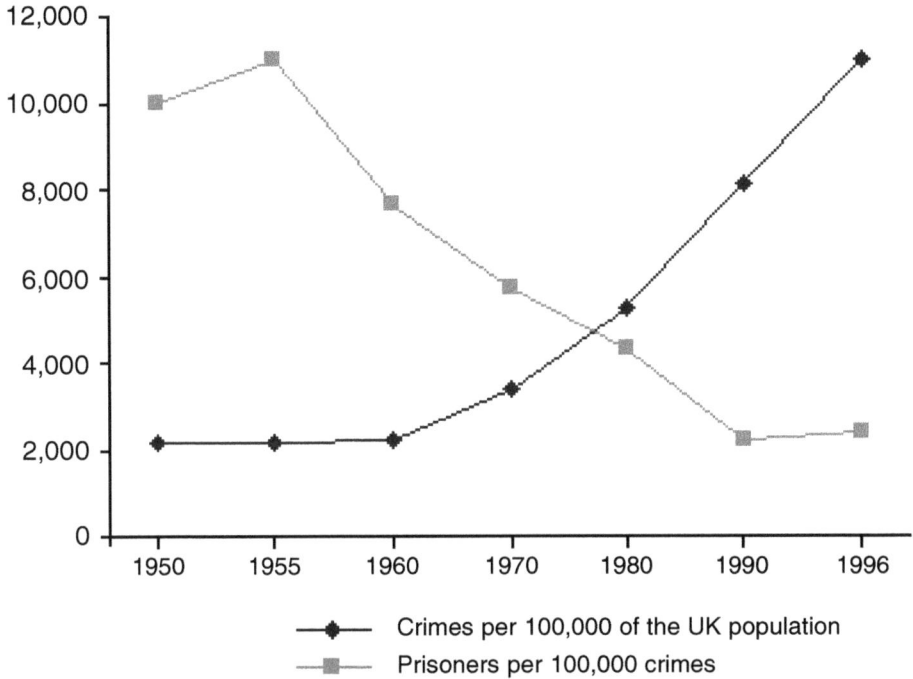

Crimes per 100,000 of the UK population
Prisoners per 100,000 crimes

Source: C. Murray, *Does Prison Work?*, Choice in Welfare Series No. 38, London, Civitas, 1997

one out of three criminals convicted of robbery were sent to jail. In 1994, it was one in twenty. In 1954, one in ten burglars were sentenced to prison, but by 1994 it was one in a hundred, a drop of 87 per cent.[16] Nothing could make clearer the utter foolishness of the Lord Chief Justice's recent and repeated guidelines to judges to send fewer burglars to jail.

Another way to bring this point home is to compare, for the UK and the United States, the incarceration rates for assault, robbery, burglary and vehicle theft – See Figures 5.5–5.8. Prison does work because, as stated, once an offender is incarcerated he is out of harm's way and cannot victimise the public. Both in the USA and the UK, it has been shown that as the risk of imprisonment goes down, so the crime rate goes up. Between 1960 and 1974, the USA sent fewer and fewer criminals to prison. If this was intended as an experiment to discover what happens when such a policy is followed, they soon found out. Over the next fourteen years, their

Figure 5.5: Number of incarcerated assaulters per 1,000 alleged assaulters, 1980-1995

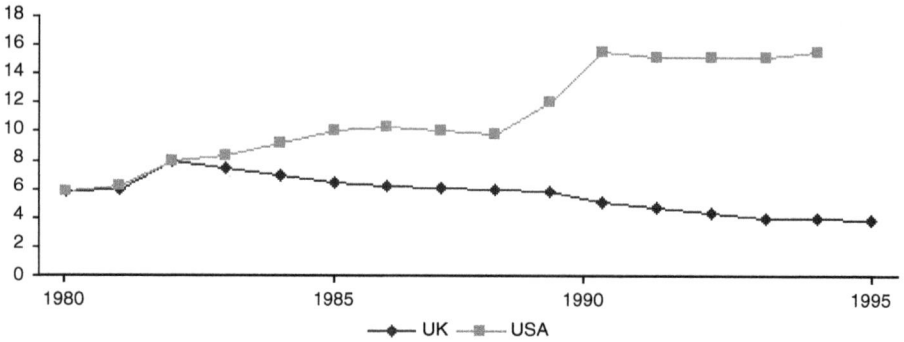

Source: D. Green, *Reducing Crime: Does Prison Work?* London, Civitas, 2000

Figure 5.6: Number of incarcerated robbers per 1,000 alleged robbers, 1980-1995

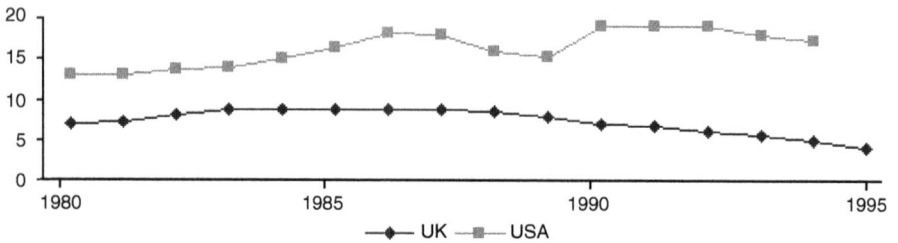

Source: D. Green, *Reducing Crime: Does Prison Work?* London, Civitas, 2000

Figure 5.7: Number of incarcerated burglars per 1,000 alleged burglars, 1980-1995

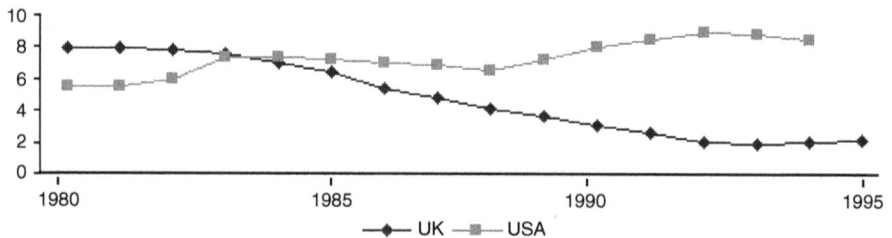

Source: D. Green, *Reducing Crime: Does Prison Work?* London, Civitas, 2000

crime rate soared to unprecedented levels and America became known as one of the crime centres of the world. This period also saw an increased emphasis on the protection of offenders' 'individual rights', which were often seen to frustrate natural justice; the

Figure 5.8: Number of incarcerated vehicle thieves per 1,000 alleged vehicle thieves, 1980-1995

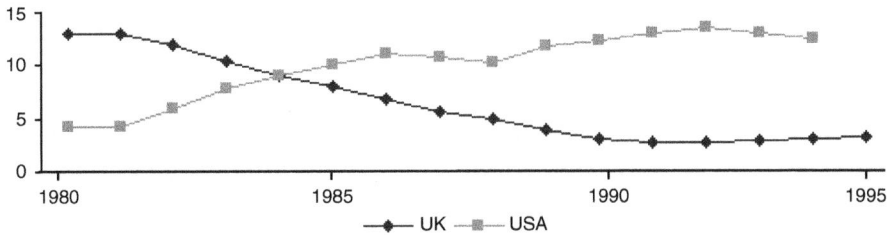

Source: D. Green, *Reducing Crime: Does Prison Work?* London, Civitas, 2000

perception developed that criminals need only appeal to their 'constitutional rights' to block legitimate attempts to convict them of crimes they had committed.

By the 1970s the public's growing resentment of this state of affairs on both sides of the Atlantic had been astutely tapped by such commercially successful films as *Dirty Harry*, 1971, and *Death Wish*, 1974, which portrayed members of the public and the police re-establishing the rights of the public to be protected from crime over the so-called individual rights of the criminals. When the first *Death Wish* film was screened in the USA, audiences spontaneously cheered the scenes which showed the victim-turned-vigilante making sure that the criminal received what many judged to be his 'just deserts'. Taking the law into one's own hands must not be condoned, but such reactions serve as a barometer indicating the depth of feeling amongst the public over the helplessness they felt in the face of non-stop crime, and their anger over the increased opportunities for offenders to escape any form of justice.

By 1974, the US crime rate had reached such epidemic proportions that it stopped its experiment of sending fewer and fewer offenders to prison. It reversed this policy and has since significantly increased its use of prison. As a result, the crime rate for most types of crime in the USA has, with a few exceptions, gone back down to the levels of twenty or more years ago. For example, in 1995 property crimes had fallen to the 1975 levels; homicide rates were down to 1969 levels; and robbery rates were also back to 1975 levels. Anti-prison ideologists have expressed their dismay at the increase in the size of the US prison population; for example, Jock Young has argued that 'it is not part of the social contract which underpins

99

liberal democracy that it should imprison and oversee so many of its citizens'.[17] However, he remains silent on the question as to whether it should be part of this contract to allow persistent offenders freedom to commit crime almost at will and cause untold misery for the general public.

Some have argued that the crime reductions experienced in America can be explained by demographic changes. However, a number of separate studies have demonstrated the crucial role prison has played in bringing down crime levels. For example, a study published in 1996 concluded that an increase of one thousand in the prison population prevents about 4 murders, 53 rapes, 1,200 assaults, 1,100 robberies, 2,600 burglaries and 9,200 thefts per year. In other words, for the cost of imprisoning one offender about fifteen crimes are prevented.[18] A previous analysis of this data showed even larger effects of prison – twenty-one crimes prevented, not fifteen, per additional prisoner.[19] Another study, by the American Bureau of Justice Statistics, concluded that the increase in the US prison population between 1975 and 1989 reduced violent crime by 10 to 15 per cent of the figure it would have been, thus preventing a conservatively estimated 390,000 murders, rapes, robberies and assaults alone.[20]

It has also been pointed out that the USA, despite imprisoning almost two million of its offenders, still has a high crime rate. But this does not mean that 'prisons fail'. What it means is that when crime rates are low it is easier to maintain a high risk of imprisonment because the numbers of offenders are not so huge as to prevent the system keeping on top of the problem. But if the crime rate is allowed to get out of hand, for example as happened in the USA between 1960 and 1974, and in the UK after 1955, when the risk of imprisonment was reduced, it is very difficult to get back to the previous ratio of prisoners to offences. In other words, if the crime rate is allowed to become high, large increases in the prison population are necessary just to enable the risk of imprisonment to keep up with the continued increases in crime. What is more, this catching-up process takes time. In the USA, for example, it was only in the mid 1990s with more than a million people in prison, that the ratio of prisoners to crime reach the level that prevailed in 1961.

We can make an analogy with the railways in the UK. They have been neglected for over forty years, and the rate of deterioration in the track, signalling and other equipment has been allowed to increase markedly, so much so that in reality the railway system is now breaking down and no longer functions properly. The investment level required just to keep up with the effects of under-investment are so huge that it is now far more difficult to keep pace with the current repair work than it would have been had the investment level been maintained at a high level when the deterioration rate was still low. Just dealing with current repair work makes no difference to the overall problem of breakdowns and system failures due to previous neglect.

In the same way, it is easier to lock up higher proportions of those committing crime when there are less of them. But once crime has been allowed to spiral, it is extremely difficult to catch up and get back to being able to lock up higher proportions of those committing offences when there are far more of them.

In addition, many who oppose Murray's thesis do so on the grounds that it is oversimplified. They argue it is wrong to look for a simple relationship between imprisonment and the crime rate. Left-wing academics are never happier than when they have an opportunity to present crime as 'highly complex', beyond the understanding of the general public, and therefore best left to them as 'experts' to offer solutions for its cure. According to them, the social forces at work which influence crime are far more varied and numerous than allowed for in Murray's thesis. They say, for example, that the social world is a complex interactive entity in which any particular social intervention (such as a prison sentence) can only possibly have a limited effect on other social events. According to this view, a large number of factors, such as levels of deterrence, informal controls, employment, child rearing, cultural, political and moral climate, and so on, can combine together to influence the crime rate.

This is an easy point to make, but one which is without any evidence to back it up. The results of studies assessing the influence on crime, for example, of unemployment, child rearing and other social factors, have always been far from conclusive. However, even if it were unanimously accepted that these factors were important in understanding crime, it would not obviate the fact that when offenders are in prison they cannot commit offences against the public.

Nevertheless, many also point to the fact that the USA has a higher imprisonment rate than many other countries, for example Switzerland, yet it still has much higher crime rates for certain types of offences. But this is because their imprisonment rate is chasing after a much higher crime rate than is found in Switzerland. A point frequently missed by those ideologically opposed to the use of prison is that if the USA, despite imprisoning large numbers of criminals, still has a higher crime rate than other countries such as Switzerland, it is because there are, in the USA, still far more offenders not locked up who are committing crimes in the community.

Some academics cite international comparisons of the relationship between changes in the risk of imprisonment and changes in the crime rate, as providing evidence that Murray is wrong. For example, Table 5.2, taken from Murray, appears to show quite clearly that a drop in the risk of imprisonment leads to a rise in the crime rate. However, the counter-argument of the anti-prison lobby is that the causal direction between these two factors is the reverse. They argue that crime increases because of the many interrelated complex factors previously mentioned, and this in turn leads to a fall in the risk of imprisonment because the prison capacity cannot keep up with the increase in crime. They argue that Murray's thesis does not hold up, and point to the example of Scotland where the risk of imprisonment stayed constant yet the crime rate went up. But the flaw in their argument is that what is important, from the point of view of the public, is not the factor or factors (outside of prison) which cause crime to rise, *but what causes crime to fall.* Even if we were to subscribe to the view that rises in crime are associated with 'complex social factors', this does not alter the fact that by increasing the risk of imprisonment it is possible to arrest the crime rate and eventually bring it down.

What is important for the safety of the public, therefore, is not

Table 5.2: The relationship between changes in the risk of imprisonment and changes in recorded crime, 1987–1995

	% change in risk of imprisonment	% change in recorded crime
England & Wales	−17	+31
Scotland	0	+4
Republic of Ireland	−13	+20
France	−9	+16
Austria	−33	+24
Netherlands	+91	+8
Denmark	+4	+3

Source: C. Murray, 'Does Prison Work?', *Choice in Welfare*, No. 38 (1997)

a debate about why the crime rate has gone up, but to bring it down by increasing the numbers of offenders sent to prison, which has been shown to work both in the USA and the UK. For example, from 1993 to 1998 the UK prison population rose by 22,240, or 51 per cent, and at the same time the crime rate fell by 21.4 per cent, representing almost a million fewer crimes.[21] To be distracted at this point by arguing that we should not send offenders to prison because it does not address the 'underlying causes' of crime is no use to the public who need protection from persistent criminals *now*. It is beyond all reason to allow them to go on being victimised whilst the search goes on to identify and remedy the so-called underlying complex, interrelated social factors hypothesised by some to be the cause of offending.

Prisons – An Overview

Let me pull together what has been said so far about why prisons work as a means of protecting the public against crime. The public debate about prisons is often confused because the issue of how to stop crime and protect the public is needlessly mixed up with the separate question of how to solve the complex stresses of society, including such factors as unemployment, poverty and family background, seen by anti-prison factions as the root causes of offending.

However, the evidence shows that prison can prevent crime and reduce crime rates; if you lock up enough offenders for long enough the incarceration effect is considerable and thousands of offences will be prevented. This, of course, does nothing about the so-called 'underlying causes'; this is simply locking up known persistent offenders. The critics of this view say that in some countries crime rates remain high even though more and more offenders are locked up; hence, they deduce that prison does not work. They miss the obvious point, which is that even though a country like the USA for example, may be locking up more offenders, what is critical is how many offenders it does *not* lock up. No matter how high the imprisonment rate, whilst even *larger* numbers of persistent offenders remain at large, the crime rate will stay high.

The point to grasp is that it is possible to have falling crime rates due to locking up more offenders and at the same time still be left with a high level of crime. This is because it takes time and considerable investment in prisons for the imprisonment rate to catch up with the crime rate, once the crime rate had been allowed to get out of hand. No Western country apart from the USA has been prepared to go down this road, and, as a result, against all expectations, the crime rates in America are now generally lower than those of the UK.

However, whether the idea that 'social stresses and strains' are the root causes of crime is correct or not, it is irrelevant to the question of whether 'prison works'. It is irrelevant because, first, prison has been demonstrated to be able to bring crime down, whatever may cause it to rise. Second, by the time an offender becomes persistent, any understanding of the so-called root causes of crime is too late as far as he is concerned; such insights will not stop him. Armies of social workers and probation officers have for years consistently failed to reform persistent offenders using interventions based on such 'insights'. His habit of persistent offending has become ingrained, just as much as his expectations that the benefits he gains from crime are well worth the small risks of being caught and the even smaller risks of losing his liberty.

My years spent working with offenders made it abundantly clear to me that an individual *chooses* to commit offences; with the exception of those who are mentally ill, people are responsible for what they do. As a probation officer, I repeatedly saw that many of those who chose to commit crime would have been prevented from becoming persistent offenders if they had been stopped early on in their criminal careers by a firm response from the authorities. Turning a blind eye to wrongdoing encourages more wrongdoing. We are all creatures of habit and the offending records of criminals show it does not take long for them to establish a routinised criminal pattern of behaviour if it is left unchecked. The rich rewards of their criminal life, coupled with the very small risks they run of being captured and/or imprisoned, compound to create within them a deep criminal persistence.

We should not be critical of prisons for failing to do what we should not expect of them. The fact that they do not address the underlying causes of crime, if these exist beyond the greed and laziness of those who commit it, is no reason for not valuing them as the best means at our disposal for stopping persistent offenders in their tracks, protecting the public and providing justice for the victims.

Prison and Probation: An Unfair Comparison

There is also a great deal of other evidence, little known to the public, which shows that prison is both more effective at protecting the public and at reforming criminals than is supervising offenders in the community. However, the anti-prison lobby frequently attempts to put prison in a poor light compared with these other methods, by measuring reconviction rates for those released from prison from the date of discharge, whereas for those on probation and other forms of supervision order they are measured from the date the supervision started. Thus they ignore the incarceration effect of prison, which is a denial of the primary purpose of sentencing – protecting the public.

For example, to compare a two-year probation order with a two-year prison sentence, both from the date of sentence, would reduce the post-prison reconviction rates by about 50 per cent, as only half the sentence is served. Thus the 63 per cent reconviction rate for all males placed on probation should be compared with about 29 per cent reconviction rate for the one year in the community following a two-year custodial sentence.[22] Government research carried out in 1996 showed that 664 drug and alcohol abusers had committed more than 70,000 crimes in three months, on average eight crimes a week each.[23] At any one time there are about 155,000 persistent offenders being supervised by the Probation Service.[24] If only half of them committed a modest estimate of two crimes a week, they would account for at least 8 *million* crimes. If they had been given a custodial sentence in the first place, the fall in the crime rate would have been dramatic. The evidence that prison works for persistent offenders is unarguable.

Home Office data has also shown that longer prison sentences are significantly more effective at reforming criminals than short prison sentences.[25] These show that reconviction rates, which for those discharged after a sentence of up to one year are 60 per cent, fall dramatically to 33 per cent for those discharged after a sentence of between four and ten years, and to an even lower 27 per cent for those who served sentences of ten or more years. Thus the statement from a previous Conservative Home Secretary, Douglas Hurd, that 'prisons threaten to become an expensive way of making bad people worse' flies in the face of the evidence.[26]

The Penal Affairs Consortium, one of the self-appointed UK anti-prison organisations, has argued that Home Office figures (from

March 1997) which showed a higher reconviction rate for offenders on probation than those released from prison can be largely explained by differential characteristics of the offenders concerned. They argue that those jailed for one-off serious offences are less likely to offend again than many persistent property offenders on probation, and this contributes to the poor comparison of probation reconviction rates with those of offenders discharged from prison.[27] This is an entirely fallacious point, because it is not the number of such offenders in prison at any one time which impact on the comparative reconviction rates for probation and prison, but the number who are released in any one-year. It follows that the number of serious 'one-off' offenders being released into the community each year will be small compared with the very much larger numbers of persistent property offenders, so their impact on the reconviction rates will be insignificant.

In any event, Home Office prison data published in 1996 showed that the numbers of offenders convicted of serious offences in the prison population with no previous convictions to be as low as 15 per cent. This was precisely the same percentage of this category of offender under probation supervision.[28] Thus the Penal Affair's Consortium's argument is undermined.

The reconviction rates for prison become even more impressive when they are considered against the reality of the prison population, which includes drug addicts, serious alcoholics, those with psychiatric illnesses, the unstable, violent, professional criminals, persistent offenders, psychotics, drug dealers and so on. Compelling evidence for the effectiveness of prison in reforming offenders early on in their criminal career comes from an analysis, carried out in London, of the effects of different sentences on four separate groups of offenders. These groups consisted of those with no previous convictions, one previous conviction, two, three or four previous convictions and those with five or more. Measured over a six-year period, as Table 5.3 shows, those with no previous convictions who were given a prison sentence had a low reconviction rate of 15 per cent compared with the much higher 38 per cent reconviction rate for those in this category who were given probation.

The high rates of further offending associated with those released from prison in the higher previous conviction groups confirms prison was the right sentence for them in the first place. Prisons do not create criminals or make criminals worse; prisons are mere bricks and mortar and therefore cannot be held responsible for further

106

Table 5.3: Reconviction rates (%) according to sentence (measured over 5 years)

Sentence	No. of previous convictions			
	0	1	2, 3 or 4	5+
Discharge	19%	50%	90%	85%
Fine	19%	41%	61%	84%
Probation	38%	46%	54%	88%
Suspended sentence	27%	56%	73%	88%
Prison	15%	51%	69%	90%

Source: N. Walker et al., 'Reconviction Rates of Adult Males, after Different Sentences', *British Journal of Criminology*, 21:4 (October), pp. 357–60, 1981

offending; this is solely the responsibility of the individual who chooses to continue a life of crime. Similarly, the argument that some offenders are vulnerable to being made 'worse' by learning new crime skills from other, more criminalised inmates is based on an entirely false premise. (If there was credence to this idea, how much more does it apply to criminals left free in the community to corrupt the vulnerable wherever they meet them, a fact reported on regularly in probation reports up and down the land?) However, the records of the vast majority of offenders receiving their first prison sentence show that they are already experienced and established criminals with little new to learn. It is wrong to say that prisons fail; it is their inmates who fail. If they do acquire new criminal skills in prison, they are not obliged to use them; this is entirely a matter of choice for the offenders concerned.

'Prisons are human dustbins – their regimes are entirely negative'

This criticism is frequently made of our prison system, often by those with little or no practical experience of life in custody. It is true that some prisons are overcrowded, but I repeat that this is not because they are 'overused', but because there are so few places even for the tiny minority of offenders who are sent to jail. In any event, all prisoners are volunteers, and prison conditions, both good and bad, are well known to them at the time they risk their freedom by committing crime.

Nevertheless, offenders in UK prisons have access to trained prison and probation staff who are available to deal with any problems that may arise. Help is provided with many financial and practical problems not always available to those on the outside. Many prisons have excellent sports facilities and trained instructors, who offer inmates *free* physical training and recreational programmes in well-equipped gymnasiums that would be the envy of many in the outside community. Prisoners in need of medical or dental help not available in the prison are taken to outside hospitals where they receive treatment with a promptness not enjoyed by the majority of the law-abiding public.

Every effort is made to help the offender mend his ways by the provision of special programmes and courses, designed by the prison psychologists, probation and/or prison officers. In addition, each prisoner serving more than one year has an individually designed 'sentence plan' to encourage him to reform. Advice and help is provided by staff inside the prison and by many outside agencies on drug, alcohol and other problems. 'Life Skills' courses are run in increasing numbers of prisons to encourage the prisoners to lead crime-free lives on release. In 2000, UK prisons provided about 10 million education study hours to large numbers of prisoners.[29] Free tuition and educational facilities, not available to many of the law-abiding public on the outside, have enabled many offenders to obtain degrees and other higher-education qualifications, which, it is arguable, they would not have achieved otherwise.

It is a myth that prison 'breaks up families'. It is offenders who by their criminal way of life break family ties. Prison staff encourage prisoners to re-establish family contacts broken long before the offender started his prison sentence, and every effort is made to facilitate visits by family and friends.

Much effort is put into ensuring a smooth passage from prison to the outside world. Generous financial grants are paid to those who need them on release. Numerous organisations such as NACRO make free job training schemes available to many about to be released. In 1995, the *Prisoners' Information Book* was published for circulation to all inmates, which is updated every year. Among other things, it contained information on no less than sixty-three organisations offering inmates help over a wide variety of issues.[30]

In sum, prisons in the United Kingdom provide their inmates with free meals and laundry services and ensure free legal advice is available; they also provide prisoners with access to free medical and dental treatment, free training and help from experts on a range of psychiatric, personal and social issues, free job training, free high-calibre sports and recreational facilities, free taxi services when required, free transport to their home, and grants of money when needed. The sustained efforts and money (quite properly) spent on criminals in our prisons to look after them during their sentence and to encourage them to reform are largely obscured from the public by the misleading propaganda of the anti-prison lobby. These facts make a mockery of the criticism that prisons are human dustbins offering a 'no-hope negative regime'.

'Prison Are More Expensive Than Supervising Offenders in the Community'

The claim that prison is more expensive than supervising offenders in the community is entirely misleading. It would be true if the offenders concerned committed no more offences. But it is known that whilst under supervision they commit millions of offences.[31] Crime costs us at least a staggering £60 billion per year, in addition to the emotional and personal costs to the victims.[32] As shown in Figure 5.9, in 1998/99 prisons cost us only £1.9 billion, which was less than we spent on sports and media; by 2003 the costs of prisons had risen to £2.7 billion, but they are still a bargain we cannot afford to miss.

It is salutary to compare the £1.9 billion (1998/99) costs of our prisons with the following amounts relevant for that period. The

Figure 5.9: Central & local government expenditure, 1997/98 (£ billions)

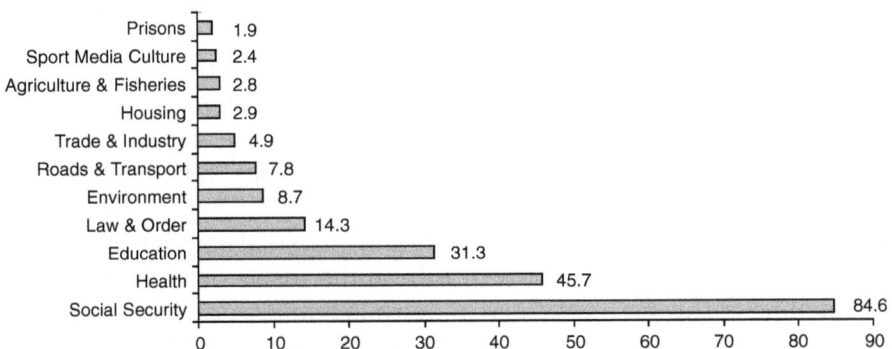

Source: Home Office Research & Statistics Department, *Digest 4: Information on the Criminal Justice System in England & Wales*, 1999

Association of British Insurers estimated that in 1998 crime costs each household £31 per week.[33] The Essex Police Force, in their 1997 annual report, calculated that youth crime costs £10 billion per year, or the equivalent of a hundred new hospitals per year.[34] Homicide costs £1.4 billion; burglaries £2.7 billion; sex offenders £2.5 billion; and drug offences, not including drug-related theft and violence, costs £1.2 billion per year.[35] Although only a small selection of crime costs, these sums totally overshadow the amounts of money we spend on our prisons. Yet as early as 1988, a senior lecturer at Leicester University calculated that prison sentences were the cheapest way to cut crime. He showed that, for example, in order to gain a 1 per cent cut in *reported* property crimes (which, based only on thefts of bikes, cars, robbery and burglary for the year 2000, equals approximately 640,000 offences), would cost no more than £3.6 million if prison sentences were lengthened, or £4.9 million if more offenders were sent to jail.[36]

If we make the conservative assumption that the 155,000 persistent offenders under supervision in the community are only responsible for half the present costs of crime (£60 billion), then by imprisoning them we save £30 billion per year, against the additional costs of approximately £3 billion for the extra prison places required. Given these calculations, the argument that it simply is not financially practical to lock up 150,000-plus offenders is shown to be false.

As huge as the financial costs of crime are, they take no account of the personal costs paid by victims. The loss of family heirlooms and items of sentimental value often results in a lifetime of distress. A debilitating loss of confidence as well as physical and emotional damage can be but part of the grim legacy of many targeted by criminals. A pervasive sense of anxiety and loss of peace of mind can result from being the victim of so-called 'minor' crimes, as well as more serious offending, and undermine feelings of personal safety, security and privacy. According to a government report published in 2000, dealing with the deleterious health effects of crime costs the National Health Service £1.1 billion;[37] it estimated that the cost of the direct emotional and physical impact on victims of crime was £18 billion and £14 billion the result of violent crime.[38]

Yet none of this has prevented numerous home secretaries, including David Waddington and Douglas Hurd in the late 1980s and more recently David Blunkett, from trying to persuade the British public that prison resources should be used sparingly, that only serious sex and violent offences should be dealt with by means of a prison sentence, and that property offenders should be dealt with in the community. What is quite extraordinary about this appeal is that very few property offenders are, in any event, sent to jail. For example, based on Home Office figures for 2000, 101,800 male offenders were sentenced for theft and handling stolen goods. Only one-fifth were sent to prison – in the majority of cases for very short terms of three months or less. The remaining approximately 70,000 were either given discharges, fines or community sentences.[39] Likewise, less than 1 per cent of the 1.64 million burglaries committed every year results in a prison sentence, and the number of male offenders sentenced to prison for this crime fell by 4 per cent between 2000 and 2001.[40]

The Dissemblers

Yet despite this mountain of evidence which shows that prisons are used very sparingly, but that when they are they protect the public and reform offenders more effectively than any other disposal, the public is frequently subject to irrational outpourings, from a variety of individuals and organisations, including judges, politicians, prison-reform groups, the media and sometimes even the Church of England, about the evils of prison.

Former Home Secretary Lord Douglas Hurd has called for a campaign against imprisoning criminals; as pointed out by Brian Lawrence (a former Clerk of the Court with thirty-seven years experience), this is tantamount to him calling for a campaign urging people to commit crime whenever they like, which would quickly lead to a complete breakdown in law and order. Furthermore, Lord Hurd's concern for criminals led him to say, and repeat, on television that burglary was a relatively minor offence.[41] His dismissal of one of the most physically and emotionally injurious of crimes as 'minor' is breathtaking in its arrogance.

Announcements from senior members of our judiciary sometimes show how unclear their thinking is about prisons. For example, the Lord Chief Justice, Lord Woolf, known for his anti-prison views and his non-stop advocacy of lenient sentencing, especially for burglars, suddenly announced in January 2002 that mobile phone muggers should be sent to prison for five years. He justified this

111

apparent about-face by saying these offences involved violence and therefore the public should be protected from these offenders.[42] But Lord Woolf has argued that 'prisons make people worse'. If he believes this, then isn't a prison sentence just as likely to make a violent offender worse, as it is a non-violent one? And, using Lord Woolf's own logic, couldn't it be argued that the consequences for the public are far more dangerous if you make a violent offender even more violent by sending him to prison, than a non-violent property offender?

The inconsistency in the thinking of criminal justice officials was also seen in the announcement, in May 2003, that the penalty for dangerous drivers who kill will increase from ten to fourteen years in prison, under the government's latest move to cut the death toll on the roads. But if prison is seen as the answer to protect the public from dangerous drivers, why is it not viewed as the way to protect us from other forms of crime?[43]

And what are the public to make of the fact that in May 2002 the Sentencing Advisory Panel, a supposedly independent body set up by Parliament to advise on sentencing guidelines, recommended a first-time burglar receive nine months in prison, and a few months later Lord Woolf stated they should not go to prison at all?[44] This inconsistency and lack of direction among judges is not new. The day after Lord Woolf's predecessor, Lord Bingham, had announced that fewer criminals should be jailed because 'prison did not work', a London judge sentenced a burglar to seven years, appearing to make a deliberately pointed reference to Lord Bingham's guidelines by saying that 'the good thing about prison was that it would stop the defendant burgling and terrifying members of the public'.[45]

In 1989, in a published newspaper interview, the director of NACRO talked of her dream of a society without prisons by the 21st century.[46] Such a dream would be a nightmare for society. In 1999, the Church of England, in an embarrassing display of its naivety and ignorance of the facts, published a report saying most prison inmates should not be locked up and that prisons were 'a bad bargain for taxpayers'.[47] A newspaper reported a bishop as saying that the Church should lobby for community service to replace prison sentences wherever possible. It appears that he did not know this had been the situation for years, or that the offences for which community service was being imposed were becoming more and more serious. What is more, had he enquired, the bishop would

112

have discovered that the previous offending records of offenders sentenced in this way were getting longer and it was becoming difficult to find work for an increasing number of them to do. The bishop was also unaware, no doubt, that the vast majority had no motivation to do any work once some was found – why should they have? They knew their indolence was likely to go unpunished. Neither, as shown by their reconviction records, did community service stop them committing crime.[48]

In 1994, Baroness Faithful made a major speech at a conference on government proposals for young offenders, in which she claimed that 'sending young people to prison will greatly increase their chances of becoming adult offenders' and that 'supervision in the community is the best hope of steering them away from crime'.[49] Such statements are as factually wrong and on the same level of foolishness as arguing that bridges would be stronger if they were built of plywood and plasticine.

Judge Tumin, a previous Inspector of Prisons, in a published interview in *The Times* in 1997, appeared to dismiss the needs and wishes of the public to be protected from crime when he said that he thought Michael Howard was just 'seeking popular support' by increasing the imprisonment rate.[50] A number of journalists poured scorn on the increase in numbers of offenders being sent to prison but made no comment about the number of offences that were prevented as a result, or the benefits this would bring to the wider public. Stephen Shaw in a published article in 1998 described prison as the 'black hole' in Labour's approach to criminal justice.[51]

Thinking Straight about Prisons

Based on one government estimate of the number of crimes committed each year by offenders it can be computed that the effect of imprisoning an additional 20,000 offenders prevents between 3 and 5 million crimes for a twelve-month sentence.[52] It is therefore no surprise that we have had some benefit from the rise in the prison population since 1993; but the supposed drop in crime to the present level of 12.6 million offences still leaves the community with a dreadful crime problem, even before we take into account that these British Crime Survey estimates are only a *partial* measure of all crime.

However, we must recall that a significant factor in the rise in prison numbers has been the large increase in other categories of prisoners, such as those serving life, foreign prisoners and those on remand, and not just those sentenced for persistent theft, robbery, burglary and so on. As will be touched upon later, increasing numbers of these latter prisoners, having been released early from prison would be on licence at the time of their further offending, leaving no option for them but a prison sentence. Therefore to see the overall increase in the number of prison sentences as entirely the result of the courts becoming more punitive is wrong. That there are millions of crimes still being committed, despite the rise in the prison population, indicates that far more offenders need to be jailed, and not be allowed to continue to predate on the public; we need, as will be discussed in later chapters, to plan for a prison population that is at least three times the present level of 75,000.

We should resist being bullied by ill-informed arguments to think negatively about prisons, or be frightened into thinking that we imprison too many offenders. Whilst, since 1993, more offenders have been sentenced to custody each year, there was, between 1997, when New Labour took office, and 2001, a sharp fall in the *rate* of the yearly increase. For example, as displayed in Figure 5.10, the numbers of offenders sentenced to custody in 1998 represented an increase of 7 per cent over the previous year; for 1999 the increase was 5 per cent, and for 2000 the rate of increase was down to 1 per cent (see Note 1).

However, this trend was hidden by the hysterical outcries from the anti-prison lobby about the increase in overall prison numbers.

Figure 5.10: Percentage change in numbers sentenced to custody and community service (CS)

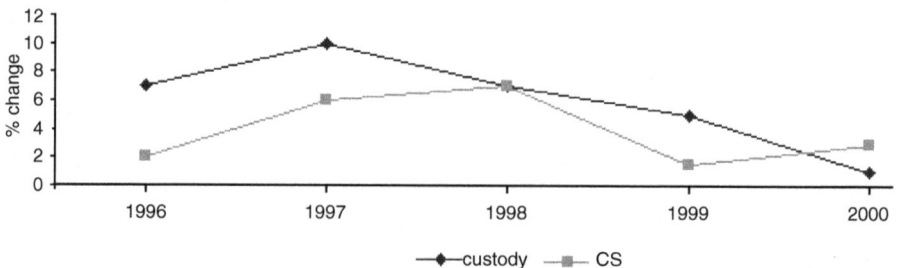

Source: Home Office Statistics, 'Offenders Sentenced for all Offences by Type of Sentence or Order, 1995–2000'

More recent data (reported in *Home Office Bulletin* 15/04) shows that the prison population increased at a lower rate between 2002 and 2003 (up 3 per cent) than the increase observed between 2001 and 2002 (up 7 per cent). The greatest value of prison to the public is the millions of offences that are not committed by persistent offenders whilst they are locked up. This enormous social benefit is deliberately undervalued or ignored by those who unfailingly point to those released from prison who continue to commit crime as evidence that prison has failed, whilst turning a blind eye to the even higher reconviction rates of offenders supervised in the community.

Nevertheless, a sustained misinformation campaign has persuaded many into adopting a negative mindset in relation to prisons. How else can we explain the community's apparent willingness to support sentencing policies that directly conflict with its own safety and well-being, by allowing unrepentant criminals their freedom to go on committing crime? What other explanation is there for the phenomenon whereby we knowingly follow lenient sentencing practices which predictably result in the misery and significant harm to many millions of people victimised by criminals every year?

Although anti-prison propaganda has poisoned the view of many towards prison regimes, in reality, as we have noted, they have much to offer prisoners, both to enhance their lifestyle inside and to prepare them for life outside. If prisoners continue to commit crime after their release it is in spite of the determined rehabilitative efforts made by prison staff and the considerable financial and practical resources which are committed to this objective.

The fact that many continue with their life of crime shows how determined they are to persist with their offending because it pays so well, not that 'prison has failed'. Although, as I have shown, prison regimes make huge efforts to encourage inmates to 'go straight' on release, offenders are entirely responsible for their own reform.

Prisons keep in safe conditions many who are unlikeable, difficult, dangerous, unrepentant and sometimes insane, thus saving countless people from the misery of criminal victimisation. Yet because of the success of anti-prison propaganda prisons are more often vilified than praised.

It is true that there are problems in prisons, but such problems can be addressed. Overcrowding is artificially induced by maintaining a deliberate shortage of places and it can therefore be solved by a significant prison expansion programme. Bullying, baroning and drug-trafficking are other problems that are also unacceptable, but it is the inmates who generate these problems by importing their criminal attitudes, not the regime, which is constantly trying to overcome them.

An Illusion

As already stated it is an illusion that we have too many offenders in prison. If prisons are full, it is because we have too few places even for the tiny minority of offenders who are sentenced to prison. The public need have no bad conscience about locking up, for increasingly long periods, those persistent offenders who fail to reform. They are all volunteers who have all been given numerous chances to go straight and who have consistently abused these opportunities by continuing to victimise the public. Their motive is profit. They earn large sums of money from crime and have almost no risk of being caught. For the tiny minority who are, a short prison sentence is nothing more than an irritant, a short break in an otherwise active and lucrative career. As demonstrated, it is longer prison sentences which encourage them to reform. Losing their freedom for increasingly longer periods means that the advantages to them of pursuing a life of crime will be outweighed by the disadvantages.

Chapter 6

Failure, Deception and Cover-up

The previous chapter has demonstrated that the reason why prisons are looked down upon by so many as a way of dealing with offenders is that the truth of their success in providing a bulwark against crime and reforming criminals has been suppressed. At the same time, officials in the criminal justice system, both inside and outside of government, have developed strategies to cover up the chronic failure of non-prison sentences, such as probation supervision of offenders, to protect the public. To the surprise of his audience, in 2000 a retired senior Home Office director of statistics admitted at a conference that statistical information was commonly presented in a way that allows for deception.[1]

It is not comfortable to be told that we are being misled by officials who we rely on to keep us safe, and it took me a long time to accept this unpalatable truth. For example, I knew, as did my colleagues that the probation orders we were supervising, particularly from the 1970s onwards, did not stop offenders from committing more crime, yet this was never recognised or admitted to by the management of the Probation Service or the government. However, I told myself that they could see the 'big picture', and I couldn't.

Thus for a long time I made the mistake of believing that my superiors knew more than I did, and that it was my fault that I could not square what they were telling the public with what I knew was happening on the ground. When the penny dropped and I finally realised their claims of success were false, I felt a sense of betrayal, as perhaps may some who read this book. We have every right to expect that criminal justice officials should be straight with us over the results of sentencing policies. But the ugly truth is they are not, and in this chapter I will identify some of the techniques they use

117

to keep the public in the dark concerning their failure. This will reveal how the impact on the public of their failed sentencing policies is minimised by misrepresentation, the abuse of statistics, and, as I will show in the following chapter, by the blatant presentation of their failure as 'success'. I will also identify examples showing how officials have deliberately clouded the evidence trail which would otherwise show their success claims are a sham.

Supervising Offenders in the Community: A Failed and Discredited Policy

The evidence that the supervision of persistent offenders in the community fails to protect the public is unequivocal, and can be found in statistical bulletins published by the Home Office. However, it is unlikely that the majority of the public know of the existence of these publications, and few would know where to look for them. In most cases, they have to rely for their information on crime, prisons and other forms of sentencing on what they are told by MPs and government officials via TV, radio and the press; nothing could make them more vulnerable.

Success or failure of those on community supervision orders is measured by the offender's reconviction rate, measured over two years from the start of the order. It is important to realise that for this purpose the Home Office only takes account of one court appearance that occurs during this two-year period. Thus the latest figures which show a 60 per cent reconviction rate for the majority of offenders on probation, disastrous as it is, gives no clue as to the total number of court appearances, or the number of offences these offenders have committed whilst under supervision.

The table in Note 1 shows the full extent of the failure rates for all types of community supervision. However, what I will highlight here are the reconviction rates for offenders on probation orders: for those under 21 years, 73 per cent, 21–24 years, 68 per cent; 25–29 years, 62 per cent; and for those aged 30 or over it is 46 per cent.[2] What is even more significant is that these high reconviction rates are based solely on those offenders who were caught and so only provide a hint of the extent of their failure. Viewed against the 5.5 per cent detection rate their *reoffending* rate will be nearer 100 per cent.

118

In the past community supervision sentences were used for offenders who showed motivation to go straight and capacity to reform, and for those who were assessed as low risk to the community. Such orders were made on the back of a promise from the offender that he would commit no more crime. On that basis, the court trusted him with his freedom. Such orders met with considerable success. For example, a Home Office investigation of 2,311 offenders placed on probation by fifteen courts in 1933 found that 70 per cent *had not* been reconvicted during a three-year follow up.[3] This is in stark contrast to the Home Office figures published in 2000 which showed that 60 per cent of all probationers *had been* reconvicted over a follow-up period of only two years.[4]

However, over the last twenty-five years this policy has been turned upside down. Those whom the Probation Service assess as being of high risk of further offending are specifically targeted for supervision in the community. The evidence, as illustrated by Figures 6.1 and 6.2, shows that young and adult offenders now placed on probation are far more likely to have long criminal histories than in the past and therefore represent a real threat to the community.

The purpose of the Probation Service in targeting high-risk offenders for supervision in the community is to divert as many of them as possible from a custodial sentence, despite the certainty that almost all of them will continue to offend. Further, the reader will be surprised to learn that when probation officers assess the risk of serious harm to the public posed by offenders awaiting sentence, burglary is not thought to be relevant. As a result, the courts frequently follow their recommendations and each year sentence

Figure 6.1: Percentage of adult offenders on probation with previous convictions

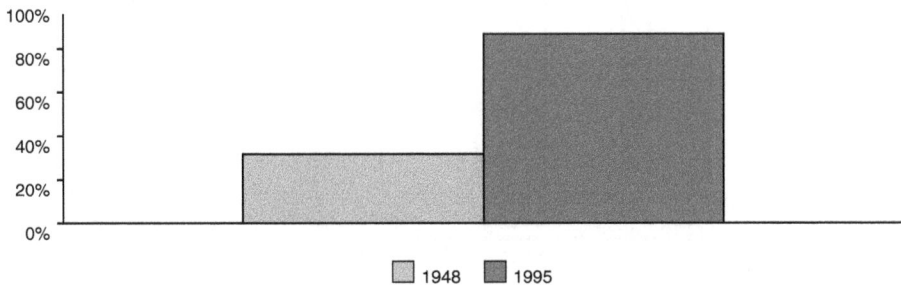

☐ 1948 ■ 1995

Source: W.A. Elkin, *The English Penal System*, Pelican, 1957; P. Coad and D. Fraser, *Community Sentences: A National Disaster, Criminal Justice Association*, 1999 (see Note 2)

119

Figure 6.2: Percentage of offenders under 21 years on probation with previous convictions

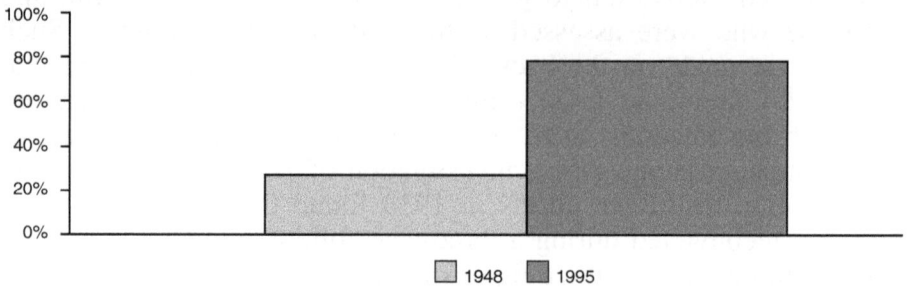

Source: W.A. Elkin, *The English Penal System*, Pelican, 1957; P. Coad and D. Fraser, *Community Sentences: A National Disaster, Criminal Justice Association*, 1999 (see Note 2)

thousands of offenders unmotivated to reform to a period of supervision. The threat they pose to the public is illustrated by Figure 6.3.

Furthermore, the Probation Service specifically targets offenders with four to sixteen previous convictions for certain types of 'what works' community supervision programmes, which I will discuss in more detail in Chapter Seven.[5] As can be seen from the table in Note 1 the reconviction rates for this group of offenders are over

Figure 6.3: Offenders on community supervision (per reconviction rates as %)

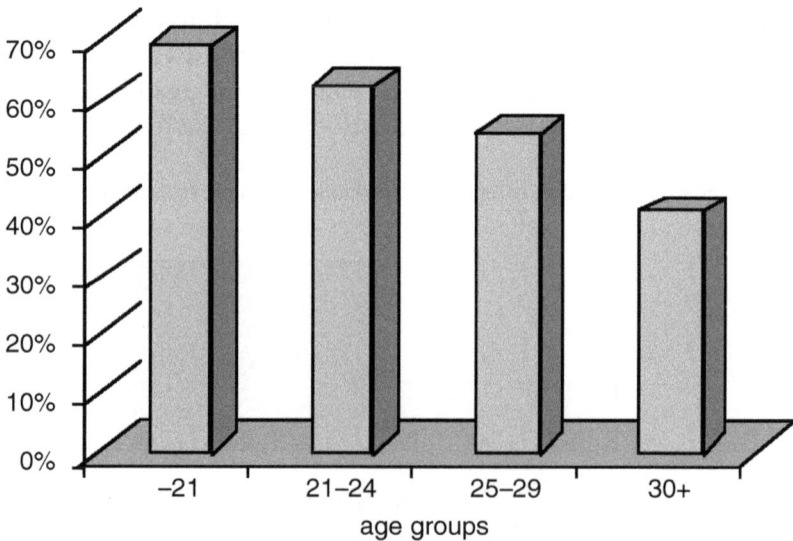

Source: Home Office, *Prison Statistics England & Wales*, 1999, 2000

120

90 per cent. These figures provide a powerful demonstration of the impact on the community of the Home Office and Probation Service's campaign to keep out of gaol thousands of offenders with a high risk of reoffending and who are unmotivated to reform.

Yet, despite this evidence, the government has tried to create the fiction that only low-risk offenders are placed under supervision. A leaked government report from Downing Street in 2003 said that probation programmes and supervision were so ineffective that 'it would be better to use the resources on more serious offenders and impose fines on the rest'. But this was a cunning piece of fiction designed to mislead the public with a phoney explanation for the failure of their sentencing policies. The truth is that the majority of offenders currently under supervision *already* do have a high risk of reoffending. The report also misleadingly implied that the fine system was not working because 'of the poor level of collection' and because 'many offenders could not afford to pay'. What the report failed to acknowledge is that large numbers of offenders simply *refuse* to pay their fines, showing themselves to be unsuitable candidates for such sentences.[6]

The continued offending of the 155,000 offenders under supervision in the community results in millions of offences, none of which would have been committed had the offenders concerned been sent to prison.[7] It cannot be stressed enough that the price paid by the victims for these failed policies is catastrophic. Not only do criminals inflict on them grievous loss and strain but many endure anxiety and fear and are robbed of their peace of mind. The quality of their lives is seriously eroded by their experience of being victimised and the nagging anxiety that it may be repeated.

In this regard it is chilling to note that, for example, in 2000, over 14,000 offenders were sentenced to community supervision orders for offences involving violence, over 10,000 for burglary, 1,400 for robbery and 41,500 for theft and handling stolen goods, despite the clear evidence of the likelihood of their reoffending.[8] Furthermore it is known that in 1998 offenders under supervision to the Probation Service committed 56 murders and attempted murders, 20 manslaughters, 33 rapes, 5 attempted rapes and 13 arsons with intent to endanger life.[9] What is remarkable is that the Home Office have known for years that offenders on probation pose a serious risk to the public, not only during the period of their supervision, but, as illustrated by Table 6.1, *for years afterwards.*

Table 6.1: Reconviction rates of those placed on probation in 1979

% reconvicted	Aged 17 and under 21 years	Aged 21 years and over
Within 2 years	56	43
Within 3 years	64	49
Within 4 years	68	53
Within 5 years	70	56

Source: Home Office Statistical Bulletin, Issue 34/86, *Reconvictions of Those Given Probation Orders*, 1986

It shows the percentage of those males placed on probation in 1979 who were reconvicted within three, four, and five years from the start of their order (which could run for one, two or three years). Nine years later, the reconviction rates for all males placed on probation within two years and four years from the start of the order, tell the same story. Within two years, 58 per cent of males commencing probation orders in 1987 or 1988 had been reconvicted; within four years, 68 per cent.[10] Offenders become more criminal as time goes by, making nonsense of Probation Service claims that it can be 'effective' at reforming them. These figures are to be compared with the much lower 45 per cent reconviction rate for all male prisoners discharged between 1985 and 1993.[11]

The Probation Service has shown a remarkable capacity to put its head in the sand by simply ignoring its grim record in reforming the criminals it supervises. For example, during the 1980s it set up special day-centre programmes for persistent offenders, to be used as alternatives to prison, which it believed would reform the most hardened of them. In what must have been, even by its standards, one of the most brazen propaganda exercises of all time, the Probation Service convinced judges and magistrates that they should go along with this experiment. For example, one local Probation Service promoted its day centre as 'providing a demanding programme for adult, serious and persistent offenders. It has a high restriction of liberty and examines attitudes to offending behaviour and the impact on victims. 64% complete the programme which has proved effective in holding the attention of men and women for whom little else has worked.'[12] This hype, similar in style to that used by quack doctors to sell their bogus medicines in the Wild West of America in the nineteenth century, beguiled a vulnerable judiciary. As a result, thousands of offenders who showed no motivation, and in many cases no capacity to change, were let loose by the courts to be

Table 6.2: Percentage reconvicted within two years of commencement of probation order (based on 1987, 1988, 1989 and 1990 samples)

Type of Supervision	Under 21 years	21–29 years	25–29 years	30+ years
Day Centre	78	67	58	46
Other probation	64	53	47	36
Community service	66	54	48	37

Source: Home Office, *Probation Statistics England & Wales*, 1993

supervised by what the Probation Service proudly called its 'flagship' supervision centres.

As demonstrated by Table 6.2 the day centres were spectacular failures and made not the slightest impression on the criminal behaviour of the offenders referred to these schemes. Their reconviction rates were even higher than those from the general offender caseloads, and it was therefore the public who paid the price for this triumph of hope over reality. Oblivious of their failure, the Probation Service continued to run these schemes for several years. However, their performance was so consistently bad that eventually, in contrast to the publicity associated with their launch, they were quietly dropped, and no one has mentioned them, or the impact they had on the community, ever since.[13]

There can be no other government department whose policies wreak such harm on the public; but why is it tolerated? Failure in schools on this scale would result in the head teacher being retired or sacked, and the school being taken over by central government, if not closed. Hospitals exhibiting this level of incompetence and danger to the public would be the subject of high-level enquiries, sacking of key staff, exposure in the press, and other forms of censure from the voters, if not the government. Yet the Probation Service escapes any form of proper accountability. This is no oversight or accident; the government tolerates the continued failure of the Probation Service because of the wider role it plays for them; its continued existence is an integral part of the propaganda lie that the majority of persistent offenders are best dealt with in the community and not sent to prison.

In 1998 criminal justice officials again thrust this message at the public in an effort to oppose the growing scepticism of their probation policies caused by the non-stop offending of criminals under their supervision. Unable to produce evidence of real success, they invented

123

new and meaningless criteria as part of their public-relations offensive to justify their pro-criminal sentencing policies. These were unveiled in a report called *Evidence Based Practice*.[14] This stretched the English language to breaking point in its attempt to reassure the public that there was evidence to show it was in their interests for criminals to be supervised in the community. It pointed out that probation success could be measured in a variety of ways which included: the offender complying with the requirements of a period of supervision, improvements in his attitude and motivation, his undertaking training or finding a job, more control by him over the use of drugs or alcohol, improved social and thinking skills, and improved relationships. Thus they seriously expected the public to accept that a probation order could be viewed as success if the offender got on better with his mother, drank less or found a job as a trainee, but nevertheless continued to repeatedly burgle their houses, rob them in the street and steal their cars. This is reminiscent of the second-hand car salesman who tells a potential customer that he should not be distracted by the fact that the engine in the car won't work but to concentrate on the quality of the upholstery and the shiny ashtrays.

The Art of Deception

The Home Office and the Probation Service are preoccupied with 'marketing strategies' and 'communications'. What this means in practice is dressing up their statistics to promote themselves as 'successful' in protecting the public and reforming criminals, and at the same time diverting attention from their record of failure. In an almost perfect reflection of the old Soviet communist system, it can be taken, as a general rule of thumb, that the more they fail, the more blatant is their propaganda, often expressed with meaningless jargon. For example, one publication on my desk speaks about the need to 'promote a probation perspective which is positive and promotional', 'to promote well-prepared information' and to 'promote periodic key messages'.[15] Of interest in this respect is that analysis of the language used by company managers has shown that their documentation becomes more indecipherable as they slide further towards bankruptcy.[16]

Publicity campaigns, leaflets and exhibitions have become standard items in their propaganda effort.[17] Likewise, the reports of their work, often published in expensive and glossy formats, can be highly deceptive. For example, Home Office Research Study No. 167, *Offenders on Probation*, fails to mention anywhere in its ninety five pages the high probation reconviction rates. An impressive-looking Home Office document published in 1999, promoted the idea of 'Restorative Justice' as benefiting the victims of crime and the community.[18] Yet it avoids the fact that there is not a shred of evidence to show that victim–offender mediation sessions have any effect on reducing crime; in reality, their main effect is to neutralise the justified anger of those who have been victimised, and so reduce the possibility of public protest and demand for more prisons. The contents of another Home Office report entitled *Strengthening Punishment in the Community* (1995), laid out proposals to do the exact *opposite*, and would have trapped many MPs into supporting it who were too busy to read anything but the title. *Joining Forces to Protect the Public* (1998) was a Home Office document about prisons and probation that used a form of 'department speak' that could have meant anything or nothing.

The most dominant propaganda message from both the Home Office and the Probation Service is that their first priority is to 'protect the public and reduce reoffending'.[19] This is deception in its most glaring form because in reality their policies achieve the converse of both of these objectives. Recently we witnessed the collapse of a number of large companies who 'talked up' their performance and misled the public by inflating their profitability. Our criminal justice system has also trapped itself with its own lies and could await a similar fate. For example, in 1998 the Home Office published its Research Study No. 187, called *Reducing Offending: An Assessment of Research Evidence on Ways of Dealing with Offending Behaviour.* The tactics adopted by the authors of this report are worth noting. First, they gave the report an impressive title; next, to give it status in the eyes of the vulnerable public they described it as 'one of the most important pieces of research on criminal justice for years' and 'the most thorough study of crime ever carried out in the world'.[20]

Incredibly, the report questioned the value of zero tolerance and of increasing the numbers of police on the streets.[21] Yet it is widely known that when zero-tolerance policing was adopted in New York it was an outstanding success in combating crime,[22] and, likewise, when it was tried in this country, in Middlesbrough, its immediate success caught the imagination of the whole nation. The Home Office fear zero-tolerance policing because they know it works, and through it more offenders would be caught and be in danger of being sent to prison. This is not on the Home Office agenda.

The report also quoted research that argued random patrolling by the police was ineffective and other findings which conceded the effectiveness of directing police patrols to crime 'hot spots'.[23] But if patrols work in high crime areas, they will work anywhere, a truth instinctively understood by the public. Would it not be better to prevent crime by widespread patrolling than wait for crime to infest an area before sending in the police to chase it away? As the public know only too well, the relief from crime after the police have descended on a problem area is short-lived, as the criminals soon return once the police have turned their attention elsewhere.

A recent independent study by the Civitas think-tank pointed out that the police are now so overwhelmed by the sheer volume of crime that even recent additions to their numbers are making no difference.[24] Street crime, which is directly influenced by the numbers of police on patrol, has rocketed over the last few decades. For example, in the London borough of Lambeth the increase in robberies in 2002 was greater than the annual number of robberies in England and Wales throughout most of the 1920s.[25]

We should be in no doubt that the objective of the Home Office Report No. 187, *Reducing Offending*, was to provide phoney reasons for not spending the very large sums of money needed to protect the public by means of an expanded police force. Instead, the Home Office is trying to fill the gaps with much cheaper alternatives: neighbourhood watch patrols, new kinds of community support officers, and security guards. In May 2003 the government reported plans to recruit 1,200 more 'police wardens', to be used, despite the findings of its own research, 'for foot patrols'.[26] The Metropolitan Police now use about two hundred quasi-officers with limited police powers around Westminster, but significantly, in April 2003, London's police commissioner conceded that it is wrong to argue that a PC on patrol interacting with the public is not a crime-fighting measure. When hundreds of police were recently deployed from Central London to deal with a terrorist scare at Heathrow, crime in the capital soared.[27]

This highly deceptive report also played down the ability of prison to protect the community, and came out with the old confused arguments that crime must be reduced by 'tackling the underlying causes'. It even went so far as to say that the long-term impact of increasing arrests for what it called 'minor' offences 'may be to damage police legitimacy'.[28] This is nonsense of breathtaking intensity; no offence is 'minor' to the victim, and nothing reduces police legitimacy more than for them to be seen by the public to be doing nothing about crime, be it serious or minor.

However, the report did concede that police targeting of high profile repeat offenders with the aim of securing sound evidence, convictions and long sentences was an effective crime reduction strategy.[29] Many might claim this was a statement of the obvious, yet by 2003 the 'targeting of prolific offenders' was a phrase which had come to mean something quite different. Instead of going all out to arrest and prosecute them, it heralded the establishment of 'prolific offender units', where seconded staff from the police, prisons and probation formed teams to focus on the most persistent offenders in a particular area. Despite the damage and misery they were causing to the public, they were to be left in the community, so that police, probation and prison staff could join forces to 'encourage' these offenders to find regular work, to come off drugs if they have a habit, and to generally go straight. Sometimes even their offending is ignored, in an attempt to 'divert them away from the criminal justice system', as contact with it is believed to contribute to their offending.

The units purport to provide 'intensive' supervision, but on closer inspection this amounts to no more than an expectation of two hours contact per week for the first three months, and one hours contact per week for the next three months.[30] This means that in the first three months, assuming the offender is only active for eight hours per day, and assuming he submits to two hours contact per week (which is highly questionable), he has 642 unsupervised hours available during which he can commit crime at will, and the staff of the prolific offender unit will be none the wiser. During the second three-month period he will have even more unsupervised time.

The sheer naivety of this approach is hard to swallow. Do these experienced police, probation and prison staff really believe that persistent criminals commit crime because they cannot find legitimate work? And do they really think that by ignoring their offending, the criminals will not be encouraged to commit more crime? Yet these prolific-offender units base their reformative efforts on the old assumptions that unemployment and other 'social problems' are the cause of the offending which has characterised the lifestyle of the criminals for so long. The fact that decades of work with criminals based on these assumptions has never succeeded has been totally ignored.

What the public have not been told is that all of the effort and money spent on these units (five of them have been established so far – all with government funding) has been wasted. Not one has been successful in protecting the public from crime. Operation ARC, for example, was run jointly by police and probation staff in the south-west region of the country, and focused on just ten prolific offenders. Its purpose, to quote the report of the project, was to 'produce crime reduction outcomes'.[31] This naive expectation soon had to be abandoned in the face of the continued criminality of the offenders being supervised on the scheme. In an attempt to provide some meaning to a futile exercise, a progress report on the project stated 'the evaluation of the scheme would need to take a wider view than that demonstrated by crime figures'.[32] What would we think if a hospital claimed that any evaluation of its efforts 'would have to take a wider view than that demonstrated by the number of patients who were cured of their illness?'

The final report of Operation ARC had no option but to admit that it 'had not succeeded in turning the target group of ten prolific offenders away from crime'.[33] This in itself is not a surprise. What is, however, is that a group of experienced criminal justice officials should ever take seriously the idea that they could. In an effort to scrape the barrel for something positive to say, the report stated that there had not been an increase in the local crime figures as a result of leaving these ten offenders in the community.[34] Why should there have been? The relevant point is that there had not been a reduction. Most significantly, the evaluation of the project failed to take into account the damage and distress caused to the lives of those victimised by the offenders selected for this scheme, and the reduced operational abilities of the police due to the diversion of their scarce manpower to a social-work activity not in their remit. The policeman's job is to make life miserable for criminals by stopping them committing crime, and getting them convicted when they do – not to be a social worker, or worse, a pseudo-sociologist in uniform.

In at least one Prolific Offender Unit the pretence maintained by

128

the staff that they have some hope of diverting their target group of unrepentant and serial offenders from crime has reached the level of farce. My enquiries revealed that among this small group of offenders are active police informants, who would be of no use in this role if they were not hardened criminals determined to carry on with their life of crime.

The public are frequently deceived by criminal justice slogans proclaiming that alternative sentences to prison are not 'soft options'. The Probation Service is forever publicising itself as offering 'rigorous and tough alternatives' to prison. They favour words like 'demanding' and 'meaningful' when describing their supervision of offenders. The truth would make these 'hard-sell' style persuasion antics laughable if the consequences for the public were not so serious. For example, the government's National Standards for Offender Supervision, which are supposed to set minimum tough standards of rigorousness for the supervision of offenders in the community, are little short of a joke. They state for example, that:

> The offender should attend a minimum of twelve appointments – normally weekly – with the supervising officer in the first three months of an order; six in the next three months; and thereafter at least on each month to the completion of the supervision'. Based on a two-year probation order and assuming a high average of thirty minutes for each appointment, the minimum requirement works out at no more than eighteen hours of supervision in a two-year period. This leaves the offender 17,502 hours to commit crimes.[35]

In addition, the much-vaunted community service orders, which have survived on the myth that they are tough and demanding, are in reality of little consequence to the offenders who are sentenced to work under them. It is well known in the Probation Service, but generally not to the public at large, that offenders frequently fail to turn up for their work sessions. Despite the claims that it is a tough alternative to prison, one day's work a week is usually the maximum demanded of them (see Note 3);[36] arriving late as well as failing to show up at all are common experiences. Work supervisors frequently have to spend time rounding up many of the offenders who would otherwise never be seen, despite the court order which states they must report to the work site as directed.

The experience of one north-of-England probation office is typical. On one particular day in 1992, twenty-one offenders were supposed to turn up for their community work session. Four arrived.[37] Offenders who failed to keep to the conditions of the community service order were given several chances, as their supervisors bent over backwards not to invoke any formal sanctions. The Home Office has since tightened up the enforcement arrangements and offenders are now breached after two unacceptable failed appointments. However, breach action by the Probation Service does not mean prompt action by the courts, who frequently instigate long delays in issuing the necessary summons or arrest warrant. Furthermore, when arrest warrants are finally issued for these offenders, the police rarely act upon them. In the area being cited, the police would not chase community-service defaulters if they were more than twenty miles away because it was too expensive. Eventually, warrants are revoked and offenders are free men again, and they may well not have completed even one day's work. So much for community service being a 'rigorous alternative to prison'.

I have a copy of a report, written by a chief probation officer, which says 'about three out of four community service orders are completed to the satisfaction of all concerned and without a further offence during the course of the order'.[38] This statement could only have been made by an official who felt utterly confident he would never be held to account for such a misleading claim. In reality they are a failure, and they neither protect the public nor encourage offenders to go straight. The Home Office's *Prison Statistics England & Wales*, 1999, for example, reveal that 65 per cent of under-21-year-olds given community service orders were reconvicted within two years. Among the 21–24 age group, the rate was 56 per cent; 48 per cent for 25–29-year-olds and 35 per cent for those aged 30 and above. Offenders were required to attend the day centres previously mentioned for just sixty days. A 'day' often meant as little as four hours. In total, this so-called 'tough' alternative amounted to about ten days loss of liberty. If that isn't a soft option, I do not know what is.[39]

Recent publications show that the determination of the Home Office to deceive the public over the results of its crime policies remains undiminished. In March 2003, they published statistics which purported to show that the reconviction rates for juvenile offenders went down by 22 per cent between 1997 and 2000.[40] This is a clear invitation for us to believe that juvenile crime has decreased (thanks to the government's juvenile crime policy). However, this claim is as reliable as that made during the recent war in Iraq that 'hundreds of coalition soldiers were committing suicide at the gates of Baghdad', and could only be made by a complete denial of reality. For example, in 1997 the police estimated that young offenders in the UK were committing crime on a vast scale, and those under eighteen were responsible for over 19,000 offences every day or 13 crimes a minute; this was costing the victims and the nation between £5 billion and £10 billion per year. Despite this, only 3 per cent of offences committed by juveniles led to an arrest and only 19 per cent of the offences were recorded.[41] The police based their assessment on findings of an Audit Commission Report published a few months earlier, which criticised the youth justice system, costing £1 billion per year as inefficient and an expensive failure.

In 1998, the Metropolitan Police Commissioner reported that offenders aged between ten and sixteen years were responsible for 40 per cent of all street robberies in London, and made up a third of all arrests for vehicle thefts, 27 per cent of burglary and a quarter of all shoplifting arrests.[42] In 2000 even Home Office figures showed that serious crime by the young had doubled in the last seven years.[43] By 2002 juvenile offending had reached such a scale that it was decided to base police officers in secondary schools across the country in high crime areas.[44]

A closer inspection of the Home Office figures associated with their recent claim reveals the now familiar statistical sleight of hand. For example, those young people who have been sentenced to imprisonment have been specifically excluded from the analysis. They, of course, are the group who will not only commit the most serious offences but they are by far the most likely to reoffend. Even more significant is the fact that there has been a large rise in the percentage of young people receiving warnings and reprimands, with 76 per cent being dealt with in this way.[45] This fact alone renders meaningless the claim that there has been a drop in juvenile reconvictions. To bring this point home even further, the south-west region of the country recorded that, in 2002, offences committed by the young had increased by 41 per cent over the previous twelve months, but the number sentenced only increased by 4.2 per cent.[46] In 1994 only 10 per cent of youths under the age of fourteen arrested for indictable offences were found guilty of anything, whereas in

1954 77 per cent of them were found guilty.[47] Overall, all youth crime has increased by more than 35 per cent in the past ten years, while the number of young offenders taken to court has dropped by 35 per cent.[48]

Beyond all of these arguments is the fact that it is impossible to say there has been a drop in juvenile crime when we do not know who is committing the 95 per cent of undetected crime. This point was illustrated by government research in 1998 based on anonymous interviews with almost 5,000 fourteen to seventeen-year-olds. Approximately one thousand admitted having committed a crime in the past year, but only 12 per cent of these had been cautioned or brought before the court.[49]

Creative Accounting

As repeatedly shown in preceding chapters, criminal justice officials are firmly wedded to an anti-prison policy, irrespective of its harmful results to the public, and for decades this thinking has heavily weighted their advice to Home Office ministers. They are therefore highly motivated, not to say desperate, to make sure that the statistics relating to the success or failure of prison and probation, justify their arguments. But here they have a problem, because prison is obviously more effective at protecting the public from crime than is a period of community supervision. This is because, whilst they are in prison, the approximately 45,000 persistent offenders commit no crime against the public but the far larger numbers being supervised in the community commit millions of offences. They have sought to overcome these problems by some 'creative accounting', employed to make certain that the 'evidence' supports their anti-prison policy, and it is worth examining some of the devious methods they employ to bend the figures to their will.

I have already described how the success or failure of probation is measured by noting the number of offenders who commit offences during the two-year follow-up period, which runs from the start of the order. This is compared with the reconviction rates for those released from prison – from the date of their release. In the previous chapter, I discussed the unfair bias this produces in favour of probation, as it ignores the period of the offender's incarceration during which no crimes were committed against the public.

In addition, for many years the Home Office made an 'adjustment' to their statistics which resulted in them being able to *reduce* the numbers of failed probation orders. This consisted of making a six-point reduction to allow for convictions received during the period of the probation order but for offences committed before it had started.[50] (They also make a two-point allowance for convictions which occur in the two years following a prison sentence.) On the face of it, this seems fair, but a closer inspection has found this not to be the case. This revealed that they make no reciprocal adjustment for offences committed during the period of supervision which are not dealt with until *after* the order has expired. In other words, if an offender commits ten offences whilst under supervision in the community, and these do not come to light, or are not dealt with by the courts until after the order has finished, he enters the Home Office statistics as having a *nil* reconviction rate for the period under supervision.

When we first made this discovery, a colleague and I believed that we were faced with a statistical device too technical for us to understand. However, we finally wrote to the Home Office asking them for clarification. To say they prevaricated would be an understatement. It is quite obvious to me now, in retrospect, that they never expected anyone to question them on this point. I am sure they hoped that the technical nature of what they called 'pseudo reconvictions' and their statistical justification to eliminate their effects, would anaesthetise most, if not all, enquiries. In the event, they took two years to provide an answer, and when it came it proved to be a masterpiece of obfuscation; but buried within it was an admission that they did *not* make any reciprocal adjustment to include in the reconviction rates those offences committed during a period of supervision but not discovered until after it had finished.[51]

The result the Home Office achieves by only making one part of the 'pseudo reconviction' adjustment is that all failure rates of offenders on community supervision are understated, and so their true failure rate is hidden from Parliament, ministers and the public.

Rows A and B in Table 6.3 compare the reconviction rates of those with community sentences and those sentenced to immediate custody, using statistics provided by the Home Office. In row C figures preceded by a + indicate the difference is in favour of

133

Table 6.3 Percentage reconviction rates for different age groups (includes the 'one-sided' pseudo reconviction adjustment)

Category	−21 years	21–24 years	25–29 years	30+ years	All males	All females	All offenders
(A) All community sentences (%)	70	63	55	41	57	46	56
(B) Immediate custody (%)	76	66	57	41	58	47	57
(C) Differences in favour of CS supervision	−6	−3	−2	0	−1	−1	−1

Source: Home Office, *Prison Statistics England & Wales*, 1999, 2000

custody (that is, the reconviction rates of those released from custody are less than for those given community penalties); those preceded by a − indicate a difference in favour of community penalties. Officials can also claim, as shown on Table 6.3 that although the differences are not great, the reconvictions of those on community supervision are better (fewer) than for those released from prison.

However, the Home Office are only too well aware that if they were to compute the pseudo reconviction adjustment properly and

Table 6.4: Reconvictions for different age groups containing 'both sides' of the pseudo reconviction adjustment*

Category	−21 years	21–24 years	25–29 years	30+ years	All males	All females	All offenders
(A) All community sentences	76	69	61	47	63	52	62
(B) Immediate custody	76	66	57	41	58	47	57
(C) Differences in favour of prison	0	+2	+4	+6	+5	+5	+5

*6 points have been added to allow for offences committed during the currency of the supervision but not detected until after the supervision period has finished.

Source: Based on Home Office, *Prison Statistics England and Wales* 1999, 2000

include both sides of the equation, this picture would be reversed. This is because, although they would have to add to the reconvictions for community supervision, to allow for offences not detected during the currency of the supervision, there would be nothing to add to the reconvictions for those released from prison, because while they were inside they would have committed no more offences. The net effect of making these adjustments on a fair and proper basis would be to nullify the distorted picture they would prefer to present. Table 6.4 shows the dramatic effect when this calculation is carried through properly and both sides of the pseudo reconviction calculation are included. I have assumed a similar six-point allowance for offences committed but not dealt with during the currency of the supervision. Thus when the adjustments are made accurately, the reconviction rates for those released from prison are noticeably better than for those supervised in the community, which is not the picture criminal justice officials want the public or parliament to see.

Probation Supervision: Bogus Success Claims

Imagine a car manufacturer who tests a new engine design and braking system by driving several models over a test route. During the test drive almost 100 per cent of the cars break down, revealing that the new systems not only do not work, but are also dangerous. Then imagine that in large numbers of cases, rescue teams go out and tow in several of these wrecks, so that about 70 per cent of all of the cars which started the test are towed to the end of the test route. What would we say of the manufacturer if when they published their results they triumphantly told the public that 70 per cent of their cars reached the end of the test course, leaving them with the impression that they had done so unaided and without problems? This analogy may seem far-fetched but it fits exactly how chief probation officers have made highly misleading claims. For example, one chief probation officer's report on my desk states that '78% of the probation orders supervised by this service were completed successfully; and 'three-quarters of those supervised on community service orders completed their orders successfully'.[52] In 1995 a different chief probation officer made a similarly brazen claim in a letter to the *Independent* newspaper.[53] Nothing could be more contrary to the truth.

135

Table 6.5: 'Successfully terminated' probation orders by local Probation Service

Probation Service	Percentage 'successfully terminated'
Leicestershire	85.3
Hertfordshire	87.0
Inner London	86.0
Cornwall	84.0
Teesside	84.0
Cheshire	75.0
West Midlands	84.0
Cumbria	84.5
North East London	76.0
Kent	83.0
Essex	84.7
Bedfordshire	85.0
Lancashire	83.0
Middlesex	84.0
Lincolnshire	84.4
East Sussex	79.0

Source: Compiled from Probation Service annual reports for the areas shown for 1996–97

Table 6.5 shows other examples of this deception made in Probation Service annual reports, which refer to the percentage of probation orders 'successfully terminated (or which ran their full course)' for 1996/97. These phrases have been carefully chosen, and they can be a trap for those uninitiated in the ways of probation 'statistical speak'. They can leave, not surprisingly, the clear impression that the probation orders reached their termination point without the offender committing further crime or breaching the conditions of the order. One particular chief probation officer was even more explicit. In 1995 he publicly declared in his annual report that 'ultimately the Probation Service will be measured by its success in preventing reoffending. The record of this service is one of which we can be justifiably proud: 81% of probation orders which ended in 1993 ran their full course.'[54]

What is not explained is that offenders commit a vast amount of crime whilst under supervision, and the courts frequently sentence them in such a way as to allow their community supervision orders to continue and so reach their normal completion date. Thus the order is recorded in the probation statistical returns as 'successfully completed' or as an order which ran its 'full course'. This remains the case even when an offender is sent to prison and his probation order remains undischarged, if, on release, he serves the remainder of his probation order until its normal completion date. Thus many MPs as well as members of the public are misled, victims of those desperate to keep them in the dark concerning the true failure rates of community supervision orders. One such MP was then Home Office minister David Maclean. In 1994, based on figures supplied by his officials, he acknowledged the effectiveness of the Probation Service in a House of Commons written reply, in which he praised the '81% success rate of probation orders'.[55] Exactly one year later he realised he had been misled and declared the '80% success claim to be a myth'.[56]

However, the details behind these specious claims are never spelt out, so the public is denied any opportunity to learn of the duplicity of these calculations; nevertheless, they can be found in a variety of scenarios which allow thousands of probation orders to be counted as 'successfully terminated', despite the clear evidence of failure on the part of the offender to stop committing crime and keep to the terms of the order. Here are some examples:

Scenario One

Where offences are committed by an offender during the currency of the probation order but do not come to light until after the order has reached its normal termination date.

This order goes into the statistics as a 'normal completion'. This is despite the fact that the offender has treated with contempt the expectation that he will not reoffend, and continued to victimise innocent members of the public.

Scenario Two

Where an offender commits further offences during the currency of his probation order, and the court deals with these offences in such a way as to allow the probation order to continue.

When the order finishes, in spite of the crimes committed by the offender *whilst under supervision*, it is recorded as a 'normal completion'. This remains the case even when the offender is sent to prison, if, on release, he serves the remainder of his probation order until its normal termination date.

137

Scenario Three

'Where no action is taken after an offender disappears, thus breaching his order.

For example: an offender is placed on probation, and one of the basic conditions of the probation order which he must agree to before the order is made is that he keep in touch with the probation officer and inform him or her of any change of address. This is explained to him in court and repeated in the typed order which he receives and signs. A few weeks after the order has started, he disappears without informing his supervising officer of his whereabouts. Nothing more is heard from him. The probation officer then takes out a warrant for his arrest.

Months go by and the warrant is never executed. If he thinks of it, the probation officer may apply to the court to have the warrant withdrawn. The magistrates normally agree, and that is the end of the matter. It is known, however, that in many cases no application is made to the court, and the outstanding warrant is left not dealt with. Home Office data indicates that there are more than 100,000 such warrants which have not been acted upon.[57] However, evidence given by magistrates to the All Party Home Affairs Committee reviewing alternative sentences in 1998.[58] suggests that the scale of the problem is much larger, with as many as half a million warrants remaining unexecuted on criminals at large in the community.

The Probation Service, the police, the courts and the Home Office all know that the persistent offenders concerned are roaming free and committing more crime, yet no action has been taken to apprehend them. Either way, the offender has breached his order, showing his disregard for the sentence of the court, and has got away scot-free. Yet these probation orders will go into the statistics as a 'normal completion' because the Probation Service can argue that the court has taken no action to bring that order to an end before its normal completion date.

Scenario Four

Where further offending whilst on probation is discovered during the currency of the order but is not dealt with until after the order has expired.

138

For example: an offender commits further crime whilst on probation. He is arrested and then remanded to a later date. Owing to delays he is not brought before the court to be sentenced until after the probation order has passed its normal completion date. Hence, nothing has occurred during the period of probation supervision to bring the order to an end prematurely. Thus, on reaching its normal termination date, although the offender is on remand awaiting sentence, either on bail or in custody, it is recorded as yet another 'normal completion', despite the clear evidence of its failure.

Clouding the Audit Trail

One of the important 'performance indicators' set by the Home Office for the Probation Service is the 'number of community orders completed without early termination for breach or further offence'.[59] Thus they ensure that this deception is built into the Probation Service's statistical returns which the Home Office publish in their bulletins devoted to probation statistics. Incredibly, these publications do *not* contain the actual reconviction rates for offenders on supervision; but instead they display, as referred to above, the highly misleading figures relating to the number of probation orders 'which ran their full course'. For example, Table 6.6 is taken from Home Office digest *Probation Statistics England & Wales 1998* and Table 6.7 from *Probation Statistics England & Wales, 1999*. Why do they include this highly misleading data, and yet leave out the crucial figures which show the true picture – an overall 60 per cent failure rate? Towards the back of these bulletins is a small note which says that the reconviction figures can be found in another journal concerned with offenders discharged from prison – but why put this data elsewhere?

It is difficult to avoid the conclusion that the authors intended to

Table 6.6 Percentage of probation orders that ran their full course – 1998 statistics

	Under 18s	18–20	21–29	30+	All ages
Ran their full course (%)	68	69	71	75	72

Source: Home Office, *Probation Statistics England & Wales, 1998*, published 2000, with kind permission from the Home Office

Table 6.7 Percentage of probation orders that ran their full course – 1999 statistics

	Under 18s	18–20	21–29	30+	All ages
Ran their full course (%)	69	68	71	75	72

Source: Home Office, *Probation Statistics England & Wales, 1999*, published 2000, with kind permission from the Home Office

mislead by leaving the impression in the minds of those who read this document, that the category 'orders which ran their full course' is synonymous with success. This illusion would have been shattered if they had published the true reconviction rates in the same bulletin. But by leaving them out they ensure the reader is given sufficient prompts to believe, quite erroneously, that supervising offenders on probation orders is highly successful in terms of protecting the public from crime. Thus the vulnerable public are further victimised by yet another deception.

Thus, if the false success claims of 70 to 80 per cent by the Probation Service have any meaning, it is only that the majority of those under probation supervision are protected from the consequences of their further offending during the currency of their order.

Fine Tuning the Techniques of Deception

In Chapter Three I discussed how some of the clauses of the Criminal Justice Act 1991 had tried to outlaw the use of prison for the majority of offences. We saw how this attempt was frustrated because these clauses proved so out of touch with reality that they had to be abandoned after only seven months. This was a major setback for anti-prison officials, but in 1999 they were to get a second chance to impose their nightmare scenario on the public when drafting a White Paper – the Auld Report entitled *Justice for All*[60] – and the Criminal Justice Bill which followed it. Their previous failure had taught them valuable lessons and this time their approach was more subtle. The White Paper's true objective of putting even more constraints on the use of prison was concealed by its promise to make victims and the safety of the public its first and main priority. In fact, *Justice for All* was an attempt to solve a number of problems that were piling up for the Home Office; and an

140

understanding of what caused them is important in being able to see through the deceptions that were employed to solve them.

The Criminal Justice Act 1991 provided for the early release on licence of the majority of prisoners. Prisoners sentenced to up to four years automatically receive 50 per cent remission, and serve the remainder under licence in the community. Prisoners serving over four years can be released at the 50 per cent point but only at the discretion of the parole board. In any event, they must be released at the two-thirds point of their sentence. For example, an offender serving a six-year sentence who is refused early release at the halfway point must be released at the two-thirds point, and so would serve four years in prison and be under licence for the remaining two years in the community. Thus, since 1991, thousands of persistent offenders, with no motivation to stop offending, have been released into the community enabling them to start victimising the public even sooner than they would have otherwise done.

Yet it was another seven years before the Crime and Disorder Act 1998 stipulated that offenders released under this scheme who committed offences during their licence or 'at-risk period' would be automatically recalled to serve their remaining time in prison, irrespective of the sentence they received for the fresh offence. In addition, in 1999 stricter rules of enforcement were introduced in relation to offenders failing to comply with community supervision orders.

As illustrated by figures published in Hansard (March 2003), the consequences of these two provisions have been that since 1998, thousands of offenders have been sent back to prison as a result of breaching their prison licence or because of their failure to comply with the terms of their community order.[61] For example, in February 2005 I learned from a serving probation officer that he alone was dealing with *at least* two such recalls per fortnight. In addition, *Home Office Statistical Bulletin England & Wales, 15/04*, published in December 2004, reported that in just one year (2003), 10,854 prisoners who had been released on various forms of licence were recalled to prison and that a further 8,740 were sentenced to custody under the stricter rules governing breaches of community supervision. Furthermore, because the court has no choice as far as breached prison licences are concerned and knows that these offenders are going back to prison in any event, it is more likely to pass a prison sentence for the new offences. For the same reason, if a period of remand is

141

necessary, it is more likely to be in custody. As touched upon in the previous chapter, the result has been that the numbers of individuals being returned to prison under these arrangements have become an important contributory factor in the rise of the prison population. For example, when the total of recalled prisoners (19,594) is added to those sent to prison for whom there was no choice plus the number of foreign prisoners, we are left with only just over 32,000 persistent offenders domiciled in the UK sent to prison by the courts. As can now be seen, it would be entirely wrong to interpret this increase as a result of the courts getting 'tougher on crime' because these mandatory arrangements leave them with no choice.

From the public's viewpoint this is to be applauded because it has given them, albeit for a short period, increased protection from the offenders who have breached their prison licence or their community order. However, an increase in prison numbers is not what the government wants; neither will it suit their purposes for the public to start taking notice of how many licensed prisoners in the community are found guilty of fresh offences committed during their 'at-risk' period. The Home Office needs to keep alive the myth that these offenders can be released under arrangements that safeguard the public. The spectacle of thousands of persistent offenders being shuffled out of prison, a long time before the end of their sentence, only to return straight away to their life of crime, is a reality they would prefer to keep hidden.

The question is why were these provisions brought in at all, when, as can now be seen, they contradict the government's undeclared aim of keeping down prison numbers at all costs. It must be remembered that these arrangements were enacted by the new Labour government still in the flush of its electoral success, and heady with its new power and belief that it could quickly make an impact on the crime problem. Thus these recall provisions were unusually realistic; they had bite and they gave the courts no opportunity to exercise any misplaced leniency toward the offender.

With the exception of Michael Howard, previous Tory home secretaries had for the most of their seventeen years in power, ruled over a relentless increase in crime, in tandem with their proliferation of anti-prison measures. As a result, the general public were disillusioned and restive in the face of the non-stop assaults by criminals on them, their homes and their property. Thus New Labour felt compelled to follow up their electoral promises to get 'tough on crime'. However, although they wanted to be seen as doing something with the power given to them by the electorate, I believe they had little or no understanding of the scale of the crime problem presented to them by persistent offenders or how to protect the public from them. If they did, they quickly stepped back from instigating the fundamental changes in sentencing that were needed. In one sense, therefore, this provision was a present to the electorate, a way of thanking them for New Labour's resounding election success, rather than a break with anti-prison philosophy. Thus I strongly suspect that the Labour cabinet has, for some time, regretted introducing these new sentencing provisions, as their officials would have soon made them aware that they were having a major influence in increasing the number of offenders being sent to prison.

The government had now tied itself in knots. Contrary to their own undeclared policy aims, the recall measures were playing a significant part in increasing the prison population. Home Office officials were now faced with the embarrassing possibility that the public would realise that, despite their glib reassurances on this matter, these offenders were highly unsuitable for release into the community. What the government needed, therefore, was a damage-limitation exercise, a new and separate measure to reverse the effects of the 1998 recall procedures, which by its own admission had resulted in a substantial increase in the number of recall requests.[62] It did not take them long to devise a strategy to suit their purpose. They introduced a White Paper deceptively publicised as 'providing sweeping and fundamental changes which would put the victim and the public centre stage of the criminal justice system'. In reality, it was designed to introduce measures that would offset the thousands of prisoners being recalled into prisons from which they had only just been prematurely released, and the large numbers jailed for breaching their community orders.

First, to throw everyone off the scent about their true objectives, the government orchestrated another vigorous publicity campaign, via the press, which blamed the courts for sending too many offenders to prison, and targeted the public with an unprecedented number of appeals, many by senior members of the judiciary, to accept that fewer offenders should go to jail. Then, in 1999, losing no time, Sir Robin Auld was commissioned by the Lord Chancellor to produce a report ostensibly based on an enquiry into ways that would ensure the criminal justice system 'works in the interests of justice'. The ensuing White Paper, *Justice for All*, was published in July 2002.[63] Its introduction said: 'The public rightly expect that the victims of crime should be at the heart of the criminal justice system. This White Paper aims to rebalance the system in favour of victims, witnesses, and communities and to deliver justice for all, by building greater trust and credibility.'

No introduction could have been more misrepresentative of its true objectives. These were to find yet more ways of reducing the use of prison, and eventually abolish it completely as a sentencing option in magistrates' courts. Being aware of this makes it possible to decipher this report, whose meaning otherwise remains heavily encoded. Contained within every one of its recommendations, which masquerade as ways of 'protecting the public', and 'dealing effectively with offenders', are proposals that will severely *reduce* the use of imprisonment for thousands of offenders and so effectively expose the public to more danger from criminals, not less.

Getting Rid of Prison by Stealth

The sentencing proposals and the philosophy behind them as outlined in the Auld Report will have dire consequences for the safety of the public. The following examples in italics, taken from the report, illustrate this point.

Prisoners are more likely than the general population to have been in child care, or unemployed, or to have a family member convicted of an offence.[64]

This is getting the public to accept that it makes sense to deal with the majority offenders in the community, where they can receive 'treatment' and help for various social problems. This will bring no relief to the public, who will go on being victimised by persistent offenders dealt with in this way.

We should focus custody on dangerous, serious and seriously persistent offenders.[65]

This seeks to once more reassure the public that when it is necessary, the government fully intend to protect the public from dangerous

144

and persistent offenders by making sure they are sentenced to custody. However, it is an attempt to distract the public from realising how almost meaningless the term 'custody' has become in the light of the other Auld recommendations.

...extend sentencing powers of magistrates from 6 to 12 months.[66]

This sounds like exactly what the crime-beleaguered public wants. The public are being invited to think that they are going to get more protection from persistent offenders. But once decoded, it can be seen as a classic deception, because, as will be explained, this measure will result in offenders serving no more than six months in prison.

...require magistrates to sentence all those they have found guilty, rather than committing some to be sentenced in the crown court.[67]

This is so worded as to convey the impression that some offenders who are found guilty at the magistrates' court are somehow *escaping* from immediate justice, as a result of the delays incurred when they are sent to the crown courts for sentence, and that this will be stopped by making sure they are all dealt with there and then. However, what the White Paper did not explain was this would result in, once again, *fewer* offenders being sent to prison, as the Crown Court sentence more offenders to prison than the magistrates' court and for longer periods.

The majority of crime is committed by a relatively small number of persistent offenders.[68]

The purpose of this message is to get the public to accept that only a small number of offenders need be sent to prison. In fact, it is not true. It contradicts the government's own latest estimates that there are at least 100,000 persistent offenders.

To prevent offending on bail we will give police new powers to impose conditions on bail.[69]

This is another example of a deliberate attempt to lull the public into thinking they are going to get more protection from criminals.

However, as we shall see in a moment, these bail proposals are so worded that the offenders will have no trouble in evading the new bail conditions and avoid remands in custody.

Sentencing must protect the public, punish offenders, and encourage them to make amends for their crime and contribute to crime reduction. Technology such as Tagging and voice recognition, give innovative ways to deny liberty, reduce offending and ensure community sentences are not a soft option.[70]

This is a subtle message that punishing offenders and getting them to make amends for their crimes does not mean they have to go to prison. It seeks to reassure the public that technology can be harnessed to make sure that community sentences will protect them from criminals and that they will not be a soft option for offenders. The reality, as previously discussed, is that the exact opposite is true. Although never admitted by the government, tagging (as will be discussed later), as well as other forms of community supervision of offenders, has been a disastrous failure in terms of protecting the public from crime.

Courts should have clear discretion to pass a non-custodial sentence, even when a short prison sentence could have been justified – bearing in mind their ability to re-sentence in the event of repeated breach of conditions.[71]

This is telling the public that they have no reason to be alarmed when an offender, whose offence warranted prison, is given community supervision instead. What the Auld Report does not go on to explain is that such risk-taking with the public's safety is almost certain to result in more people being victimised by the offender, and that, despite previous government reassurances, no action has been taken in relation to hundreds of thousands of failed community supervision orders.

The Home Secretary should disseminate information (to courts and other criminal justice practitioners) about the effectiveness of sentencing, its costs and the contributions of sentencing to crime reductions.[72]

This sounds very progressive, but in practice it will provide the Home Office with unbridled opportunity to feed the courts with propaganda, which will mislead them and others about the results of sentencing. This will help quieten any anxieties that may soon otherwise occur when it is realised that millions of innocent members of the public are continuing to be targeted by offenders. Information relating to the true failure rates of community supervision of offenders has never been made available to the public in an understandable format and will continue to be hard for them to find.

We will introduce a new sentence of Custody Plus which will allow for a maximum period of 3 months in custody, followed by a period of supervised activities in the community.[73]

The term 'Custody Plus' creates the impression that the community is getting something extra with this sentence, over and above protection from the offender for a maximum of three months (early release arrangements under the Home Detention Curfew Scheme will not apply to these sentences). The report fails to mention that the 'Plus' element will consist of supervision requiring the offender to undertake various activities in the community which have all been shown to fail in persuading offenders to reform.

The new sentence of Custody Plus could eventually replace all custodial sentences of up to 12 months.[74]

This implies that the new styled three-month sentence, because of its attendant period of supervision for the offender when he is released into the community, will give the public better value and more protection than a straightforward twelve-month sentence. It can be taken as a clear signal that in the near future all sentences in the magistrates' courts will be no longer than three months, which will play a significant role in reducing the prison population.

Severity of punishment should reflect the seriousness of the offence or offences as a whole.[75]

This coded language confirms the practice which has been used for a long time. Not sentencing an offender for each offence he has committed is a way of minimising the impact of his offences on

147

the public, and his subsequent sentence. In any case, this statement should be read in conjunction with the proposal that eventually all sentences of twelve months may be replaced by the three-month 'Custody Plus' sentence. Thus the net effect is that no matter how seriously the magistrates view the offence, they will be able to give the offender no more than three months in prison and, in addition, be prevented from sending him to the crown court when they think the seriousness of the offence warrants more punishment than they can give.

Research shows that prisoners are six times less likely to reoffend if contacts with their families are maintained.[76]

They make this point to support their claim that too many offenders are sent to prison – because they argue that high prison numbers increase the chances of a prisoner being transferred away from his local area. It is entirely false to suggest that keeping contact with their families will prevent reoffending. It has not stopped them in the past. In the majority of cases, it has been their offending which has caused their family ties to be broken. The research is far more likely to indicate that the offenders who are more motivated to go straight are the ones who will keep in touch with their families.

Cautions have value in reducing offending.[77]

This gives the reassuring message that criminal justice officials *know* this, and therefore it should not be questioned. In fact, it is meaningless propaganda. The low detection rate of 5.5 per cent means that we do not know how many offences are committed by offenders who have been cautioned. What we do know is that thousands of offenders who are cautioned are reconvicted, often several times.

Many of these alarming proposals were incorporated into the Criminal Justice Bill, which was presented to Parliament in November 2002. It was heralded as bringing 'far-reaching changes to the heart of the justice system', and in particular that it would 'shift the balance in favour of the victim'.[78] This was an exciting promise indeed, but for any one who dared believe that at last something was going to be done to significantly reduce crime, it proved to be a woeful disappointment. This legislation is an exercise in 'fiddling while

148

Rome burns'. Of course, the issues it addresses are important in themselves, but tinkering with sentencing arrangements, scrapping the 'double jeopardy rule', restricting the right to trial by jury, and allowing juries to hear about a defendant's previous convictions in certain cases, of themselves do nothing about the central problem faced by the public. This is that they are surrounded by thousands of hostile criminals who predate on them at will and are allowed to do so by lenient courts who have lost sight of their primary duty to protect the public from crime.

The new bail provision which might have given the public more protection from criminals in some limited cases was, once again, rendered meaningless by various qualifications and the usual 'get out' clause. For example, the Bill created the presumption that bail will *not* be granted for a person who is charged with an imprisonable offence *and* who tests positive for a specified Class A drug *and* refuses treatment, *unless there are exceptional circumstances*. Even without the exceptional circumstances clause, it will not take the criminal fraternity long to work out that if they are charged with an imprisonable offence, and they test positive for a Class A drug, all they need to do to make sure they are not remanded in custody is to opt for treatment. In fact, their defence lawyers will advise them to do so. In most cases, having been given bail, they will fail to attend for their 'drug treatment' appointment, and so remain at liberty whilst on bail under their own terms, having defied the law yet again.

The Bill's proposal to increase the sentencing powers of magistrates' courts from six months to twelve months, marked a high point, I believe, in the application of the government's deceptive, not to say Machiavellian skills. This clause may trap many into believing that the government is toughening up its stance towards offenders. Not so, I am afraid, because under present rules, offenders sentenced one to four years benefit from early release under the Home Detention Curfew Scheme in addition to the 50 per cent remission rule. Thus, under these arrangements, the effect of a twelve-month sentence handed down by the magistrates would be that the offender would serve no more than six months and frequently far less. Furthermore, according to Prison Instruction 31/2003, for many prisoners given longer sentences the Home Detention Curfew Scheme has now been extended to operate up to four and a half months before the normal release date.

Lord Falconer, the then Home Office minister, speaking for the Bill in the House of Lords in November 2002, said, 'The fight against crime is one of the biggest issues that affect people's lives; people want policies that actually make a difference and that is why we think the criminal justice system needs a fundamental reform'.[79] But exactly how is the public protected by a reform whose impact is to reduce a twelve-month sentence to only three months? What is clear is that these early-release schemes undermine the government's claim to put victims and the public centre stage of the criminal justice system.

To encourage magistrates to hear more serious cases, rather than send them to crown courts, their sentencing powers are to be extended to allow them to pass a fifteen-month sentence in respect of two or more offences.[80] The hidden motive is to ensure that such offenders will only face seven and a half months in prison due to the 50 per cent remission, which will be *further* reduced because of the early-release scheme, even though they have committed multiple offences, and lessen the chances of their receiving longer sentences in the higher court.

What in effect the government has done is to make sure that even fewer offenders will be sentenced to prison in magistrates' courts than at present. The few who are handed down a term of imprisonment are likely to receive the new Custody Plus sentence and spend no more than three months in prison; those receiving the new maximum for the magistrates' court of twelve months (should this be introduced) will, as previously stated, serve no more than six months because of the 50 per cent automatic remission rule, and possibly far less if the new arrangements, when they are introduced, allow them to benefit also from the Home Detention Curfew Scheme. Those receiving the new Custody Minus sentence will not go to prison at all and will stay in the community.

I am quite certain that the final curtain has not yet fallen on this sentencing travesty. It will not be long, as indicated in the Auld recommendations, before they make *all* prison sentences in the magistrates' court no more than three months. After these new sentencing proposals have been in existence for a while, I anticipate that the Home Office will argue that because offenders jailed by magistrates receive only very short terms, it is not worth their going at all, given the high administrative costs and burdens on the prison service of the more than 8,000 short-term prisoners currently serving less than twelve months.[81] Right on cue the Lord Chief Justice has argued that jail terms of less than a year are useless and have no rehabilitative value.[82] It will therefore be but a short step for the government to completely abolish prison sentences at the magistrates' court, and rely on the proliferation of supervision arrangements of offenders by the Probation Service. No doubt, for the criminal justice officials denied their victory in 1991, revenge will be sweet, but for the public a new dark age of victimisation by criminals will have arrived.

An Unbroken Thread

One of the main themes of this book has been to expose the ruthless, uninterrupted war against the use of prison conducted by every government since the 1950s, and there should be no doubt that this most recent piece of legislation continues this policy. This idea will not resonate well with those who have been misled to believe that it will increase the use of prison, a view that the government's deception machine has worked hard to promote.[83]

For example, it was no coincidence that in August of 2003 the contents of a Home Office report, which criticised David Blunkett on these grounds, was prematurely 'leaked' to the press.[84] Thus the spectacle of one government body appearing to criticise another, in this case the Home Secretary, for being 'too tough' served to promote the government as a whole as being on the side of 'law and order', which was the effect wanted. Whilst it is true Blunkett sought to increase prison terms for murder, he knew this could be achieved with minimum opposition from the Treasury because the numbers of offenders involved will only be a fraction of the much larger offender group who *should* be facing longer prison sentences, namely persistent property offenders. Instead, they will face shorter jail terms and *fewer* of them will be dealt with in court because of the diversion tactics that will be introduced, such as the 'cautioning plus' schemes and other arrangements under the general heading of 'restorative justice'. Yet David Blunkett was frequently referred to as a hard-liner keen to push through tough anti-crime measures, a view which could not be more removed from reality. Likewise, in January 2003 Tony Blair's office seized another opportunity to falsely promote itself as being tough on crime. It was reported in the *Daily Mail* (8 January 2003) that Lord Irvine had said that most people in Britain accepted that repeat burlgars should not go to jail. According to the same newspaper, the Prime Minister's official spokesman bluntly insisted that repeat offenders *should go to jail* (my italics). Presumably, he hoped no one would notice that it is the government's sentencing strategy, cleary sanctioned by the Prime Minister, which ensures that most of them do not.

Even some criminal justice commentators basically in sympathy with the arguments presented in this book have, in my view, failed to understand how determinedly the present Labour government has disguised its sentencing intentions. For example, many have argued that the anti-prison policy line maintained since the 1950s was reversed by Michael Howard's 'prison works' policy whilst he was the Conservative Home Secretary between 1993 and 1997, and that the continued rise of the prison population since Labour came to power indicates it has carried on with tough pro-prison policies.[85] This is an incorrect analysis.

Whilst Howard's policies caused prison numbers to rise, this did not mean that sufficient offenders were being jailed to properly protect the public. Indeed, in 1997, an international crime survey report described the UK as 'one of the most pressurised by crime in the Western world, despite the small fall in the official police crime figures since 1993'.[86]

During his reign as Home Secretary the even greater numbers of offenders *not* imprisoned continued to commit millions of offences against the helpless public. As can be seen in Figure 6.4 he did

Figure 6.4: Decline in use of prison in the UK after 1953 as a means of protecting the public against crime (prisoners per 1,000 recorded crimes)

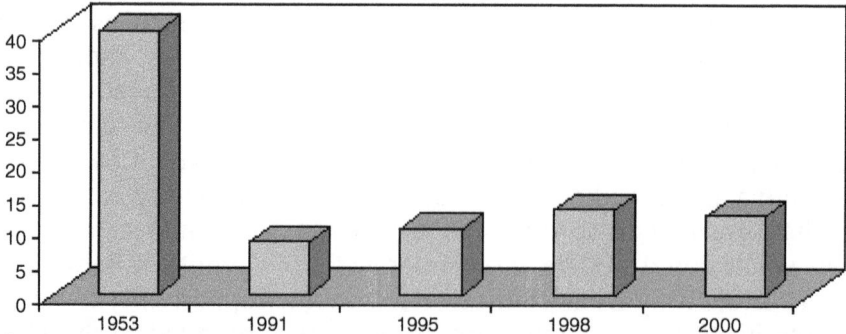

Source: *Crime Rates in the UK, 1898–1998*, Civitas, 2003

Figure 6.5: Offenders sentenced to immediate custody as percentage of all offences (UK courts, 1950–2000)

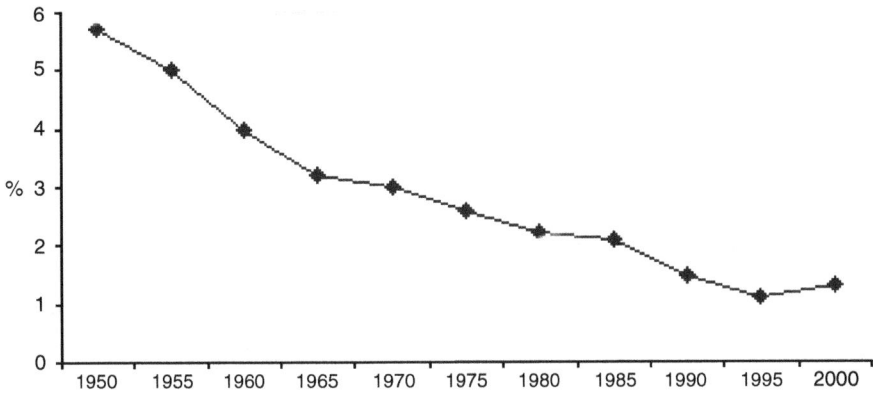

Source: Civitas, 2000

not reverse the anti-prison policy followed for the previous forty-five years, although I believe he wanted to; he was allowed only to weaken it under the onslaught of the fierce anti-prison lobby, both within Westminster and outside of it. Figure 6.5 tells a similar story.

As I have previously described, the main thrust of the present Labour government's sentencing policies, apart from ensuring that prisoners let out on the early-release scheme and sentenced offenders who breached their licence were more likely to be returned to jail, or be jailed, has been to ensure *fewer* offenders ever get to court, *fewer* go to prison, and increasingly large numbers are released long before their sentence has finished.

While prison numbers have gone up since they took office, the hysteria promoted over the steady increase in the prison population grossly exaggerates the numbers of UK-domiciled sentenced persistent offenders being put behind bars; the increase in prison numbers should not be interpreted as the courts sending *too many* offenders to jail, a view the government peddles with ever increasing vigour. Despite this rise, it must not be overlooked that the vast majority of offenders who are put before a court are given a community sentence. As I have already pointed out, a very large proportion (approximately 25,000) of the present prison population of 74,000 consists of foreigners, remand prisoners and those serving life sentences for murder, and therefore are those for whom either no

153

other disposal is possible or, in the case of the foreign prisoners, are not part of the argument concerning how many offenders we jail, as they will go home after their release. It must also not be forgotten that the number of prison sentences has been significantly *inflated* because courts are more frequently passing jail sentences for crimes committed by offenders on licence following their early release, knowing that they are going back to jail whatever they decide. Were it not for this they might well have passed a non-custodial sentence.

The offender group from which the public needs urgent protection is the persistent mainly property offenders who cause millions of members of the public great harm and distress each year. Yet the number of these in prison is now down to approximately 45,000, compared to the 155,000 which the courts have placed at liberty in the community under the supervision of the Probation Service; if we include the number of offenders being supervised following a prison sentence the total comes to 200,000.[87] To provide the public with proper protection their numbers in prison need to be considerably expanded. Yet the government's (albeit disguised) sentencing intentions laid out in its latest criminal justice legislation will ensure even fewer of them go to jail, and the tiny minority that do will be guaranteed an even shorter stay.

Chapter 7

The Research Confidence Trick

Over the last few years the Home Office and other government departments have produced a plethora of 'research' to support their objective of keeping the majority of persistent offenders in the community. The studies have purported to show, for example, that community-based drug treatment, employment schemes, electronic monitoring and other types of community-supervision programmes, are all effective ways of sentencing offenders as they reduce crime without recourse to jail. An objective review of this research shows that these claims are bogus and that they should be more realistically viewed as yet more government deception tactics.

What is surprising is that no independent body has challenged the tenuous nature of this research or its claims. There is no watchdog to guard the safety of the public in this respect, as there is for example in the field of medicine, seen for example in 2003, with the Royal Society's investigation that dubious research was reaching the press and misleading the public.[1] Likewise, in 1998 it came to light that the Committee on Publication Ethics, which endeavours to ensure high standards in the publication of medical research, was becoming alarmed at the number of research papers being submitted for publication whose research methodology was unacceptably poor, leading to unsupportable conclusions, or whose results were bordering on the fraudulent.[2] All this is alarming, of course, but at least there are bodies in place to force these issues into the open and deal with them in order to protect the public. One problem highlighted by the Ethics Committee involved experiments by GPs using different drug treatment methods without telling the patients concerned what was going on. What would the Ethics Committee make of the fact that in the field of criminal justice the general public are *consistently* used as unconsenting guinea pigs in dangerous community-based supervision experiments with offenders that result in thousands of people being victimised by the criminals concerned?

The Crime–Drugs Link

The government wants the public to accept the idea that drug abuse is the driving force for the majority of acquisitive crime. If they can persuade the majority to believe this, it then becomes but a simple step for them to also accept that these offenders need 'treatment' and not jail, and so should be supervised in the community. Research studies used by the government to support this claim have been a sham because they have ignored any results which have conflicted with their preconceived intentions, and they have resulted in thousands of drug offenders being allowed to stay in the community, despite their prolific and harmful offending.

In 1998 this was illustrated by a study funded by the National Health Service (NHS) which reported on the community treatment of over a thousand drug abusers.[3] The results showed that despite being given methadone as a substitute to aid withdrawal from drugs such as opiates and cocaine, the offenders concerned continued to commit crime. Another initiative contained in the Criminal Justice and Courts Services Act 2000 gave the courts power to order the drug testing of offenders under the supervision of the Probation Service, and this 'community treatment' programme was piloted in three different areas of the country. Between November 2001 and February 2002, over a hundred offenders were put on the scheme and well over half were known to have breached its conditions by their continued drug use.[4]

In a third example, in 2000, the Home Office reported on a study of 221 drug addicts being treated in a London clinic, to assess the impact of methadone treatment on their drug abuse and criminal behaviour.[5] All were prolific offenders. Only 81 were able to be interviewed for the all-important six-month follow-up interview, and of these only 31 remained in treatment. Thus, despite being given free methadone to support their withdrawal from other substances, 86 per cent had already dropped out by the six-month stage. The treatment period had no impact on non-drug related crime. If only half the 221 addicts on the scheme committed five offences per week (a conservative estimate for these offenders), then it can be computed that during the six-month treatment period alone they committed over 13,000 offences against the public.

Although their results were presented in positive up-beat terms, the reductions in crime and drug use reported for some of the offenders in these studies cannot be taken seriously, as they were based entirely on 'self-report' information from the drug addicts on the schemes, who are known to be highly unreliable informants. Furthermore, in each case the assessment data was based on only a small proportion of those taking part. For example, the NHS study reported a high concordance between the results of urine samples and self-report on drug use. However, urine samples were taken from less than half of the 769 offenders on the scheme. But why was the majority not tested in this way? Was it because they had made themselves unavailable, perhaps due to drug taking, reoffending, or just failing to keep in contact? Or were there other reasons why the researchers were prepared to base their findings on a minority? It would have been more accurate for them to have concluded that there were doubts about whether the results of the urine tests supported what the offenders were telling them about their drug use and that therefore the results were inconclusive.

In any case, little can be inferred from such observations, as some temporary reduction in illegal drug use would not be a surprise as the offenders were being given a free substitute drug during treatment. Even so, many of the offenders on the scheme continued to commit crime.

First Crime – and then Drugs

The simple hypothesis the government wants us to accept is that the vast majority of prolific offenders are drug users who commit crime to feed their habit. In September 2003 this naive view gained support from Simon Hughes, the Liberal Democratic home affairs spokesperson, who argued that if all offenders in prison who needed it were treated for their drug addiction, there would be a fall of about 3,000 offenders.[6] However, it is entirely wrong to conclude that we have crime because of drugs; acquisitive and persistent offending existed a long time before illegal drugs became as available as they are today.

In 1999, the government initiated the NEW-ADAM national research programme.[7] Under its auspices, offenders from sixteen different locations throughout the United Kingdom who had been arrested by the police were tested for drug use and interviewed about their drug habits and offending behaviour. Contrary to their expectations, the researchers found that there was a connection between drug use and offending behaviour in only 40 per cent of those arrested, and that almost half the sample who had taken drugs reported no offending in the previous twelve months. Similarly a large study in Leicester of almost a thousand juveniles found that the majority of those who were delinquent started crime before taking to drugs and there was little evidence to show that anyone stole to feed their drug habit.[8] In 1999, a study by South Bank University's criminal policy research unit called into question the simple view that drug use draws people into a life of crime. It argued that most of the drug users in their sample became career criminals long before their drug use spiralled out of control, rather than the other way around.[9] These studies militate against the all-embracing view that drug use by offenders leads to crime, and that the bulk of crime is almost always linked to drug use. They seriously challenge the belief that if we can rid the community of the drug problem, we will rid it of crime.

What was also interesting was that a significant minority of the 40 per cent in the NEW-ADAM sample who reported a connection admitted that crime came first. Drugs are expensive and few can afford them on normal incomes. Criminals, on the other hand, have money to spare, and so drugs become just one more item on which they spend their ill-gotten gains. Likewise, my own research with a large sample of persistent offenders who spent money on drugs indicated that, for the vast majority, offending came first. During the 1980s, I gathered information on this topic from large numbers of offenders serving a prison sentence in a young offender prison. This institution had an enormous catchment area, which took in the whole of the south-west of the country, plus large sections of the Midlands and south-central England, as well as parts of the south-east. The offenders I interviewed, therefore, could be said to be reasonably representative of most seventeen to twenty-year-old persistent offenders sentenced to a period of imprisonment. Over a long period of time the picture which emerged was that these persistent offenders earned huge sums of money from their crimes. They spent their criminal earnings on holidays, eating out, buying clothes, drinking with friends, on cars and, because they had money over, they started to buy drugs which were then becoming more available. The drug problem was not then on the scale it is now, but their use was on the increase and recognized as a major potential problem.

It is easy to understand with such a lifestyle how some of them went on to become dependent on whatever substance they were using, and this then led to them stealing in order to feed their habit, thus establishing a drug–crime link. However, as previously stated, it is important to emphasise that for most of them this link started with crime. But whichever came first, we should resist the idea that offenders who 'steal for drugs' need to be approached as if they were patients who needed treatment. By responding to them on this basis, we deny their criminal motivation, and it is this that needs to be the focus of sensible sentencing policies. Of course, treatment, help and encouragement should be extended to offenders who are drug-dependent, but this should be carried out in an environment which is totally safe for the public, and that can only be when the offender is in prison. In 2003, a judge sitting in a crown court in the south-west provided an all too rare example of this approach. He turned down an application by the defence that a 22-year-old criminal with fifty previous convictions, who had robbed a woman in the street, should go to a 'residential' centre for drug addicts. Instead, he was sent to prison for three years.[10] This is, however, not the line the government wants the courts to take.

Drug Treatment and Testing Orders

Separate from the community treatment schemes mentioned above, Drug Treatment and Testing Orders (DTTOs) were introduced as a community sentence for offenders under the Crime and Disorder Act 1998.[11] Between October of that year and March 2000, they were tested in three pilot areas for offenders who were serious drug misusers, with a view to reducing the amount of crime committed to fund their drug habit. These orders involve supervision by the Probation Service and monitoring of the offenders' drug use by means of regular testing by medical staff.

When read objectively, the results of the pilots showed they were a failure; they neither protected the public nor weaned the offenders from their drug habit. But the government ignored this and went ahead with its plans to legislate for DTTOs. The so-called 'pilot studies' were, once more, a sham. Their purpose was to deceive both public and Parliament into believing that 'research' had shown this to be an effective method of sentencing. What the results actually revealed was that, despite a lenient attitude by their supervisors towards the offenders' continued drug use (contrary to the supposed requirements of the order), fifty-seven per cent were breached (taken back to court) and almost half the orders were ended owing to non-compliance with the terms of the DTTO. In fact, the majority of the offenders on the scheme continued to test positive for drug use throughout the term of the order, which was usually for twelve months, despite their claims they were obeying the rules and were drug-free.

However, as indicated, the supervisors frequently turned a blind eye to these contraventions of the requirements and allowed the order to continue. What is more, the evaluation of the scheme's effectiveness, in terms of reduction in drug use and offending, was based, as with the schemes previously discussed, on 'self-report' information obtained in interviews with only a small number of offenders from the original 210 made subject to the orders.[12] Even though the report admitted we should be circumspect about information gathered in this way, no genuine research enquiry would base its findings on such unreliable data; information obtained in this way is useless, particularly as already indicated, drug offenders are known to be highly unreliable informants. However, any reduction in drug use (if it were true) would not be a surprise as many were given methadone as a substitute to support their withdrawal from other substances. Yet on this basis the Home Office evaluation of the scheme was that the DTTOs had resulted in 'substantial reductions in crime and drug use'.[13]

No attempt was made to verify offenders' claims that they were committing less crime, for example by asking the police about the numbers of offences they were suspected of or checking objective sources such as their record of actual convictions during the currency of their DTTOs. Furthermore, no attempt was made to find out about their drug use or offending behaviour in the longer term, which is equally important from the point of view of protecting the public.

Despite attempts by the Home Office to put these results in the best possible light, the failure of these orders was apparent even to the National Association of Probation Officers (NAPO), not known for its willingness to criticise community schemes for offenders. In 1999, NAPO publicly admitted that DTTOs did not appear to be having any impact on drug-related crime; their failure rates were all the more worrying because the offenders had been carefully chosen from among those put forward for the (pilot) scheme.[14] Nevertheless, DTTOs were fully implemented and by January 2003 almost five thousand offenders had been sentenced in this way.[15]

Since then, the Home Office has succeeded in keeping the news of their continued and dramatic failure away from the public. However, in 2002, a police survey of all offenders subject to a DTTO in a major UK city revealed that at least 73 per cent of the offenders had committed between one and ten offences whilst being supervised under the terms of their DTTO.[16] The majority of these offences were property crimes such as burglary, theft, shoplifting, handling stolen goods as well as drug offences. What is more, since the scheme started in 1998, the survey discovered that only one offender had been taken back to court, following a long period of repeated offending.

The Probation Service refused to reveal the figures showing how many offenders had failed the drug testing requirements of the order (that is, had tested positive for drug use), but it became known that this was the case for almost all of them, and that the supervision of the offenders had descended to a level of farce. For example, it was common practice for the offenders to tell their supervising officer that they had not taken drugs since they last reported, but because of the 'stress' involved in visiting the probation office 'they gave in and had a shot'. The supervising probation officer nevertheless accepted this obvious fabrication, intended as the offender's cover story for testing 'positive' yet again.

The Probation Service has an interest in keeping the DTTOs going, despite the failed drug tests and the continued offending, because they are under pressure to meet the targets set for them by the Home Office. As a result, they have developed the practice of recording that the offender has reduced his consumption of drugs, entirely on the basis of what he has told them, even though this frequently conflicts with the objective results of the drug test. The farce of the DDTOs has tragic consequences. In December 2003, a policeman was killed by an offender escaping from the scene of his crime. It was revealed that the criminal had repeatedly failed

161

drug tests while under supervision and should have already been recalled to prison. The policeman's widow claimed that the Probation Service admitted that the offender had failed as many as thirteen previous drug tests.[17]

The police survey also revealed that 20 per cent of those who had committed offences during the currency of the DTTO were in the local remand prison as a result, either serving a sentence or on remand.[18] However, their DTTOs were still current. No action had been taken to revoke them because of the further offending. It also became known that when such offenders were released from jail, the Probation Service maintained the pretence that they were still supervising them under the terms of the DTTO and did so until the end of the order, which they then recorded as having 'satisfactorily reached its conclusion'.

In practice, the Probation Service found it impossible to keep in contact with these offenders once they had been released from prison. Despite appointment letters from the probation officer, which maintained the fiction that they were still supervising them, they were in fact out of contact for the rest of the order and never seen again. It was revealed that because no action was taken by the Probation Service to revoke the order, they were able to record it as having reached its termination date. It therefore went down in the Home Office statistics as a 'success'.

In June 2003 the Home Secretary suddenly and vehemently criticised the management of the criminal justice system for being two hundred years out of date. The target for his outburst was the Lord Chancellor and his department, whom he accused of presiding over a justice system that undermined victims' confidence that criminals will be punished and which allowed 'addicts on the street to commit more crime'.[19] This was a telling observation. Why did the Home Secretary suddenly choose this particular issue to throw in with his more general criticism? The answer is, I am sure, that his officials must have by then briefed him on the disastrous reconviction rates of offenders on DTTOs, and his tirade was a convenient way of preparing the public for yet more bad news about another failed sentencing policy and, at the same time, deflecting the blame onto someone else. The reality, of course, is that the failure of DTTOs has nothing to do with the administration of the criminal justice system by the Lord Chancellor's office. It was the Labour government, which, ignoring the results of the so-called pilot studies which made it clear that these offenders were highly unsuitable for any form of community-based treatment, went ahead with its legislation anyway, allowing these offenders to be supervised under the auspices of DTTOs.

The bad results feared by the government were confirmed by the National Audit Office in March 2004. They reported that three-quarters of offenders sentenced to DTTOs drop out before they finish the course.[20] However, the government can take no solace from even the small number reported to have completed the programme because they did not stop committing offences. This dire picture was confirmed by the publication of Home Office figures published in December 2004 (Offender Management Caseload Statistics, 15/04), which showed that the reconviction rate for offenders given DTTOs was a staggering 90 per cent. Thus there can be no hiding the fact that the scheme is a disaster, and that its only results are to allow hundreds of thousands of people to be victimised by drug-using criminals – something that could have been avoided had they been sent to prison instead.

Other Court-based Drug-rehabilitation Schemes

The police survey also found evidence of interventions being made by workers from other types of court based drug-rehabilitation schemes;[21] some of these have a charitable status and often receive financial assistance from the Home Office or the National Health Service. Their staff are frequently young and idealistic, and some have had drug-taking histories.

The survey discovered that the practice had developed for these drug workers to visit offenders who have been arrested for drug possession to offer them help and support for their drug dependency. Where the offender is held in the larger custody centres found in cities, the drug 'counsellor' visits the prisoner in the cells. If the prisoner rejects his help, the drug worker reports this to the custody sergeant, and the prisoner is then processed normally, and he is placed before the court. Despite his help being rejected, it has become known that many drug counsellors record the visit as an example of 'drug treatment' because this enables them to maintain their case for future funding and so keep their jobs.

163

It also came to light that if the offender accepts the offer of help, the custody sergeant scraps the charges and simply leaves the offender in the hands of the drug rehabilitation worker. The offence is not recorded and is thus forgotten. Thus the rule of law is flouted, the offender gets away with his crimes yet again and their impact on the victims is not considered. Where an offender is taken, after arrest, to a smaller custody centre which only stays open for a limited number of hours (as opposed to the twenty-four hours for the main centres), the drug counsellor rarely carries out his interview in the cells. In these cases, the offender is released on bail, and the drug worker sees the offender during the bail period. In these situations, the practice has developed for the drug worker to ring the custody sergeant and tell him that he has seen the offender but for him not to tell the police the results of his interview. Following this one telephone call, the custody sergeant brings the criminal processing to an end and no charge is brought against the individual concerned. The police can rationalise that the offender is now in touch with 'community-based help' for his drug dependency. It was found that this happens even though in the majority of cases offenders refused the help offered by the drug counsellor. The fact that the law had been broken was routinely forgotten.

The Employment Scheme Myth

The Probation Service and the Home Office have long been fixated on the idea that persistent offenders could be reformed if they had jobs. I will say more about this in the next chapter, but suffice it to say here that there is not a shred of evidence to support this belief which the Probation Service clings to despite the decades of contrary evidence accumulated from its own work with offenders. Nevertheless, a number of criminal justice research projects have attempted to keep this myth alive, but, as with the drug offender research, when the results are read objectively, they are all found to have failed in their objectives; not one has had even a modest effect on the offending behaviour of the offenders concerned.

For example, Home Office Research Study 218 reported on the results of two schemes whose objectives were to improve the employment and training prospects of unemployed offenders on probation.[22] Both started in 1997 and ran for three years. The project title 'Working their Way out of Offending' could not have been more misleading. In the first year alone, 175 (43%) of the 16 to 25-year-olds on the first programme (called the Asset Scheme) had been reconvicted, and for the second (the Springboard Scheme) it was 163 (45%). If we conservatively estimate that each of the 238 offenders who were reconvicted in the first twelve months committed only five offences each per week, then between them they were responsible for at least 60,000 offences.

Despite the intense advice and support to find work offered to the 1,634 offenders over the three years of the Springboard Scheme for example, only 452 actually did so, and by six months only 74 were still employed. Only 13 per cent (102) of the offenders on the Asset Scheme found work but it is not known how long they remained employed. However, the one central question of relevance to the public is, did attendance on these employment schemes make the offenders concerned law-abiding? The answer is plainly no. Whether the offenders found work or not is irrelevant to this all-important concern. Yet the write-up of the report focused on irrelevances. For example, the researchers noted that 'the probation officers spoke highly of the projects' and that 'generally there was a feeling there should be more schemes of a similar type'. Would the thousands of victims agree? Not one sentence was given over to assessing the impact of the scheme on them. Almost reluctantly the Asset report admitted that it had failed in its objectives, which was equally true of the Springboard Scheme. All that can be said of these programmes was that they were a waste of the £2 million spent on them and that they brought untold misery to thousands of members of the public.

Scraping the Barrel – Failure Presented as Success

Sometimes criminal justice officials scrape the barrel for something positive to say when reporting on supervision programmes which have lamentably failed to reform the offenders referred to them. In this respect, a favourite trick is to focus on the results of offenders who complete schemes such as these, and not on those who dropped out. This is a failure to acknowledge that members of the public are victimised by both the finishers and the non-finishers alike. For example, in 1995 a local Probation Service reported that 'one year

165

after commencement, of the 50 per cent of offenders who completed their employment course, almost two-thirds had not been convicted of further offences'.[23] Put more objectively this meant that 70 per cent of all of the offenders who started the programme were likely to have been reconvicted within twelve months. With a low 5.5 per cent detection rate the true reoffending rate would be nearer 100 per cent.

The results of another project, published in November 2000, examined the long-term impact on offending of probation supervision on a sample of offenders in Scotland.[24] The results showed its impact had been nil, as none of the 106 offenders included in the study stopped committing crime. Yet in its findings the report said, 'the majority of probationers believed that their circumstances had improved since they were on supervision';[25] this is as relevant as pointing out how well the seats are upholstered in a car that won't start. Another of its findings was that 'across the sample as a whole the rate and frequency of reconviction were lower following the imposition of the probation order than before'.[26] Given that most crimes go undetected this claim is without meaning, but despite this the results showed that 84 per cent of the offenders under the age of twenty-one years and 62 per cent of those aged twenty-two and above were reconvicted within two years of the start of the probation order. The implications for the public of this level of failure do not bear thinking about. Yet, as we have seen with other projects, their experience of being victimised by the criminals being researched did not rate a mention.

In short, the research showed that those who had a persistent criminal history before the period of probation did exceptionally badly. For example, all of those who had failed previous probation orders were reconvicted within two years, whereas 40 per cent of those who had done well on previous probation orders were reconvicted within two years. What this demonstrates is that probation supervision of even the more hopeful cases cannot stop offending.[27]

Another example is provided by a Scottish Office report (Research Findings No. 31) of an employment scheme for offenders called Cue Ten.[28] Its purpose was to reduce offending among juvenile persistent offenders by teaching them employment-related skills over a twenty-six week programme during 1999. Only 40 per cent completed the programme, and predictably it was found that the more criminal they were before starting the programme the less likely they were to complete it. Both finishers and non-finishers continued to commit crime and there was no evidence that any of them stopped offending. However, the researchers reported reductions, for some offenders, in the *rate* and *type* of their offending, and based on the target group of twenty-four young offenders, they suggested that this programme *may* have prevented about thirty crimes. Had these persistent offenders been sent to prison *all* of the hundreds of crimes committed by them whilst on this programme would have been prevented. But once again the programme evaluation failed to take into account the heavy price paid by those who were victimised.

Don't Be Taken in by the Tag

The government has also produced research to report on the results of electronic monitoring of offenders released from prison, and once again it is highly misleading.

Sections 99 and 100 of the Crime and Disorder Act 1998 enabled the government to introduce the Home Detention Curfew Scheme. This allowed for the majority of prisoners sentenced for up to four years to be released two months before the end of their prison sentence on a Home Detention Curfew (HDC) order. During this sixty-day period the order stipulates they must remain at home or other location from 7 p.m. to 7 a.m. They are required to wear an electronic watch-sized tag around their ankle or wrist. This emits a signal via the telephone line which will stop if the offender moves away from his home base, thus breaking the terms of his early release. This signal is monitored by a private contractor who is responsible for informing the Home Office when an offender has broken his curfew. Violations of the curfew conditions should lead to a recall to prison. The scheme began in January 1999, presaging the early release of a possible six thousand prisoners during that year.[29]

Whilst it may sound as if the arrangements described above protect the public, in reality they put them at great risk. However, the initial concerns of the Probation Service were not for the potential victims of those criminals released early from their sentence, but that the tag would be an infringement of the offender's civil liberties.[30]

Home Detention Curfew – Lighting the Fuse for a Crime Explosion

From the start, the system was poorly thought through and riddled with a level of incompetence that almost defies belief. For example, it may shock many to learn that in the early months of the scheme the three private companies employed at a huge cost to the taxpayer to implement and monitor the scheme were not provided with a photograph to enable them to be certain they were tagging the correct person when they called at the offender's home address following his release from prison. The offenders, who are never slow to look a gift horse in the mouth, immediately exploited this blunder. There were soon known examples of their arranging for associates to be tagged instead of them, allowing them to go where they liked, free to commit offences as they chose.[31] In one case, a prisoner paid a fellow criminal £1,000 to be tagged in his place. Why would he pay such a large sum just to avoid the relatively minor inconvenience of a nighttime curfew for two months? It is difficult to avoid the conclusion that the motivation for this deal was the prospect of lucrative night and daytime crime.

Despite the enormity of this error, which should have resulted in sackings or at the very least resignations from the Home Office, the press made very little of the affair, and it was only reported in one or two newspapers. The officials concerned kept their heads down and when questioned tried to keep the matter low key, as if it were of little consequence. The Home Office minister at the time said, 'we are concerned there has been an abuse of the system and are looking at tightening it up', as if somehow the opportunity to abuse the system was not of their making.[32]

However, the government was much more vocal about what they saw as the benefits of the scheme. Only seven months after it started, the parliamentary under-secretary of state for the Home Office stated that tagging had been a 'qualified success'. He reported that only 1 per cent of the 7,226 prisoners released by that stage on HDC had been charged with new offences whilst on curfew.[33] On 30 November 2001, a Home Office spokeswoman was more fulsome and announced that 'tagging had been a huge success'. She said that by November of that year only 893 of the 42,853 prisoners released under the HDC scheme had been convicted or cautioned or were awaiting prosecution for offences committed whilst subject

168

to HDC.[34] What she did not make clear was that many offences committed during the curfew period will not come to light until after it has finished.

Home Office research published in 2001 likewise painted a rosy picture of the first sixteen months of the HDC system.[35] It reported that those released under the terms of the HDC and their families were very positive about it, which is hardly surprising (it is unlikely they were going to be against it), and that only 5 per cent of the released prisoners had been recalled following a breach of the curfew restrictions. To those uninitiated in Home Office speak this result sounds reassuring. However, as demonstrated, it is meaningless and only serves to highlight the wishful thinking of Home Office officials and their willingness to deny reality. For example, the research included a cost analysis of the scheme which claimed a net benefit, but it totally ignored the personal and financial costs to the victims of the crimes committed by tagged prisoners. Likewise, it failed to acknowledge that had these offenders still been in prison these offences could not have been committed. In this respect, how can the Home Office regard prison, which prevents all crime against the public, as a failure and the tag as a success?

Because of the low crime detection rate (5.5%), most offences committed during the tag period will never be known about. The best that can be said is that no one knows what the actual reoffending rate is of prisoners released on the tag, but it is likely to be considerably higher than the acknowledged reconviction rate. Moreover, some members of the public may be surprised, not to say alarmed, to learn that the electronic tag only operates for a maximum of twelve hours (with some rare exceptions) and a minimum of nine hours in every twenty-four-hour cycle.[36] The conditions of the curfew therefore leave the prisoner with ample time to move away from his base, unmonitored and able to commit crime at will. Yet at the inauguration of the HDC ministers and officials heralded it as an effective and safe way of supervising the prisoners in the community.

In January 2004 the Home Secretary intervened in the case of Maxine Carr and changed the rules to prevent her being released early on HDC. This prevented the spotlight falling on the government's early release arrangement for prisoners, which would otherwise have come under close public scrutiny, an outcome I believe he preferred to avoid.

The Crime Explosion Is Triggered

By 2000, examples of offenders committing large numbers of crimes whilst on HDC licence began to surface in some newspapers. Faced with growing public disquiet the Home Office had to admit that more than one thousand offences had been committed by offenders during their HDC licence.[37] These included rapes, arson, attacks on the police, burglaries, robberies, thefts, and drug offences. Government ministers played down the seriousness of this for the public by emphasising that only 5 per cent of tagged criminals had committed further offences and had been returned to prison.[38]

Although this claim impressed many, it is one which, as I have already made clear, cannot be taken seriously. The victimisation of just *one* person by a prisoner on HDC licence would be an abrogation of the government's duty to protect the public. It brings no comfort or relief to the thousands who have been robbed, attacked or burgled to be told that, according to the government's view of events, only a small number of prisoners on the scheme commit more offences.

Any lingering belief that criminal justice officials in the Home Office are genuinely concerned for the safety of the public should be dashed by the shocking revelation that at the outset of the scheme they *expected* a failure rate of at least 10 per cent. Thus they were quite prepared to entertain the fact that the early-release scheme would result in thousands falling victims to 'tagged' criminals.[39]

The Story the Public Has Not Been Told

My enquiries among those closely involved with the day-to-day working of the scheme revealed that when it was first introduced in 1999 prison governors exercised great caution over who they released, and only the safest prisoners were granted HDC licence. The governors had been told their jobs were on the line if the scheme got off to a bad start.[40] In fact, so cautious were they that at first, very few prisoners were released and then only for a few weeks. This suited the tactics of the Home Office because they wanted a good run of early results so they could tell the world that HDC was a great success.

Thus during the early days of HDC when the Home Office felt that the eyes of the country were watching its progress, great sensitivity was shown to public opinion in the way the scheme was operated. The private monitoring companies gave the offenders no leeway and reported them quickly to the Home Office if they violated their curfew. Likewise, the police, having informed the Home Office that an arrested offender was wearing a tag, were immediately instructed by them to return the prisoner to jail.

In time, public anxieties about the scheme lessened. This was due, as described above, to the highly abridged, not to say misleading, version of its progress fed to the public and Parliament by the Home Office, which proved to be highly effective in quelling growing concerns about crime committed by prisoners on HDC. As a result, the scheme, in contradiction to the public's actual experience of it, generally earned, in the eyes of the press at least, the reputation of being safe. As one newspaper headline put it: 'faith in the tag has grown as fears of re-offending fade'.[41]

During the first few months of its operation, the small number of prisoners being granted HDC was creating another problem. The private monitoring stations had been set up and financed to cope with large numbers of released prisoners, and unless numbers increased, their viability would be threatened. Therefore in 2002 the Home Office, judging that the public was by then sufficiently off its guard, set about relaxing its HDC arrangements, and during that year over 20,000 offenders were released under the scheme.[42] Despite the shallow claim by the Home Office that the early-release programme was aimed at 'rehabilitating inmates more quickly', it was clear that their intention from the beginning had been to exploit it as a means of reducing the prison population. Once the public had been lulled, by misleading information, into a false sense of security about its impact on their safety, this real purpose of HDC licences could be pursued with vigour. Within sixteen months of its start, over 21,000 prisoners had been granted early release on the scheme, an average of 1,300 prisoners a month.[43]

As a first step to achieving these reductions in the prison population, the Home Office held a meeting with all prison governors and told them to be more relaxed about who they released, as it was imperative to increase the numbers of HDC licences. Perhaps to the surprise of the officials, the governors refused. These clumsy tactics failed to recognise that the governors knew they would be held responsible should there be an outcry about harm done to the public by prisoners they had released. The Home Office dealt with this united front by inventing the concept of 'presumptive HDC'. In other words, and without the public being made aware, the governors were told that from then on they were under instructions to grant HDC licences to a widening category of offenders, including burglars and others who clearly presented a real threat to the safety of the public. As it was the Home Office, and not them, who were seen to be taking responsibility for this step, the governors fell into line.

There was, of course, no ombudsman to protest on behalf of the public, whose safety, as usual, did not figure in these new arrangements. By September 2000, they had resulted in the early release of more than 1,000 convicted robbers, 2,500 burglars and 2,000 convicted of grievous bodily harm, as well as others convicted of manslaughter and attempted homicide.[44] By 2000, as reported above, this relaxation of the scheme resulted in over a thousand members of the public being victimised by these criminals during the two-month period of their licence. What makes this far worse is that, as I have previously described, these are just the offences that are known about. For this reason, the true victimisation list of those released on the 'tag' is likely to be much longer than the latest figures available, published in December 2004, in *Home Office Statistical Bulletin 15/04*. These show that 13 per cent (2,720) of all tagged prisoners released in 2003, had to be recalled to prison and that 15 per cent of these recalls were the result of new offences.

But even this was not the whole story. The caution that was exercised in administering the HDC system in its early days soon began to break down. Staff involved in its day-to-day operation have revealed that many probation officers tasked by the prison to check addresses of prisoners being considered for the scheme, do so by ringing a mobile phone number, with no back-up home visit or call to the home landline to check the address. To make matters worse the mobile number is supplied by the prisoner and is not independently checked.[45]

In addition, evidence began to pile up that the monitoring stations were becoming increasingly lax in their surveillance of tagged prisoners. Staff in prisons responsible for operating the scheme began to see examples of prisoners accumulating as many as eighty curfew violations before they were recalled, and soon such examples were not uncommon. This apparent reluctance on the part of the contractors to investigate violations may well point to their fear of intimidation at the hands of the offenders concerned, and the Home Office has admitted that this has been a feature in the behaviour of some tagged prisoners.[46]

In addition, tagged prisoners began to find ways of playing the system. For example, officials have been loath to make public the fact that many offenders have avoided surveillance by the monitoring station by the simple tactic of switching off their electricity over night. Sometimes the prisoner will ring the monitoring station and tell them, for example, 'I am at a friend's house watching TV or playing cards', and the monitoring station will accept his story. The prisoner, of course, could be anywhere, at the point of burgling a house or committing some other crime.

What is more, the Home Office conditions for recall are worded so as to make it unlikely that the prisoner is deemed to have failed his HDC licence. For example, if he loses his address he is usually recalled to prison, but it is deemed not to be his fault. This means that he is *not* recorded as having failed his HDC licence (despite as stated being recalled to prison). This is the case even if he has lost his address as a result, for example, of excessive drinking, drug taking, committing crime, or being dangerous and violent. The effect of this bizarre arrangement is that he can be considered for early release again, which would not be the case if he was recorded as having *failed* on a previous licence.

Some Disturbing Questions

My enquiries have revealed that in at least one area of the country it has become known to the police that there are a number of serious anomalies in the arrangements by which prisoners are released early from their prison sentence.[47] They had become aware (not surprisingly) that many tagged offenders were committing offences during the daytime when the tag was not operating. It was a sure certainty that persistent offenders tagged in this way would take advantage of these free and unmonitored periods, and these huge gaps in the surveillance cover point, at the very least, to an appalling level of naivety on the part of those responsible for the scheme's design.

In addition, large numbers of offenders have been arrested for committing offences, having, it was discovered, removed their tags. However, the private company responsible for their surveillance appears not to have known or, if they did, have taken no action.

This raises very serious questions about the limits of the monitoring equipment. If the offender moves sufficiently far away from his base, can he remove his tag without the monitoring station being aware of it?

In one case known to the police, an offender removed his tag and broke it in the process. He then committed more offences. He was caught and the police informed the company, who, however, were reluctant to take action. (Might not the cause of this relectance be that the private companies have a vested interest in keeping these tagged prisoners in the community?) Eventually the police managed to get the offender into court (no longer an easy, straightforward task even for the police). Despite offending whilst on the tag and removing it, he was only given a two-month prison sentence. Because prisoners were then released two months before the end of their sentence, he was immediately sent home and tagged again the next day.

In another example, a released prisoner robbed a victim in the street of her purse whilst on the tag. The Crown Prosecution Service downgraded the offence to the lesser charge of theft, and the offender was sentenced to eight months in prison. The 50 per cent automatic remission scheme reduced this immediately to four months, and the application of the Home Detention Curfew scheme would have reduced this further. However, she appealed against her sentence, and *despite* being on the curfew scheme when she committed the robbery, and *despite* being caught red-handed at the time of the offence, her appeal was upheld and she was given a suspended sentence.[48] Few examples could illustrate more clearly the fraudulent nature of the Home Detention Curfew programme.

The Perfect Alibi

What the Home Office has unwittingly created are the circumstances for the perfect alibi for persistent offenders who commit crime whilst on an HDC licence. A tagged prisoner can commit an offence and then claim he was in a friend's house playing cards at the time the crime was committed and that he informed the monitoring station of his whereabouts by telephone. Such a call would have been necessary because their equipment would have recorded that he had moved away from his base. If the staff at the station failed to notice

174

or check this story, the authorities might not be too keen for the alibi to be investigated, lest this loophole in the system came to light. A number of tagged prisoners recalled to prison have told staff, for example, that the checks made by the monitoring stations on them were few and far between. In any case, the system only requires contractors to check the location of the tagged offender at certain specified intervals, and between these intervals the offender can move away from his home without detection.

Despite such failures, the government seems determined to extend the programme. In 1999 prisoners were released on an HDC licence two months before the end of their sentence, but on 16 December 2002 this was quietly increased to three months and again in July 2003 to four-and-a-half months in some cases.[49] I have little doubt that the government will watch for an opportunity to extend it again. As already illustrated in the previous chapter the combined effect of the Home Detention Curfew and the 50 per cent automatic remission on, for example, a twelve-month prison sentence means the offender will serve just three months inside. The effect of the Home Detention Curfew Scheme on shorter sentences will mean that the offenders will spend hardly any time in jail. Thus HDC licences have not only allowed thousands of prisoners to be freed before the end of their sentence but they have rendered meaningless the prison sentences given to thousands of others.

Curfew Orders Made by the Court

Electronically monitored curfew orders for offenders aged sixteen and over were made available to the courts throughout England and Wales from December 1999.[50] Section 12 of the Criminal Justice Act 1991 provides for a maximum sentence of six months, and a curfew period for between one and seven days a week. They can be made for a minimum of two hours and a maximum of twelve hours a day, and generally they have been used as alternatives to custody.[51]

Trials of these orders were run in three separate areas of the country between 1996 and 1997.[52] The research reports detailing their results showed the extent to which the courts were prepared to expose the public to offenders with a high risk of further offending for the sake of yet another dangerous community experiment. For example, in the second year of the trials 77 per cent of the 374 curfew orders were made on offenders with between two and twenty previous convictions.[53] What is more, the main offences attracting curfew orders included theft, burglary and violence.[54]

The reconviction rate measured two years from the start of the order was nearly 73 per cent, which showed beyond argument that the experiment had failed either to protect the public or reform the offenders.[55] Yet in February 2002 the Home Secretary announced proposals to extend tagging to include offenders aged twelve to sixteen years old who were bailed following an offence. He was no doubt responding to public concern about the alarming number of muggings carried out by young offenders, and that in nine London boroughs street crime had increased by 44 per cent between April 2001 and January 2002 alone. The police expressed their well-founded fear that tagging of itself would not stop determined criminals breaching their bail conditions. They were only too well aware of the large numbers of offenders who repeatedly committed crime whilst on bail and that their hardened and deep seated criminal attitudes would ensure this would continue, whether tagged or not.[56]

It also became known that curfewees and solicitors were abusing the stipulation that breach cases (offenders accused of breaking the terms of their curfew order) could only be presented before the end of the sentence. For example, solicitors were attempting to get breach cases adjourned beyond the end of the sentence and curfewees were absconding for the last two or three days of the order.[57]

Despite this the research frequently focused on banalities. For example, it reported that over 80 per cent of the offenders completed their orders 'successfully'. For all the reasons previously described, this is meaningless, not the least because the researchers knew that the reconviction rate for the offenders remained very high. Indeed, the researchers admitted that there was no connection between the so-called 'completion rates' and subsequent reduction in offending.[58] Yet this did not stop one Home Office research paper from reporting that 'the results of the trials were generally positive'.[59] It would be interesting to know how many members of the public have to be victimised by offenders on schemes such as this before the researchers judge them to be harmful.

The average length of the orders made in the second year of the trials was 3.3 months.[60] Given a reconviction rate of 73 per cent for the 374 offenders given curfews in this period, it can be deduced that, assuming a modest estimate of five offences per week each, these offenders, in only just over three months, committed almost 18,000 offences. But once again, the government failed to take into account the harmful impact of these curfew orders on the public and introduced legislation making them a permanent sentencing option (see Note 1).

'What Works': A Classic Misnomer

Over recent years the Probation Service, the Home Office and other organisations concerned with the criminal justice system have claimed that evidence exists to show that particular kinds of community offender supervision programmes can be effective in reducing reoffending. They have been labelled as 'what works' programmes. Those responsible for such claims appear not to be aware of the all-important difference between reoffending and reconvictions; the former refers to all offences committed by an offender, whereas the latter refers to only those that are known about. It follows that no one can know about reoffending rates, as offenders in the community are not supervised for twenty-four hours a day.

These 'what works' claims of success are based on data from Canada and the United States where the results from large numbers of supervision programmes have been combined and analysed as one dataset.[61] A number of researchers have claimed that by using this 'meta-analysis' technique they have been able to show evidence of an overall positive effect of these interventions not previously identified from the analysis of data sets from smaller programmes.[62] These programme 'effects' have been taken to indicate reduced criminality of offenders following attendance of these schemes.[63] As a result 'what works' exponents have put forward a number of principles underlying the management and content of these programmes as guidance for agencies working with offenders.[64] In particular, they claim successful results for programmes based on 'cognitive therapy' aimed at changing the way offenders think.[65] Over recent years similar claims of success have been made for a number of UK probation supervision programmes based on these principles.[66] However, such claims are unsupportable as indicated by the programmes' high reconviction rates, usually falling in the 65 to 80 per cent range. For example, the Cognitive Therapy

Programme launched by the Inner London Probation Service in the 1990s 'achieved' a reconviction rate of 67.5 per cent for those who completed the course and 76.6 per cent for non-finishers.[67] An evaluation of the national Motor Projects of the late 1980s showed them to be even less successful, with a reconviction rate of 80 per cent.[68] It would have been more realistic for those responsible to have used these as examples of programmes that should *not* be used, as they exposed large numbers of the public to the certainty of being victimised by the criminals concerned. Yet, as we have seen so often with other research previously discussed, none of these 'what works' programmes took into account the impact of these crimes on their victims when assessing their performance.

All too frequently, their claims of success were based on results specially selected to support that conclusion, whilst ignoring the data that did not. For example, the Hereford and Worcester scheme reported success on the basis of the 16 per cent fewer reconvictions for offenders on their programme than for a custody group used as a comparison;[69] this ignores the 68 per cent of those offenders who continued to commit crime within two years of the start of the scheme. Likewise, the researchers of the probation STOP programme concluded that their project represented better value than a custodial sentence by emphasising that those released from a young offender institution had a higher reconviction rate than those attending the STOP programme, thus ignoring the fact that offenders were specially selected for the scheme as opposed to the less hopeful cases sentenced to imprisonment. In any case, the fact that at least 70 per cent of the STOP offenders continued to commit offences means that this comparison has no meaning as a measure of its ability to protect the public. They also failed to comment on the comparison of this high failure rate with the lower 57 per cent reconviction rate of a group of adults who received custodial sentences. They failed to offer any explanation of this result, which was achieved despite the influence (as described above) of selection of the more hopeful cases for the STOP programme and against the general expectation of poorer results from the more criminally sophisticated adult offender group.[70]

Similarly, a claim by a major 'what works' exponent of a 10 per cent average reduction in offending based on his review of over 400 schemes is ambiguous.[71] Does it mean that out of 100 offenders who attended a 'what works' style community supervision programme that 90 reoffended during the six-month follow-up period? If so this cannot be viewed as success. In terms of the impact on the public, this represents a 90 per cent failure rate, quite apart from the fact that the six-month follow-up period is too short to be meaningful. Furthermore, this author failed to take into account the low 5.5 per cent detection rate, made no distinction between reoffending and reconvictions, and gave no indication of how often offenders came to notice during the follow-up period. The all important role of motivation will be touched on a little later on, but suffice it to say now that, apart from all of these other objections, the 10 per cent reduction, if it is to be believed, only indicates the difference between more hopeful offenders chosen for the schemes compared with higher-risk cases dealt with in other ways. It does not reflect the effect of the programme per se.

Of particular interest is an admission by the same 'what works' exponent that 'it is well established that the effects of many interventions are relatively short-lived. It is also recognised that in criminal justice settings, the reoffending rates of any pre-selected group will accumulate steadily with the passage of time'.[72] This surely sounds like a retraction of his original argument that supervision programmes can be effective in reducing offending.

Likewise, the Inspectorate of Probation's advocacy for the 'what works' approach was based on flimsy evidence.[73] The majority of the research programmes they used as the basis for their case were found to be methodologically unsound and the results of the few that merited serious evaluation fell far short of out-performing prison reconviction results.[74]

Clutching at Straws

As indicated, it was from the early 1980s onwards that the UK was bombarded with 'meta-analysis' results of North American programmes purporting to show 'evidence' that community supervision programmes for offenders based on cognitive behavioural techniques worked. Many of these programmes were not even concerned with crime, yet the Probation Service and others who identified with this line of thought did not approach these claims objectively. Rather, they seized upon them as a way of pressing their unrealistic ideological claims about the ineffectiveness of prisons and the effectiveness of alternative sentences for offenders. To this end, as previously described, a number of group work programmes were run in the UK along the so-called 'what works' principles. The obvious gap between their stark failure and the 'what works' claims from North America was ignored. What is more, the UK programmes were reported as 'successful' and probation committees, judges, magistrates and others were targeted with this misleading propaganda.

During the early 1990s in the wake of these catastrophic results, the Home Office and the Probation Service played a confusing double game. They continued to portray these 'what works' experiments as successful but at the same time they let slip that they knew there were significant problems which undermined their credibility. This gave rise to a number of reports from the Probation Inspectorate that were masterpieces of confusion and double-talk.[75]

Referring to 'what works' programmes, the Probation Inspectorate Report *Evidence Based Practice* stated that the 'best probation practice can substantially reduce reconviction rates' – but then equivocated with the warning that such programmes might not always work.[76] An earlier report, *Strategies for Effecive Offender Supervision*, was couched in the same ambiguous terms. It stated that 'what works' programmes can reduce reoffending by 10 per cent – and sometimes by 25 per cent, but then implied doubt about their efficacy by arguing that there should be comprehensive arrangements for 'programme evaluation'.[77] This classic piece of double-think was then encapsulated in the official policy of the Home Office which directed that the Probation Service should base its entire effort on running 'what works' style programmes.[78] The Probation Service was directed to submit offender group work schemes to be considered for 'accreditation' by a panel established in 1999, as part of the rapidly expanding 'what works' bureaucracy within the Home Office.[79]

Once 'accredited', they could then be run and their results, as indicated above, evaluated to see if they were successful. This was despite the fact that the Home Office emphasised that only group work with offenders planned on known 'what works' principles would be accredited because these principles were drawn, so they argued, from programmes with proven success. Not surprisingly, magistrates, judges and others soon fell victim to the confusion caused by this circular argument, and many believe that when a programme is 'accredited' it means that there is evidence that it works. Nothing could be further from the truth.

A Burgeoning Bureaucracy

In the short space of a decade, this highly confusing apparatus has burgeoned into a substantial bureaucratic empire within the Home Office, with the creation of many new layers of specialists and Civil Service jobs. Adverts have appeared for highly paid senior- and middle-management posts to staff the What Works Unit of the National Probation Directorate based in London. In addition other adverts for such posts as National Programme Implementation Manager, Programme Implementation Manager, Head of Young Adult Offenders, Training Manager, Senior Policy Officer, and National Trainers have likewise been advertised as posts within the What Works Unit of the Home Office.[80] Below these are tiers of 'practice managers', senior practitioners and group workers.

But what has it achieved? If its offender programmes were as successful as the propaganda indicates we would be well on the way to solving our crime problem. However, our homes on estates, in town centres, in suburbs, and in the countryside are still predated upon by burglars, and crime generally, violent and otherwise, is still a major problem for almost every community in the land. Nevertheless, against this background the 'what works' exponents have continued, for at least a decade, to make unrealistic and misleading claims.

For example, in 1998 the then Home Office minister Joyce Quinn, in a conference speech said, 'The government believes that the "what works" initiative is of the utmost importance and that it will ground probation work in techniques *which have been proven to reduce offending*' (my italics).[81] She offered no evidence for this statement. She did however refer to 'research from North America which has enabled us to identify factors which help to make interventions with offenders successful – but there is still some way to go'. Does not this vague, not to say obscure, statement contradict the firm claim referred to above? She went on to say, 'a reduction of 5 to 10 per cent in offending rates is commonly believed to be attainable. Some put it as high as 25 per cent'. Likewise, the National Association of Probation Officers (NAPO) stated, 'Virtually all accredited programmes are likely to result in a fall of between 10 and 25 per cent in reoffending'.[82] How could anyone know that before the results were in?

A few months earlier, the Penal Affairs Consortium, a leading member of the anti-prison movement, had gone one step further and claimed 'What Works' programmes could achieve a reduction in reoffending of between 15 and 50 per cent.[83] A Home Office circular[84] introduced the 'What Works' theme by declaring that 'it had been shown to reduce offending', and then contradicted itself a few pages later by stating that 'the evidence base which underpins effective practice ("What Works" programmes) is still thin'.

Over the last five years, I have written to a number of senior criminal justice officials, including a minister of state, asking them to identify the programmes whose results substantiate their claims that 'What Works' has reduced offending. Not one of them has been able to do so. In 2001 the then Home Office minister (not the same one referred to above) passed one such written request to his senior official and he referred me to 'What Works' programmes whose results were not yet known. When I pointed this out to him, he failed to answer any more letters.[85] A number of chief probation officers similarly have also failed to produce evidence for such claims when I have asked them. In 2000 a chief probation officer chaired a high-profile conference which the Home Secretary, the Lord Chief Justice and many other senior officials attended as either speakers or guests. At this conference a member of the royal family presented awards for 'What Works' programmes which were said to have been particularly successful. I wrote and asked the chairman if he could identify which programmes had received these awards so that I could follow them up.[86] My request was ignored. I asked another chief probation officer to specifically identify the research whose results were such that it gave her confidence to embark on these 'What Works' programmes in her local Probation Service, bearing in mind her brief to protect the public. Her reply was classic obfuscation. She wrote back saying, 'a panel rigorously assesses the programmes for accreditation'[87] which, of course, tells one nothing.

In May 2000 an article was published by a chief constable which contained bold claims for the success of 'What Works' programmes.[88] He quickly threw in the towel when faced with my request for evidence to back up his claim. Unable to supply anything to support what he had said about 'What Works', he forwarded my request to his local probation service, who he indicated would answer my query. Their silence was deafening and thus they failed to come to his rescue.

It is self-evident that anyone who makes a claim that offender community supervision programmes are effective in protecting the public must be able to back it up with reliable research results which are available for review. Otherwise, such claims are meaningless and run the risk of misleading the public into believing that they are being protected from criminals who are placed on these schemes when this is not the case. This requirement is particularly true for those who hold high office as the public are all the more likely to be persuaded by what they say because of their high-profile position.

A Confidence Trick in the Making

Behind these wild and unsupported claims the Home Office hoped to pull off what amounts to a confidence trick intended to convince the public that 'what works' programmes reduce offending and so result in fewer victims. A senior Home Office official privately admitted that the pressure to do this came from the new Labour government, who had already decided to use these programmes and wanted data to fit these preconceived ideas. To this end, the Home Office instructed the Probation Service to put no fewer than 60,000 offenders through these group work courses by 2004.[89] The reason they wanted large numbers to be dealt with in this way is because *big* samples will be statistically sensitive to *small* differences that occur between the reconviction rates of those who attend 'What Works' programmes and their theoretical 'predicted' reconviction rate.[90]

This suggests that despite all the hype which forecasted big drops in reoffending following attendance of 'what works' programmes, they were playing it safe and preparing for the possibility that the differences may be small when the reconviction results of offenders on the programmes became known. Let me put this another way. The Home Office knew that its results must at least *appear* to have followed the rules of proper scientific analysis to be regarded as statistically respectable. Vital to this is that the differences in reconviction rates between the 'what works' offenders and the comparison groups are amenable to tests of significance, so it can be demonstrated whether the results are meaningful or have occurred by chance.

A proper scientific analysis normally also requires that the offenders be randomly allocated between the 'what works' group and the comparison group. But this is just not possible in the criminal justice setting. On the contrary, as we have seen, offenders go through what is in fact a two-tier selection for 'what works' courses. Probation officers recommend those whom they feel are suitable, and then magistrates will decide whether to follow their recommendation or not. I shall say more about this in a moment, but suffice it to say here that this selection process invalidates any comparison of reconviction results of those on accredited schemes and those sentenced in other ways.

We can draw a parallel with an educational psychologist who sets out to test the effects of a new reading scheme on the reading skills of a sample of schoolchildren. To do this he must compare the reading results of a group of children who used the new method with a group who used the traditional method. To run the experiment properly, common sense dictates that children of the same reading ability should be randomly allocated between the two groups. In this way, any differences in their reading scores recorded after the reading scheme has been used can be attributed to its benefits or otherwise, as opposed to the differing abilities of the children. If, on the other hand, the psychologist deliberately selects children with higher reading abilities for the new reading scheme, he destroys the validity of the test because any differences in reading scores between them and the traditional group noted after the test will reflect the differences in the children's skill in reading and not the different methods used by the two schemes.

In its guidance notes covering how to conduct 'what works' research programmes issued to the Probation Service the Home Office has said that where random allocation is not possible the programme researchers should compare the reconvictions of offenders completing 'what works' programmes with their theoretical 'predicted' reconviction rate.[91] (These have been computed by analysing the offending and background details of thousands of offenders.) As previously indicated, both the Probation Service and the Home Office confidently predicted, well before the results were published, that the actual reconviction rates of offenders on 'what works' programmes would be 5 per cent less than their predicted rate. (As I shall discuss later, the results eventually showed that the programme had failed disastrously.)

184

A senior Home Office statistician told me that an anticipated drop of this order in reconviction rates measured in this way, would be translated into an estimate of crimes not committed and a corresponding reduction in the number of victims – all due to 'what works' programmes.[92] Therefore, even though the difference between the actual and predicted reconviction rates is small, the more offenders they put through the programmes, the larger the number of offences they can argue have not been committed. The then director of the National Probation Service left no room for doubt that this was their strategy. In March 2000 she spelt it out in a message to all probation staff: 'Our target is to put 60,000 offenders through accredited programmes, together achieving a 5% reduction in reconviction rates by 2004. When we succeed our communities will have been spared some 900,000 crimes. Just think how many fewer victims this represents.'[93]

Of course, in reality this would have been no more than a theoretical result and it is vital that sentencers, MPs and the general public see through this statistical sham. The comparison of actual and predicted reconviction rates is an irrelevancy. What matters to the public is how many offences are actually committed against them by offenders on the 'what works' schemes, and as previously emphasised these figures are catastrophic. Even if the 'what works' claims were real, the reductions in crime would be nowhere near those achieved by even short periods of custody.

Pseudo Science

The claims of success referred to above, made years ahead of the results being known, sufficiently embarrassed some members of the National Association of Probation Officers into warning that such practice can only debase genuine research enquiry.[94] But that, of course, is the point. It is not genuine research. As described above, reconvictions provide only a hint of the true reoffending rate; the time period used to measure many of the programmes has often been too short; there are no properly constituted control groups because there can be no random allocation between what works programmes and other ways of sentencing offenders; and the use of predicted reconvictions as a substitute comparison method provides only a theoretical result.

185

In addition, the way in which offenders are selected for 'what works' programmes only serves to underline the pseudo scientific nature of 'what works' research. As already noted, in July 2001 it was reported that the Home Office objective, set some time before, was that 60,000 offenders should be put through these 'accredited' programmes,[95] and in order to process such huge numbers, offenders were at first targeted with little discrimination. The experience of probation staff running these groups, confirmed later by figures reported by NAPO,[96] was that few of those selected attended regularly or completed the programme, and none of them gave up crime. The Home Office, in a renewed bid to make sure sufficient numbers were processed through these groups, began to insist that only offenders who were 'suitable' should be chosen for them and that attention should be paid to their motivation to complete the course.

This, of course, is the *opposite* of random allocation and the antithesis of genuine research enquiry because it represents their attempt to rig the design of the tests to make sure they get the result they wanted. It was not long before this theme appeared in probation training material. One document on my desk spells it out. 'The crucial thing is motivation. This is what we should look for in offenders being chosen for "what works" programmes'.[97] As previously stated, choosing the more motivated offenders for accredited programmes invalidates at a stroke any comparisons of their actual reconviction rates with other offender groups used for comparison purposes. This also undermines the case for using their theoretical predicted rate as a comparison. Offenders who are *selected* for 'what works' programmes can be argued not to be from the same sample base – theoretically regarded as 'all offenders' – on which the prediction scores are based.

What is interesting is that one major 'what works' exponent has felt it necessary to admit that motivation can influence the results of 'what works' programmes. He states, 'The effect of self selection and motivation may also have played a part in the results obtained in [What Works] studies'[98] – an admission totally at odds with the view that 'what works' research can be taken seriously.

However, trying to solve attendance problems by selecting offenders they judged to be more suitable and more motivated caused the Home Office to jump from the frying pan into the fire. With what appears to be nothing less than disdain for the safety of the public, the Home Office decided that only offenders with relatively large

186

numbers of previous convictions should be chosen for 'what works' programmes and that they were to be identified by using the Offender Group Reconviction Scale (OGRS) designed to assess the offender's risk of further offending.[99] The Home Office guidance for probation officers is that offenders with an OGRS score of between 41 and 74 per cent are those who should be selected for the Think First 'what works' programme.[100] Another probation document on my desk instructed staff to target 'what works' programmes at offenders whose OGRS score exceeds 54 per cent.[101] But offenders with a high risk of reconviction are those who are poorly motivated to change, and this has predictably resulted in confusion and muddle in Probation Service practice, as well as yet more victimisation by criminals for the public.

Cracks Appear in the 'What Works' Initiative

The experience of many probation staff running 'what works' groups has been that very few offenders attend all of the sessions, and that, not infrequently by the second or third session of a twelve-, sixteen- or twenty-week programme, there are only one or two, from an original group of about eight, who bother to turn up. In 2002 a Home Office report admitted that between 40 and 80 per cent of offenders dropped out of some programmes.[102] One internal probation document I have seen reported that only 70 offenders completed an accredited programme compared with their target of 550.[103] Others have commented that the highly regimented programmes, far from inspiring offenders to change the way they think, are boring as well as patronising.[104] By 2001 the writing was on the wall and the Home Office briefed the Probation Service that the feasibility of getting 60,000 offenders through programmes by 2003, their revised date, was looking increasingly uncertain.[105]

Prisoners serving jail sentences were also targeted for attendance of 'what works' programmes, and some prison funding was linked to numbers of prisoners who completed these programmes.[106] In a bid to make sure their targets were met, prison psychologists designed selection criteria to ensure that they chose those prisoners who would attend regularly, yet another example of rigging the design of the test to make sure you get the results you want.[107] However, prisoners motivated to attend programme sessions regularly are the very people whose 'thinking skills' are not a problem. In other words, the selection criteria made sure that those who needed 'thinking skills' type courses were not chosen.

Given these built-in contradictions, it was no surprise when it became known that even in prisons with a captive audience, it was found, not infrequently, to be difficult to find sufficient numbers of prisoners who were interested or suitable. In some cases, to make up numbers, even those serving life sentences were dragooned onto these programmes despite the fact that, because of their long sentence, they were unlikely to be included in the assessment of the programmes impact on reconviction rates.[108]

By June 2003, definite signs of unease could be discerned in the announcement by NAPO that completion figures for 'what works' programmes for offenders in the community throughout the country showed that as many as two out of three offenders were failing to even start their programmes or were dropping out after only one or two sessions. It was also reported that NAPO strongly suspected that the Accreditation Panel, the Home Office body which oversees the development and practice of the 'what works' programme, was sitting on figures which showed that the effect on the offending behaviour of those few offenders who complete a programme was minimal or zero.[109]

A press release barely two months later proved their suspicions to be correct. This announced that Home Office researchers had reluctantly admitted that 'what works' programmes run in prisons had been a failure; inmates who had attended the courses were just as likely to commit offences as those who had not, and in some cases it appeared to make them worse.[110] The Prison Reform Trust described the results as deeply disappointing, something of an understatement given that the £200 million pounds of public money spent on them had therefore been wasted.[111]

But this is not the worst of it. At least these offenders were in jail while they attended these courses, and so could not predate on the public, at least until their sentence was finished. But these courses have also been used as an alterative to jail for thousands of offenders, and it was not to be too long before probation officials were forced to find a formula of words which enabled them to quietly admit that these had also been a failure, allowing the offenders concerned to continue their life of crime.[112]

This was confirmed in March 2004 by a Home Office report that admitted only 22 per cent of offenders in the community referred to programmes during 2002/3 completed the course.[113] They blamed these disastrous results on poor case management, lack of support for offenders, and insufficient programmes, all of which were feeble excuses for a scheme which never stood a chance of success. A further research report published in 2004 put the final nail in the 'what works' coffin. It found that none of the several community-based programmes it reviewed came anywhere near protecting the public from the criminals who attended them; their reconviction rates were as high as 84 per cent and completion rates to be as low as 28 per cent. It guardedly remarked that the results of 'what works' programmes held in prisons 'were a cause for concern', as they too showed no evidence of being able to deter prisoners from future offending.[114] The conclusion is obvious. Persistent offenders are persistent because they make a good living from crime and are not in the least motivated to change, and whilst this is so, efforts to get them to be different are a waste of time.

'What Works' Doesn't Work

This calamitous news was not welcomed by senior Home Office and probation officials, who wanted so much for the public to believe the myth that 'what works' programmes could reduce offending. The Probation Inspectorate must now rue their report which recommended this method of work to the government, especially as the then Chief Inspector described its foreword as the most important he had ever written.[115] The inaugural speech by the new director of the National Probation Service, which based the future of the organisation's work entirely on the outcome of its 'what works' programmes, must now be an unwanted and almost unbearable weight on her shoulders.[116] (In fact, in the wake of such disastrous results, she was allowed, a short time later, to slip quietly away from her highly prestigious post in the National Probation Directorate to join a Home Office unit concerned with 'Islamaphobia'.) It will be particularly embarrassing for the Chief Probation Officer, who, in 1996, in the full flush of 'what works' enthusiasm, stated in a Home Office document: 'They [the offenders] are not changing because they have been told to, but because we have managed *profoundly* to change the way they think.'[117] The Head of Corrections, who had also thrown his weight behind the 'what works' campaign, was made to suffer his embarrassment a little longer, and it was not until the summer of 2005 that he was allowed to depart. The *Observer* (3 July 2005) reported that he had been removed from office as a result of serious differences with the Home Secretary. I am sure this was a mask for the real motive for his removal which was that he was associated with the inevitable but dramatic failure of the 'what works' programmes to deter offenders from crime. Much more difficult for the government, however, is to shed the vast bureaucratic machinery set up to run this debacle. Despite being in no doubt that these programmes are useless in the fight against crime, hundreds of civil servants are continuing to process offenders through this system. It is a scandal whose proportions are only matched by the failure of the press and media generally to identify an example of gross mismanagement and incompetence by politicians and civil servants alike without parallel in recent times.

The import of this failure cannot be overemphasised. Hundreds of thousands of people have been victimised by criminals attending these courses as an alternative to jail, but their fate will not preoccupy those responsible for pursuing this disaster. Their concern is how to extract themselves from this debacle with the minimum of damage to their reputations and dignity, and to devise ways of breaking the news of their failure in such a way as to attract as little attention as possible.

Such criminal persistence shown by these results is no more than should have been expected. From a common-sense viewpoint the idea that persistent offenders can be 'programmed' to behave in a law-abiding way is not only naive but preposterous. Professional psychotherapists who employ cognitive group therapy techniques have recognised how difficult it is to achieve behaviour change even with highly motivated fee-paying patients, and that not infrequently it is impossible. With persistent offenders unmotivated to reform, such programmes have no chance of success.[118]

The 'what works' programmes' initiative has been an invention of academic psychologists and criminologists; indeed, I have discovered that certain aspects of the 'what works' programme structure were dreamed up by their author from his deckchair whilst on holiday. The Home Office has paid large sums of money for these ideas; the failed prison programmes alone have cost the taxpayer between £150 and £200 million, quite apart from the costs to the victims,[119] and some of those arguing in favour of 'what works' have a commercial interest in doing so. Their assessments of the programmes cannot therefore be said to be objective.

Managing Bad News

What is certain is that these programmes have not protected nor ever will protect, the public from crime committed by the persistent offender unmotivated to reform, and, as indicated above, it has dawned on the Home Office and probation officials that they are going to have to extract themselves from this foolhardy, not to say disastrous, venture, and in order to do so with the minimum of embarrassment they have put together a two-point escape plan. First and almost within days of the news concerning the 'what works' debacle, the government announced another and entirely different initiative called 'Restorative Justice' aimed at keeping persistent offenders in the community, which they hoped will serve to distract attention from the failed 'what works' schemes.

The concept of 'restorative justice', which is not a new idea but one that has been waiting quietly in the wings for some time, encourages criminals to meet their victims, apologise to them and face up to the 'consequences of their offending'.[120] As with 'what works' programmes, there has not been a shred of evidence offered from restorative justice schemes so far that they protect the public or reform criminals. The restorative justice fanfare was followed up in September 2003 with an almost unbelievable announcement by the Commissioner for Correctional Services in England and Wales, who, despite admissions to the contrary from his own department, said that 'whilst the evidence from what works programmes was *encouraging,* the Probation Service should put *less* emphasis on them and concentrate more on teaching offenders basic skills in reading and writing' (my italics).[121] This could not make clearer their tactic of attempting to slither away from a major embarrassment under the smokescreen of yet another panacea for crime.

Second, a separate government report lost no time in twisting the failure of 'what works' programmes into a bizarre argument that blamed the Probation Service for their lack of success.[122] The Home Office have invented the myth that the reason the programmes failed is because they only work with a *relatively small number* of offenders

191

– about 10 to 15 per cent, the more serious (high-risk) ones – and accused the Probation Service of not targeting those most suitable for 'what works' schemes. Yet in 1998 it was the Home Office who, in their Circular 35/1998, instructed all probation areas to ensure that '*every offender* was supervised in accordance with "what works" principles' (my italics), which is what they have attempted to do, at great organisational cost.[123] Thus the Home Office's claim that the wrong offenders have been targeted can be seen as a clumsy attempt to avoid any responsibility for an enormous error of judgement, which has resulted in a massive waste of public money and harm to the public on a frightening scale.

In August 2003, a senior Home Office probation official repeated the claim that the reason the 'what works' programmes had not worked was because the 'wrong people had been put on them'.[124] However, this time he was referring to programmes for offenders *in the community.* This admission was slipped into an article that dealt with an entirely different problem, namely the growth of paperwork in the Probation Service. This was clearly an attempt to bury embarrassingly bad news and hope few would notice.

Is it feasible that Home Office officials do not understand that 'high risk' offenders are those who are established and persistent (and largely property) offenders – and that they are *least* motivated to change and therefore the *most unsuitable* for any type of community sentence? I doubt it. And if, as the Home Office now announces, these programmes will only work with a *small* proportion of offenders (even though there is no evidence that they work with any), why is it that, at the outset of the 'what works' campaign, they instructed the Probation Service to target as many as 60,000 offenders for these programmes?

And why is it that after fifteen years as the spiritual centre of the 'what works' message, which preaches that 'cognitive therapy is known to reduce offending', Canada still has a very high crime rate? Figure 7.1 shows how much more effective is Singapore's method for controlling crime, with its prison population of 388 per 100,000 population, more than twice that of Canada, which has only 119 per 100,000 population. Singapore, still untouched by the 'what works' missionaries, who no doubt view that country as still being in the criminal justice dark age, has a crime rate of 693 per 100,000 of the population, dramatically lower than Canada's which stands at 7,733 per 100,000.

192

Figure 7.1: Comparison of crime rates and prison populations both per 100,000 of population, Canada and Singapore (2003)

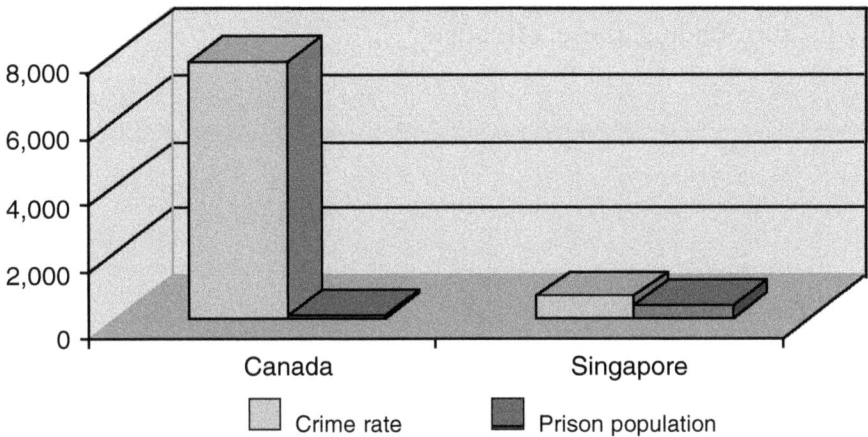

Source: *Prison Population and Crime Rate in Singapore*, World Prison Brief on the International Centre for Prison Studies, 2003; *Prison Population and Crime Rate in Canada (2003)*, Crime Statistics, Canada On Line

As far as the UK is concerned, after more than ten years of 'what works' hype, reconviction figures for all male offenders under community supervision have shown no improvement. The Home Office's *Prison Statistics, England & Wales, 1997* showed that for community orders made in 1994 the reconviction rates were 55 per cent; and *Prison Statistics, England & Wales, 1998*, reported that for those made in 1995 they were 58 per cent. The 2001 reconviction rates, published in *Home Office Statistical Bulletin 15/04* in December 2004, were 61 per cent, but these have not been adjusted for 'pseudo-reconvictions' (these were discussed in Chapter Six). It must be borne in mind that these figures for 'all males' hide the higher reconviction rates for the *majority* of those who are given community supervision. Likewise, the failure rate of those with a proven track record of previous criminality is significantly higher. For example, those with eleven or more previous convictions who were given community orders have a reconviction rate of more than 90 per cent. It must be again stressed that all of these figures are based *only on the 5 per cent of crimes* which are detected. Thus the true failure rate for these orders is likely to be almost total.

Those who may have genuinely believed that 'what works' programmes, restorative justice or indeed *any* community based initiative could bring about significant reductions in crime have severely misunderstood the nature of persistent criminals unmotivated to reform, and in the next chapter I will endeavour to dispel the myths surrounding these offenders.

Chapter 8

The Persistent Offender

Few people have been so misunderstood or so misrepresented as the persistent offender unmotivated to reform. Few have been allowed to wreak such havoc on the community and yet be so indulged and protected from the consequences of their destructive behaviour. But who is it I am referring to when I describe someone as a 'persistent offender' – what kind of person fits this description?

Let me first say who the persistent offender is *not*. He is quite different, for example, from the majority of those offenders my colleague probation officers and I supervised in the 1960s. Many of these were first- or second-time offenders; they were usually people in desperate straits, facing financial, personal or social problems who had turned to crime as a way of escape or as a way of solving their troubles. Of course, it never worked. They were no good at hiding their tracks, their offence was obvious and they were easily caught. Standing in the dock before the magistrates with their head down, eyes glued to the ground, they were often the very picture of dejection and shame.

I can recall numerous such offenders who were placed on probation. Terry, for example, who was an immature 21-year-old who had 'borrowed' money from the firm's cash box to tide him over until pay day at the end of the week. He had become a prolific gambler, and, as he said later, due to an 'unlucky streak', he had simply run out of money. It was mid-week, and he needed cash to eat, pay his rent and to feed the electricity meter to keep warm. He was living alone in a flat in North London. He wasn't socially gifted and was quite lonely. He had fallen out with his parents a long time before and was making his way on his own. He was a pleasant, shy person, and although twenty-one years old, he was immature. His firm had sacked him as a result of the theft and he was mortified with shame and frightened. I capitalised on this and in a stern but not unfriendly manner never let him forget what would happen to him if he stole again.

I saw him every week for eighteen months. He never gave up betting on horses but he gradually learnt to accept that money for food, rent and heating had to be put away and not touched. He found another job with help and encouragement from me and did well. He had moments of temptation when he wanted to spend more on betting than he could afford, particularly, as with all gamblers, during those periods when he was convinced he was going to win. But he learned to talk to me about these temptations, and he slowly but surely got on top of this otherwise destructive urge. By the time his probation order was finished, he was noticeably more confident and altogether more capable. He had grown up. Terry displayed features that are not to be found in a persistent criminal – genuine remorse, a healthy fear of authority and a willingness to change.

Charlie was quite a different sort of person. He was fifty years old, disgruntled, untidy, and often wore tattered and dirty clothes, making him unpleasant to be with much of the time. He tended to snarl at the world and was always looking for arguments and trouble. He was basically a disappointed man and was envious of others who had done better in life than he had. One day it all became too much for him and he stole a briefcase and all of its contents. It was made of beautiful leather and looked expensive. It symbolised for Charlie the sort of moneyed, successful life he felt shut out from, or, put another way, he gave in to greed and envy. He had not stolen before, and fifty years old was a bit late in the day to start on a criminal life, but Charlie might well have gone on to become a persistent thief if he hadn't been caught and given a fright by the magistrates. They told him that even though it was his first offence, they had come close to sending him to prison, as a man of his age and previous good character should have known better. Instead they told him they would give him his one and only chance. He was fined and placed on probation.

He grumbled his way through his period of probation supervision but, despite this, slowly revealed himself as a lonely person, ashamed of his poor status in life, and who admitted he was frightened of growing old on his own. As with Terry, he gradually plucked up courage to talk about these painful topics. There was no neat solution for him. He never learned enough social skills to be likeable, and although he was never completely able to stop feeling resentful about the fact that other people seemed to have more than he did, he learned to be a little more accepting of himself and his lot in life. As with Terry, he showed willingness, albeit grudgingly, to do the right thing and not offend again. He did not want to go to prison, which I promised him I would recommend to the magistrates if he committed any more offences. As far as I know he never did.

Mary was caught shoplifting. She was fifty-seven years old and had plenty of money. Although theories abounded as to why some people behaved this way, I never really understood why Mary did what she did. She never knew either. It might have been the proverbial 'cry for help', but I never worked out what she wanted help for. She was happily married and had a comfortable home. The only thing that was obvious was that she was full of shame and driven to make amends in any way she could. She had not stolen before and, although she was compelled to talk endlessly about what she had done, nothing she ever said helped her or me understand it. But this turned out to be less important than her obvious determination not to do it again. She relished the idea of being on probation as a punishment because she felt she had done wrong. Nothing could contrast more with the response of the persistent offender for whom feelings of guilt are unknown.

Donald was a wreck when I met him in prison – a serious alcoholic who had lost everything – job, family, home and his self-respect – in a downward spiral of drinking and crime, punctuated with spells in prison. Yet, one day sitting alone in his cell he had caught hold of the idea that life could be better, that he wanted it to be different; he wanted to reform himself; and crucially he did not want to spend any more of his life in prison. That prospect was beginning to frighten him. Nevertheless, shortly after his release he went on a drinking binge and committed more offences. Somehow he convinced the court he was genuine in his intentions of wanting to build a new life free of alcohol and crime, and they took a chance and placed him on probation. So began a long and troubled three years for him and for me during which he see-sawed between periods of stability and dark times of drinking and crime.

I would sometimes find him very drunk, staggering through the streets of Islington where I then worked as a probation officer. I would frogmarch him to his flat, frisk him for his door key, open

197

the front door and push him into the hall, where he would crumple onto the floor and remain inert for hours. On these occasions, I frequently emptied his pockets of his money and bank-book, take them to the probation office and throw them into the office safe. He would almost certainly have been robbed otherwise. Invariably he would show up next day, shamefaced, head held down and say he hoped it was me who had taken his belongings. Eventually he became quite taken with the idea of his bank-book being kept in my safe and asked me to keep it there from time to time so he would not spend its contents on drink.

Eventually, following yet another of his crime spates, I recommended to a judge that he send Donald to prison for as long as his powers allowed. The judge concurred and gave him eighteen months in prison (I thought it should have been more). This intervention brought him to a point of crisis; these experiences represented the final humiliation for him and he felt he could sink no lower. But it was this sense of utter humiliation and self-disgust that fuelled his determination to reform and go straight. Following his release from prison, he was a frequent visitor to the probation office, and he set out to show me he could lead the straight life and that he was a capable man who could work and lead a decent, crime-free life.

And so he did. By the time he died several years later, he had more than amply demonstrated his ability to change and reform. He had held down a job, saved money, kept away from alcohol, and even built a social life for himself. Donald's case underlines a powerful truth. For years he had been a persistent offender, but he had reformed because *he wanted to*, and not because he had been programmed by a group work course run by the Probation Service on how to think differently. It is true he remained vulnerable for a long time and needed lots of help and support, and sometimes a lot of controlling, but none of this would have meant anything had he not decided that he wanted to reform and to show his pride in leading the straight life.

Feelings of guilt, a sense of shame and a wish to make amends were the characteristics that led to the reform of these offenders. Without them, no intervention by a probation officer or anyone else, whatever form it took, would have made the slightest impression on them. To have thought otherwise would have been to have allowed hope to triumph over reality.

Persistent and Determined Criminals

The persistent offender, as I understand the term, is clearly illustrated by Billy, who was fourteen years old when the court placed him on probation for stealing and burglary. Soon after his supervision began, it became apparent that he was already a determined and persistent offender. Local enquiries revealed that he had been stealing from the age of eight, even though he was fourteen before he was first put before the magistrates. I had no influence on him. Unlike the probationers I have described above, he was not at all impressed by authority and showed not the slightest remorse for his crimes. He avoided seeing me at every opportunity and when he did he said very little. What I learned about him came mostly in the form of complaints by local people who thought he was a menace.

We could speculate about the reasons for his criminality. Perhaps it was down to the influence of his parents, or perhaps the lack of it. Or maybe it was due to his criminal friends, because he certainly had plenty of those. It might have been because of the way he was reared as an infant; perhaps the run-down area in which he lived had something to do with it. My point is that to try and identify the social and psychological factors that have been so often theorised to be the cause of crime would have been a waste of time. Because even if such causes had been identified this would not have stopped him from offending. It was too late. Billy had developed a persistent criminal habit, and as I have pointed out many times in previous chapters, interventions based on insights into the assumed psychological and/or social causes of an offender's crimes, consistently fail to influence those who show no motivation to change.

Billy had already enjoyed several years as a criminal and found that it paid well. He also knew that he was rarely caught. Crime promised him a well-financed future without the need for schooling and qualifications. He was quite untroubled by guilt and appeals to him on the grounds that he was causing harm to his victims fell on deaf ears. He was without conscience. He was the very model of a persistent offender unmotivated to reform, who would exploit any chance the system gave him to go on offending.

Billy is typical of thousands of repeat offenders who cause immense problems for the community. In 1998 the Association of Chief Police Officers drew attention to the fact that persistent criminals could be identified at the age of eight years, and that once the pattern of criminal persistence had become established it was all but impossible to divert the offender away from crime. They made the altogether sensible point that intervention needed to be made with very young children to prevent their criminal behaviour becoming an established pattern.[1]

Persistence and Profit

Studies that purport to show a connection between crime and unemployment should be treated with caution.[2] Figure 8.1 – a graph of recorded crimes between 1898 and 1998 – enables us to put such assertions into context. During the 1920s in the UK when unemployment reached 1.5 million and poverty was a very serious social problem, the annual crime rate was only about 300,000.[3] Thus what the graph reveals is that when high unemployment and poverty were a fact of life for hundreds and thousands of working-class men and women in this country recorded crime was only a fraction of what it became during the years of increasing prosperity from the 1960s onwards. For example, the crime rate for the first nine months of 1974 showed a 19 per cent increase over 1973, yet during the same year real incomes for the majority of the population rose by an unprecedented amount.[4] If the poverty and deprivation which results from unemployment are the causes of crime, how is it that almost all offenders are male? As pointed out by Lewis,[5] there is no evidence to suggest that in this country more boy babies are deprived than girls.

A Newcastle University sociologist, Norman Dennis, argued in his book *The Invention of Permanent Poverty* that the notion that poverty

Figure 8.1: Recorded crimes per 100,000 population (UK), 1898–2000

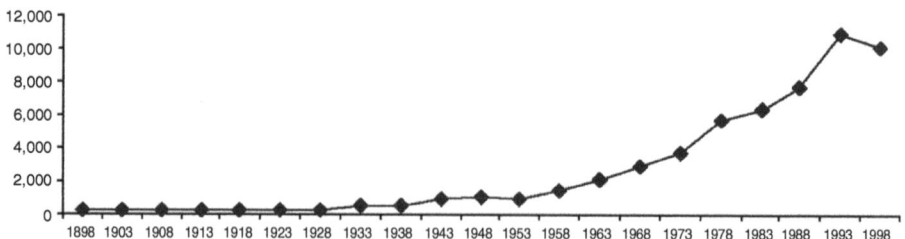

Source: *Crime Rates in the UK*, Civitas, 2003

200

causes crime is wrong. He criticised a 1995 Rowntree Foundation report which claimed a vast gap between rich and poor had opened. He pointed out that the Rowntree report had noted that poverty had lessened between 1961 and 1979, but this was also a period of rapidly rising crime.[6] Likewise, a 1994 Home Office Research study found no relationship between unemployment and crime.[7]

Earlier in our history, R.A. Butler, who was Home Secretary from 1957 to 1962, noted that the marked increase in crime during this period coincided with 'the most massive social and educational reforms for a century'. These years were a phase of distinct economic and social progress. They were years of full employment, higher wages and rising consumption. During this time, well over a million new houses were built and there was a massive movement of the British working classes away from their drab slums into new council houses. In 1961, as Butler pondered these developments and the escalating crime rate which had paralleled them, he said, 'today the link between poverty and crime has been severed'.[8]

However, even if this had not been the case, the existence of a poverty–crime link would be of no relevance to the persistent offender; to harbour beliefs that he steals because he needs to would be to completely misunderstand him; avarice and jealousy, not poverty and need, are the mainsprings for his crimes. Thousands of persistent criminals fail to take up employment even when it is offered to them. For most of them, crime pays very well, often producing an income of many hundreds of pounds a week.[9]

For example, in 1999 an offender known as the 'Boomerang Boy' was still on the streets after committing more than a thousand offences.[10] What drove him wasn't hunger or desperation, but greed for the profits he knew his crimes brought him. In the same year, a newspaper carried a report of a £60,000-raid on a bank by black youths.[11] It reported that 'the thrill of being able to spend a grand on a pair of jeans is irresistible to the poor black kid born in south London poverty'. But this is to misrepresent them and what they were doing. They did not rob the bank because they were poor. They robbed it because they wanted to be rich, and they were not prepared to wait until, as result of study, training and hard work over many years they could become rich by conventional, honest means. This underlines my experience of over thirty years' work associated with persistent criminals; they steal because it is profitable. It is an easy way to make a lot of money.

From his point of view, why should the persistent offender give up crime when it earns him thousands of pounds a year, tax-free, with easy hours and the freedom to work when and where he likes? His criminal activity is almost risk-free, and if he is caught the penalties, as described in Chapter Two, are light and come nowhere near outweighing the financial rewards he earns from crime. It follows that offending does not result from 'distorted' thinking by the offender. This is an invention of psychologists, who themselves have failed to see that criminals know exactly what they are doing and why they are doing it. Is it any wonder that 'what works' programmes providing 'cognitive therapy' for offenders aimed at teaching them to 'think properly' have significantly failed to impress the criminals referred to them?[12]

During the late 1980s and early 1990s, I conducted a survey in the young offender prison where I worked for seven years to find out how much money the inmates earned from crime and how they spent it. None of them had given this much thought, and a few of them had the decency to look embarrassed when we discovered, after some discussion and arithmetic, just how much this was. I discovered that many of these seventeen to twenty-year-old persistent offenders committed between two and fifteen crimes per week, totalling hundreds of crimes each per year. A typical haul from a burglary could often include a hi-fi system, jewellery, cash, small clocks and other items such as watches, CDs, cameras and TVs. They admitted that items stolen from each house earned them anything between £50 and £200. On this basis, it was not difficult to arrive at a figure of £500 per day earned from the proceeds of burglary. This equates to approximately £25,000 per year, tax-free, which they spent on rent, holidays, expensive clothes, eating out and drinking with friends. How much would we have to earn in order to be left with a net income of this amount? The scale of the problem can be deduced from the estimate made by the Office for National Statistics that 'fencing' or the receiving and selling on of stolen property adds £0.7 billion to the UK's gross domestic product.[13]

It is easy to understand why persistent offenders are contemptuous of suggestions from probation officers that they should give up crime and find a regular job, which would, by comparison, earn them small change. Here we can explode another myth. Many well-meaning commentators, for example Roger Graef in his book *Living Dangerously*, argue that the provision of educational and job training opportunities for persistent offenders will divert them from crime.[14] Such views are dangerously naive and are based on the mistaken belief that it is the lack of these that make it difficult for them to find work, which then results in them offending in order to survive. Worryingly such ill-informed views have also been expressed by the Prime Minister, Tony Blair. In August 2002, in a major speech on criminal justice matters, he said that the record investment in prison regimes was intended to give offenders the basic skills and the education they needed to survive on the outside. This almost Salvation Army view of prisons as *saving* persistent offenders from the need to commit any more crime by the provision of basic skills and education would be laughable if it were not so serious.[15]

What they fail to understand is that it is not the *lack* of educational and training opportunities which dictate their criminal lifestyle, but their *refusal* to make use of them and to spend the time and effort required to obtain a well-paid job and a comfortable lifestyle. They are simply not prepared to wait; they want wealth *now.* The persistent offender also knows that even if he did follow the conventional route to a lucrative occupation, it is unlikely to bring him anything like the income he could earn from crime. In 2003 a ruthless gang of robbers who had preyed on wealthy London victims for months were known to have stolen millions of pounds worth of property from them, often using violence. They were eventually caught because their victims recognised them in their expensive designer clothes. Their Prada shoes cost hundreds of pounds and their Gucci and Armani suits each cost thousands of pounds, yet none of the robbers had a legitimate income or had ever worked.[16]

If anyone is tempted to think these sums of money earned from crime are fanciful, they pale into insignificance compared with the amounts identified in other similar studies. For example, research carried out in 1998 at Manchester Metropolitan University among a group of young male persistent criminals revealed that individual thieves could earn much larger sums from stealing.[17] One of them asked a researcher, 'What would I want with a job? I can get as much cash as I want, when I want. I can turn £250 in 10 minutes. Beat that. What do I want to work all week for?' Another prolific offender targeted by the police in the south-west of the country admitted to earning as much as £1,000 per day from crime. In one three-month spate of offending he committed more than 180 burglaries, stealing property with a total worth of about £750,000.[18]

In 1999 inmates from another young offenders prison admitted to earning large sums from dozens of robberies which they said they spent on items such as expensive clothes and jewellery.[19] One was asked if his ability to go into an exclusive sports outfitters and pay for a thousand pounds' worth of sports clothes *in cash* was worth two years inside? He replied that he 'would be out in three months', the result of 50 per cent automatic remission, three months early release on the tag and some remand time taken into account. From a business point of view, his is a difficult case to knock down.

Another unrepentant young offender interviewed in his cell also asked why he should go straight and earn £100 per week when he could earn over £1,000 a day from crime. On a good day he said he could earn £1,250 from theft and burglary, while a bad day earns him just £100 – hardly worth going out for in his opinion.[20] Another group of prolific offenders were identified as making £100,000 a year from their crimes.[21]

Figure 8.2, based on 2000 Home Office data, shows the percentage of prisoners who are reconvicted within two years of their release by their original offence. For example, 57 per cent of those sentenced for robbery are reconvicted within the two-year period, whilst for burglars it is 78 per cent. There may be a number of reasons for these differences in reconviction rates, but one way to view this chart is to see it as a measure of how determined burglars are to return to crime – because it pays so well. The tiny risk the burglar

Figure 8.2: Percentage of prisoners reconvicted within two years by original offence

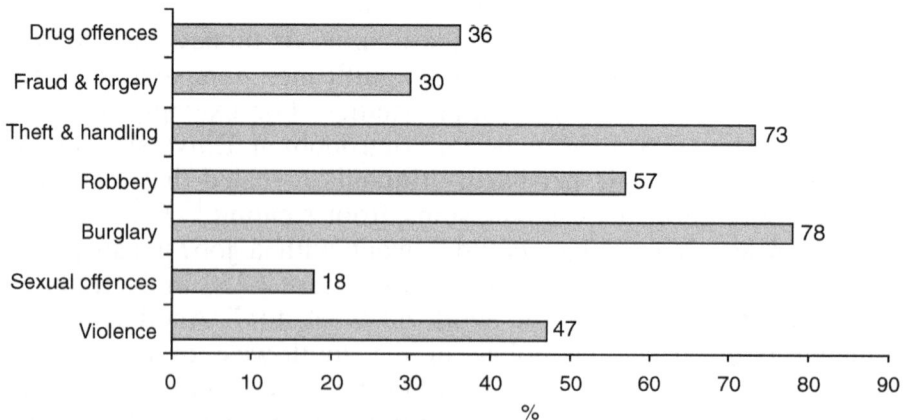

Source: Home Office Findings 154, *Prison Population in 2000: A Statistical Review*

runs of imprisonment is well worth taking against the considerable financial gains from their crimes. The recent pronouncement by the Lord Chief Justice that burglars should get their first job 'for free' and not be sent to prison will no doubt have increased its popularity even more than is displayed in these figures.[22]

Persistent Offender Myths

Apologists for persistent offenders have described them as disadvantaged, leading a chaotic lifestyle, having low self-esteem, as being poor achievers with few life and job skills, and whose offences are frequently 'spontaneous' and unplanned. These are inventions, dreamed up by those who wish to excuse them their criminal behaviour. None of the persistent offenders I knew came anywhere near fitting this description. Indeed, what stood out about them was their sharpness, their ability to think and move fast, and their willingness to exploit any opportunity to carry on offending. They were confident and often audacious; having a poor self-image was the least of their problems.

Those who come from disadvantaged beginnings are not obliged to commit crime. I know people who have lived in care, and others whose early home life was broken by divorce or other reasons. None of them has become criminal. They chose to struggle against the odds in a law-abiding way. Some of them have done well in life; others have not and are still poor and disadvantaged. Yet they have chosen to lead the straight life and show respect for others and their property.

'Poor Achievers'

Persistent offenders do not turn to crime because they are 'poor achievers'. They have, as I have said, forsaken the conventional and slower route to personal achievement in favour of a quicker route offered by crime. I have interviewed hundreds of persistent offenders during my career in the Probation Service and I can assure the reader that they do not see themselves as 'under-achievers', a label given to them by others. On the contrary, they are often very successful. Most never work in the conventional sense, yet they are able to buy expensive clothes, spend large amounts on enjoying themselves, and generally live well. Occasionally they are caught, but they treat the community penalties they are almost invariably given as a licence to offend. Should they be in the tiny minority who go to jail, it is only for a short period, often measured in weeks, which they experience as no more than a minor irritant. The inmates' property room in the young offender prison where I worked was full of the most expensive designer jeans, top-of-the-range trainers and very expensive leather jackets, not holed shoes and ragged clothes. These young men were not underprivileged, pushed unwillingly into crime by crushing social and psychological circumstances beyond their control. On the contrary, they were, in the main, determined and resourceful individuals who had got the taste of easy money in their mouth.

This is not a taste they are willing to give up, even when increased security measures appear to thwart them. For example, in 2002 the outbreak of 'carjacking' in which at least one victim was killed by his assailants because he resisted them, was a direct result of the improvements in the security of expensive cars, making it difficult for the thieves to overcome their sophisticated alarms and locking devices. As a result they used the simpler method of ambushing the driver while he or she was in the car and using violence to eject them, or of stealing the keys from their home.[23]

'Out of Control and in Need of Help'

Many probation officers will protest at this picture I paint of persistent criminals. They will point out that they often live in substandard accommodation or sometimes have no fixed address, living casually with different friends. This is true of some, but their living conditions are self-imposed, not forced on them by necessity. This sometimes disorganised lifestyle, their disruptive behaviour at school when younger, their propensity for violence and sometimes heavy drinking, and their persistent offending are portrayed by the Probation Service as evidence of the offender's 'criminogenic' needs for which they require help. But the idea that his *bad* behaviour (a word that those who work with criminals are not allowed to use today) is beyond the offender's control and represents a 'need' is, as already pointed out, a preposterous myth created by his probation minders to protect him from the consequences of his criminal way of life.

I can recall that the case histories of many of the young offender prison inmates typically spoke of their unruly and destructive behaviour at school, an inability to concentrate, and their uncontrollable temper outbursts and violence, all of which had kept them under the constant attention of child guidance clinics, psychologists and social workers for years. However, in many cases this view of them as damaged individuals, at the mercy of behavioural forces beyond their control, turned out to be false, because in the prison they showed normal self-control and generally behaved themselves. During my visits to the school wing in the prison, for example, I saw these young fourteen to seventeen-year-olds, sitting quietly at their desks and concentrating on their work. What had happened to all of those uncontrollable behavioural problems which had made them unmanageable in the classroom before they came into prison, and for which many of them had been treated by psychologists and child guidance clinics for so long?

I came to the conclusion that the major factor in their transformation was that these young prisoners knew that disruptive behaviour of any kind would result in the teacher immediately summoning an impressively large prison officer, who was always on duty at the door of the classroom in the event he was needed. This could result in the prisoner spending time in the isolation block, which, though not harmful, was an extremely unpleasant experience. So to avoid this, they behaved themselves, and some even made respectable progress with their schoolwork, an achievement long thought impossible by those who regarded them as beyond control and impossible to teach.

One particular example of this kind stands out. The institution received a fifteen-year-old prisoner who, his file warned, defecated at the first sign of conflict with adults. He had learnt from an early age that this was a very effective form of blackmail which he could use to get his own way. As a result he had been the subject of psychological assessment and treatment for this 'problem' for many years. On his reception into the prison, this young offender was given an instruction by the reception officer which he did not want to carry out. He employed his well-rehearsed tactic and promptly defecated. The prison officer was not thrown by this act of defiance, and he calmly and firmly pointed out to the boy that he could repeat this infantile behaviour all day if he so wished, but he would still have to do as he was told. The boy was told to clean himself up, which he did, and later, wearing his prison issue clothing, he was

207

moved from the reception area to his accommodation in the prison. He was with us for approximately three months and during the whole of that time he never repeated this behaviour, providing ample evidence that, faced with well-disposed, authoritative adults who were prepared to use the sanctions available to them, he was able to control himself and do as he was told.

In 1998 Britain's first privately run jail for twelve to fourteen-year-olds came to grief only seven months after it was opened because the teaching and supervisory staff, having been told to approach the inmates 'nicely' as they were 'disturbed' and in need of 'help', were left without any suitable back-up when faced with violence and rule breaking by the inmates. The young prisoners saw the absence of control as an opportunity to show how much they resented being locked up and indulged in outbursts of destructive and violent behaviour and constant attempts to escape. A riot brought things to a head, and staff, on whom the inmates had inflicted non-stop misery, cheered with relief when the police arrived with dogs to regain control. Prison officers were then imported into the jail. After a firm regime was introduced, based on the clear knowledge that sanctions would be used to control violent and other forms of disorderly conduct, the inmates demonstrated they could behave themselves and no similar incidents have been reported since.[24]

'The Myth of Low Self-Esteem'

It is often argued that one reason why the persistent offender commits crime is because it helps him prop up his poor self-image. The apologists argue that we should therefore help the offender develop feelings of self-esteem by answering his need for psychological and other forms of help, including the provision of job skills and regular work.

Two well-known criminologists, in a paper published in 2001, have written: 'Those who work with offenders often identify a connection between perceptions of self-worth and the social and educational circumstances of those who habitually break the law.'[25] I have always rejected this as a pure fabrication, dreamt up by those more interested in protecting the criminal than changing him. Certainly I never recognised any of the persistent offenders I knew as a probation officer as being short of self-confidence. Most of them positively bounced with self-belief. They could not have stolen lorries, burgled houses, robbed post offices, mugged individuals, stolen cash, or planned raids on shops and warehouses, to name but some of their crimes, had they been shrinking violets.

Research results published by the London School of Economics in November 2001 found that people with 'high self-esteem' could pose a greater menace to society than those with less high opinions of themselves. Furthermore, it concluded that low self-esteem is one of the most popular explanations for social problems such as crime, violence, drug and alcohol dependence, but that, based on the research findings, these beliefs were shown to be myths.[26]

Soft Targets and Easy Pickings

Another excuse put up for many persistent offenders is that their offending is spontaneous and unplanned, to be seen, as it were, as a feature of their disorganised, chaotic and underprivileged lifestyle, and for which they need help rather than condemnation. Even if this were so it would be irrelevant; it makes no difference to a victim whether he or she was robbed and terrified by an unwashed and unshaven criminal, who having fallen out of bed late, attacked his target on the spur of the moment whilst on his way to collect his social security benefit, or as a result of a well-laid ambush. However, all that we know about persistent offenders tells us that his choice of victims and criminal targets is anything but spontaneous.

This was starkly revealed by research from Manchester Metropolitan University, which in 1998 identified that in areas where zero-tolerance policing had been introduced, criminals had responded by altering the times and areas they operated in an attempt to become less predictable and harder to catch. Others, identified by the researchers as 'crime surfers', shifted between different offences in order to confuse the police.[27]

In December 2001 it was reported that up to 300,000 pensioners were being robbed of £40 million a year as a result of distraction burglaries. Three-quarters of the victims were women, with an average age of 81, and nine out of ten victims lived alone. It is known that some of the criminals involved travelled up to 400 miles a day to commit as many as 33 offences in 10 different police force areas. This cold-blooded targeting of the frail and elderly who are

Figure 8.3: Percentage of burglaries occurring at different periods

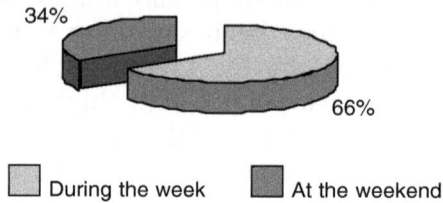

34%

66%

☐ During the week   ■ At the weekend

Source: Home Office Bulletin 1/03, *Crime in England & Wales, 2001/2002*

easily confused and unlikely to offer resistance hardly fits the description of chaotic and unplanned criminality.[28]

Likewise, there is nothing unplanned about the majority of burglaries in the UK, which, as reported in Home Office crime figures for 2001/02, and displayed in Figure 8.3, occur when there is less likelihood of the burglar being disturbed and detected by anyone in the house. Similarly, data from the same source (Figure 8.4) shows that the majority of burglars prefer to work under the cover of darkness, which again flies in the face of their crimes being 'spontaneous'.

There is nothing new about these patterns. Research carried out at Cambridge University showed that twenty-five years ago crime figures relating to the time burglaries occurred told the same story. This (1975) data displayed in Figures 8.5 and 8.6 shows that during weekdays burglars preferred to target houses in the middle of the day, when most people would be out. For Saturdays and Sundays the picture was reversed, with fewest burglaries occurring in the middle of the day, when the majority of people would be at home. There is nothing here that speaks of 'spur of the moment crimes'. This pattern shows planning and forethought.

Figure 8.4: When burglaries occur

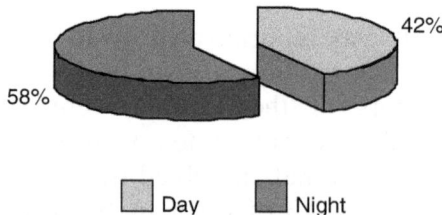

42%

58%

☐ Day   ■ Night

Source: Home Office Bulletin 1/03, *Crime in England & Wales, 2001/2002*

Figure 8.5: Thursday – burglary data for Thames Valley, 1975

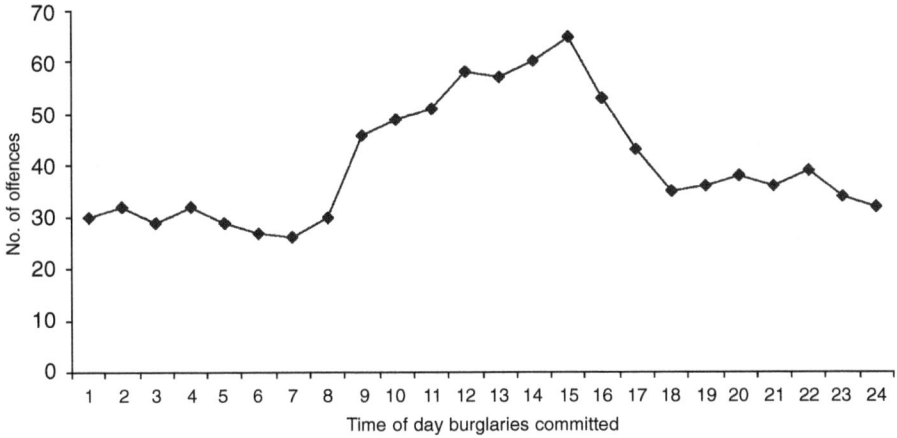

Source: T. Bennett and R. Wright, 'Burglars on Burglary', unpublished paper, Cambridge University, 1975

In 1994 a government study of a sample of 130 repeat property offenders nearing the end of their prison sentence revealed that their criminality was not 'opportunistic', as they calculated very carefully the risk of capture before committing a crime. In addition, they predicted their likelihood of reoffending following their release,

Figure 8.6: Saturday – burglary data for Thames Valley, 1975

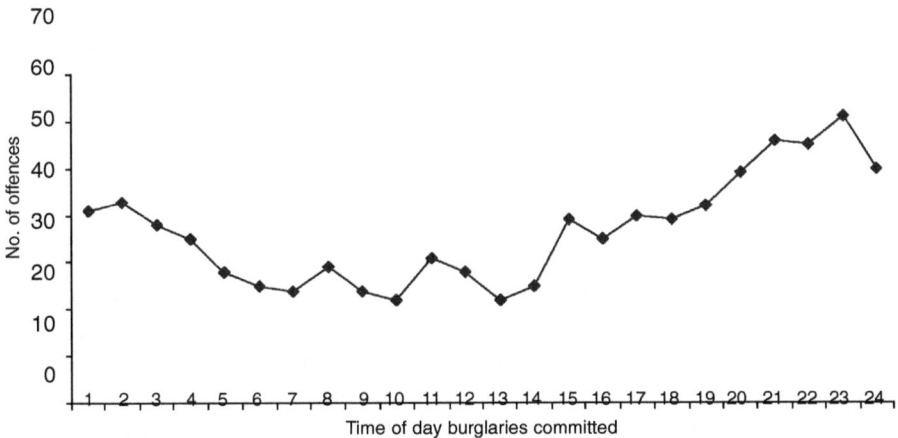

Source: T. Bennett and R. Wright, 'Burglars on Burglary', unpublished paper, Cambridge University, 1975

211

which completely undermines any notion that their crimes are committed 'on the spur of the moment'.[29]

Similarly, a 1995 Home Office enquiry into crimes against retail premises found that they were most at risk of burglary at night, at the weekend, and when there were no staff on the premises. Likewise, they were most likely to be the subject of a robbery after 6 p.m. and when shopkeepers were alone in the shop.[30] Again, none of these sound remotely like crimes committed on the spur of the moment by disorganised, chaotic individuals with low self-esteem who are not thinking properly. On the contrary, they reveal, from the criminal's point of view, confidence, a clear head, well-judged planning and lots of determination.

These features were well displayed by criminal gangs reported on in 1998 who were ambushing cars in broad daylight and stealing laptop computers, mobile phones, briefcases and handbags from the drivers. These attacks were well coordinated with the thieves communicating with each other using mobile phones to strike their victims while they waited at traffic lights.[31]

It is also the case that many crimes are committed by those said to be drug addicts; whilst this may be true the details of their offending reveal that their heads are clear enough to enable them to choose their victims with great care, indicating a measure of preplanning in order to minimise the risk to themselves. I have several reports on my desk which illustrate, for example, that many burglars and thieves deliberately target old people. One of these, dated 2001, describes how a criminal, who was also a drug addict, singled out a 77-year-old woman living on her own and broke into her home and robbed her of hundreds of pounds. Another tells how a crack-cocaine addict preyed on old people's homes, carefully targeting them for burglary.[32]

In 2002 three violent drug-taking offenders were sentenced for a string of robberies at a crown court in the south-west of England. At their trial it was revealed that in order to steal money to feed their crack-cocaine habit, they had driven around looking for women, elderly women or otherwise, with a view to robbing them. In this way they had robbed and terrorised several defenceless female victims, two of whom were in their eighties.[33] Drug addicts these offenders may have been but it did not prevent them from carefully choosing victims who would offer little or no resistance. Likewise, it is a known fact that burglars are particularly active at Christmas

Figure 8.7: Coded messages left by burglars on front doors and gate posts

wealthy house	burglar alarm	good target for burglary	soft women easily conned
nervous and afraid	nothing worth stealing	already burgled	too risky

time. Again this points to thought and planning before the crimes are committed.[34]

Whilst working as a criminal intelligence analyst, I came across a particularly powerful example of the cold-blooded way in which persistent offenders go about their business. I was given a copy of coded messages left by burglars (Figure 8.7), which had been scratched on the front doors of houses or gate posts; these indicated to other burglars whether the house was worth burgling, whether it was a soft target, or too risky, as well as other features they should know about. These coded messages speak to us from a dark and criminal underworld; they provide a powerful illustration that what separates repeat offenders from the rest of society is not deprived or underprivileged backgrounds but their greed and lack of conscience.

This last point was illustrated by a particular experience I had whilst working in a Young Offenders Prison. I was called to the hospital office to help the staff who were concerned by an eighteen-year-old prisoner who, I was told, 'was very upset and would not stop crying'. I sat quietly with the six-foot, fourteen-stone youth for a while, and he eventually told me he was 'missing home' and that he 'didn't like it in prison'. I told him I was glad to hear it and that the remedy was in his own hands. I then suggested to him that whilst he was crying he should shed some of his tears for the victims he had hurt and whose lives he had severely disrupted. He stopped crying immediately, and his mood changed from one of self-pity to resentment. I handed him back to the staff dry-eyed.

Pardoned, Protected and Excused

It is a peculiarly unhealthy aspect of our criminal justice system that it goes out of its way to indulge those who continually commit crime. In his very fine book *They Call it Justice*, Brian Lawrence, a lawyer with thirty-six years experience of work in the magistrates' courts, contrasts the leniency shown by magistrates towards criminals who have committed offences such as burglary, theft, assault and so on, with their draconian punishments for driving offences.[35] I am not arguing against tough measures to deal with driving offences; such an approach is entirely consistent with the need to uphold the law and protect the public. What is wrong is the way in which the courts in the UK indulge persistent criminals, and others make excuses for them. By contrast, in the early 1990s many law-abiding people who were struggling to make ends meet were not given a second chance by their town hall when they had difficulty in making their 'poll tax' payment. They were not allowed to plead a special case and no excuses were accepted from them.

This could not contrast more to the pitiful mitigation pleas taken account of by the courts when dealing with criminals. I have actually heard solicitors say, for example, 'My client agrees there was a fight outside of the café but he does not know how the knife came to be in his hand, your worship, it all happened so quickly.' In relation to a burglary prosecution where the defendant had been caught red-handed equipped with housebreaking tools in a house, another solicitor said, 'My client had consumed a large amount of alcohol and does not know how he got there.' In another example known to me, the police found a criminal standing next to a smashed parking meter with a lump hammer in his hands. He later told the magistrates that he had no idea how the meter came to be smashed. No other evidence was offered and he walked free.

A more recent indulgence for offenders allows them to plead guilty so that they can get a discount on the sentence. They then submit a basis of plea, which is a written statement describing their offence. These are frequently worded as to almost amount to a

214

denial of their guilt. Faced with such a document thirty years ago, the court would have responded by making the defendant change his plea to not guilty. Not today. The court accepts the near-denial of his guilt implied in his statement, and so is able to treat him with *additional* leniency. The system is more than willing to collude with this malpractice as it cuts down the chances of a prison sentence.[36]

I have heard barristers and solicitors claim that their client committed offences because he was 'bored and had nothing in his life to engage his energies'. A frequent tactic of defence lawyers and probation officers is to blame someone else for the crimes committed by an offender. 'He was misled by more experienced criminal minds' was a phrase I heard many times. In 1995 the then Chief Prison Inspector offered the excuse for offenders jailed for violence that their offences were the result of 'stupidity'.[37] Even if this was the case for a minority of such cases (which I very much doubt), what difference does it make to the victims? Their injuries and trauma remain the same.

Most of the offenders I have known who committed crimes of violence were anything but stupid. They were callous, sometimes psychopathic individuals who above all else wanted their own way and were prepared to hurt others to get it. This was illustrated by a brutal attack against a probation officer in 1992 when a criminal resident of a probation hostel in south London broke into the staff quarters during the night where a lone female staff member on duty was sleeping. The criminal bound and gagged her and then hit her over the head with an iron bar. He then stole money and her car. She needed eighteen stitches to a head wound and was lucky to survive.[38] At 4 p.m. one Wednesday in 1967, a criminal whose parole licence I was supervising presented himself to me in my office in north London; it later emerged that he was setting me up to be his alibi for a violent robbery which he had perpetrated in Birmingham around midday. His excuse was that he could not have carried out the crime and had time to reach my office. He had, of course, and had driven at high speed down the motorway in order to make his entrance. Such violent acts as these are not instigated by stupidity, and to describe them as such is to deny their cold-blooded, criminal purposefulness.

The variety of excuses offered for persistent criminals never ceases to amaze me. In 1988 a chief probation officer took me to task in a letter, over my stance towards persistent offenders (they often did). With the most blatant example of psycho-babble I believe I have ever heard, he excused their criminal behaviour by saying that 'offenders were ambivalent about their criminal actions and it was the duty of probation officers to engage with this ambivalence'. When I reread this sentence in his letter (I have it still in my possession) words fail me, as they did then.[39]

In that same year I rang the organiser of a community supervision scheme for offenders in Basingstoke which had been reported in the press as a successful alternative to imprisonment. It did not take long to discover that this was not true. Well over two-thirds of the offenders had committed more offences while still on the scheme, and they were only the ones known about. When I pointed this out, I was told in all seriousness by the organiser that it was the architect's fault for creating a design of house in this particular town that made it too easy for offenders to burgle them.[40]

In April 2004 during a discussion on Radio 4's *Today* programme on rape I actually heard a local community worker say that gang rape 'can be a cry for help on the part of the young men who carry it out'.[41] For once, even the programme's presenters were speechless.

In Chapter Five, I have identified how few offenders are caught, and even less prosecuted or sent to prison. A visit to any magistrates' court will show the extent to which the persistent offender is indulged and cosseted; the courts bend over backwards to find any excuse to keep him in the community. Government figures show for example that in 2000 36 per cent of those found guilty of violence against the person were cautioned, the equivalent figure for those found guilty of burglary was 20 per cent.[42] As a result, the persistent offender is allowed to go around the sentencing tariff system several times before he is even considered for a prison sentence. He knows he can offend with impunity because if he is caught he can expect to repeatedly receive conditional discharges, fines, probation supervision, community service and deferred sentences, stretching over a long period. These indulgences allow him, as the evidence shows, to go on pursuing his career as a criminal.

Sometimes the courts seem paralysed by the sheer bravado of persistent offenders. In 2001, for example, a 37-year-old repeat offender was placed on probation by magistrates in the south-west of the country for committing several crimes. Instead of taking the view he was lucky not to go to jail, he abused the leniency shown

216

to him and refused to cooperate. He was eventually returned to court for failure to comply with the conditions of his order. As if transfixed by his defiance, the court gave him more of the same and passed a community service order. No one, it seems, not even the clerk of the court, was able to ask them why they expected him to fulfil the conditions of a community service order requiring him to work for so many hours a week when he had totally failed to comply with a probation order. Such examples are legion.[43]

A parliamentary report, issued by the 1998 All Party Home Affairs Committee on Alternatives to Prison, highlighted that probation officers frequently protected the criminals they supervised by failing to record violations of their probation conditions, and that three out of four who failed to comply were not punished.[44] Likewise, I have made previous reference to the fact that thousands of arrest warrants taken out in respect of offenders under supervision in the community have been ignored. The scale of this problem can be deduced from evidence given to the same All Party Home Affairs Committee, which was that in a number of counties there were as many as 20,000 warrants outstanding.[45] If we assume that only half of these were for breach of probation or community service orders, it can be computed that for the whole of the country there are at least half a million unexecuted arrest warrants relating to criminals who have broken contact with their probation officer and disappeared. It is salutary to work out that even on the very conservative estimate of five offences each per year, this cosseted and protected group of criminals would have committed over two and a half million crimes in the space of twelve months (see Note 1).

The Right to Riot

The excuse offered for the immense damage caused by prisoners in the UK jail riots of the early 1990s was that they were protesting about poor and overcrowded prison conditions. Whilst no one would condone unsanitary and overcrowded jails, this excuse overlooks that generations of prisoners had previously tolerated sharing cells and slopping out prior to these orgies of violence and destructiveness. As pointed out by Lewis[46] not only were similar toilet arrangements standard for many of the working class before the Second World War, it was also common practice for them to only change their underwear once a week (one of the riot causing issues according to the then Archbishop Runcie). Lewis recalls from his long experience of working in prisons that many prisoners in open conditions petitioned to be returned to close conditions despite the conditions of three to a cell, slopping out and scant exercise, and that he never met any inmate who regarded the often quoted 'bad conditions' as crucial.

More recent rioting has all but destroyed some new state-of-the-art prison buildings, with single cells, modern toilet facilities, gymnasiums, libraries, gardens and modern visiting facilities, thus indicating the irrelevance of poor conditions as the cause. Committees of Enquiry have blamed management errors, poor physical conditions, the behaviour of some prison staff, lack of physical exercise and poor visiting conditions; indeed anything and everyone except the inmates. They fail to see the riots as demonstrations of *why* these prisoners are locked up in the first place. In 1995 the clampdown by prison staff on illicit drugs in one prison was all the excuse the inmates needed to indulge in two days of serious rioting.[47] Whilst these and other similar control measures resented by the inmates may often be the spark for a disturbance, what fuels them is that many prisoners are anti-authority, indulge in gratuitous violence, do not like being told what to do, are unrepentant and resent their incarceration.

Don't Blame Them – It's Not Their Fault

In September 2003 government figures were released which showed that many criminals who were also drug addicts were not being treated whilst in prison.[48] An opposition party spokesperson inferred it was therefore the government's fault that these offenders, when released, would continue to commit crime. His naive view was that if only the government ensured the offenders received adequate treatment whilst in jail, they would stop committing crime. This assessment is as removed from reality as it is possible to get. Such MPs should stop and ask themselves why these addict offenders did not seek help for their addiction in the community? The responsibility for their cure and reform lies entirely with the offender. If they are motivated to go straight and kick their habit, they will do so, whether the government provides them with treatment in jail or not.

218

Likewise, it is frequently reported that young people who are excluded from school as a result of behavioural problems are more likely to turn to crime.[49] The implication is that they have become criminal *because* they have been excluded from school. This, of course, is nonsense, as anyone who has worked with young persistent offenders will know. For example, in 1998 research from Southampton University found that 63 per cent of a sample of 227 young adults aged between sixteen and twenty-three who had attended an exclusion unit had a criminal record, and that their crimes had cost millions of pounds. The researchers concluded that they became delinquent because, after leaving the unit, they were 'hanging out with other delinquents with a bad reputation and there was little chance of them getting a job'. In other words, it was the fault of the system that excluded them from school that they had turned to crime. One might ask, if all delinquents can be excused their crimes because they have been 'misled by someone else', who misled the mysterious 'someone else'? The possibility that those who are disruptive at school are also those who are motivated to commit crime seems to have escaped the researchers' notice.[50]

In 1989 the then minister of state at the Home Office wrote to the Chief Probation Inspector and said, 'I know that many offenders lead chaotic and disorganised lives and *are so lacking in understanding that they do not appreciate the consequences of their actions*' (my italics).[51] Naivety of this depth from a Home Office minister is frightening, but he was expressing a view that has held on in the minds of many officials to the present day. Anyone who has knowledge of persistent offenders will be aware that they know exactly what the consequences of their crimes are and that many of them would be affronted if they knew that they were viewed in such a patronising way.

Another familiar excuse made for criminals is that committing crime is a normal part of their development. In 1995 the Association of Chief Officers of Probation expressed this ridiculous view in a document that said, 'it seems reasonable to conclude that for most young men some involvement with crime is part of their 'normal experience of growing up'.[52] The corollary of this argument, which I have often heard, is that they will eventually grow out of crime, so it would be counter-productive to criminally 'contaminate' them by sending them to prison, even though nothing else can stop them from offending.

Table 8.1: Number of offences according to age (1997)

Age of convicted or cautioned male offenders for indictable offences	10 years	18 years	26 years	34 years	42 years	50 years	56 years
No. per 100 population	1	9	3.8	1.9	1.0	0.8	0.5

Source: Home Office, Digest 9, *Information on the Criminal Justice System in England & Wales, 1999*

Although it is true that the peak age for offending is eighteen and then tails off noticeably as shown in the following table, this should not distract us from the fact that large numbers of offences are committed by criminals well into their forties and beyond (see Table 8.1). Thus the idea that all we have to do is to wait for criminals to mature, implying that their offending life is short-lived, not only ignores the effects on their victims, but is also a

Table 8.2: Percentage of males participating in offending and drug use by age group (1992)

Offence type	14–17 year olds	18–21 year olds	22–25 year olds
Property offences	17	25	27
Violent offences	12	9	4
Vandalism, graffiti, arson	8	8	0
Drug use	17	47	31
All offences (excluding drug use)	24	31	31

Source: Home Office Research Findings No. 24, *Young People and Crime, 1995*

misconception. Although some may start offending later in life, many criminals remain active for a period of at least thirty years. In addition, Table 8.2, taken from a Home Office investigation, suggests that the frequency of certain offences committed by offenders between fourteen and twenty-five years increases as they get older.

An Opened-ended Amnesty

During 1991 and 1992, the government closed all of the prisons which catered for fourteen to seventeen-year-old male persistent

220

offenders. They ignored the fact that non-custodial sentences, though tried repeatedly, had failed to reform them, and that therefore prison was the last line of defence left between these young criminals and the public. Instead, government officials were more than willing to follow the argument that it was wrong to lock up 'children', and so they removed prison as an option for them altogether.

In 2000 crime figures were released which showed that from 1992, the exact year of the prison closures, there had been a sharp rise in offences among boys aged fourteen to seventeen years.[53] It could have been predicted. Closing prisons for this age group was as good as giving them an opened-ended amnesty for their then current and future crimes, and they took full advantage of it. Before the end of the decade, their unbridled criminal activity was regularly making the headlines,[54] and in 1998 the Prime Minister announced his intentions to tackle juvenile offenders who were then thought to be responsible for 40 per cent of all street robberies in the capital as well as a third of the car theft and burglaries.[55]

By the turn of the millennium, the problem was so acute that the shadow Conservative Home Secretary was promising beleaguered members of a crime-ridden estate in east London that her party, if elected to government, would send child gang leaders to jail, only eight years after it had closed prisons for juveniles when it was in power.[56] The Labour government, not wanting to be outdone, jumped in with an announcement of a new law allowing the courts to impose custodial sentences on offenders as young as twelve years old.[57] It emerged that local authority secure units, which had been used as an alternative for juvenile offenders, had been a failure; there were far too few of them, and most were unable to properly contain the sometimes acute discipline and behavioural problems of these offenders, who, whilst young in years, were often hardened and remorseless criminals. It was also revealed that in one eight-month period, between April and December 1999, more than one thousand boys aged fifteen and sixteen were remanded in custody. The figure for boys under seventeen years remanded in custody was 1,068. Significantly, this was *more than double* the 440 who were held on remand in 1992.[58]

Nothing could demonstrate more powerfully the adage that if you reward bad behaviour you will get more of it. This misplaced and disastrous act of generosity towards young criminals in the form of an unrestricted prison amnesty is paralleled by a similar gesture

221

associated with the eighteenth-century French philosopher Jean d'Alembert. He believed that it was possible to transform the most evil human by kind and considerate behaviour. He persuaded an official to allow one violent criminal to avoid a prison sentence and instead be allowed into his custody. D'Alembert sent the man to stay in a comfortable chateau near Provence, where he slaughtered the cook, his wife and her lover.[59]

Similarly, the police, probation staff and others in the UK pay a high price for their daily contact with unrepentant and sometimes dangerous criminals who, from the point of view of justice and the safety of the public, should be in prison. In the next chapter, I will discuss how the growing defiance of the persistent offender, his refusal to change, and obvious triumph at repeatedly defeating the forces of law and order, have sapped the morale and sense of purpose from the police, probation staff and others forced to deal with him. In chapter ten I will focus on the equally high price paid by the public for being compelled by the government to play host to hundreds of thousands of offenders, many of them psychopathic and beyond reform, whose sole interest is to do them harm.

Chapter 9

Subversion, Defeat and Statistics of Terror

Persistent offenders allowed their freedom place huge financial burdens on individual victims and on society generally; in addition, they are without conscience for the harm they do to others, abuse the leniency shown to them by the courts, take advantage of every opening they are given to commit more crime, are contemptuous of probation 'help' and supervision, can be violent and menacing, flout their disregard for the police and revel in their ability to escape justice by whatever means. Yet despite this, because of government policy, approximately 155,000 of them are on community sentences at any one time.[1] As a result of this indulgence, the effects on the police, probation and other criminal justice staff, who on a daily basis are forced to engage with them, have been highly destructive.

The Subversion of the Probation Service

In the 1970s a shift in government policy caused a significant change in the focus of the Probation Service's work. No longer were they to concentrate on supervising low-risk first and second-time offenders in a bid to divert them from a life of crime; their new mission was to divert persistent offenders from prison by persuading courts to place them on probation, in the mistaken belief that by so doing, they could reform them.

Not once did senior probation management challenge or question the wisdom of this extraordinary turn of events, and the service has paid a high price for their unwise and more than willing acceptance of this new brief. This once noble service has been brought to its knees by the non-stop torment from contact with offenders who

223

refuse to reform, flagrantly ignore the rules governing their supervision in the community, gloat at the court's unwillingness to imprison them, and who have increasingly subjected probation staff to intimidation and violent physical attacks.[2]

Sickness and Denial

As a result, the morale of the Probation Service in general has declined to an alarming degree, and many staff now exhibit a sense of hopelessness, with high levels of stress and sickness increasingly evident.

Faced with such relentless and incontrovertible evidence of failure, it is not surprising that research involving a large sample of UK probation staff discovered that their mental health and stress levels compare badly with other employment groups. It also found high levels of 'burn-out' among staff; this and absence from work were all outcomes significantly associated with a sense of failure.[3] My contact with other probation areas suggests that this is widespread.

As a result, much of the effort of probation officers is devoid of real meaning and assumes the offender will carry on offending; there is no longer any conviction in the endeavour to strive against his criminality,[4] and the pointlessness of supervising offenders who refuse to reform has left many staff with a sense of meaninglessness about their work. Yet this cannot be acknowledged, and the strain associated with maintaining a pretence of effectiveness and success has resulted in many probation officers retreating into denial or illness and long periods of absence from work. High sickness rates are now common. For example, the Kent Probation Service annual report for 2001–02 states: 'We continue to suffer from high sickness rates.'[5] In 2003 the West Midlands service reported an average sickness rate of more than four working weeks (twenty-one days) per year for each probation officer;[6] at the other end of the country in Gwent the average number of days lost each year through sickness for probation staff was almost eighteen.[7] For the Avon and Somerset Probation Service it was seventeen and a half days.[8] Added to their annual leave, this means that on average, probation officers are away from work for almost three months a year.

Denial of failure and defeat can take many forms. Staff in one service refused to accept the evidence I showed them that offenders under supervision victimised millions of members of the public each year. Similarly throughout my twenty-six years in the Probation Service it never once acknowledged its inability to reform persistent offenders under its supervision, even though it stood knee-deep in the evidence of its own failure; instead, as mentioned earlier, it turned to the invention of meaningless success criteria to provide the illusion of achievement. The futility of the Probation Service in hurling itself at one failed work method after another – such as group work, pro-social modelling, family therapy, cognitive therapy and restorative justice – is, I believe, a clear demonstration of this denial mechanism.

In 1997 a local Probation Service known to me organised a conference called '2001 … A Probation Odyssey' to display and discuss its ambitious work objectives for the coming period. These included its plans to embrace the latest legislation, a strategy to 'demonstrate its effectiveness', another to embrace 'quality assurance'. To show it meant business, senior members of the criminal justice world were invited to attend as guest speakers.[9] However, the zeal demonstrated by this impressive agenda was a mask for deep strains and stresses caused by the service trying to achieve the impossible with unrepentant persistent offenders. Shortly after this conference, dominated by themes of 'effectiveness' and 'quality assurance' and backed up by propaganda proclaiming a 94 per cent success rate[10] with young offenders, it was judged by the Home Office to be a 'failed service', and the chief officer and the chairperson of the employing committee were invited to fall on their swords, bringing their probation odyssey to an abrupt end.

Make Work and Management Babble

The Probation Service has wrecked itself on the rocks of self-delusion by believing it could achieve hopelessly unattainable goals such as reforming criminals who are unmotivated to change. Rather than acknowledge this failure, it has retreated into an unreal world of 'probation speak'. A continuous stream of 'action plans' policies and papers frequently expressed in meaningless jargon have been the only results of their wasted effort. For example, one article published by *The Journal of the Association of Chief Officers of Probation* in 1998 states:

225

'There is a tendency in courts and other social agencies toward decoupling performance evaluation from external social objectives...'[11]

Another paper in the same journal urged probation officers to be aware that:

'Professional discretion is imperative to effective practice, but it ought to be informed by a coherent vision of a service perspective that encapsulates certain common objectives which transcend the bounds of individual practice.'

A little later, the directorate of the National Probation Service (NPS) issued a statement which said:

'The NPS will use its reform programme to weave its values and expectations into its development and planning.'[12]

One local probation area described itself thus:

'We have a system of strategic management based on the concept of effectiveness.'[13]

The senior management team of another local service chose to describe itself to staff in a statement that read:

'We are leaders of leaders and this will be reflected in our thinking and actions.

Faced with deadlines and limited resources we continue to strive for both task and process achievement.

Our purpose of providing credible alternatives to custody is urgent and important but we maintain enjoyment in our work.

We delight in the differences between people.

Our organisation will be healthy and holistic; endorsing staff commitment to home, family, self and acknowledges that the whole person needs to function.'[14]

226

Given the chronic sickness rates of the staff they managed this must stand out as one of its more memorable if vacuous aspirations.

Refusing to engage with the evidence from the real world which shows a horror story of reconvictions of those under its supervision, the Probation Service has instead created an industry of 'make-work', consisting of countless meetings and policy edicts, the production of propaganda news bulletins as well as detailed plans for group work programmes for offenders which the majority ignore and none are influenced by.[15] Life is a merry-go-round of reviews, organisational changes and form filling, in response to an insatiable appetite for more and more questionable information used for the production of hollow and misleading statistics. In October 2002 the NPS started the process of introducing yet another method of collecting statistical information for the Home Office that requires at least twenty-five pages to be completed every time a probation officer writes a court report on an offender. Form filling for probation staff now takes up more of their working day than anything else. In addition, even the chief executive of the National Probation Boards Association has been moved to comment on the paperwork blizzard cascading from the Home Office down to the forty-two probation areas, who, as a result, have had to cope with a deluge of manuals, circulars, protocols, reports, returns and statistics from an ever-increasing number of civil servants.[16]

Over recent years the Probation Service has turned to producing hollow Stalinist-like slogans whose purpose is to keep alive the myth that it is 'tackling offending',[17] or 'confronting offending',[18] or offering 'enforcement, rehabilitation and public protection',[19] whose specious terms protect the Probation Service from any real accountability. As its management style has become increasingly frenzied, calling on staff to 'strive' to reach unobtainable objectives, it has had to become more and more authoritarian in response to dissent. The constant flurry of management-instigated 'policy reviews' and the monitoring of results are frequently a sham, as they are carried out without reference to the only meaningful criterion for success, namely the numbers of criminals under supervision who stop offending. The pursuit of policies aimed at keeping persistent offenders out of prison has resulted in the Probation Service losing its heart. Over the years the crime rate has soared in the face of its unreal claims of success; it appears to have anaesthetised itself against reality by retreating more and more into a make-believe

227

world filled with pseudo-activity, couched in the language of management babble.

The Retreat into Political Correctness

During the 1980s and 1990s the Probation Service generally became obsessed with political correctness, particularly with regard to anti-racism and issues of gender. There is of course a place for these principles in our society; no right-minded person would agree with oppression and intolerance, whatever its source. However, in many probation areas, for almost a decade stretching into the 1990s, these issues took precedence over all else, and self-appointed political gatekeepers became the oppressors of an increasingly bewildered and frightened workforce. In a bid to challenge this preoccupation with political correctness, Melanie Phillips wrote in the *Observer* on 1 August 1993, that training courses (for trainee probation officers) were full of 'illiberal gobbledegook' which, for example, made sure they understood the 'processes of structural oppression, race, class and gender', and made them aware of 'individual and institutional racism and ways to combat both through anti-race practice'. What is more, Professor Pinker, Professor of Social Work at the London School of Economics, pointed out (*Daily Mail*, 2 August 1993), that unless students followed this ideological line they would not get their qualification.

In some areas, probation chiefs, aware that they had failed to impact on crime, all but abandoned their normal responsibilities and turned themselves into twentieth-century witch-hunters, on the lookout for examples of 'racism' or 'sexism'. In the early 1980s, in one service known to me a hapless middle manager working in a prison mildly rebuked a visiting probation officer for the decrepit state of her identity card. He described it as 'Mickey Mouse', which accurately described the card in question. The probation officer complained to the senior management that by using this phrase he had behaved in a racist manner towards her. This surprised him for a number of reasons – not the least of which was that he had thought she was a white person. She was in fact very pale-skinned and of Anglo-Indian extraction; however, she thought of herself as black. The bewildered middle manager was arraigned before a formal disciplinary board and put through a degrading and farcical 'trial'. His accuser was never present, and the senior managers and members of his employing committee who sat in judgment over him ignored his perfectly reasonable defence that 'Mickey Mouse' was an accurate description of the card and was in no way a reference to the probation officer. The board found against him and the chief officer claimed his first anti-racist scalp. Those who climbed onto the anti-racist platform in this way enjoyed enormous power over the workforce, who, though innocent of any racist intent, soon became afraid that anything they said might be wrongfully interpreted as racist by ideological zealots.

In another example, again in the 1980s, a black senior probation manager gave an interview to the press and said that 'all white people in the criminal justice system were racist'.[20] This sweeping comment caused offence and amazement to large numbers of people, who nevertheless kept quiet because of the intimidating atmosphere at the time. One white staff member did speak out and complained that, apart from being very foolish, this was a violently racist statement. His protests were crushed by the management who publicly sided with the black manager.

In just one year, one particular local Probation Service spent £60,000 on 'gender awareness' from its training budget and only £4,000 on training associated with work with criminals.[21] Probation representatives generally took every opportunity to flex their politically correct muscles. In 1990, at the NAPO annual conference in Brighton, officials, in a public display of their 'anti-sexist' credentials, covered the naked breasts of angels adorning the sides of the platform.[22] In 1993 the NAPO conference was to have been held at Bridlington but was moved because the resort was thought to be 'racist and heterosexual'.[23] The Probation Service also found other ways to express its political correctness. For example, on one occasion a local Probation Service in the north of the country offered financial compensation and a formal apology to a drug dealer for his 'hurt feelings' after reading a probation report suggesting a long prison sentence.[24] The offender complained that the report had caused him a 'high anxiety level as he waited to be sentenced'. NAPO also campaigned for prisoners to have the right to vote. They clearly hold the view that convicted thieves, burglars, robbers and murderers have a legitimate role in deciding how the country is governed.[25] A London Probation Service recommended that a professional pickpocket should be sentenced to a 'period counselling young offenders'.[26]

The Criminal's Champion

Unable to reform persistent criminals, the Probation Service has, over the last thirty years, become their champion. Perhaps to find purpose for their existence, they are for ever on the lookout for every opportunity to defend the reputations and rights of the very criminals who torment them with their violence, continued offending and displays of contempt. According to one internal document I have seen, the Probation Service sees itself as having to 'fight for a share of resources in order to *access services for offenders*' (my italics).[27] This can be taken to extremes. I have been told that, in a bid to maintain their numbers and Home Office funding, probation hostel staff will sometimes overlook drug use and possession by their residents rather than take them back to court.[28] In 1992 the then Home Secretary Kenneth Baker launched a car-crime prevention scheme and probation chiefs expressed their concern at the campaign's portrayal of offenders as cowards preying on the defenceless victims, causing misery and death. Almost unbelievably, they complained that this created a climate of intolerance.[29] In 2001 the Probation Service criticised what it saw as tougher sentencing plans because it feared that it would cause overcrowding in the prisons.[30]

Many years ago I was directed by my then probation superiors to ensure that certain phrases were not used in probation reports written for the courts. We were forbidden to describe an offender as a 'recidivist', as this was thought to stereotype him, despite the fact that it accurately described the majority of offenders being reported on. We were also told to avoid undermining the defendant's credibility with phrases such as 'he presents a surface appearance of compliance with supervision requirements', even when this was the truth.[31] In other words, no matter how guilty an offender was of criminal or devious or untruthful behaviour, we were not to say anything that put any blame at his door. Likewise, I have on my desk a document issued by a Probation Service in the late 1980s which directed its staff not to recommend or even mention 'custody' when writing reports on offenders for the court.[32] This resulted in the making of thousands of unsuitable recommendations for leniency, in both court and parole reports, even in respect of criminals who posed a serious threat of reoffending.[33]

In 1998 the Probation Service objected to a pilot scheme that allowed courts to take away a criminal's driving licence. It was

230

intended to take many of them out of circulation by depriving them of the means of offending. The Probation Service argued that it was an 'extraordinary' penalty that would make some offenders act even more irresponsibly and drive anyway'.[34] Likewise, in 1987 the Association of Chief Officers of Probation (ACOP) criticised what they saw as an increased use of custody,[35] and, in May 1996, it complained that 'despite the Citizens Charter of 1991 and the Courts Charter of 1992, there was little evidence that offenders have actively participated in the standard setting of criminal justice'.[36]

Shell Shock

Supervising persistent offenders has created a deep sense of exhaustion and futility among probation staff, which over the years has corroded morale and not surprisingly resulted in poor work standards. In the 1980s many services developed the practice of letting offenders simply 'sign in' at the probation reception office to avoid any contact with them. Also during the 1980s the practice of home visiting was more or less abandoned. Supervision requirements were often said to have been met on the basis of a chance meeting in the street with the offender or even a telephone contact. During this period I was responsible for the Home Office Probation Training Unit in the south-west of the country, and the majority of case files handed to me by probation staff for transfer to probation trainees were in an appalling condition. In some cases, the supervising officer who handed me the file was not even aware that the probation order he had been overseeing had been cancelled months before.

In 1999 the Chief Probation Inspector's report on the work of the service was damning, and spoke of 'poor and unsatisfactory supervision plans, poor understanding of objective setting, and showed little evidence of management guidance of work with offenders'.[37] In the same year a shell-shocked Probation Service was forced to admit that thousands of hard-core offenders, who failed to carry out the terms of their community sentence, by failing to show up for their community work or other probation appointments, had faced no disciplinary action.[38] This prompted the then Home Secretary to accuse the Probation Service of being too soft,[39] and to threaten them with privatisation.[40] Yet almost a year later, little had changed, and in 2000, despite pledges to 'toughen up the system', it was

231

reported that large numbers of offenders who broke their probation conditions were still not brought back before the court.[41] Eventually, new regulations were introduced to force the Probation Service to take action against an offender after two failed appointments and this has, since 2000, resulted in thousands of arrest warrants being issued. However, the police have generally failed to execute them, leaving the offenders free to predate on the public.[42]

The Defeat of the UK Police Force

As already outlined, the effect of almost every Criminal Justice Act passed by our Parliament since the 1960s has been to leave thousands of persistent offenders on the streets, rather than to imprison them. Some of the problems this has caused the police in terms of stress, overload and falling morale have already been touched upon in Chapter Two, but they will be returned to here to illustrate the overwhelming difficulties faced by the police in their struggle against mounting lawlessness.

As previously argued, the sheer volume of crime has now overwhelmed the police, who have lost control of the problem, leaving the British public to look to its own defence against criminals. Any sense of police urgency over probation arrest warrants has become lost in the ever-growing morass of crimes not dealt with.

The knowledge that several indicators of their performance underline their failure to protect the public must be highly corrosive to police morale. Yet when they are allowed the opportunity to properly police an area they can be noticeably effective in curbing crime. In 2001, in the Knowsley district of Merseyside, for example, police reintroduced night-time foot patrols to curb youth crime. In just three months, this led to a drop in offences by as much as 71 per cent,[43] raising the quality of life for the local people and boosting police morale at the same time. However, such intensive police efforts cannot be sustained and is only achieved by leaving other parts of the community unprotected. This problem was highlighted in March 2003 when a chief constable of an overstretched police force refused to sign up to the Home Secretary's crime-cutting targets on the grounds he did not have enough police officers.[44] Over the last fifty years, as indicated by Figure 9.1, the proportions of reported crimes cleared up has steadily fallen, and depressingly, in October

232

Figure 9.1: Percentage of crimes cleared up, 1950–2000

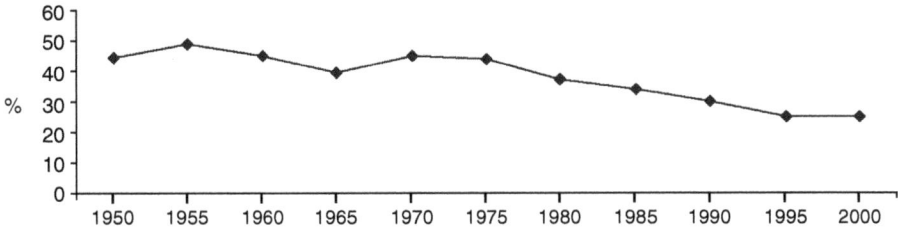

Source: *Detection, Conviction and Punishment, 1950–2000*, Civitas, 2003

2003, it was reported that once again detection rates had dropped.[45] However, the detection rate for *all* crimes is far worse, at little more than 5 per cent. The sense that the police are battling against the odds will have been increased even more by the steady decline in the number of guilty verdicts seen over the last fifty years (see Figure 9.2), despite the enormous increase in crime during that period.

Despite government claims that some crime is falling, the public experience is that it is exploding on all fronts and that the police are powerless to stop it. This is particularly so for robbery and burglary, crimes which are especially able to mobilise fears about public safety and the inability of the police to protect individuals and their property. By April 2003, the number of street attacks by criminals on members of the public had risen to more than a million.[46]

In addition to householders, thousands of small businesses all over the country have found themselves alone and unprotected in the face of a vicious onslaught from criminals who rob them at will, terrorising, injuring and sometimes killing staff members in

Figure 9.2: Percentage of offences leading to cautions or guilty verdicts, 1950–2000

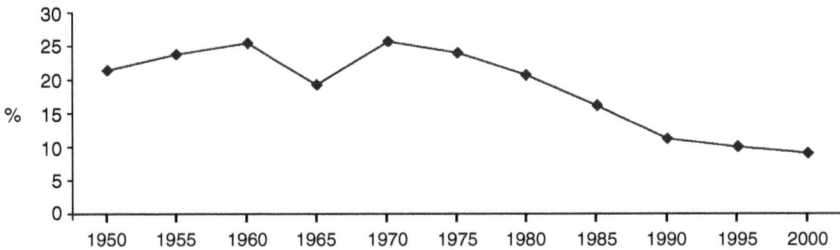

Source: *Detection, Conviction and Punishment, 1950–2000*, Civitas, 2003

233

the process. The small general store near my home has been robbed three times in as many weeks, traumatising the store assistants and leaving the owner at his wits' end to know what to do. He has installed every security device possible and followed the advice of the police and the insurance company to the letter, but it makes no difference. The robbers, armed with weapons, keep returning. This local store situated in a once-safe street, has become a dangerous place to work.

While this local shop owner is just about hanging on, many others are giving up and closing down their business because of the onslaught from criminals. In a story replicated all over the country, it was reported in September 2003 that a Birmingham businessman had given up his off-licence business which he had run successfully for eighteen years. Over the last ten years, he had been robbed and attacked so many times that he felt unable to go on. He had made increasingly desperate attempts to seek help and protection. He found the police sympathetic but powerless to stop the criminals attacking and plundering him. Four years before he gave up the unequal struggle, he even launched a petition calling for more policing, but to no avail. In the end he had to face the hard fact that as far as crime is concerned, he was on his own and undefended.[47]

It has become necessary for the police to mount more and more armed operations against criminals increasingly willing to use guns to terrify their victims.[48] In October 2003 it was reported that gun crime had doubled since Labour took office in 1997,[49] and in the same month robbers attacked a jeweller's shop in Nottingham and shot dead the jeweller in front of her daughter and husband. They escaped, and even though four men were arrested two weeks later, nothing could illustrate more the depth of helplessness experienced by individuals and their families in this country, in the face of victimisation by criminals.[50]

The incidence of robbery against individuals has spiralled out of control. It was reported in April 2002 that, owing to insufficient manpower, the police in the London Borough of Lambeth were only attempting to follow up a third of all muggings, leaving large numbers of the public with the conviction that the police could no longer look after them. One such victim was a young TV director who was attacked in the winter of 2001 as he walked home across a Lambeth park carrying a Christmas tree. He felt a tap on his shoulder and as he turned round he was punched viciously in the face and knocked unconscious. When he came round, he found one robber sitting on his chest holding a knife to his throat, who warned him he would stab him if he moved. The other four attackers were rifling his pockets; they stole all of his money and his credit cards. Before they left him, just for good measure, they all took it in turns to punch and kick him. Later he had to walk to a police car where he gave a statement, which turned out to be the police's only involvement as a result of this terrifying attack. He was then taken to hospital by ambulance.[51]

If this were the only robbery of its kind it would be one too many, but figures compiled by Dr David Green, director of Civitas, the Institute for the Study of Civil Society, show that in 2001/2 there were 6,500 in the London Borough of Lambeth, whereas in 1972 there were 8,900 robberies in the *whole* of England and Wales.[52] In just one month (December 2002), there were 282 robberies of personal wealth in Lambeth. This exceeds the figures for *all* robberies, personal and business, for all of England and Wales in any year between the two world wars, with the exception of 1932 when there were 342, and 1938 when there were 287. (These of course are recorded police figures and are only a fraction of the robberies estimated by the British Crime Survey which showed that in 1999 there were almost 900,000 robberies in the UK.)

When Tony Blair's New Labour government came to power in 1997 there were 27,000 recorded robberies in London; in 2002 there were 45,000 – a 63 per cent increase. If we go back a little further, the figures show that in 1991 there were 22,000 robberies in London and in 2002 there were 44,600, an increase of 105 per cent. This

Figure 9.3: Robbery convictions per 1,000 alleged robbers

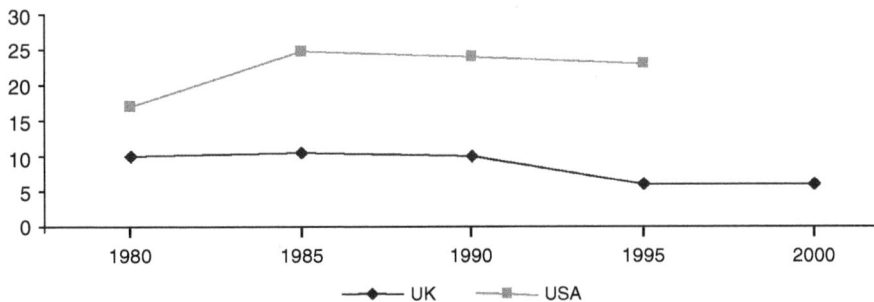

Source: D. Green, *Reducing Crime: Does Prison Work?*, Civitas, 2003

contrasts with New York where in 1991 there were 99,000 robberies and in 2002 the figure was 27,000, a decrease of 73 per cent.[53] These statistics are bitter pills for our already bewildered and battered police force.

Not only have the police had to cope with an avalanche of robberies, but they have, as illustrated by Figure 9.3, also witnessed a fall in the number of robbery convictions; comparable figures from the USA which show an increase in their conviction rate for these offences can only make worse the sense of defeat for the UK policeman. Reference has already been made to the inability of the police to combat burglary and its effect on undermining the public's belief in their ability to keep them safe. British Crime Survey figures for 1998 indicated that there were at least 1.7 million burglaries per year,[54] yet as shown in Figure 9.4, the numbers of burglary convictions in the UK has consistently fallen over a period of twenty years, whilst in the US they have risen.

The reality that they cannot protect people even in their own homes must be highly stressful for police officers and has no doubt seriously undermined their confidence. In 1999 the house of a close friend of mine was burgled in broad daylight, whilst he and his wife were out. On discovering the burglary, they immediately called the police who did not visit them until twenty-four hours later. A young constable called with a clipboard and pen and started to write down the details of the crime. My friend asked him what the police were going to do about catching the criminal who had violated their home and stolen a number of their treasured possessions. To his surprise, he saw tears well up in the eyes of the young policeman,

Figure 9.4: Burglary convictions per 1,000 alleged burglars

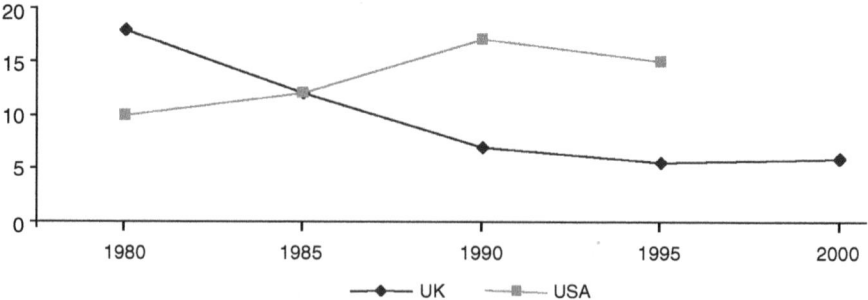

Source: D. Green, *Reducing Crime: Does Prison Work?*, Civitas, 2003

Figure 9.5: Percentage of all offences leading to custody

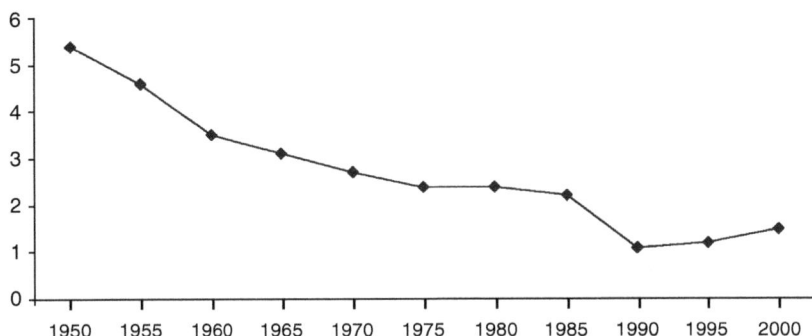

Source: *Detection, Conviction and Punishment, 1950–2000*, Civitas, 2003

who, burdened almost to breaking point with a sense of defeat, confessed that all he ever did was to call at people's houses and record the details of their burglary.[55]

At the root of his frustration lay the knowledge that it was extremely unlikely that he would find the offender and that if he did he would have to fill in at least seventeen forms all requiring great detail (see Note 1).[56] Beyond that was the near certainty that the Crown Prosecution Service would either throw the case out or downgrade the offence, allowing the criminal to walk free at the end of a meaningless judicial process.

In addition to these pressures, even when successful, police hard work in finding and arresting criminals, often at considerable risk to themselves, is frequently wasted because the courts fail to jail the offender concerned. Nothing can be more disheartening for the police than to see convicted persistent criminals allowed back into the community by a court brainwashed against the use of imprisonment (see Figure 9.5). It is little wonder that the police have been overwhelmed by the sheer volume of crime. In 1931 there were three reported crimes a year for every police officer and in 2001 there were forty-four.[57] Table 9.1 shows how this problem has worsened over the last thirty years.

Measured by *reported* crimes in relation to each police officer, the police force would need to be two and a half times larger than it is to maintain the ratio of crimes per police officer that we had in 1971.[58] However, as shown in Chapter Two, when measured by the 13 million crimes found by the latest British Crime Survey

237

Table 9.1: Crime and police numbers

Year	Crimes reported (thousands)	Police officers (thousands)	Crimes per police officer
1971	1,666	97	17
1981	2,794	120	23
1991	5,075	127	40
2001	5,527	126	44

Source: D. Green, *Forces of Law and Order Have Lost Control*, Civitas, 2002

(BCS), such an increase would still leave the police with impossible odds. Yet we know that the BCS figures also considerably understate the crime figures; therefore, to give it even a fighting chance of getting on top of the crime problem, the police force needs to be between four and ten times its present size.

The Widening Gap Between the Police and the Public

Table 9.1, compiled by the Institute for the Study of Civil Society, also suggests that there has been a dramatic drop over the last ten years in the numbers of crimes being reported to the police, and Home Office data indicates that now only 45 per cent of known crime is reported.[59] Such a decline supports the view that the public are becoming increasingly alienated from the criminal justice system.

Not only has the public witnessed a sharp decline in the number of criminals brought to justice, but it has also found the police increasingly unable to respond to their calls for help. One example, now all too common, involved a young couple who at 7.15 p.m. one evening in the winter of 2003 were subjected to a terrifying robbery by a criminal armed with a knife and an axe. Five minutes later at 7.20 p.m. the mother of one of the victims rang the police. She rang again at 8.30 p.m. and was told that all officers were busy. At 9.45 p.m. she rang again, but still no one came. At 12.10 a.m., almost five hours after the robbery, two police officers arrived at the victims' home.[60] It was no surprise that the British Crime Survey, published in 2001, reported that confidence in the police force was at its lowest for twenty years.[61]

Police in different parts of the country report having to cope with impossibly low staff numbers. In October 2003, the Chief Constable of Nottingham admitted that his officers were being forced to ignore

238

thousands of burglaries, thefts and car crimes because there was not enough money or staff to investigate all crimes.[62] In 2002, a police sergeant from the south of the country told me that within five minutes of the start of her 10 p.m. shift the previous day she had taken two calls from the public. She sent out two men to the first incident and the remaining two officers went in response to the second call. Those jobs tied them up for the best part of the shift. She had no other police to call on. In other words four policemen and one female sergeant were expected to police the whole area where they were based. From five minutes past ten onwards all callers were told that there was nothing the police could do. Effectively that meant that thousands of people who lived in that city did not have a police force at all. This is a story that is replicated throughout England and Wales.

Police Burn-out

The problem of police burn-out was touched upon in Chapter Two and I deliberately return to it to illustrate how pervasive this largely unacknowledged problem has become. In 1985 I went for a walk on Christmas Day evening. Once in the high street, I saw, on the other side of the road, a man sitting on the shoulders of another; one by one he was unscrewing the coloured light bulbs strung out over a shopfront and dropping them into a large bag on his shoulder. I rang the police straight away from a well-placed call box and told them what I was watching. They said 'stay there' and within two minutes a police car arrived. The police jumped eagerly out of the car but the thieves had left the scene a minute earlier. Undeterred, they put me in the car and drove around the streets looking for their quarry until they found them. The men were arrested.

In contrast, I was shocked by the results of a call I made to the police just over ten years later, when I reported a burglary in progress. They said they were too busy to respond. I recently rang the police on a 999 call while witnessing a street drug deal. I believed that my call would provoke a rapid response leading to an arrest. I was subjected to a painfully slow, and unnecessarily detailed, grilling from the policeperson I spoke to which made me feel as if I was a suspect. By the time this laborious process was over the drug dealer had disappeared from the scene.

239

Overburdened police are more likely to respond poorly to members of the public. In the summer of 2000 a foreign postgraduate student was attacked and robbed in a large university city on a Saturday evening. Frightened and hurt, and minus her bag and money which had been stolen, she ran in a panic to the police station, confident of help. In an obviously distressed and emotional state, she blurted out to the desk officer what had happened. To her shock and dismay, he said, 'What do you expect? This sort of thing is always happening here at the weekend.' The police did not even stir from the police station in answer to the victim's entreaties for them to try and find her assailant and retrieve her bag and other possessions.[63]

Sometimes the police respond to the stress of too many demands by sinking into apathy. During my career as a criminal intelligence analyst, I once tracked a dangerous sex offender over a period of twelve months or more. I was able by various means to place him at the scene of at least four undetected sex crimes involving attacks on children in swimming pools. In one instance, I was even able to identify the first names of two victims, both girls aged about eleven years. I rang the police in the town concerned, thinking they would be pleased with this information, as with a little more enquiry work, I was confident they could find the girls concerned and build a good case against my target and so arrest him. To my surprise, they said they could do nothing with my information, as I could not tell them the surnames of the children or where they lived.

The town in the north of England where the offences took place was small, and as I had already found out there were only two junior schools in the vicinity, I suggested that all they needed to do was to contact the two schools and make enquiries for two children aged approximately eleven years with the appropriate first names. I said it would take them probably no more than forty minutes at the most. Once they had found the girls, they would then know their address and they could then interview them and build their case. The swimming pool had kept a record of the original offences with dates and descriptions, so they could be confident of obtaining a result. However, the police would not do it. The policeperson I spoke to sounded tired and uninterested. And that was that. Nothing was done. I came across numerous examples of this kind where the police exhibited classic symptoms of burn-out.

A glaring example of a tired and burned-out police response to crime was provided in 2003, on a crime-ridden inner-city London

240

estate. In 2003, seven young criminals who had terrorised the area for two years with crimes such as burglary, robbery, violence and intimidation were made the subject of anti-social behaviour orders by a district judge in a magistrates' court.[64] These provisions were introduced in 1999 in order to give authorities the power to ban troublemakers from particular areas for 'anti-social behaviour', such as intimidation, bullying, violent behaviour, drunkenness, despoiling property with graffiti and other forms of vandalism. In this case, the bans were for periods of five years to life, an indication of the serious nature of the problems caused by these young criminals. However, the public would be forgiven for asking why the police had resorted to applying for these orders, instead of presenting the Crown Prosecution Service with a criminal case against them.

Given that they were known to be prolific offenders and strongly suspected of being responsible for large numbers of robberies on the estate in question (the incidence of robbery fell 25 per cent as soon as they were removed), there was good reason to think that the police could, with some effort, have found evidence that could have resulted in their being sent to prison, which would have given the public the protection they desperately needed from these offenders. As it was, the banning orders left them free to carry on their crimes elsewhere. Was it the case that, because the rules governing the gathering of evidence are now so stringent and protective of the rights of the offenders, that the police had simply given up hope of building a criminal case against them? The burden of proof required for an anti-social behaviour order is lighter than that required for a criminal offence. However, although the provision exists to imprison those who break the conditions of these anti-social behaviour orders, the burden of proof required to prove such a breach is as stringent as for criminal matters, and in all likelihood they will be ignored for as long as possible.

Retreat into Sickness

As with probation staff many police personnel have retreated from the stresses and pressures of their job into illness. In 1997, the cost of sickness in the police in England and Wales was reported to be £210 million a year; by 2002 this had increased to £240 million or 1.5 million working days lost each year. A report by Her Majesty's

Inspectorate of Constabulary revealed that in 2002 the equivalent of 6,400 police officers were off sick every day, slightly more than the total police strength for the whole of Kent and Essex combined. Jack Straw had, in 1998, stamped down on what he called unacceptable levels of police absenteeism. This resulted in police sick days falling from 1.6 million in 1998 to 1.4 million in 2000. However, by 2001 they were back up to 1.5 million.[65] Whether or not some sickness absence can be avoided, the high incidence of illness is a reflection, I believe, of low morale brought about by their failure to provide even the semblance of protection for the public, impossibly high demands, and the almost daily taunting from guilty criminals allowed to escape justice, as well as physical injuries sustained on duty, badly organised work practices and domestic disruption.[66] To this list must be added the frustrations brought about by the Crown Prosecution Service who have targeted the police rather than the criminals, by refusing to prosecute hundreds of thousands of cases.

In 2002 I interviewed a former policeman who now lives in the rural peace and quiet of the Yorkshire Dales. He had been a member of a police force for a number of years in a large northern city, and he said he left because he had taken one beating 'too many'. He was frequently the only policeman available to be called to scenes of violence and mayhem and was frequently attacked and almost as frequently injured. On the last occasion, he was deliberately ambushed by a crowd of about twenty men well known for their antipathy towards the police. He responded to a call for help and when he arrived they all set about him. My policeman informant was a large, strong man, keen to do his job well, but after he was released from hospital he resigned from the force. He decided he could not go on policing large sections of this city on his own and risking serious injury. Many have gone that way before him. In some police forces it is known, for example, that more than three-quarters of all officers retire or go early for medical reasons.[67]

Losing their Focus on Crime Fighting?

Despite being chronically short of staff, many police services allow their officers to find their way into 'non-police' jobs in schemes involving 'shared working' between police, probation, social services and other agencies, designed to 'address crime and its causes'. The job requirements are often woolly. Typical is the example on my desk for a 'criminal justice coordinator', a post that was eventually filled by a *police inspector*. His task was described as 'assisting the key criminal justice agencies to deliver the joint Area Criminal Justice Strategy'. This was to involve him in 'working across all key agencies'.[68]

Such jargon leaves us guessing as to what exactly he was required to do, but my previous experience leads me to be confident it would certainly involve a lot of meetings, minute-taking and administrative work. But is this really what the public want a highly paid police inspector to be doing when they are increasingly told there are not enough policemen to detect the crimes committed against them and bring the offenders to justice? How can the police force, which is rarely able to put on duty enough officers to provide even basic policing for our villages, towns and cities, justify secondments to these research and administrative posts? I know examples where there are as many as three of these posts, all filled by policemen, in one city probation office.

Another 'joint agency' project that provides 'community support' for persistent offenders included a police sergeant who was pulled away from his crime fighting duties in order to interview persistent offenders referred to the scheme.[69] There were other staff, such as probation officers, who could have carried out this task. What has happened to the priorities of police senior management that they can agree to the transfer of an experienced detective sergeant to a post that involves him in non-police work? Would it not have been a better use of his time to carry on leading a team of detectives to pursue and bring to justice the criminals he and they are paid to catch? There are numerous examples of police filling such posts throughout the country.

Sometimes so-called local 'initiatives' taken by the police appear to miss the point. In one recent example, the police announced they were going to 'work with local NCP car park staff to crack down on car park thieves'. This 'work' turned out to be no more than them turning up at various car parks and handing out leaflets advising people not to leave valuables in their car, and others which told the thieves 'not to bother' as there was nothing of value in the car. Again, I suspect the public would regard it better use of police time for them to flood the car parks with policemen and women in a determined effort to catch, arrest and prosecute these offenders, rather than with leaflets to divert them and their criminal behaviour elsewhere.[70]

It appears odd, to say the least, that the police have to launch special initiatives to 'crack down on crime'. Isn't that what they are supposed to be doing all of the time? In one case, it was reported that 'for the next two weeks the police will focus on criminals wanted for robbery, burglary and theft of motor vehicles'.[71] Another example on my desk actually says: 'Police Notice: For two weeks from 6th March 2000, the police are having a crime crackdown campaign'.[72] Two more examples stand out. One states: 'The police are set to launch a four-week campaign to reduce muggings and burglary in the city'.[73] The other proclaimed that 'in a series of Days of Actions this police force will launch its biggest ever campaign to target criminals'. But what about the rest of the year? Have we reached the absurd state where the local police need to run a special operation in order to pursue and catch criminals? If so, what are they doing in the long intervals between these short-lived periods of crime fighting? In another example, local police announced they were going to launch a special initiative to concentrate on offenders with more than six previous offences.[74] Yet public safety requires that they are stopped and imprisoned long before they become that prolific.

In an area known to me, more than fifty cars were recently vandalised during one evening, many of them in the street in a direct line of vision from the police station. But not one of these incidents was spotted by the police. During the same period and in the same location, however, they found time to affix a £30-fine notice to the vehicle of one local resident for apparently having one digit in his car registration plate two centimetres too far to the right.[75]

It is also known that some police forces have set quotas for the number of motorists they must fine each month;[76] and in one area of the country speed camera fines are being handed out at the rate of £2,000 per week.[77] None of this fits easily with the knowledge that the police in many areas have, by their own admission, all but given up investigating burglaries, car thefts and other forms of crime because they do not have enough staff. It is increasingly difficult to avoid the conclusion that a number of police forces have given up the unequal struggle to catch local criminals and instead have turned their policing energies onto the law-abiding public, who make much easier and more lucrative targets.

'Politicising of the Police'

Equally disturbing have been the numerous examples of the way in which some senior police officers have described the objectives of so-called 'modern day policing'. Aware that their political masters want to divert offenders away from expensive court hearings and prisons, they are placing less emphasis on their traditional role of catching criminals and refocusing on the 'causes of crime'.

In 1996 research suggested that, bizarrely, a number of Britain's most senior police officers spurned the hard-line crime policies of the then Home Secretary, Michael Howard. It was revealed that a new breed of university-educated chief constables, despite being paid out of the public purse to protect our communities from crime, were lining up with judges in opposing key parts of the government's law and order policy.[78] Incredibly, the majority of these new chief constables doubted Michael Howard's policy of jailing more criminals would cut crime, and echoed the threadbare argument that 'prison does nothing to tackle the root causes of crime'. One chief constable, in 1997, told a conference of the Howard League for Penal Reform, that despite the huge increases in crime, especially among the young, that it was better not to lock them up because community penalties were likely to be cheaper and more effective in the long run.[79] Other senior police officials even cast doubt on zero-tolerance policing despite the unarguable evidence pointing to its success in New York and later in Middlesbrough, England.[80]

Two years earlier, in 1995, many police chiefs had thrown their weight behind a report entitled *Crime and Social Policy*, compiled by academics, criminologists, police and economists, which had laboured once more their a priori assumptions about the social dynamics of crime.[81] Under its influence, several chief constables launched a number of schemes to test what they described as the more 'progressive' style of policing. These included making offenders face a special conference of local people who discussed the effects of their crime; having young offenders fostered by trained volunteers; moves (in one force) to find a de-facto red-light zone for prostitutes away from residential areas; offering counselling to young offenders as a substitute for prosecution; and establishing large numbers of 'mediation' services throughout the UK which bring offenders face to face with their victims, again as an alternative to prosecution.[82]

As usual, the public were never consulted about whether they

245

agreed to be used as guinea pigs in these dangerous experiments, all of which failed utterly to protect them, but which gave the offenders concerned unbridled opportunity to go on offending. Yet one chief constable, who is also a visiting fellow of a well-known college, said that the 'police service has changed radically in recent years – we are now looking at the roots of problems in communities and looking for social solutions'.[83] At no stage however, have the public been consulted over this new role for the police. If they were, I am confident I know what they would say. In response, the rank and file spokesperson for the police made what the public might judge to be a more sane observation on this nightmare scenario: 'It is all madness. Officers just don't know what they are supposed to be doing. There are so many crimes now where policemen are told they can't take firm action.'[84] This is not what the public are paying its taxes for. What is disturbing in this context is the statement made by the Police Management Training Directorate that the job of chief officers is to 'manage large organisations – *not to mess about chasing criminals all day*' (my italics).[85] Some chief constables have spoken out against this philosophy. In 1998 one senior Essex policeman went public and told a journalist that the police force was monitoring itself to death and had lost sight of its basic objective of fighting crime.[86] Another pointed out that management training for the police had lost its emphasis on technical abilities to fight crime, and instead concentrated on management skills and the 'political delicacy' of the role of chief constable.[87]

This last observation may explain why significant factions of the Association of Chief Police Officers (ACPO) appear to have tuned in to the government's wavelength and now openly support schemes to keep persistent offenders out of prison. They are now unashamedly making recommendations they know the government wants to hear. This is a disturbing indicator of the extent to which many of the leaders of our police forces have become politicised. Whilst some police chiefs still advocate the use of prison for persistent offenders,[88] others are involving themselves in dubious social policy initiatives, and anti-prison schemes for the management of persistent offenders in the community. It was reported in October 2003 that one particular police force was handing out 'welcome packs' to convicted criminals on their release from prison, containing advice on alcohol- and drug-related problems. Is this not the job of the probation staff and other social work agencies?[89] These self-adopted agendas are a million

246

miles away from the one the public want and expect the police to follow, namely to make life miserable for criminals by ensuring they are caught and brought to justice.

A national newspaper, in October 2003, was several years too late with its warning that the police force in the UK should not become 'politicised'.[90] Fifteen years before, a police inspector in the area where I worked as a senior probation officer persuaded his police force to run a local 'cautioning policy' as a trial, with a view to cutting down the number of criminals going to court. I can still recall my amazement that a senior policeman of all people should come up with a plan to let criminals off the hook. I came to the conclusion that he had understood what his senior management and government officials wanted, and I believe in order to promote his career he had come up with a plan that fitted their political agenda.[91] If this was the case, it worked, and he was later promoted to chief constable. Years later he was forced to admit that his force had made a major error when it destroyed crucial records on the Soham killer, Ian Huntley, which contributed to Huntley getting a job as the village school caretaker. But was it an 'error', or did political correctness play a part in the decision not to keep those all-important records beyond a certain limited time period?

In 2002 we were treated to the spectacle of one chief constable publicly declaring that drug addicts should be given free heroin. Whatever the rights and wrongs of this view, the question the public should ask is why is this chief constable using his time and energies to involve himself in this debate? It should be regarded as outside of his remit. His job is to track down and arrest those who import, distribute and use heroin, not to involve himself in matters of social policy.[92]

The same year the ACPO submitted a plan to the Home Office which proposed that some offenders should be given a 'conditional caution' and not be prosecuted. Under the scheme, offenders who admit their crimes will sign a special contract and submit to certain conditions, the chief of which is to apologise to their victims. It is bizarre in the extreme that it is the police who should come up with a scheme that is so advantageous to criminals, allows them their freedom, and which blatantly denies justice to their victims. Of course, the government were very impressed, and it was made a clause in the Criminal Justice Bill 2002 then being debated in Parliament.

Given the enormous problems faced by the police, it is a wonder they function as well as they do. In recent years there have been reports of some forces massaging their figures – further possible indicators I would argue that they are under enormous pressure to present the outcome the politicians want to see.[93] Yet, notwithstanding some of the more critical parts of my analysis, it must be recognised that many policemen and women work tirelessly to protect the public, often at the cost of their own safety and well-being; in 2002 there were 24,000 assaults against police officers,[94] amounting to almost one in four of the police force. But local policing generally in the UK has become chronically ineffective and distracted by odds too big for it to cope with. On the one hand, the courts and the Crown Prosecution Service not only fail to back them up, but, as I have shown, actually undermine them; on the other, they are kept under-strength in the face of an unprecedented number of crimes committed every year – the direct result of government policy which allows hundreds of thousands of persistent offenders their freedom.

The Statistics of Terror

But just how many crimes are committed against the public? The figure for crimes *recorded by the police* is currently 5.9 million per year. We should think of this statistic as the casualty rate in the undeclared war that criminals wage on the public. It becomes far worse if we consider there are at least two victims per offence, and if this were the true extent of crime it would be calamitous. However, the grim reality is that recorded crime represents only a fraction of the true number of crimes committed against the public. Since the 1980s the Home Office has also been measuring crime by finding out from samples of the population how often they have been victimised by criminals, and the figures obtained from these British Crime Surveys (BCS) tell a very different story from those recorded by the police. For example, the BCS figures for domestic burglary, woundings and bicycle thefts were three times those recorded by the police; likewise there were six times more crimes of vandalism, four times as many thefts from vehicles, and seven times as many robberies and thefts from the person.[95]

British Crime Survey Estimates

Official statements about crime have become a minefield for the public, giving an entirely false impression that government sentencing policies are working but the reality is that crime is out of control. In 1995 the BCS estimates for the number of crimes committed against individuals and their property was 19.1 million per year.[96] The government has been keen to emphasise that this figure was down to 12.6 million by 2001/02. Even if this were true, it still represents a serious betrayal of the government's first duty to protect its citizens. The amount of psychological and physical damage caused to individuals and families represented by these statistics is beyond comprehension for most of us, yet even they are far from the whole story.

The government, however, is keen for the public to see these BCS estimates as the final crime account, and the previous Home Secretary has gone so far as to describe them as the most accurate measure of crime ever. But they are not, and what is more the government knows this; the BCS can only interview those in households which are prepared to open their doors to interviewers and let them ask the questions. It is well known that it can be difficult to get access to people in high-crime, inner-city areas, who are most likely to be the victims of crime in the fist place.[97] In addition, the government's own separate studies indicate a crime rate at least four times the almost 13 million crimes estimated by the latest BCS survey.[98]

The Home Secretary's statement was no more than propaganda. He knew that journalists would pick up on his comments and propagate the myth that crime was under control. Such proved to be the case, and by September 2003 both national and local newspapers as far apart as London and Cornwall were reporting that 'overall crime was down by 22%'.[99] What the Home Secretary's comments gave no hint of was that there are significant omissions in the BCS figures. They do not include crimes related to illegal drug use, murder, sexual offences, or crimes against those under sixteen years old, crimes against commercial premises, thefts of commercial vans and trucks, and shoplifting.

Recent research has shown that as many as one in four of those between the ages of twelve and sixteen is a victim of crime.[100] Table 9.2 shows the Home Office estimates, elicited by Dr David Green, director of Civitas, of the number of crimes committed against those under sixteen years (not included in the BCS), for the year

Table 9.2: Crimes against eleven to fifteen-year-olds (2002/03, estimated)

Crime Category	Home Office estimates of actual crimes committed against 11–15-year-olds
Wounding	122,908
Robbery	79,457
Theft from person	55,858
Assault	342,507
Total	**600,730**

Source: D.G. Green, *Do the Official Crime Figures Tell the Full Story?*, Civitas, 2003

2002/03. Similarly, Table 9.3 shows data relating to the number of crimes against shops, offices and other commercial premises and commercial vehicles, not included in the BCS estimates, for the year 2002/03. Shoplifting is another category not included in BCS statistics, but the Home Office estimates that some 7,700,000 offences were committed in the year 2002/2003.[101]

Thus the total of these offences not counted in the BCS is in excess of 11 million crimes, and when added to the official 12.6 million identified by the BCS for 2002/03, totals almost 24 million crimes. It must be said that even this is an incomplete calculation because it does not include sex offences or drug offences. Also the shoplifting figure is a low estimate. Professor David Farringdon of Cambridge University has estimated the number of these crimes as being between 7 and 31 million.[102] Using the high figure for shoplifting, the total number of crimes committed every year based on the above data, would not be almost 24 million, but 47.4 million.

Table 9.3: Crime against commercial victims (2002/03, estimated)

Crime category	Home Office estimates of actual crimes against commercial victims
Vandalism	2,484,846
Theft from motor vehicles	184,686
Theft of motor vehicles	24,513
Attempted theft of motor vehicles	18,008
Attempted theft from motor vehicles	30,098
Vehicle interference and tampering	15,903
Total	**2,758,054**

Source: D.G. Green, *Do the Official Crime Figures Tell the Full Story?*, Civitas, 2003

Yet in September 2002 the Office for National Statistics (ONS) claimed that, on the basis of the original BCS figures, crime had fallen 22 per cent since 1997, and that the chances of being a victim of crime were the lowest since the BCS began in 1981.[103] But at the same time many police forces were admitting to an ever-increasing avalanche of crime, which the public were aware they were powerless to stop,[104] and in some areas was driving businesses out of city centres.[105] The meaninglessness of the claim by the ONS was further underlined, when less than a year later, it was reported that there had been a significant rise in burglary and car offences.[106]

A more accurate picture of the crime problem can be seen from Figure 9.6. This shows, for comparative purposes, the number of crimes committed each year as recorded by: the police; the British Crime Survey; the BCS plus its omissions based on both (a) low estimates of shoplifting and on (b) high estimates of shoplifting; the Home Office Research Study 217, published in 2000; and my own estimates, based on the 155,000 offenders placed on community penalties under the supervision of the Probation Service. What this comparison shows is that the BCS figures, previously thought by some to be an accurate measurement of crime, pale into insignificance next to more realistic assessments, and reveal the emptiness of the government's claim that its crime policies are working.

The author's estimate of 63 million offences is based on his research into the number of offences committed each week prior to their sentence by a sample of prisoners aged seventeen to twenty in a young offender prison (1990). This discovered that approximately

Figure 9.6: Comparison of estimates of number of crimes committed each year (millions)

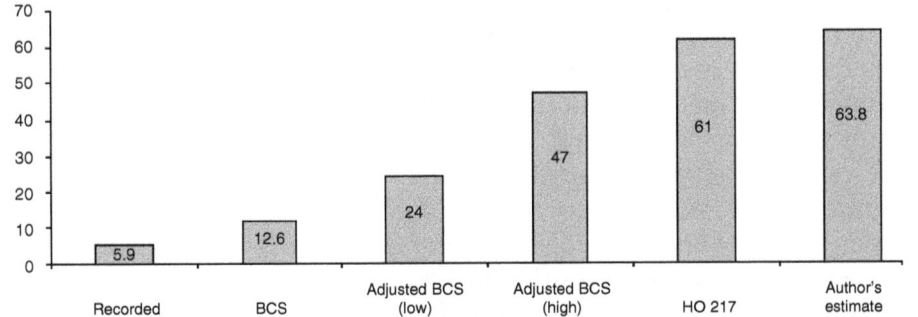

Source: Home Office, *Crime Statistics, 2001*; BCS, 2002/03; D.G. Green, *Do the Official Crime Figures Tell the Full Story?*, Civitas, 2003

251

Table 9.4: Estimate of annual total crimes committed by offenders

Number of offenders	% of total	Number of crimes committed per week per offender	Number of crimes committed each year per offender	Total number of crimes committed per year (millions)
40,000	25	15	750	30.0
40,000	25	8	400	16.6
31,000	20	6	300	9.0
20,000	13	4	200	4.0
15,000	10	3	150	2.2
9,000	6	2	100	0.9
155,000	100			Total = 62.7

Source: Author

a quarter of the young prisoners in the sample of about 500 committed very large numbers of offences a week, and the figure of fifteen is by no means the highest that was admitted to. Another quarter said they committed at least eight to ten per week, whilst just over 20 per cent admitted to carrying out as a minimum six offences per week, 13 per cent four crimes per week, 10 per cent approximately three crimes a week and a smaller group of 6 per cent revealed they committed about two offences per week. These rates of offending and the percentages of offenders involved have been used as a template and applied to the total number of offenders under supervision to the Probation Service (taken to be between 154,000 and 155,000). The results are displayed in Table 9.4.

The total of 63 million offences per year (which is very close to the government's latest calculation of 62 million,[107] may seem breathtakingly large, but I have deliberately used the lower end of the crime rate estimates given to me by the prisoners in the sample and therefore my instinct is that it is *an underestimate* of crime committed against the public. In 1998, for example, police in one major town in the south of England calculated that a hard core of just twenty young persistent offenders were responsible for 7,000 crimes in one year alone, a rate of 350 per year each.[108] In the same year, it was reported in another town on the south coast that a group of sixty persistent offenders admitted having each committed an average of 330 crimes *per month*, a total of almost 4,000 crimes each per year.[109] In 1999, I interviewed two detectives; one told me he had arrested a criminal who had committed 700 burglaries in

Figure 9.7: Estimates of number of offenders involved in different crime rates per week

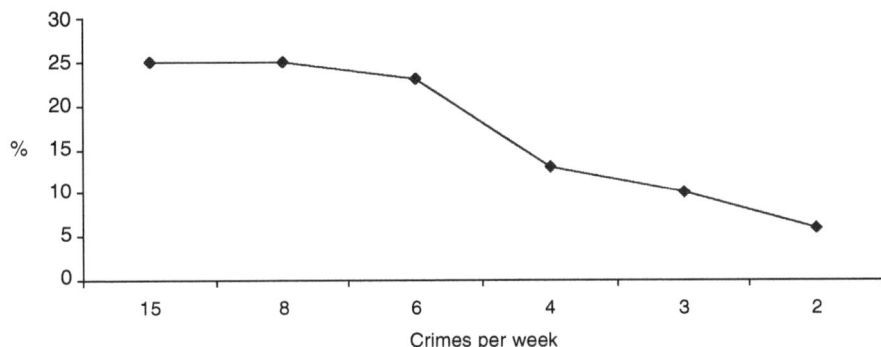

Source: Author

four years; the other had tracked down a criminal responsible for 600 crimes in seven months.

The earlier findings of the Home Office Janus Studies concluded that a minority of persistent offenders were responsible for large amounts of crime,[110] while a later government assessment was that about 100,000 hard-core offenders were responsible for half of all offences.[111] However, the very high numbers of crimes referred to above fall more in line with a much more recent Home Office study, which revealed that as many as 1.7 million boys aged between fourteen to seventeen years were persistent offenders.[112]

Of further interest is that the curve displaying the spread of the crime rates over the different groups does not go in the direction we might expect. For example, it might have been believed that a small number of offenders commit the highest number of crimes per week, and that the largest group of offenders commit the smallest number of crimes per week. But the results, displayed in Figure 9.7, show the opposite trend. This makes immediate sense if we apply it to what is already known about persistent offenders, namely that offenders commit more crime the longer they remain criminals. This is supported by Table 6.1 that shows offender reconviction rates remain high for long periods following the end of their probation orders. Likewise, the official reconviction figures show that those who have more reconvictions go on to commit more crime than those with less reconvictions. Given that it takes months or years to accumulate high levels of reconvictions, we can deduce that it is the experienced, longer-term persistent offenders who, because of

253

the passage of time, become more numerous and commit the most offences, and that it is they who are represented in the higher offending rate groups shown in Table 9.7. On the other hand, the new and relatively fewer inexperienced persistent offenders start their criminal apprenticeship by committing a smaller number of offences per week, but will in time, if not checked, build up their offending rate.

The majority of the higher crime estimates shown in Figure 9.6 are government figures and are filed away in their archives. Whilst their existence is not exactly denied, they are not advertised (although it is true they are on the government web site if you know where to look); nor do they appear in the government's propaganda. However, if asked, Home Office officials will provide this data. But unless you ask or embark on time-consuming research, you will not find out about them. But how can a busy member of the public, occupied with their own daily demands, possibly reach the point where he or she feels able to search for or ask a government department about specialist statistics whose presence is simply not generally known about? It does not happen, and so information about crime which the public should be informed about, and which is vital to their safety, remains unknown to them, leaving them vulnerable to the misinformation it suits the government to give them.

Financial Costs of Keeping Persistent Offenders in the Community

The government report *The Economic and Social Costs of Crime* estimates the total cost of crime for England and Wales at a staggering £60 billion.[113] Table 9.5 displays this data and relates these costs to each major crime category. However, the report warns that this figure is by no means comprehensive – costs of precautionary behaviour, quality of life, drug crime, low-level disorder, undiscovered fraud, costs in terms of attitudes and social structures and other costs are not included in this figure.

Around £32 billion of the total costs are due to crimes against individuals and households. (Police targeting criminals in one area of Milton Keynes in 1995 discovered that the offences of *just one* offender had cost at least £2 million).[114] A measure of the impact

Table 9.5: The cost of crime

Offence Category	Average Cost (£)	Number of incidents (thousands)	Total Costs (£billion)
Violence against the person	19,000	880.0	16.8
Homicide	1,100,000	1.1	1.2
Wounding	18,000	880.0	15.6
Serious wounding	130,000	110.0	14.1
Other wounding	2,000	780.0	1.5
Common assault	540	3,200.0	1.7
Sexual offences	19,000	130.0	2.5
Robbery/mugging	4,700	420.0	2.0
Burglary in a dwelling	2,300	1,400.0	3.2
Theft	600	7,300.0	4.4
Theft (not vehicle)	340	3,800.0	1.3
Vehicle theft	890	3,500.0	3.1
Criminal damage	510	3,000.0	1.5
Crime against commercial victims	260		9.1
Fraud & forgery		9,200.0	13.8
Traffic & motoring			4.8
Total cost of crime			**60**

Source: Home Office Research Paper 217, *The Economic and Social Costs of Crime, 2000*

crime makes on us can also be seen from the fact that around £19 billion is the cost of stolen or damaged property, and £18 billion is the cost of direct emotional and physical impact on victims of crime.

Figure 9.8, also taken from the Home Office report *The Economic*

Figure 9.8: Costs of crime by cost category, as a proportion of total costs (£60 billion)

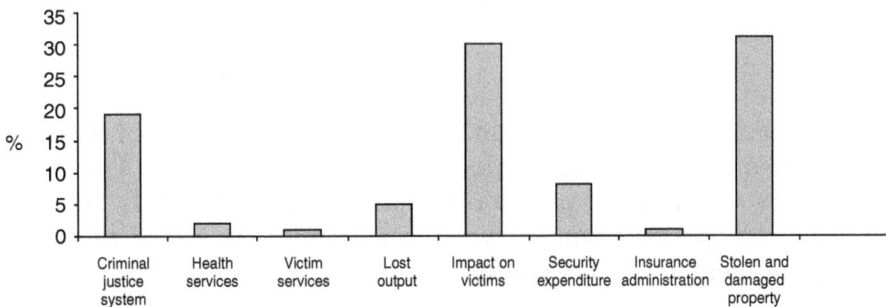

Source: Home Office, *The Economic and Social Costs of Crime, 2000*

255

and *Social Costs of Crime*, shows the distribution of crime costs over different categories of expenditure. Some of these costs relate to huge sums which are wasted on inefficient and drawn-out legal processing of offenders, contributing to the massive £12 billion bill for our criminal justice system, which represents nearly 20 per cent of the total costs of crime. The following is a real but anonymous example, replicated by the thousands every year, of the pointless and highly expensive time-wasting procedures followed by our courts which allow persistent offenders to play cat and mouse with the judicial process to no one's gain except the lawyers involved.

Catch Me If You Can

Many prolific and persistent offenders who for long periods of time have successfully avoided capture by the police for their repeated property crimes are often caught for driving offences. This may well be because a drunk or disqualified driver is an easier target for the police to spot, chase and catch than is a burglar, and may explain why magistrates' courts up and down the land have to deal with enormous numbers of such cases. In the following example, the criminal, whom I shall call Smith, had a string of previous convictions for a variety of offences, going back several years.[115]

April 2001

He appeared before a magistrates' court charged with Driving Whilst Disqualified, Excess Alcohol and No Insurance. He was given a six-month sentence suspended for two years. As a result of being allowed his freedom he continued to offend.

September 2001

He was back at the same court for yet more offences of Driving Whilst Disqualified, Excess Alcohol and No Insurance. The court bailed him to allow a probation report to be prepared. He was instructed to appear again in two weeks' time. He failed to attend the appointment with the probation officer.

256

1 October 2001

He also failed to appear at court in answer to his bail. The court issued a warrant for his arrest. Two weeks later he was arrested and brought to court again. The court *once again* released him on bail for a probation report to be prepared. Once again he failed to keep the appointment with the probation officer.

22 October 2001

At the same court, the case was once more adjourned until 12 November for a probation report. For the third time he failed to keep the appointment with the probation officer.

12 November 2001

He failed to appear in court as instructed. Another warrant was issued for his arrest. Five months went by before the police once again picked him up.

26 April 2002

He was put before the same court again, and almost unbelievably the court remanded him *once again* on bail, in order for a probation report to be prepared. He was instructed to reappear at court at a date in May. He failed to attend the fourth probation report appointment.

At this point in the proceedings any member of the public reading this sequence of events would be forgiven for questioning the sanity of the court's decisions. To make matters worse, it became known that Smith, such was the level of his contempt for these farcical procedures, had on this last occasion even left behind his copy of the bail instructions given to him by the court. It also became clear that the court had not bothered to make a condition of the bail that he cooperate with the probation department in the preparation of the report – clear evidence that the magistrates no longer believed in what they were doing but were just going through the motions, and in doing so had abandoned their first duty to protect the public.

20 May 2002

The court once again, and *for the fifth time*, adjourned the case for a probation report to be prepared, and instructed Smith to reappear on the 10 June. Smith once again failed to keep the appointment with the probation officer.

10 June 2002

Smith failed to appear before the court. Once again a warrant was issued for his arrest. Smith was eventually arrested on the warrant.

15 August 2002

He appeared at the same court and, despite the fact that he was on a suspended prison sentence, which should have been activated when he committed more offences, the magistrates still did not sentence him but once again requested a probation report. This time, however, they remanded him in custody and he went to Prison A. The probation officer rang the prison to arrange a visit to find that he had been transferred to Prison B, much further away. The probation officer made the appointment with Prison B. Too late to do anything about it, the probation officer discovered that Smith had been produced at another court for other offences and as a result he had been taken back to Prison A. The probation officer was therefore not able to keep the appointment to prepare the report.

September 2002

He appeared before the same court and was finally sentenced to twelve months' imprisonment.

However, the nightmare sequence did not end here. As if he had not made enough mockery of the court procedure already, Smith was allowed leave to appeal against his sentence. The appeal court requested a probation report. By this time, Smith had been transferred to serve his sentence in Prison C, 120 miles away from the original court area. This meant that the original probation department had to bear the additional costs involved in arranging for the report to be completed at long range, as an alternative to incurring the even higher costs of a local probation officer making the long journey to Prison C. The report was written, and his appeal was refused, thus bringing to an end a grotesque farce of discredited legal and procedural ritual.

The whole episode resulted in a colossal waste of public money, much of it from the legal-aid fund, but such time-wasting and pointless court pantomimes are by no means the exception, *they are common*, and shows that much of our sentencing procedure is wasteful beyond words and without meaning. This waste is put into perspective when we consider that youth crimes alone and our procedures for dealing with it costs the equivalent of building a hundred new hospitals every year.[116]

Justice would have been served had this offender been sentenced to imprisonment when he appeared in court in September 2001. He was, after all, on a suspended prison sentence for other offences, and the public might well ask what exactly was achieved by the twelve months of prevarication, who benefited from it, and why the magistrates felt hostage to a criminal whose only response was to show his contempt for the law.

Another example of the massive waste of time and money occurring daily in our courts was provided by magistrates who, in February 2001, remanded a criminal thirteen times before sentencing him. Finally, after months of unnecessary delay, he was sentenced to just four months' imprisonment for theft, four months for motoring offences and unpaid fines totalling £900, and two months for failing to comply with community service and probation orders imposed for numerous previous offences. These sentences were concurrent (of course) which meant he only actually received four months' imprisonment. As a result, with automatic remission and time spent on remand taken into account, his punishment for these numerous current and past offences was no more than three weeks in jail. Such sentencing is not only pointless, but an expensive farce played out for the sole benefit of lawyers who earn large sums from the legal-aid fund by encouraging offenders and gullible lay magistrates to spin out these legal proceedings.[117]

A number of justices of the peace have told me they feel under pressure not to lock up even habitual offenders; others have expressed their frustrations that their organisation has chosen to bow to political demands for them to avoid using prison, rather than challenge them.[118] One JP told me that her court had a policy of imprisoning repeat driving offenders, but were stopped in this practice by a directive from the Lord Chancellor. What, one wonders, was his authority to interfere with our so-called system of local justice? His preparedness to sweep aside the sentencing practices of local magistrates makes hollow the recent claim by a senior judge that our 'JP system is a jewel of democracy'.[119] The politicisation of the courts is as serious, if not more so, than the politicisation of the police. Both are highly dangerous and, as well as making a mockery of our much-vaunted constitutional 'separation of powers', carry the seeds of future problems we would do well to avoid.

As one journalist put it:

> There can be no doubt that the persistent offender unmotivated to reform is the despair of the authorities who have sunk millions of pounds into a bewildering variety of initiatives, community punishment schemes, task forces and judicial procedures designed to curb his behaviour. He is the mainstay of an entire academic discipline that researches his motives and make-up. He has spawned large numbers of White Papers and official reports, and every Home Secretary since the Second World War has promised to 'crack down' on the persistent offender.[120] Yet all of this effort has been wasted because governments do not want to pay for the only sentencing option that will stop him, namely increasingly long prison sentences. The next chapter will discuss how this has led to a serious erosion of peace and security for the citizens of this country and, most significant of all, the removal of any sense of justice.

Chapter 10

If You Value Peace, Guard Justice

Justice Is Not Revenge

Thomas Keneally's brilliant, factually based novel *The Playmaker* (1987), tells the story of one of the earliest penal colonies established by the British in 1789 at Sydney Cove, Australia.[1] It reveals how, in addition to water, food and shelter, the naval officers, ratings and their convict prisoners soon realised that, for their fledgling community to work, they needed a transparent and fair system of justice; rules and sanctions were every bit as important for their survival as food and water. Likewise, whilst walking in north-eastern Spain, I came across a deserted village perched high on the slopes of the precipitous and craggy mountains which form the southern foothills of the Pyrenees. The old village church, though long abandoned, still stood intact and over its wooden front door was an inscription – 'If You Value Peace, Guard Justice'. It made a deep impression on me, as I reflected that the community of farmers and their families, who had lived and worked out their lives in the surrounding fields almost two hundred years ago, had discovered, no less than the early penal colonists in Australia, that justice is a vital ingredient for the orderly functioning of their society.

They understood that justice is not revenge; that it is the cement that maintains order and peace between persons in all communities and therefore it is society's first concern. They had grasped that justice is the cornerstone of stability and orderliness and that, without it, there is disaffection, lawlessness, anarchy and no peace. Jack Straw put his finger on it when, in 1997, he talked of justice as a system of responsibilities and rights, and said, 'without it, *society breaks down*' (my italics).[2]

The Archbishop of Canterbury, in a statement attacking the government's criminal justice policy in 1996, appeared not to share this conviction. He stated that the government's sentencing policy placed too much emphasis on revenge rather than rehabilitation.[3] His remarks showed him to be out of touch with the plight of millions who are victimised by criminals; in addition, he had failed to understand that despite the government's tough talk they were following soft sentencing policies which also placed, contrary to his view, a heavy emphasis on rehabilitation. He had also failed to make the distinction between justice as the public's right to be protected from criminals by laws sternly but fairly applied, and the drive for naked personal revenge.

In 1998 a survey of public attitudes to crime found that there was widespread support for criminals to be locked up for longer and also for the introduction of the 'three strikes' sentencing rule for offences generally.[4] But it would be wrong to interpret this as wanting *revenge*; the respondents of the survey were asking for *justice* by registering their wish to go about their daily lives unmolested by criminals.

In a different context entirely, Paddy Ashdown, the former leader of the Liberal Democrats, talked on the radio in May 2003 of his work as an international civil servant in Bosnia, helping the government there to re-establish a peaceful and thriving community following the devastations of the wars between the former states of Yugoslavia.[5] Significantly, he said their first task was to re-establish law and order and a proper system of justice. He emphasised that 'nothing could be achieved unless that were established'. Happily he reported that over the previous six years a justice system had been re-established which had gained the confidence of the people; the rules governing the peaceful functioning of their society had been put in place, and criminality was opposed by the enforcement of laws that ensured the protection of the law-abiding community. He said that as a result his wife now felt safer on the streets of Sarajevo than she did on the streets of London.

Dismantling of Justice

But while a fair and effective justice system has been put back in place in Bosnia, it has been dismantled in the UK as a result of the State's willingness to ignore large swathes of offences and pass lenient sentences. Every day our system metes out procedural and sentencing injustices, and officials frequently display their indifference to the harm caused by crime. For example, David Faulkner, a previous senior Home Office official, arguing against the use of prison, has publicly stated that 'prisons are full of people who have committed minor offences – normally theft and who are more of a nuisance than a danger to the public'.[6] To trivialise theft as minor and only of nuisance value is grossly offensive towards the millions of people who every year become victims of crime.[7]

Yet this callousness is seen in almost every aspect of our criminal justice system, which has become increasingly organised around the needs of criminals. For example, probation chiefs, instead of supporting custodial measures aimed at protecting the public, criticise them on the grounds that they may cause the prison population to rise.[8] The Probation Service expressed its 'surprise' when the government included grievous bodily harm on the list of offences judged to be serious and warranting a mandatory life prison sentence on the second appearance of the perpetrator. The Probation Service failed to express its support for this measure, which was aimed at offering the public greater protection from dangerous and violent offenders. Instead, it expressed its concern that, because of the numbers of violent offenders who are convicted for a second time for this offence, this measure would result in a rise in the number of those serving life sentences.[9]

In June 1992 magistrates at one court completely ignored the safety of the public when they released on bail a dangerous criminal charged with rape, when they had it in their power to remand him in custody. During the remand period, he raped and murdered a woman.[10] The magistrates made their decision *despite* being provided with a long list of the murderer's previous convictions, which included sex crimes. The chief probation officer of the area denied that his service was responsible for the bail decision by pointing out it was the court's job to decide on these matters. He added that the Probation Service simply had to be satisfied that the individual met the criteria for bail. But the public might ask how could anyone representing such a danger to the public, as evidenced by his previous convictions, be considered to meet criteria making him suitable for release into the community?

In 2003 a burglar was jailed for seven years for raiding no fewer than 600 homes in one eighteen-month period, which meant that for each burglary he received a little more than four days in prison.[11] This can be compared with a seven-year sentence passed on a burglar six years earlier, for six burglaries involving elderly people. Even though by comparison this appears to be a more realistic sentence, in fact it still only represents just over twelve months for each burglary.[12] In July 2001 a victim was assaulted by several attackers. The victim was kicked and punched as he struggled to escape them. The incident was captured on CCTV, but despite the brutal attack and its potential seriousness, the main aggressor was sentenced to only two months in prison, which must have left the victim convinced the courts did not consider the attack upon him as serious.[13]

As we have seen the Crown Prosecution Service (CPS) routinely discontinues thousands of cases presented to them by the police. This was illustrated in 1992 when the CPS refused to prosecute two thieves caught red-handed by their victim, a café owner whose premises they had robbed of money. One young burglar, realising the game was up, admitted he had committed the crime and pointed out his accomplice. Both were taken to the police, who presented the case to the CPS. All concerned were optimistic the burglars would be sent to court. But the CPS discontinued the proceedings against them and nothing was done. No consideration was given to the café owner's need for protection from crime, but, instead, the CPS ruled that the admissions of guilt made to the police were not in the presence of a lawyer, and therefore they would not hold in court.[14]

In the mid-1990s two young teenage girls, who kicked to death a thirteen-year-old in a spate of dreadful violence, were released after only one year's detention. The Attorney General appealed against the sentence on the grounds that it was too lenient, but the law lords turned it down, and no one listened to the protests by thousands of people in response to a decision that devastated the dead girl's family and shocked the public.[15] A few months later an eleven-year-old boy from a different part of the country was released after prosecutors decided not to pursue a charge of manslaughter against him. He had earlier punched to death a 93-year-old, partially sighted grandmother. She died a few days after the attack as a result of a blood clot, an injury entirely consistent with the assault. However, pathologists thought there was a 10 to 15 per cent chance that it could have occurred naturally and on this slim basis the decision was made to drop the charge. The dead woman's daughter could not speak through her tears.[16]

A couple whose house was burgled in 1991 wrote an impassioned letter to their MP, complaining of the increasing crime in the area and pleaded to be given better protection from criminals who were burgling unopposed when and where they chose. They received the usual wordy reply from an official which told them that the Home Office believed community sentences were better than prison for property offenders and the new Bill then going through Parliament would make provision for this. In 2003 the Home Office dismissed the trauma caused to victims of robbery by issuing guidelines to courts which said street robbers should be spared jail and given community sentences if their threats of violence did not end in actual harm to the victim.[17] Examples such as these could not make clearer how detached and, indeed, unbothered are the Home Office about the effects of crime on the public.[18]

In the mid-1990s the police interviewed a prisoner already serving a sentence for burglary. They were shocked at his admission that he had committed a further two hundred burglaries in the six months before he was caught. The police were able to declare these crimes 'cleared up' under Home Office guidelines that gives immunity from further punishments to those already serving sentences who choose to admit to other crimes. In other words, the Home Office was prepared to ignore the two hundred extra burglaries for the sake of improving their clear up rates. The suffering and loss of the victims who took the brunt of this crime deluge were not considered, and while it was the burglar who looted hundreds of homes of their property, it was Home Office procedures which looted the victims of any justice.[19]

Tony Martin, sentenced to five years for the manslaughter of a teenage burglar in 2000, was refused parole in early 2003.[20] Probation reports had recommended he should not be released. They expressed the view that the public support Martin had received had 'influenced him to think that what he had done was appropriate', and he would therefore represent a danger if released. But a danger to whom? Burglars? The report made no attempt to weigh the fact that burglars would not be in danger from anyone if they stopped breaking into people's property. The probation officer also recommended against releasing him because of Martin's refusal to admit he had done anything wrong. This is to be contrasted with the hundreds of

Table 10.1: Projected effect of longer prison sentences on the crime history of Jones (projected effects are *italicised*)

Date	Offence	Actual sentence	Actual time served in jail	Effect of increasingly long prison sentences after first appearance	Offences prevented if given long prison sentences
1984	theft, deception, burglary,	12 m s/o	none		
16/9/86	handling, assault	£25 fine + b/o for 12 m	none	*2 years*	
25/9/87	theft	£75 fine	none	*in prison*	*offences prevented*
29/1/88	criminal damage, breach of b/o	£50 fine	none	*in prison*	*offences prevented*
28/9/88	criminal damage, fail to surrender	£70 fine	none	*3 years*	
3/5/89	criminal damage	£50 fine	none	*in prison*	*offences prevented*
11/3/91	attempted burglary, theft, handling*	200 hrs com. service	none	*in prison*	*offences prevented*
11/10/91	burglary, theft, equipped for burglary	2 m suspended sentence	none	*4 years*	
21/8/92	theft	1 m prison	2 weeks	*in prison*	*offences prevented*
18/2/94	handling, fail to surrender	3-year c/d	none	*5 years*	
7/7/94	burglary, theft, handling	19 m prison	9 m	*in prison*	*offences prevented*
15/5/96	poss. drugs, handling stolen goods	£40 fine	none	*in prison*	*offences prevented*
6/12/96	deception, breach of c/d	60 hrs com. service	none	*in prison*	*offences prevented*
13/3/97	wounding	12 m prison	6 m	*in prison*	*offences prevented*
27/5/98	poss. drugs	£60 fine	none	*6 years*	*offences prevented*
28/6/99	handling	140 hrs com. service	none	*in prison*	*offences prevented*
January 2000	conspiracy to burgle	3 yrs prison	16 m	*in prison*	*offences prevented (including burglary of Tony Martin's farm)*

Abbreviations: M = months; b/o = bound over, c/d = conditional discharge, com. service = community service; hrs = hours; handling = handling stolen goods; s/o = supervision order

*Burglary is often down graded by the Crown Prosecution Service to the lesser charge of handling stolen goods

Source: Compiled by author from data reported in the *Daily Mail*, 14 May 2003

thousands of probation reports which recommend leniency for burglars and other criminals who, throughout their long careers in crime, have never showed the slightest remorse. The Probation Service was also highly critical of Martin's belief that life was safer forty years ago, and this contributed to their view that he was still too dangerous to let out. The injustice of this attitude is breathtaking, because whilst it may not have fitted the world-view of the probation officer who wrote the report, the evidence shows that Martin's assertion is 100 per cent correct.

One of the serial burglars involved in the raid on Tony Martin's farm – I will call him Jones – was given three years in prison for this crime. There were no 'exceptional circumstances' for the judge to call upon, as the defendant had a long history of criminality. The only exceptional feature was that, despite his determined life of crime, the offender was even now only being given a sentence that would leave him in jail for one year and two months. A review of Jones's crime record illustrates that the lenient sentences he had received did nothing but encourage him to continue offending.[21] Table 10.1 illustrates the effects that increasingly long prison sentences *would have had* on his criminal career (as opposed to the lenient sentences he actually received), and shows the large numbers of crimes that he would *not have been able to commit* had he been incarcerated at the time. Significantly, had such a more realistic sentencing policy been in operation, Jones would not have been able to carry out the fateful raid on Tony Martin's farm in August 1999, when his younger cousin and co-burglar was killed.

Alienation of the Public

The continued indifference shown by the justice system towards the safety of the public has resulted in such dramatic loss of trust in the forces of law and order that it poses a threat to our social and political stability. This issue will be returned to in the final chapter, but suffice it to say now that public confidence in the machinery of justice is fast disintegrating, as illustrated by the British Crime Survey (BCS) data displayed in Figure 10.1. Seventy-seven per cent of those questioned believed that the system looked after criminal's rights but only 32 per cent believed that it met the needs of the victims of crime.[22] Whilst the Home Office Minister was forced to

267

Figure 10.1: Public attitudes towards crime and the criminal justice system

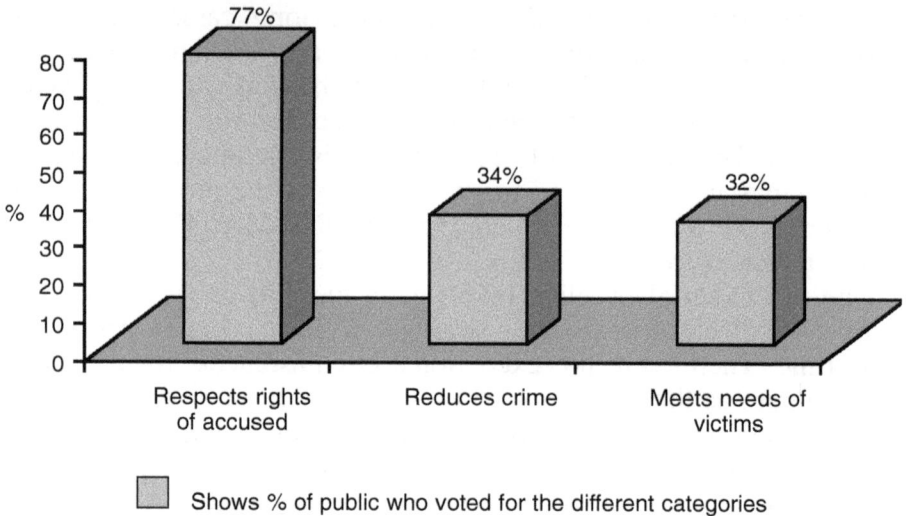

Shows % of public who voted for the different categories

Source: Home Office Bulletin 1/03, *Crime in England & Wales, 2001/2002*

admit that this showed a 'worrying lack of confidence on the part of the public in the system',[23] nothing has been done to reverse this trend, and the government's drive to prevent offenders from going to jail has not only continued but increased in its intensity.

The Distortion of Justice

The catalogue of injustices suffered by the public in the face of crime has reached such proportions that Britain's most senior police officer has described the criminal justice system as appalling and has pointed out it treats victims with 'utter contempt'.[24] He has called for more criminals to be locked up, and for there to be a clampdown on the use of bail for hardened and persistent offenders. In March 2002, in response to yet another appeal by the Home Secretary and the Lord Chief Justice for magistrates to send *fewer* offenders to jail, the Commissioner for the Metropolitan Police said that the court system is used as a shield for criminals and allowed the guilty to walk free, and far from protecting the public and providing justice, the system actually contributed to the current rise in crime.

He pointed out that, in effect, criminals were above the law. The intimidation of witnesses by the accused was a regular occurrence. In one recent example, a criminal with a history of violence walked free from a crown court because he had successfully scared off the witnesses to his violent hammer attack on a sixteen-year-old girl which had left her seriously injured. This was despite the fact that forensic tests found her blood on his T-shirt and shorts.[25] The Commissioner also argued that criminal trials have lost any real meaning. They are an uneven game of tactics played out by lawyers in front of a vulnerable and uninformed jury while the disillusioned victim looks on. He pointed out that the public were more than disenchanted with the criminal justice system in the UK – they were alienated from it because the system actually encourages the criminal to believe that crime is merely a game of no consequence to society, local communities or their victims.

Nothing is more contrary to the purposes of justice than the frequent sight of robbers, with strings of previous convictions, strutting across the estates of inner-city London, having won their most recent game in court – arrogant, untouchable, fearless and ready for anything. It is not uncommon to have muggers released on bail eight or nine times before they face trial for their first attack. Yet, as previously pointed out, despite the massive increase in crime, there has been a sharp fall in the number of offenders being brought before the courts; the figure of one million for the year ending in March 2002, was a 9 per cent fall over the previous year.[26] At the same time, the number of offenders found guilty of burglary fell from 55,200 in 1990 to 31,000 in 2000; for crimes of violence the numbers found guilty in 1990 were 60,600 compared with 47,100 for the year 2000; and for theft the numbers fell from 174,700 to 142,100.[27]

This is not a recent trend. In one police district alone, in 1989, it was reported that of the 4,729 reported crimes committed by juveniles, only 34 per cent were 'proceeded with', that is, taken to court.[28] The rest were 'diverted' from the system and so got away with their crimes. This approach to juvenile offenders, which is still used today, makes a mockery of any claims that juvenile crime is decreasing; it also means that the loss and anxiety experienced by their victims is routinely ignored.

Victims and their witnesses are often treated as if their wholly understandable fears, as well as their time, were of little consequence.

In one crown court, for example, out of 140 people summoned as witnesses in a two-week period, only 19 were called to give evidence. In one particular case, a highly dangerous gun gang walked free because a judge would not allow a terrified witness to give evidence from behind a screen. In another case, the mother of a murdered child was forced to sit in court within feet of the man who admitted killing her son.[29] Many volunteer witness support workers have given up because they could no longer stomach the injustices perpetrated on a daily basis by a court system many of them describe as rotten. Is it any wonder a survey found that 83 per cent of witnesses who had appeared in court wanted nothing more to do with the system?

Criminals No Longer Fear the Daylight

Thousands of crimes occur in broad daylight because the criminal is now unafraid of being caught and knows he has little to fear. In July 1995 a woman was abducted and raped in the middle of the day in London's Regent's Park. During the fifteen years before this offence was committed the risk of becoming a victim of violence had increased by at least 15 per cent.[30] What is more the level of violence we are witnessing by robbers intent on stealing is escalating. In recent times a young girl was shot in the head in a suburban street in mid-afternoon for her mobile phone; an estate agent was fatally stabbed in front of his fiancé for his car; and a family were shot at and one of them killed for a Rolex watch. Drug deals, street robberies and other thefts are now frequently carried out not only in daylight but in full view of scores of passers-by, so confident are the criminals that they will escape justice.

Yet despite this disturbing trend, the government has stuck to its liberal sentencing policies and at the beginning of the twenty-first century, only 1.6 per cent of the thousands of violent offences taking place every year resulted in a prison sentence.[31] In fact, as described in detail in an earlier chapter, criminals generally, and rapists, robbers and burglars in particular, are more likely to avoid prison in Britain than ever before, as the chances of them going to jail has dropped by 80 per cent since the 1950s. This, plus a dramatic drop in the detection rate as well as a significant increase in the use of cautions, is the reason for the twelve-fold increase in crime over the same period.[32]

Table 10.2: Percentage of sentence served, 2000

All lengths of sentence less than life	44%
Up to 3 months	39%
Over 3 months and up to 6 months	38%
Over 6 months and less than 12 months	37%
12 months	37%
Over 12 months and up to 18 months	39%
Over 18 months and up to 3 years	41%
Over 3 years and less than four years	42%
Four years	54%
Over four years and up to five years	54%
Over five years and up to ten years	54%
Over ten years and less than life	54%

Source: Home Office, *Prison Statistics England & Wales, 2000*

A Redefined 'Justice' System

In 1999 the government forecast a massive 40 per cent increase in property crime within three years.[33] This was destined to have a huge effect on the public with burglaries rising to more than a million each year and car crimes to 1.4 million. However, nothing was done to avert this thus ensuring their forecast became a reality. Whilst the length of prison sentences continued to be derisory, the time *actually* served was even less as shown by the 2000 data in Table 10.2.

As stated, these figures are for 2000, and so the percentage of the sentence actually served in prison will now be *far less*, due to extensions to the Home Detention Curfew scheme. However, whilst these mechanisms exist to shorten the sentence of the criminal, there is nothing that can lessen the victim's anxiety and fear which are frequently the legacies of burglary, robbery, theft and other crimes.

In October 2001 a 'rehabilitation' scheme was launched by the Home Office following an initiative taken by a senior law lord, Lord Justice Kay, chairman of the Criminal Justice Consultative Committee. His view was that it was time for judges to become involved in the rehabilitation of offenders.[34] Under the scheme, judges visit prisons and interview prisoners with a view to finding out what the offender thought about his sentence and the rehabilitative efforts being made on his behalf. Lord Justice Kay underlined this extraordinary development by saying that the judge's role should not end with the passing of a sentence. The rationale for this nonsense was that judges 'should have a databank of prisoner's experiences [of sentences] to draw on so that next time they would know whether that sentence is a good idea'.

So what the public are being asked to accept is that criminals' views on their likes and dislikes of prison now have to be taken account of by judges when they decide on sentences. In contrast, no senior law lord or other official has put forward a scheme whereby judges are required to interview the victims of crime in order to take their views into account before sentencing. In fact, only a few years earlier, Lord Chief Justice Taylor had argued that the feelings of victims should *not* be allowed to dominate judges' sentencing,[35] but now it seems the view of the criminals who victimised them are so important that judges are now making special visits to prisons in order to canvass their opinions.

The built-in absurdities as well as the injustices of this scheme make it impossible to take seriously. There is already an army of professional workers whose job includes assessing the impact of the prison sentence on prisoners. I cannot believe that the majority of judges, who jealously guard against any interference with their sentencing role, submit willingly to this scheme, and probably privately resent being dragooned into what is an embarrassing 'rehabilitative' charade. Its real purpose, I am certain, is to bring yet more pressure to bear on the judges to send fewer offenders to jail.

Jailed offenders were the focus of a leaked report from the Social Exclusion Unit set up by Tony Blair in 2002 to tackle poverty. It said that public funds should be used to pay for enhanced discharge grants for prisoners leaving prison and to pay offenders increased housing benefits to keep them out of prison in the first place. Their proposal was that such financial help should be given in exchange for the prisoner signing a document promising to be good in the future.[36] The depth of naivety in this idea is unfathomable; but it rests on two worn-out and incorrect assumptions. These are, first, that criminals commit offences and end up in prison because they are poor, and, second, that it is the responsibility of the State to reform the offender and therefore it must be seen to be making financial and practical gestures to this end. The idea that the *community* bears a heavy responsibility for this process is itself a form of injustice because, whilst it is right to provide help and encouragement for those who truly intend to lead the straight life, the criminal is responsible for his own reform. If he is truly sorry for what he has done, then he will reform with or without help.

Chapter Nine referred to Anti-Social Behaviour Orders (ASBOs) introduced in 1999 as a measure to deal with persistent offenders and troublemakers, by banning them from a particular area for a period of time. These are now known to have wrought their own brand of injustice on the public; an undercover investigation carried out in 2003 revealed that the majority of offenders simply ignored the restrictions placed upon them by these orders and the authorities did nothing about it. The few that were taken back to court for failure to comply were all given a non-custodial penalty which left them on the streets to carry on offending as before. The undercover cameras used in the investigation showed there was frequently no one around to see the offenders breaching their orders, while the street wardens, appointed by some authorities to supposedly control anti-social behaviour, were powerless to stop the offenders from offending or behaving in an anti-social way because they had no powers of arrest and could only observe. The street wardens were often the targets of intimidation by those whose behaviour they were supposed to be controlling.

In addition, many youths made the subject of these orders are hardened, vicious criminals with long histories of offending. One example concerned a youth who had, prior to being made the subject of an anti-social behaviour order, viciously attacked a man living on an estate in London. He had repeatedly beaten him around the head with a bat, fracturing his skull. His trial for this crime was halted on a technicality and so the criminal walked free. As a result it was the victim, suffering from memory loss and epilepsy as a result of the attack, who had to move house in order to get away from his tormentors. More recently it was reported that almost 50 per cent of all ASBOs are known to have been breached.[37] The real figure, I am sure, is very much higher because only about 5 per cent of crimes are detected. Therefore, it is likely that the vast majority of the 3,826 orders made between 1999 and March 2005 have been broken, often by further acts of crime.

The Policy of 'Double Think'

I have repeatedly drawn attention to the fact that for years the government has talked tough in relation to its crime sentencing policies, but has done nothing to properly ensure the protection of the public. The ineffectiveness of the ASBOs mentioned above provides an illustration of this. Another example can be found in the National Standards[38] set by the Home Office for the supervision of offenders by the Probation Service. It states that the purpose of a community sentence is to:

provide a rigorous and effective punishment.

As previously explained, this requires offenders to be supervised for no more than 18.5 hours in a two-year period. In reality, such 'supervision' amounted, in the majority of cases, to a talk with the probation officer or attendance at a programme (if the offender turned up) for, at most, half an hour every couple of weeks. To call this 'rigorous' and/or indeed a 'punishment', is stretching the English language to breaking point.

reduce the likelihood of reoffending.

Nothing could be more meaningless. For years the evidence of their reconviction rates has demonstrated beyond all argument that persistent offenders are not deterred from their life of crime by community sentences. All Probation Service and Home Office initiatives aimed at reforming persistent offenders, many of which were based on special community programmes, have lamentably failed to do so, most recently evidenced by the disastrous 'what works' offender group work programmes, naively seen as being able to change the way offenders think.

rehabilitate the offender, where possible.

This had meaning forty years ago when the Probation Service worked with offenders early on in their criminal career and who showed some motivation to change. It is now meaningless, as the offenders on community supervision are, in the main, hardened and persistent offenders who make a lot of money from crime and who do not see themselves as in need of rehabilitation.

274

enable reparation to be made to the community.

This is empty rhetoric because nothing can undo the experience of being victimised by criminals. Visits from well-meaning counsellors or offers for windows and doors to be repaired and made secure by local organisations cannot remove the sense of anxiety and loss of peace of mind which is the frequent legacy of those targeted by criminals.

minimise the risk of harm to the public.

This has to be the most vacuous of the supposed purposes of community supervision. The Probation Service *deliberately* targets the more persistent offenders for community supervision, despite them showing no evidence they want to change. Thus not only do they not *minimise* the risk of harm to the public, they *maximise* it. The evidence could not be clearer that offenders determined to carry out violent and/or property offences are not the least deterred by being supervised; and there is nothing probation officers can do to stop them.

The Growth of Public Despair

It is not only probation officers who cannot stop offenders from committing crime. Neither can our police force, as the lack of police on patrol means that the offenders have free rein of the streets to do as they want. In particular, over the last decade the number of attacks by vandals and thieves on parked cars in our communities has increased alarmingly.

Following one of these systematic attacks in the 1990s, my neighbour's car was vandalised for the second time. Several other vehicles in the street were also extensively damaged and one was stolen. The repair bill for my neighbour's car alone was several hundred pounds. The change in the victims' attitude over this period has been noticeable. Ten years before they all expected that something would be done about it. Now they are in despair and no longer have any expectations that the police will even bother to look for their cars when they are stolen or will show any interest in catching the vandals who damaged or destroyed them. If it were not an insurance requirement, many have said they would not bother to tell the police at all. When the police do find stolen cars, they submit the victims to more injustice by towing it to a private pound without their consent, where a substantial fee must be paid to have it released. Thus the public's attitude to the police is now not only one of despair over these matters but also of growing resentment.

When my neighbour reported her car had been vandalised the police limited their involvement to telling her that car theft and burglary had increased dramatically in recent years and she would be well advised to spend at least another £200 on fitting a good-quality car alarm. She then wrote to the local MP, expressing her concern over the rising crime rate and pointing out that the Criminal Justice Bill that was then going through Parliament failed to address this problem adequately.[39] She received the usual bland reply, saying that her letter had been forwarded to the Home Office and that a reply was expected soon. When it came, it consisted of twelve photocopied pages of a wordy and meaningless departmental report on crime. Nothing could have compounded the feeling of helplessness and despair more than the receipt of such an empty and meaningless reply.

If it meant anything, it was that nothing was going to be done to stop the steep slide into lawlessness. Yet the misery caused to the public by criminals and vandals has been ignored, and all governments since the 1960s have maintained an attitude of denial towards the deeply destructive effects that the explosion in crime, particularly property crime, has had on the health and standard of life of the public. Those in power have done nothing to stop it and everything to encourage it. These injustices have been made worse, if that is at all possible, by the presentation of their crime policies as being in the public interest, thus treating the citizens of this country with a degree of contempt which is hard to imagine.

Alarm bells began to ring loudly in the 1980s when a series of reports revealed the state of crime levels in the UK. In 1988 a Home Office report admitted that crime had risen relentlessly over the previous years, and that millions of ordinary men and women were living in fear and of being attacked in the streets. With a display of arrogance, the researchers tried to claim that the crime problem was not as bad as the public felt it to be and added that the best way to reassure them was to provide accurate information about the levels of crime. They even claimed that more police action would not help improve the crime problem and that in some cases it would make it worse. It is difficult to understand how officials could be so dismissive of the experiences of the millions victimised by ruthless and persistent criminals. Much to the relief of the public the then Police Federation Chairman struck a note for common sense by declaring such claims to be nonsense, and that the way to tackle crime was to put more police on the streets to deter and catch the criminals responsible.[40]

However, he was not heeded and these injustices were allowed to continue. By 1991, government research was showing the crime situation had deteriorated even further and it attempted to quell rising public concern by organising the first national 'Crime Prevention Week' to focus attention on burglary, car crime and crimes of violence, all of which had shown a marked increase. The then opposition spokesman Roy Hattersley was right to declare this an effort to 'create the illusion of activity'.[41] I believe it was also deeply patronising to a public that was and is desperately in need of practical measures to protect them from crime, not propaganda which lays the blame for it at their door. These make-believe attempts to deal with the problem continued. By 1992 it was reported that only seven in every hundred crimes were being solved, and only three led to a court conviction.[42] Local and national newspapers were again reporting that policemen on the streets of our towns and cities were a rare sight, and almost non-existent in rural areas.[43] The public were bothering to report only a fraction of the crimes being committed against them. Out of 3.4 million offences of vandalism each year, only 750,000 were reported; likewise, less than half of the 70,000 cases of wounding were brought to notice because the public believed the police were not interested or could do nothing. In addition, only half of the 1.4 million burglaries committed in 1992 were recorded by the police.

But worse was to come. In 1998 the then Home Secretary Jack Straw was said to be 'in shock' after reading a report prepared by one of the country's most distinguished criminologists, which revealed, as summarised in Tables 10.3–5, that most crime was by then worse in the UK than in America, and that our methods of dealing with it were far less effective.[44] The report detailed the evidence which showed that while rates of robbery, assault and burglary were plummeting in the US, they were rocketing in the UK. In particular, it pointed out that there had been an 81 per cent increase in robbery in the UK since 1981, while over the same period in the US there

Table 10.3: Crimes per 1,000 people – UK and USA compared

Crimes per 1,000 people 1995	England & Wales	USA
Robbery	7.6	5.3
Burglary	82.9	47.5
Assaults	20	8.8

Table 10.4: Convictions per 1,000 alleged offenders – UK and USA compared

Convictions per 1,000 alleged offenders 1995	England & Wales	USA
Robbery	6	22
Burglary	6	14
Assaults	14	25

Table 10.5: Average sentence – UK and USA compared

Average sentence (in months) 1995	England & Wales	USA
Robbery	40.3	88.8
Burglary	14.9	43.1
Assaults	13.7	47.8

Source: A Report on Crime in the UK by Professor David Farrington and Dr Patrick Langan, 1998, reported in the *Mail on Sunday*, 11 October 1998

had been a 28 per cent drop. Equally startling was that the rate of muggings in the UK was shown to be 1.4 times higher than in America. One especially chilling section of the report showed that in 1981 the chance of becoming a murder victim in America was nearly nine times higher than in the UK. But despite some of the toughest gun laws in the world, the UK was gaining ground, and the US rate was now less than six times greater.

The report blamed these crime figures on the UK's soft policing and sentencing policies, and on Home Office policy makers who for years, it said, had been primarily concerned with reducing the prison population. That this was the conclusion of a highly respected academic criminologist meant that it could not be easily dismissed. Nevertheless, whilst the report may have shocked Jack Straw, it did little to change the direction of sentencing policy, which has continued to heap injustice upon injustice on victims and the public.

Crime Victim: Cinderella of the Criminal Justice System

I have already identified that the justice system shows a disregard for the victims of crime that frequently amounts to contempt. In October 2001 a youth was sentenced to only six months supervision in the community following his dangerously violent attack on a cyclist.[45] The defendant had ambushed his victim and beat him around the head with a large heavy stick. He needed seven stitches for his wound and was lucky not to have been more seriously injured. This excessively lenient sentence told the criminal that no one minded too much if he used violence; that it was not that serious to hit someone on the head with a large, heavy stick; and that he risked very little if he did it again. To the victim, the message of the sentence was clear. No one was too bothered about him; he was left feeling unprotected; and the court was not prepared to recognise that what happened to him was very serious or give him justice.

A different example was provided in September 2003 when Simon Hughes, the Lib-Dem spokesman on Home Affairs, implied that burglary was no more than a minor intrusion into someone's house. Speaking at the Lib-Dem Conference he said that, 'Where there was no contact between the burglar and the victim, the burglar should not go to prison'.[46] Brian Lawrence, in his book *They Call it Justice*, points out that in March 1987, the then Conservative Home Secretary Douglas Hurd, whilst discussing crime on the television programme *This Week Next Week*, also described burglary as a relatively minor offence.[47] Such statements amount to a major injustice for those affected by these crimes. Brian Lawrence also recalls from his experiences in court that probation officers frequently referred to such crimes as 'only against property', as though they did not matter. Likewise, newspapers often criticise courts for sending property offenders to prison, despite the fact that these crimes cause millions great distress and unhappiness.

The few property offenders who are caught are frequently fined, yet for many this has become a meaningless exercise. Figures published in 1997 showed that a quarter of the total fines imposed by the courts were written off because the offenders refused to pay them. By the late 1990s this sum amounted to over £100 million, yet the system could (apparently) do nothing about it.[48] Writing the fines off meant that the criminals got away with their burglaries

279

and thefts, and the courts' refusal to follow up with alternative sentences for the non-payers, signals to the victims of those crimes that they are of little consequence. In November 2002 a Radio 4 news item reported that the problem of unpaid fines was still chronic.[49] Yet these injustices were made worse by government proposals put forward in July 2003 to place a surcharge on home insurance policies to make up for the shortfall in fines collection.

In 1991 a conference was held in Long Lartin Jail, near Evesham, attended by Home Office officials, prison reform groups and welfare pressure groups.[50] The audience were the inmates who were encouraged to make angry speeches about their dissatisfaction with the arrangements governing their family visits and other prison conditions. In speeches from the platform, prisoners demanded the installation of telephones *before* improvements to the sanitary conditions, because they said keeping contact with their families was so important to them. They also demanded better pay so they 'could send some money to those at home', and they demanded to be moved to jails nearer home areas. These demands were met with loud cheers and applause from the inmate audience.

That this conference was ever organised was an affront to the tens of thousands of individuals who were victimised by the inmates of Long Lartin Jail. These offenders chose repeatedly to steal, rob and burgle the public; the latter had no choice about being victimised, and being left, in some cases, with a life sentence of fear. The Home Office have never organised a conference to encourage the victims of crime to give voice to their demands for better protection and to be left in peace by criminals who predate on them. Yet this conference, aided and abetted by the Home Office officials, helped create an atmosphere where the criminals were encouraged to feel hard done by and that they had the right to make demands.

Yet, in reality, they and other prisoners have nothing to complain about, as they are aware that they have got away with most of their crimes. In 1999 it was revealed that one in ten defendants facing criminal charges were going free because of a catalogue of blunders committed by the Crown Prosecution Service.[51] This is apart from the thousands of defendants they *deliberately* chose not to prosecute 'in the public interest'; that is, to save money. At the same time Neighbourhood Watch information handouts were telling the public that one home in Britain is burgled every thirty-seven seconds,[52] yet Home Office statistics dated 2001 revealed that 88 per cent of burglaries were not detected, leaving these experiences unresolved for millions of victims.[53] In 2003 it was reported by an ICM poll that nine out of ten crimes *do not* end up in a courtroom.[54]

There is a hollow ring to the prisoners' claims they wanted access to telephones and better visits in order to 'stay in touch with their families'. It was their criminal behaviour which caused them to be separated from their families in the first place; in many cases, their family ties would have been broken long before they came into prison. If contact with their families were so important to them, why did they risk it by repeatedly committing offences? I know from my previous work experience that many prisoners have used access to telephones in prison to foster and maintain criminal contacts and activity. They have also used them to intimidate witnesses and victims. Likewise, moving to jails nearer their homes makes it easier to stay in touch with their criminal associates. During my many years of working in a prison, I never knew of any inmate 'who sent money home'. If prison reformers believe they do then they will believe anything.

Following the prison riots in the early 1990s, Lord Woolf recommended improved visiting arrangements for prisoners, to 'help them keep in contact with their family and friends'. Many inmates have used these contacts to receive drugs, cigarettes and other contraband. In some cases, the possession of such smuggled items provides the prisoner with a power base that can be used to bully and intimidate other inmates.

Yet many liberal commentators never cease in their efforts to raise the public's guilt about offenders who are locked up. In January 2001 one of them misused Winston Churchill's famous dictum: 'The level of civilisation in any society should be judged by how it treats its weakest members, such as those left forgotten in prison'.[55] To try and persuade the public that criminals, particularly those who are drug addicts, are 'weak' members of society is a major falsehood. Criminals are anything but weak, and to view many of them as otherwise innocent individuals driven by drug dependency to steal, rob and burgle, often with violence, is dangerously naive. Likewise, there is no danger of those in prison being forgotten because they are not there long enough; the government is only too keen to discharge them at the earliest possible opportunity. Whilst it is right that society should look to defend and care for its weakest members, these should be seen to include, not the criminals, but their victims, who are powerless to defend themselves against repeated onslaughts of theft, burglary and violence.

But not only does the State fail to prevent millions falling victim to crime, it falls significantly short of providing them with adequate help when they do. In January 2004 it became known that Ian Huntley, convicted of the murders of Holly Wells and Jessica Chapman, was entitled to receive £250,000 in legal aid to mount an almost non-existent defence. At the same time it was announced that the families of the murdered girls were to receive just £11,000 each under the Home Office compensation scheme.[56] This equates to a little more than £1,000 for each year of the girls' lives. A similar amount was paid to the family of Sarah Payne, murdered by the paedophile Roy Whiting in 2000, and also to the family of Damilola Taylor, who was stabbed to death in Peckham, London in the same year. The deep sense of injustice this must have provoked for the families concerned could only be made worse by the knowledge that the sum of £11,000 is the same figure paid to someone who suffers a damaged wrist as a result of being a victim of crime, and that it is considerably less than the £33,000 paid for receiving burn scars or the £27,000 paid for the loss of one eye.[57]

What makes this response to these victims all the more unacceptable is that in 2003 the Home Office paid £248,000 damages to a convicted criminal after he fell over in a shower whilst in jail. In addition, an asylum seeker who was jailed for sexually assaulting a 76-year-old woman in 1998 was awarded £15,000 for breach of his *human rights*. The judge ordered that he should be returned to Somalia after he finished his three-year sentence, but when released he protested and fought to stay in the country. He was remanded in jail while his legal challenge was heard, prompting the High Court to rule he had been unlawfully detained. His compensation was five times the £3,000 maximum to which his victim was entitled.[58] In another example, a policeman in 1998 received £150,000 after leaving the police force with a back injury caused by banging his head on the doorway of a police kennel, while in the same year a six-year-old was offered £7,960 from the Criminal Injuries Compensation Board after an attack by a maniac which had left her with metal plates in her jaw and a six-inch scar on her face.[59]

Justice Rationed: The Public at the End of the Queue

The public increasingly fail to receive help from the police when they need it. On 24 December 2003, an 87-year-old woman rang the police HQ in her area because she had discovered that her car had been broken into and badly damaged. Someone had tried to steal it but had been disturbed and ran off. She lived alone and was highly distressed, particularly as thieves and vandals had targeted her car on several occasions in the past. The police HQ's switchboard tried to put her through to her local police station. She waited for what seemed an interminable interlude. Finally the switchboard operator was forced to confess that she could get no answer. She was advised, 'Ring back tomorrow'. The elderly victim could hardly believe what she was being told. This was the police she was ringing after all, not a department store she had called on the wrong day. She protested that surely someone could come out and see her. Eventually, to the victim's dismay and astonishment, the operator told her that there was only one policeman available at her local police station and that was probably the reason why she could not get any response.[60]

Based on information obtained from the police station in question[61] and an investigation of the latest Census figures[62] for the area it covered, I discovered that the one policeman available for call-outs was covering a population of at least 140,000 people. This figure is hard to take in and makes a farce of local policing because it meant that effectively those local wards had no police cover and that thieves, vandals, robbers, burglars and other criminals had free rein on their streets. Further investigation revealed that twenty years ago the same area was covered by three police stations (and for a while four) in contrast to the one that exists today. I recently heard exasperated members of the public ask, 'Where are the police? We never see them around here – they are always too busy to come when we call them,' despite claims by their local chief constable that he had opened several new police premises during 2003.[63]

It was no surprise that in the same year a YouGov crime survey reported that the public remained unconvinced that Tony Blair had been true to his pledge to be 'tough on crime'.[64] The size of our police force is so inadequately small given the size of the crime problem it faces that the record number of police officers the government claimed it recruited in 2003 made no difference to the general absence of police on our streets.

Two separate crime reports from the *Bristol Evening Post* provide a telling insight into the problem.[65] One tells of dozens of bus shelters being smashed during a single night of vandalism across a wide area. This spate of violent and noisy destruction was not challenged or witnessed by a single policeman, presumably because there were none available to patrol the streets. The second report speaks of a successful police raid on a counterfeiting factory producing pirate DVDs. Several police were involved in the operation, which, no doubt, was based on an intelligence picture built up over a period of time. Whilst no one can argue with deployment of police officers to disrupt criminal organisations involved in commercial piracy, why should there not also be sufficient of them to patrol our streets and provide protection for community facilities and members of the public? Why have the public been put at the end of the queue for justice and protection – and who made this decision?

That chief constables can only deal with certain selected pockets of crime at the expense of ignoring large swathes of other criminality is an injustice the community should not be asked to bear, and one that will increase the dangerous sense of alienation many people now feel in relation to the forces of law and order. Indeed many in the police force have made public their awareness that anarchy is taking over in the hearts of many of our cities, as the rule of law slides into crisis because of a complete absence in many areas of police officers to either challenge or arrest those committing offences.[66] The thousands of robberies recorded by the police in 2000/01, for example, in which firearms were used is a powerful indication that those responsible for these very serious offences had little or no fear of the law.[67]

Disdain for the Public's View of Crime

In the early 1990s a high-ranking civil servant told me, during the course of a meeting, that she and her colleagues were so affronted by Michael Howard's tough crime policies that they had 'written a letter of complaint about him'. I asked her why she thought he was bringing in tougher sentencing measures. She said, with a great deal of disdain, 'he is only doing it to court public votes'. I replied that it seemed as if she thought little of public opinion, which must have made it hard for her to live in a democracy. This did not go down well, but she had shown that all too often the criminal justice elite assume 'they know best' as far as sentencing policy is concerned and are prepared to dismiss the views of the majority.

Frequently, even ministers show what amounts to contempt for the public by claiming to have found successful ways of coping with offenders in the community (contrary to the public's own experience) and then respond with a disdainful silence when they are challenged to produce the evidence for their claims. In January 2002, the then Minister of State for Prisons and the National Probation Service, said, 'There are too many people in jail. There are many people in prison who could be dealt with effectively and toughly in the community in a way that would turn them away from crime.'[68] Home Secretary David Blunkett, in a newspaper interview published in February 2002, claimed that the Probation Service used tough and effective programmes with offenders. Both were publicly challenged to provide evidence to back up their statements and both failed to do so.[69]

In the 1980s, the then Deputy Under-Secretary of State at the Home Office made the following astonishing statement. He said: 'The police are unsure whether their main task is simply to detect and arrest criminals – or whether they have a wider social purpose in maintaining social stability and confidence, in tackling crime *by other means*, or in protecting individual rights and civil liberties' (my italics).[70] I am sure it was the offender's 'rights and civil liberties' he had in mind when he made this absurd statement, which declared that the task of the police, to detect and arrest criminals, is outdated. The untutored public might ask if it isn't precisely by detecting and arresting criminals that the police maintain social stability and confidence. The same official could hardly conceal his contempt for public opinion when he said that reform of the criminal justice system should be based on the evidence of what works rather than what appeals to *Sun* readers.[71] The 'what works' programmes he was thinking of have since proved to be a disastrous failure, and millions of *Sun* readers, along with countless other members of the public have a right to live in peace unmolested by criminals.

'Star Chamber Justice'

In 1998 a massive injustice was perpetrated against the public by a government enquiry supposedly set up to find out if alternative (non-custodial) sentences were working as a means of protecting the public and reforming offenders.[72] From the start, the House of Commons All Party Home Affairs Committee charged with this investigation abandoned this brief and focused instead on building a case against the use of prison, entirely on ideological grounds. The laborious process they followed in collecting evidence over several months, at great cost to the taxpayer was a charade, because it had no influence on the outcome of their enquiry, which had been fixed in their minds from the start. They ignored any evidence, which contradicted their view that there were too many people in prison and seized upon anything which supported it. Their final report was never going to recommend anything else other than the extended use of non-custodial sentencing and less use of custody, thus seriously undermining the safety of the public. Just as the Court of Star Chamber was misused by some of our monarchs in past centuries to crush all opposition to their wishes, so was the parliamentary committee used to suppress all opposition to its already formed anti-prison agenda.[73]

A False Dawn

All Party enquiries of this sort have long been regarded as beacons of democracy, as they provide an opportunity for members of the public, not normally associated with politics, to submit their views to influential members of Parliament, whose recommendations are likely to be encompassed in new legislation. My small group of colleagues and I were therefore excited at the prospect of providing the committee with evidence in the form of several well-researched papers which tabulated the unarguable evidence that the community supervision of offenders was an unmitigated disaster as a means of preventing crime and protecting the public. This small group consisted of one of the most distinguished professors of criminology in the country, a senior and long-serving magistrate who was also an eminent academic, and two former senior probation officers with over fifty years experience between them. In most cases, the evidence we presented was from the Home Office archives, and for this reason I was confident the committee would be swayed by what we said.

I am now somewhat embarrassed to recall how hopeful I was that our research would sway MPs into passing laws which would better protect the public from crime. In the event, they ignored both our written and our oral evidence, and instead based their recommendations to Parliament on ill-informed opinion, half-truths and ideologically motivated misinformation provided by numerous anti-prison organisations and individuals. (One of these organisations, the Penal Affairs Consortium, was invited by the Select Committee to respond to our evidence, and it is of the greatest significance that it failed to do so.)

Tell Them What They Want To Hear

For example, the 'evidence' given by the then Chief Inspector of Prisons was significant only by its naivety and ignorance. At that time, he had barely three years experience of the penal system and lacked any significant background related to criminal justice generally and sentencing in particular. Yet he made the sweeping statement that '30 per cent of women prisoners, 30 to 40 per cent of young offenders and 30 per cent of adult offenders were wrongly given a custodial sentence'. No one asked him how he knew this. Did the committee think that he, lacking any knowledge or experience in sentencing, had read the case papers on thousands of trials and knew for certain that in every case the courts were wrong to impose a prison sentence? Of course not, but he told the committee what they wanted to hear. At no time did they challenge the basis for this sweeping statement, which was later supported by the then Lord Chief Justice.[74] In his oral submissions to the committee the Chief Inspector of Prisons, whilst discussing offenders, made reference to 'the chap who goes out and does something silly'.[75] Thus crime, which causes untold harm to millions every year, was trivialised by this official, revealing the depth of his ignorance about persistent offenders and their effects on the public.

The representatives of the Association of Chief Officers of Probation (ACOP) also provided highly misleading information to the committee. In their written evidence, they claimed a 72 per cent success rate for offenders supervised in the community,[76] and repeated this in their oral evidence.[77] Yet only a few minutes before the ACOP officials had talked to the committee about the 52 per cent reconviction rate (failure rate) for *all* offenders on community supervision.[78] Yet no one on the committee queried the obvious contradiction (see Note 1). The National Association of Probation Officers went further and told the committee '80 per cent of offenders placed on a community order completed the period of supervision *without reconviction or breach*' (my italics).[79] Once again, the committee were more than willing to be misled and no one queried this wild claim, even though Home Office reconviction statistics for offenders on community supervision made it abundantly clear that this statement was nonsense.[80] These show that for offenders under 21 years the reconviction (failure) rate is 70 per cent; for 21 to 24-year-olds it is 63 per cent; for 25 to 29-year-olds it is 55 per cent, and for those aged 30 and over it is 35 per cent.

The Chief Inspector of Probation wrote a letter to the committee in which he stated: 'Certain community programmes involving offenders significantly out-perform custodial sentences in reducing offending.' A few lines further on he wrote, 'There is a body of evidence which shows that the Probation Service *can be* more effective in reducing offending.' This second statement falls short of saying that the Probation Service *does* reduce offending and therefore conflicts with the earlier claim. Not one MP on the committee commented on this or asked him to identify the community programmes that he claimed out-performed prison in reducing offending.[81]

The committee had in any case already been informed by an eminent professor of criminology that the research upon which the Chief Inspector based his claims was without value,[82] and additionally that, by the time a prisoner has served an average prison sentence (less than three months), some 28 per cent of those given a community order will have offended again at least once,[83] and that long-term analysis of reconviction rates showed that prison *always* provided the public with more protection than community supervision.[84] This was a lot for the committee to swallow as it powerfully undermined their anti-prison agenda, so they ignored it and kept quiet on these issues.

In contrast, they were keen to stress their support for the comments made by the Lord Chief Justice who had submitted that community sentences were often more effective at protecting the public from offenders with drug habits than was prison. No one on the committee asked the Lord Chief Justice what his evidence was for his pronouncement, which, in any case, he was not qualified to make. It is just as well for him they did not because there isn't any. The committee went on to praise the work of the Bolton Drug Misusing Offenders project, as an example of an effective non-custodial drug programme. However, detailed examination reveals that after three months almost 60 per cent of the offenders on this programme dropped out,[85] thus it failed totally to protect the public. The committee made no reference to how long the remainder stayed on the programme which offered the usual mix of counselling and methadone as a substitute for other drugs. Most significant of all was that the committee's assessment of the programme made no reference to the offending rates of those involved, yet despite this, and on the basis of a discussion with only three offenders on the scheme, this programme was highly commended by the government as a good example of work with offenders which could stabilise or reduce drug use in *80 per cent of cases* (my italics).[86]

A Pre-arranged Agenda

The truth is that the enquiry by the All Party Home Affairs Committee was not an enquiry at all, but a carefully staged propaganda play in which the outcome had been fixed in the minds of those who controlled it long beforehand. The Committee sat for six months. They examined nineteen witnesses and read thirty-five written submissions, but my colleagues and I soon became suspicious of the committee's objectivity. We were not the only ones. The Police Superintendents' Association, in their written evidence, expressed concern that one of the background objectives was to reduce the prison population. How right they were. In spite of repeated requests, the association was not allowed to give oral evidence.[87]

Patrick Curran, QC, in his review of the work of the Home Affairs Committee in September 1998, correctly identified that their major concern was the rise in the prison population. At no time did any independent observer point out that this was not their brief, which was to enquire into non-custodial sentences, and Curran's review likewise failed to mention this.[88] Thus unchallenged, the chairman of the Home Affairs Committee, in May 1998, felt safe enough to

289

declare his colours in an interview for a parliamentary journal. He told the interviewer: 'The starting point [for the Home Affairs enquiry] is that everyone recognises that our prisons are too full, and that the prison population is rising out of control'.[89] I believe that in his management of the committee objectivity was sacrificed and every piece of evidence he was given was filtered through this prearranged mindset.

Stalinist Tactics

One of the hallmarks of Stalin's regime in Soviet Russia in the early part of the twentieth century was its ability to engage in 'double-think', where reality was ignored and all political and social actions were driven by ideology propped up by meaningless statistics and propaganda. There is a disturbing echo of these politics in the way the All Party Home Affairs Committee handled its investigation. Astonishingly, it concluded that community-based sentences are more effective at reducing offending than prison, despite the fact that it was given irrefutable evidence to the contrary. As indicated, it eagerly took note of evidence submitted to it that was misleading and sometimes untruthful.

It rejected our view that the prison population needed to rise to 200,000 or more in order for the public to be properly protected from criminals. This estimate was based on the number of persistent criminals supervised by the Probation Service who, because of their continued offending, should have been serving prison sentences, added to those who were then in prison. The chairman knew the basis of our calculation but he sensationalised this issue in his criticisms of us to Parliament and said nothing about the calculation it was based on. He also refused to acknowledge our criticism that the committee had no right to put a ceiling on the number of people sent to prison, and that the rate of imprisonment should be dictated by the crime rate and not by ideological or financial expediency. They took no notice of our argument that no crime is 'petty' to the victim; that persistent and serious criminals are a grave threat to the mental health and prosperity of the nation, and that they should be considered enemies of the State. As succinctly argued by Peter Coad of the Criminal Justice Association, 'If in 1942 we had decided to repatriate German prisoners of war to fight us again because we had too many prisoners, the world would have thought us to be mad.'[90]

After the publication of their report we wrote to the committee pointing out they had ignored irrefutable evidence. Their reply could have been drafted by Stalin himself. It said: 'We are not dealing solely or mainly with the facts. They are there, but at the end of the day, the committee drew its own conclusions on what we had heard and seen.'[91]

The Politics of Coercion

When presenting his report to Parliament in December 1998, the chairman of the committee said that he and his committee members had taken their cue from the anti-prison stance of previous home secretaries – the noble Lords Carr, Baker and Hurd,[92] all of whose liberal sentencing policies had allowed large numbers of criminals to go on victimising the public. In addition, it became known to us that in the build-up to the final report there had been disagreement between the members, a small minority of whom were sympathetic to our evidence and wanted it given more emphasis. The chairman agreed to water down some of his criticisms of our presentation and rewrote the draft.

I believe that this was a deliberate tactical move on his behalf. He cleverly backed down over the original objections from our supporters and wrote a draft that appeared to encompass at least some of their criticisms. As a result, the dissenters gave way and he was able to present the report as having the unanimous support of all the members, who were drawn from all of the major parties, thus making it all the more likely that its contents and recommendations would not be questioned or examined by Parliament in a detailed way. This would firmly close the door on anyone who had any doubts about the main thrust of the report. Thus its ideologically based anti-prison agenda, nurtured carefully from the beginning, was safe. That under its influence Parliament would consent to the continued use of liberal sentencing policies, resulting in millions being victimised by unrepentant and persistent criminals, represents an injustice whose size cannot be gauged or imagined.

Chapter 11

All the King's Men

A Judiciary Gone Astray

Out of place though it may seem, one source of the many injustices experienced by the public arising from crime has been the judiciary. After criminals and the Crown Prosecution Service, judges (and magistrates) bear a heavy responsibility for the high crime rate in the UK, and a public debate about the lenient and unrealistic sentences frequently handed down by many of them is long overdue. Likewise, serious questions should be asked about the appropriateness of the excessively liberal views and sentencing guidelines emanating from our most senior law lords (see Note 1). Over recent years, the judiciary have lost sight of the fact that the purpose of the law is to bring justice to the common man; instead, they have become mesmerised with concerns for the offender, based on pseudo psychosocial explanations of crime fed to them by the anti-prison lobby. The result has been that the public in general, and victims of crime in particular, are frequently let down by sentences which deny them any sense of justice or retribution.

For example, as described in earlier chapters, the British public have, since the end of the Second World War, been mercilessly targeted by burglars who have been encouraged in their crimes by misguided government policies and a liberal judiciary, as illustrated by one infamous case in Leicester in October 1997. A crown court judge was completely taken in by a persistent burglar who entreated the judge not to send him to prison because he wanted to 'go straight and look after his sick mother'. He was given a suspended sentence.[1] Almost twelve months later the burglar was back in court before the same judge, having committed another ninety-nine

293

burglaries. The judge on this occasion expressed his horror at the enormity of his error in not sentencing the burglar to prison previously. But it was too late, as hundreds of householders had been added to the list of victims because he had risked the safety of the public rather than making certain of it.

When Michael Howard took office as Home Secretary in May 1993 he was appalled by the statistics which showed that a burglary was taking place every thirty minutes in some police districts,[2] and he was equally shocked at the liberal sentences being handed down to them, as well as to other offenders. As a result he instigated Section 4 of the Crime (Sentences) Act 1997 (now Section 111 of the Powers of Criminal Courts Act 2000), which provided for a mandatory sentence of a minimum of three years for persons convicted for a third time of domestic burglary.[3] This bill was presented to Parliament at a time when crown court sentencing records for domestic burglary could not have provided clearer evidence that judges could no longer be trusted to impose realistic sentences and were protecting the interests of persistent domestic burglars at the expense of the general public.

This was obvious even to some members of the House of Lords, such as Lord Derwent who, though they disliked mandatory sentences on principle, nevertheless felt it necessary to support Michael Howard's Crime (Sentences) Bill,[4] although most judges (as well as many members of the House of Lords and the Commons) were vehement in their opposition, as they resented any reduction of their sentencing discretion. During the debate in the House of Lords in 1997, Lady Blatch, the then Minister of State at the Home Office, faced a hostile audience, as she listed the facts that showed beyond doubt that the sentences handed down by judges for burglary failed to protect the public. Of the 4,400 convicted of domestic burglary by the crown courts in 1995, only 179 received sentences of over three years, and only fourteen were sentenced to more than five years.[5] In the previous year, as reported by the Criminal Justice Association, the crown courts, for the first offence, gave burglars an average sixteen months' imprisonment and an average of only nineteen months after seven convictions; 28 per cent with six or more previous convictions were not sent to prison at all. Overall, crown courts imposed community-based sentences on 56 per cent of all offenders appearing before them.[6] In magistrates' courts, 61 per cent of offenders with seven or more previous convictions for burglary were not sent to prison.[7]

Although the maximum penalty for burglary is fourteen years, during the five-year period leading up the 1997 Crime (Sentences) Bill, only two domestic burglars received sentences of more than ten years.[8] Thus, even Lord Derwent, opposed in principle to mandatory sentences, had to acknowledge that the judges had ignored the sentence range for burglars laid down by Parliament and imposed their own of up to three years in most cases. Whilst the majority of judges were outraged at the proposed limitation of their discretion, so were the public by the way their discretion had been exercised in recent years.[9]

Likewise, research published in 2000 by the Sentencing Advisory Panel, appointed by the Lord Chancellor, showed that magistrates' courts sentenced only 25 per cent of burglars to immediate custody and then to an average of only 3.8 months; crown courts gave 24 per cent of burglars non-custodial sentences. The panel recommended a sentence of twelve months' imprisonment for a first conviction for domestic burglary and two years for a second conviction.[10]

Domestic burglary is a very serious offence. Victims often lose items of irreplaceable sentimental value as well as other expensive possessions. In many cases, they live the rest of their lives in constant fear. Research shows that 82 per cent of burglary victims suffer significant emotional effects; thus the cost in terms of human misery is incalculable.[11] By any standards, a minimum of three years' imprisonment for a third court appearance for burglary is modest. Yet many of the judiciary, for example Lord Donaldson, claimed that the 'third strike' clause was unjust, as did the then Lord Chief Justice Bingham, who claimed that such sentences prevented the court from considering the psychiatric, financial and family difficulties of the offenders concerned.[12] Whether burglars experience these problems or not is irrelevant to the victims' suffering and loss. It would have been more to the point if Lord Bingham had referred to the need to attend to the psychiatric, financial and family problems of the victims resulting from repeated assaults by burglars and other offenders.

The arguments put up against mandatory sentences were often baseless. For example, one law lord, in order to ridicule the 'three strikes' clause for burglars, expressed his fear that a tramp who put his hand through an open window and stole a bottle of milk would face an unjust prison sentence for this technical burglary.[13] But such a scenario does not stand up in the real world. An offence of this nature is not likely to be reported to the police, even if the losers noticed it. If it were, the police would not investigate it, and, as pointed out by the Criminal Justice Association, even if the offender committed the offence a hundred times it would be detected only five times.[14] In the unlikely case they chose not to ignore it, the police would deal with it by means of a caution. If it went further the Crown Prosecution Service would throw it out.

'Three Strikes and You're Out' – A Sentencing Deceit

But what makes the objections of Lord Bingham and others even more out of place is the fact that the 'third strike' meant the third *court appearance* involving convictions for burglary (not the third offence). Objectors such as William Rees-Mogg were wrong to imply that under the Crime Sentence Bill petty thieves would automatically receive a three-year sentence for a third conviction.[15] At his two previous court appearances, the offender, as shown by court records, is likely to have been charged with multiple burglaries, so by the time of his third court appearance, he may well have committed *scores* of burglaries and reaped untold harm on large numbers of victims. So far from being draconian, the 'three strikes' clause is in effect excessively lenient as it allows the criminal enormous scope to commit large numbers of burglaries before a prison sentence is even considered. This is particularly so when the effect of 50 per cent automatic remission is taken into account plus early release on the Home Detention Curfew scheme, which together reduces a three-year sentence to approximately one year and two months. Compared to the multiple burglaries offenders are frequently convicted of, this sentence makes a mockery of justice and is an insult to the victims.

But, incredible as it seems, judges have thwarted even this modest attempt to protect the public from burglars. They and others proved fierce opponents of the 'three strikes' clause and argued vociferously against it in both the Commons and the House of Lords; many were misled by their false arguments and, as a result, the successful passage of the Crime (Sentences) Bill was only made possible by the insertion of an 'escape' clause, which said that the mandatory sentence at the third strike for burglars would apply 'unless the court considers this to be unjust in all the circumstances'.[16] The judges, who, as noted, were highly resentful of what they saw as a restriction on their freedom of choice, pounced on this 'let out' clause and have used it extensively ever since. As a result, the public are no more protected from burglars now than they were before the act was passed.

To illustrate this, it is staggering to recall that between 1 December 1999, when the 'three strikes' clause came into force, and January 2001 no mandatory sentences were passed on domestic burglars, yet the records show that between April 2000 and March 2001 there were 402,984 recorded domestic burglaries.[17] Again, between 1 December 1999 and the 31 December 2001, a period of more than two years, there were an estimated 37,000 offenders convicted or cautioned for burglary; during the same period 840,000 domestic burglaries were committed. Yet information from a Home Office official indicated that throughout the whole of this period *only six mandatory sentences were imposed*.[18] Thus for a variety of misplaced considerations for the offender, as well as reasons of professional spite and jealousy, many judges (and magistrates) deliberately undermined the will of Parliament. As a consequence, the public have been denied the protection Parliament intended and burglars continue to burgle at will and laugh at the law.[19]

When David Blunkett was told by his civil servants that the figures suggested only a handful of mandatory sentences had been passed, he issued orders to his officials not to reveal them to anyone. Thus the public, who had every right to know what was going on over a matter so vital to their safety, were kept in the dark in order to save the face of a highly embarrassed Home Secretary. When the news was finally leaked to the press in June 2002, it showed that the estimate of only six mandatory sentences being passed since December 1999 was wrong, and the Home Office was forced to admit that not one burglar had been jailed under the 'three strikes' clause, despite the thousands of burglars who had passed through the courts during this period.[20]

Nothing could make clearer the judges' determination to thwart the will of Parliament in order to get their own way; and although they should not have been allowed to frustrate the will of the democratically elected House of Commons, the government did nothing about it. Only one MP, Julian Lewis, appeared to have understood the seriousness of what had happened; in January 2001 he called for the government to look again at the 'three strikes' legislation in order to combat the judges' refusal to implement it.[21]

Yet, as is often the case in the field of criminal justice, no action was taken, and MPs remained acquiescent over a matter that should have rocked Parliament to the core.

Mandatory Sentences for Drugs and Violence: The Judges Dig Their Heels In

Likewise, Lord Bingham argued against the mandatory sentence of seven years for those convicted of trafficking Class A drugs on the offender's third appearance for a similar offence. Again, in most cases, the three court appearances allowed before the imposition of the mandatory prison sentence will not represent three single drug offences but scores of these crimes. Whilst drug traffickers are largely responsible for making drugs available to addicts, it is entirely wrong to excuse addicts of their crimes because they want to finance their addiction. They are responsible for becoming addicts in the first place, and they are 100 per cent responsible for their crimes and the harm they cause their victims.

The Crime (Sentences) Act 1997 also established mandatory life sentences for offenders convicted of a second serious offence of physical or sexual violence.[22] Predictably, many in the House of Lords objected. For example, Lord Rees-Mogg argued that our very experienced judges should be free to sentence according to the circumstances of the time.[23] But this argument ignored their failure to adequately protect the public from dangerous and violent offenders, which was what prompted the legislation in the first place.

The staggering difference between the level of protection demanded by the public from repeat violent offenders and the level considered adequate by the judges was illustrated in 1999 at a crown court in the south-west of the country. A defendant was given a mandatory life sentence following his second conviction for grievous bodily harm. He appealed and the Law Lords found in his favour on the basis that the offence had occurred before the Act came into force.[24] They changed the sentence of life imprisonment to a three-year sentence. This was a derisory penalty for such a seriously violent offence, particularly as the judges would have been aware that the offender would benefit from automatic remission at the halfway stage, leaving him only eighteen months to serve. Another example was provided in July of the same year when a judge, forced by the

298

Crime (Sentences) Act to pass a mandatory life sentence, showed his resentment by setting the minimum tariff at only four years, which meant that the offender could be considered for release at that point.[25]

In 1998 Lord Chief Justice Lord Bingham added his voice to the demand for mandatory life sentences for murder to be dropped, and claimed that judges should decide on the prison sentence in these cases.[26] Earlier, when these proposals were being discussed, he had been so incensed at the prospect of judges losing their discretion over these matters that he led a revolt against the measure in the House of Lords.[27] He criticised the government for introducing 'politically driven' justice reforms.[28] In so far that the government were responding to the public's growing disquiet over the inadequate sentences for violent offenders, they were 'politically driven', but what did Lord Bingham think was wrong with that? The answer I believe is that it clashed with his elitist view that he and his senior Law Lords knew better than the public what was best for them; his disdain for public opinion over these issues could not have been made clearer.

Earlier Lord Chief Justice Lord Taylor of Gosforth had even claimed that longer prison sentences did not benefit the public, a statement which could not be more contradicted by the evidence[29] Ignoring public opinion he also cautioned against giving victims too loud a voice in the punishments and sentences handed out by the courts to their attackers. He argued that to talk of justice for victims in terms of sentencing was not only to look at the system 'through the wrong end of the telescope', but also to ignore a major section of it.[30] No statement could make it clearer that he believed that considerations for the offender should take precedence over the protection of the public. He also argued that mandatory life sentences would thwart the system of sentence discounts for guilty pleas, since someone who is aware of receiving a mandatory life sentence is less likely to plead guilty.[31] However, a reluctance to plead guilty in these circumstances would make little difference if there was a sufficiently strong case to secure a conviction. If the case against the defendant was weak, or he was innocent, the offender is unlikely to plead guilty anyway because of the fair chance of getting off.

I believe there is something artificial in the claim made by judges that their objection to mandatory sentences is that they will lead to injustices. Judges are well aware that the system can be applied flexibly, and so take into account the varying circumstances that surround different offences of violence. For example, the parole board and ultimately the Home Secretary can influence the release date of someone convicted of murder or of causing grievous bodily harm, and those thought no longer to be a risk to the public can be released earlier than others known to be dangerous. Where necessary, highly dangerous killers such as Neilson, Hindley and Brady have been imprisoned indefinitely. As already noted, judges have maintained the power to set the tariff for mandatory sentences (the judges' recommendation as to the minimum sentence to be served), and this can be used to provide a clear signal to the parole board and others of how seriously the judge viewed the crime. Thus, there is little for the judges to fear in terms of injustices arising out of mandatory sentences, and I am sure they know it. What fuels their opposition to them is professional pique at the loss of some of their power.

However, Parliament resisted their demands and listened instead to the public's demands that violent behaviour should be controlled. The victim may be knocked to the ground and suffer no more than broken bones, or he may be more seriously injured, and perhaps suffer permanent brain damage or even be killed. Whether his attacker intended these injuries or his death is not the point. What it was right for Parliament to outlaw was the act of violence itself, simply because its consequences are unpredictable.

In February 1999 a national newspaper carried a story involving a violent attack during a game by a footballer who knocked the referee to the ground and kicked him in the head until he was unconscious.[32] It was only a matter of chance that the victim was not killed or suffered permanent brain damage. That he was lucky and escaped both of these outcomes does not diminish the dangerousness of the violent attack, and it is entirely appropriate that the attacker be given a mandatory life sentence should he be convicted a second time for a similar offence. It is only reasonable that such violent offenders should be kept in prison until they no longer pose a threat to the community. In 1994, 217 offenders were convicted for serious offences of violence. All of them could have received a life sentence but only ten did.[33]

The Law Lords Turn Their Backs on Prison

In 1998 Lord Bingham in his role as Lord Chief Justice sent guidelines to judges and magistrates on when to jail offenders.[34] They followed his continuing concern about what he saw as a high prison population and were a thinly disguised attempt to persuade the courts to send fewer offenders to prison, particularly those involved in property crime. However, as argued by the Criminal Justice Association,[35] they were probably also intended to re-emphasise the courts' influence on sentencing policy in response to the government legislation concerning mandatory sentences.

But the public might understandably ask why Lord Bingham made it his business to be concerned about the number of offenders in prison. This is outside of his remit, which is to make sure trials and courts are run fairly and according to the rules of justice. However, Lord Bingham frequently showed that his concern for the offender outweighed his concern for the protection of the public. For example, one section of his guidelines said, 'Offences which are deliberate or premeditated are more serious than those which are spontaneous.'[36] It is difficult to imagine anyone saying something so absurd, let alone a senior Law Lord. How could Lord Bingham not be aware that it matters not to the victim whether the burglar who robbed his house did it on the spur of the moment or whether he planned it? How is it that he, as the then most senior law lord, could ignore that the victim's loss, fear and hurt are unrelated to the criminal's frame of mind and intentions when he committed the crime? This guideline is devoid of all common sense and is a good example of the 'pseudo intellectual' thinking which has undermined the debate about sentencing and so often misled the public.

The current Lord Chief Justice, Lord Woolf, much to the disadvantage of the public, has proved to be as liberal as, if not more so than, the previous incumbent, Lord Bingham. In 2001, for example, he opposed the government's announcement that it was going to tackle persistent offenders and build more prisons if necessary. Lord Woolf said he preferred to see prisons closed rather than opened,[37] even though, as with his predecessor, these matters of public policy were nothing to do with him. It is the government's duty to respond to the electorate's need for protection from crime; it is not the place of the judiciary to interfere with this.

Woolf also argued that if offenders were sent to jail they should go for the shortest possible time.[38] He claimed that one month in prison will achieve everything that can be achieved by a three-month sentence, and three months will achieve everything that can be achieved by a six-month sentence. There is no evidence for this; he was once again echoing the foolish and unsubstantiated ideas of the anti-prison lobby. However, such claims serve to show how he views prison from the point of view of the criminal, and not through the eyes of the public who require retribution, justice and maximum protection from further crime.

The Judiciary's One-dimensional View of Prison

These comments make it clear that Lord Woolf believes that, once prison can be said to have served its 'rehabilitative purpose', the offender should be released as soon as possible, and it was this think-ing which influenced his decision to reduce the minimum tariff for the Bulger killers, who had expressed remorse for their crimes, from fifteen years to seven and a half years.[39] But this denies the all-important role that prisons have in both protecting the public and providing justice and retribution for the victim. The fact that rehabilitation in prison has achieved all that it can does not make it necessarily either appropriate or safe for the offender to be released. A number of experts, for example, diagnosed the Bulger killers as being psychopathic and far too dangerous to be released, and the Bulger family would have every right to feel that the decision to release them ignored their justified demand for retribution and justice.[40]

Just because an offender has expressed regret for his crimes should not necessarily qualify him for a lenient sentence. Indeed, if he is truly repentant of his deeds, he will accept that he should be punished in order for justice to be done. In April 1994 a crown court judge sentenced a seventeen-year-old youth to two years' probation, following his horrendously violent attack on an elderly Sikh man.[41] The victim suffered grievous head wounds as a result of the youth bludgeoning him with a large and heavy plank of wood during an unprovoked attack. The judge decided not to send the defendant to prison for five years because he was told that, whilst on remand, the youth had made 'good progress'. Whatever that meant, it should have been treated quite separately from the question of his sentence,

302

which ought to have reflected the highly dangerous nature of the crime.

Similarly, in 2003 an Old Bailey judge chose not to send a persistent burglar to prison, despite the serious and aggravated nature of his offences and his fifty previous convictions. His reason was to give the offender a chance 'to write his poetry' and make his living other than by crime.[42] True reform on the part of the offender should be accompanied by an acceptance that he must serve a punishment to fit the crime, even though this may involve a very long time in prison; a fit punishment also crucially maintains the difference between right and wrong, without which we would ultimately slide into anarchy.

The Judiciary: Representatives of the Crown or the People?

In the summer of 2000, six-year-old Sarah Payne was abducted, sexually assaulted and then murdered by Roy Whiting. This dreadful crime riveted the attention of the public, and it soon came to light that it was not Whiting's first offence of this kind. He had abducted and sexually assaulted a nine-year-old girl in 1995; fortunately this victim managed to escape, otherwise she, too, would probably have been killed.

After Whiting was arrested for the Sarah Payne murder, the public were stunned to learn that this highly dangerous man had received just a four-year prison sentence for the previous abduction and assault offence in 1995, for which he served just two and a half years. The outcry against the leniency of this sentence was so furious that, on 17 December 2001, the judge responsible for it took the unusual step of speaking about it on the BBC's Radio 4 *Today* programme.[43] He addressed a nation who believed with very good reason that, had he given Whiting a life sentence in 1995, Sarah Payne would still be alive. Why had he not done so? Why, for example, did the judge choose to ignore how dangerous Whiting was and place an innocent interpretation on the rope and knife found in his possession, saying he accepted that it was just chance he had these items at the time?

The interview proved to be a revelation in that it provided an insight into how rigid and out of touch can be judges' thinking in their approach to sentencing. It also revealed the arrogant self-belief displayed by many in the judiciary that they know best and that the public should accept and not question their decisions. During the discussion the judge blustered and clearly did not like being held to account by direct and forceful questioning. It was as if he had expected to walk into the studio, make his statement to a deferential and silent audience and then leave. He placed no value on the opinion of those who believed he had made a terrible error. He offered no apology for what he had done and showed no regret or remorse for a decision the consequences of which robbed a child of her life and her family of happiness and peace of mind. In response to the criticism of his earlier derisory four-year sentence on Whiting, he referred to his summing-up made at the 1995 trial, and made the following statement:

> Judges must not punish offenders for crimes they have not yet committed. The public must realise there is a limit to the punishment which can be exacted against a criminal. The sentence of four years was in line with the Court of Appeal guidelines at the time and was based on the facts before me.

All of this is breathtaking nonsense; sentencing Whiting on the basis of the facts implies the offence was a 'one off', but this flies in the face of the fact that Whiting did not just pose an extreme danger for children at the time of the trial, but permanently and that he needed to be locked up for life. It was quite wrong for the judge to take the view that this amounted to punishing Whiting for crimes he had not committed; had he given him a life sentence the judge would have offered certain protection for all other children who might otherwise have crossed his path, and not doing so was a grave dereliction of his duty.

His statement that 'the public must realise there is a limit to the punishment which can be exacted against a criminal' is highly revealing. It reflects the arrogant belief that judges know what is best for the public; but why should their view on this matter prevail over that of the majority of the public? It would have been more to the point had he said that nothing should limit the degree of protection owed to the public when faced with offenders such as Whiting. That such tragedy should result in him following sentencing guidelines set down by the Court of Appeal indicates how inadequate they are, and how effectively the senior law lords have insulated themselves against public opinion by devising sentencing rules which are so dominated by their concerns for the criminal, as opposed to the public or the victim.

However, in that same year another judge stated that 'dreadful crimes must attract dreadful sentences' and sent a criminal to prison for twenty-five years for shooting and wounding two police officers.[44] That this judge was prepared to hand down a very long prison term, while Whiting received only four years for an equally serious offence indicates that judges have too wide a scope to apply their own individual, if not idiosyncratic, view of what is a just sentence and supports the case for mandatory sentences to be established by Parliament.

I believe that factors other than the protection of the public were preoccupying the judge when he sentenced Whiting in 1995: first, his fear of the senior law lords' guidelines, and the effect on his career of a successful appeal; and second, his misjudged preoccupation with the offender; and third, the unnecessary straitjacket he imposed upon himself by refusing to take into account the very long-term danger Whiting posed for children and the near certainty of future horrific crimes by him if granted his freedom. His attitude carried the message that sentencing was the prerogative of judges, and that the populace must accept the level of protection they are given and not question it. He dismissed the public's wishes for stronger sentencing as irrelevant and implied that to go down that route was somehow dangerous. Is there a historical overlay here, harking back over the centuries to the times when judges went about the country administering the king's justice, which no one dared question?

Some constitutional textbooks refer to the monarch as the 'fountain of justice and general conservator of the peace of the kingdom' and likewise as the 'reservoir of justice, whose right and equity are conducted by a thousand channels to every individual', and that 'all jurisdictions of courts are immediately derived from the Crown, and all proceedings run in the King's name.'[45] The names 'royal court of justice' (for civil matters) and the 'crown court' (for criminal matters) provide examples of this close link between the courts and the authority of the monarch. The resistance of the judges in early 2004 to the proposal to abolish the House of Lords as the senior appeal court has, at its roots, their objection to the idea that our legal institutions should no longer have to rely on their authority from the 'Crown'.

The attachment of some judges to their historical roots as the 'king's men' operating their prerogative is stronger than most probably realise. For example, in the late 1970s a judge sitting in the wardship court made a supervision order relating to two children whose custody was in dispute. The judge wanted the Probation Service to oversee the children for an interim period. However, the order was illegal. A law passed by Parliament made it clear that children who were the subject of a care order, as these children were (which effectively made the local council their legal guardians), could not also be made the subject of a supervision order. However, the judge overrode this legislation. When I queried this with him, he said that 'his arm was longer than their [Parliament's] arm' and that he was exercising the Queen's prerogative to overrule Parliament.

Judges – Torch Bearers for Justice or Just Confused and Inconsistent?

Few senior Law Lords have made more public statements condemning the use of prison than Lord Woolf. As early as 1993, in a public speech, he said, 'It has to be made clear to the public that all the experience shows imprisonment is not a cure for crime', and since then has repeatedly called for fewer criminals to be sent to prison and argued that 'prison doesn't work'.[46] However, he made no mention of the relief afforded to the public when persistent criminals are incapacitated by a prison sentence. But why has he targeted prisons in this way and not the community supervision of persistent offenders, which, as the evidence shows, lamentably fails to protect the public? A constant theme in Lord Woolf's anti-prison rhetoric has been the need to maintain the dignity of offenders in prison, but he has yet to comment on the indignities that the criminal justice system inflicts upon victims of crime.[47]

However, he is far from consistent and has contradicted himself on several occasions. In the wake of repeated claims that prison should not be regarded as the answer to crime and that community supervision was more effective in dealing with criminals, he suddenly announced, in January 2002, that 'robust prison sentences' were the only way to curb street robberies of mobile telephones and recommended sentences of between three and a half and five years in jail.[48] He denied he was contradicting his earlier position by

306

saying that the difference lay in the use of force.[49] But if prison is the way to stop offenders who use force, why is it not the way to stop other offenders? If it works with one, it will work with the other.

The Burglars' Charter

Following the liberal lead of his predecessor, Lord Bingham, who four years earlier had argued at a police conference that fewer prisoners should be sent to prison,[50] Lord Woolf, in December of 2002, unleashed another astonishingly liberal edict when he issued sentencing guidelines to judges and magistrates that said:

> For a domestic burglary displaying most of the features of a standard domestic burglary (theft of electric goods and/or personal items, damage caused by the break-in, some turmoil in the house and some trauma to the victim) but committed by a first-time burglar, the initial approach of the courts should be to impose a community sentence.[51]

The guidelines also made it clear that a non-custodial sentence would be appropriate for a first-time burglar where there were 'medium level aggravating features' such as the victim being at home or goods of high value being taken. Unbelievably, he went on to say that 'even for a second offence, a domestic burglar would receive a community sentence if there was no damage to property or if goods of only a very low value were stolen'.[52]

I believe there can be no doubt that Lord Woolf was taken aback by the public resentment caused by his expectation that they should tolerate any burglary of their homes, whether committed by a criminal novice or an experienced offender. He complained that the press had misunderstood him and had misinterpreted his guidelines. However, I am certain this was not the case. He had made himself crystal clear. I believe his protests of being misunderstood were a smokescreen to cover up his embarrassment and confusion in the face of the public's vehement protest. He confounded his position by issuing not one but two 'clarifications' that emphasised he was referring to 'less serious burglaries', apparently unaware that *all* burglaries are serious to the victim. But in any case his clarifications

307

left his guidelines, which included recommending community sentences for repeat burglars, otherwise unchanged, leaving the public aghast at his insensitivity towards householders and other potential victims of burglars.[53]

To the utter disbelief of many, Lord Woolf also said he did not want the inaccurate reporting of his guidelines to 'undermine the public's confidence'.[54] Could it possibly be that he was totally unaware that his statement on burglars had done just that? I suspect that many of his judicial colleagues were uncomfortably aware that Lord Woolf had made himself a spectacle, and perhaps to come to his aid and draw some fire, Lord Irwin spoke out on the radio in January 2003.[55] His announcement that 'first-time burglars will not go to prison *because the public know that community penalties are more effective*' (my italics) could not have been more insensitive towards an audience constantly victimised by criminals serving sentences in the community. It did nothing to diminish the public's view of senior judges as being disdainful of their plight and insulated from reality.

Almost everything Lord Woolf said in the ensuing debate and afterwards strengthened the public's view of him as not so much out of touch with their feelings concerning burglars but dismissive of them. Despite the evidence of the public's long-suffering patience in the face of escalating crime, he claimed, in 2003, that 'the criminal justice system was overly concerned with satisfying the public's and individual victim's thirst for vengeance'.[56] To support his approach, he claimed that community sentences could provide protection for the community for three years.[57] This shows his embarrassing ignorance of the disastrous reconviction figures for those on community sentences. Even the briefest perusal of these statistics would show Lord Woolf that community sentences not only fail to protect the public from criminals but actually put them in danger. He denied that his guidelines were dramatically altering the approach to the sentencing of domestic burglars, but this denial sits uneasily with his admission that the purpose of the guidelines was to reduce the number of offenders being sent to prison.[58]

Amazingly, Lord Woolf denied his sentencing rules were a 'charter for burglars', but his denial cannot rescue him from the facts spelt out to him in January 2003 by one of the country's most eminent criminologists. Less serious burglars were *already* avoiding prison; burglars have a high reconviction rate, and likewise community penalties have as high a reconviction rate as prison, which means that Lord Woolf's guidelines will result in more crime. The likelihood of conviction after one burglary is almost nil, therefore the vast majority of so-called 'first-time' burglars will already have cut a swath of numerous offences through their long suffering communities by the time they first appear in court.[59]

Lord Woolf refers to 'standard burglaries' because he wants the public to believe they are less serious in order to justify his misplaced leniency. But it is entirely wrong to subdivide this offence in this way. From the court's viewpoint it should not matter whether the criminal stole a button or a collection of rare silver; what should be outlawed is the act of burglary itself. It is well known that great distress and despair frequently accompany the loss of family and personal items of no intrinsic value. Yet Lord Woolf believes burglars should be given their freedom even after a second appearance in court if 'goods of only very low value were stolen'.[60] His dismissal of the legacy of hurt and anxiety of those who have been burgled is beyond belief.

For this reason it is equally unacceptable that Lord Woolf should recommend softer sentences for burglaries involving only 'some trauma' and 'some stress', as if they were less harmful than offences involving 'more stress' and 'more trauma'. Does he really believe a burglary victim should divide these experiences into quantifiable amounts and weigh them with different degrees of acceptability? The harm caused to the public as a result of these guideline rulings can be judged from the results of a survey taken only a few weeks after their announcement. In one crown court, out of a random sample of ten burglary cases, only four were given prison sentences, all of noticeably inadequate length.[61] Bearing in mind *all* of the sentences were for repeat offenders, the four prison sentences, which ranged from nine months to three years, were an insult to the victims. To make matters worse, because the effect of 50 per cent automatic remission and the early-release scheme, the repeat burglar given nine months would only serve a few weeks in prison, and those receiving three years would serve less than half of this sentence.

Likewise, in January 2003 a judge sentencing a criminal for seven counts of burglary made it clear that before the new guidelines he would have sentenced him to prison, instead of the lenient non-custodial sentence he felt obliged to hand down, despite the serious and aggravating features of the crimes.[62] One month later, another judge imprisoned a burglar who admitted committing no fewer than fifty-six burglaries to a total of ten years, which amounted to no more than nine weeks for each burglary.[63]

The influence of Lord Woolf's recommendations have not diminished over time. In February 2003 a prisoner serving a prison sentence for burglary offences was produced in court to face further charges. Despite being a prolific offender, the judge sentenced him to only nine months for the fresh burglary charge, which in practice meant no more than an extra few weeks in jail; he asked for forty-eight other offences to be taken into consideration and for these he received just one month imprisonment.[64] Such decisions tells the victims that their experiences of loss, hurt and anxiety are of no consequence to the court, while the message given to the burglars by these derisory sentences is that they can go on offending without fear of serious retribution.

In December 2001 Lord Woolf, showing further inconsistency, said that in exceptional circumstances paedophiles might be imprisoned even if they had not committed any offence.[65] Such an outlandish statement must have caused embarrassment even for some of his more liberal colleagues, though their reaction was not reported. How can a decision be made that someone is dangerous enough to lock up before they have acted in a dangerous way? For a Lord Chief Justice to even hint at a measure which so obviously runs contrary to the rule of law only serves to undermine further the public's confidence in this important office.

On another occasion he said that robberies in which the victims were mainly vulnerable teenagers or elderly people were undermining the criminal justice system. But it is not the robberies per se that do this, but the weak and inconsistent response of the courts. For example, *despite* his own guideline that robberies of mobile phones in which violence was used should attract up to five years in jail, he reduced, on appeal, a four-year sentence for a robbery in which a weapon was used. The substituted three-year sentence meant that the offender would serve only one year and two months, hardly an example of the 'robust' sentence he himself advocated for offences involving violence. Yet earlier he had increased, on appeal, a six-month sentence to three and a half years for an offence of robbery involving violence, which would nevertheless amount to no more than one year and five months in prison.[66]

Beyond Reasonable Doubt

Lord Woolf has said that when a judge or magistrate sends an offender to prison it should be of the greatest concern to them what happens to that offender while he is in jail.[67] But it is not for the judiciary to take this onto their shoulders; offenders in jail are the responsibility of the prison department. The first duty of the judges is to be concerned about the effects on the public of not sending an offender to prison, and to be sure beyond reasonable doubt that the offender will not commit any more crime. However, as shown in previous chapters, they all too often pass community sentences on criminals where not only is there reasonable doubt about the offender's willingness to give up crime but there is a sure certainty that he will go on victimising the public. Hence the protection given to defendants (who are often established criminals) – that they can only be convicted if their guilt is established beyond reasonable doubt – is not given to the public, who are forced to play host to criminals placed back in the community despite the overwhelming evidence that they will continue offending.

The Dislocation of Public Opinion and Trust

There is now no doubt that the public view judges (and magistrates) as being out of touch with their experience of crime and their need to be protected from criminals who too frequently are allowed to roam free and victimise them. In February 2001 Jack Straw drew attention to the fact that 80 per cent of the public were shown by research to be dissatisfied with the way judges did their job;[68] earlier research in 1998 showed that four out of five people in the UK believed that judges were too lenient.[69]

In fact, in 1998 the Home Office became very concerned about the public's poor image of the judiciary. Research published in that year showed that judges were deemed by the public to be doing the worst job among all of those involved in tackling crime. Instead of the Home Office taking this seriously and responding by ensuring that judges passed adequate sentences, Home Office officials showed their disdain for the public's view on these matters by mounting a publicity campaign to persuade them they were wrong to view judges as being too lenient.[70] They argued, with breathtaking arrogance, that public criticism of the judiciary was based on 'poor knowledge' of crime and sentencing. But the public are well versed in these topics, as they suffer the brunt of over 60 million crimes a year, and that while many of them are given long sentences of fear, anxiety and financial hardship, criminals get away with almost all of the crimes they commit.

Sometimes it seems, judges go out of their way to defy public opinion, as if to remind the 'populace' that they are the lawgivers, and that they must accept their judgments. For example, in March 1999 a senior judge placed a persistent paedophile on probation in order for him to attend therapy sessions.[71] It has to be said that there is not one jot of evidence to show that paedophiles can be 'cured' by therapy. In fact, all that is known about them indicates that their predilection for children is unalterable. The judge placed the offender back into the community, despite being warned that he was a serious child molester and that he would, even by the offender's own frank admission, pose a threat for children in the future. However, the judge's concern to keep the offender out of prison outweighed any concerns he may have had for the future protection of the public. Such sentencing decisions are legion. Later that same year a prisoner was turned down for release by the parole board because he was judged to be too dangerous to let out into the community. The prisoner took legal action against the decision and a judicial review followed. As a result, the high court overturned the parole board's decision and freed the prisoner.[72]

At other times, it seems as if the judiciary revel in the opportunity to show how powerful they are. For example, in 2003 an Iraqi was jailed for organising the illegal entry into Britain of possibly thousands of immigrants. When the police raided his shop they found him in possession of over 3,000 forged holograms intended for use in visas earmarked for Iraqi asylum seekers. He pleaded guilty but was sentenced to only nine months in prison, reduced immediately by half because of the automatic remission scheme, with further reductions possible under Home Detention Curfew arrangements.

Such a derisory prison term must have confirmed for the defendant that his lucrative illegal activities were well worth the risk. However, an even more pleasant surprise awaited him. Sometime later the Court of Appeal quashed his conviction on the grounds that the wording of the offence used at the original trial was incorrect. Not only was the offender released but he was paid compensation for a 'miscarriage of justice'. There was never any dispute over the question of his guilt, which he had, in any case admitted, but once again the Law Lords twisted the meaning of justice beyond recognition by this incredibly perverse decision.[73]

Justice: A Crumbling Edifice

The journalist Simon Heffer has perceptively described the Lord Chief Justice as a man for whom the law has ceased to be about protecting the community from crime; instead it has become an intellectual exercise in devising rights for criminals who, by any standards, do not deserve them.[74] He constantly speaks of the need to protect the dignity of those in jail, so they will not riot. The dignity of their victims does not rate a mention. Nor does he acknowledge that offenders choose to commit offences and it is therefore in their own hands whether they end in prison or not. He speaks of the futility of locking people up, but pays no attention to the fact that whilst they are incarcerated they are not able to victimise the public. He also claims he wishes to restore the public's faith in the criminal justice system. This would be almost laughable if it were not so serious, as he fails to understand that nothing erodes faith in the criminal justice system more demonstrably as judges' failure to protect the public from crime by handing down sentences which are sometimes so lenient as to be offensive to the victims.

As already mentioned, the Lord Chief Justice has claimed community penalties provide better safeguards for the public than does a prison sentence,[75] but when challenged to provide evidence for this statement he refused to answer. The public should not be expected to accept that such claims are correct just because they are made by persons in high office. Likewise, his guidelines for the sentencing of burglars ignore the unarguable evidence concerning the low detection rate and their high reconviction rate. Few other lord chief justices have done more to undermine the public's faith in the justice system and helped bring about the present dangerous alienation of the public from the forces of law and order.

Some judges maintain high standards and ensure that trials are run fairly. Too many others stick to the letter rather than the spirit of the law, causing distress for many. The judge's role in maintaining order and peace in our society is pivotal and we should not stint them their privileged work conditions which they are given to support them in their difficult task or the elevated social position which their office (as opposed to the individual) is said to require. However, they must no longer be regarded as beyond criticism; too many criminals walk free because the trial judge has paid overstrict attention to the technicalities of the judicial process and has lost sight of its overall purpose. Likewise, their sentencing record is dire, and the harm caused to victims by offenders that the judges have let back into the community should be thought of in the same way as the harm caused by surgeons or other professionals whose incompetence injures or harms members of the public.

The independence of the judiciary in deciding whether a defendant is guilty or innocent must be maintained. However, there is nothing sacrosanct about their sentencing role and this must be changed. They should be made to follow a sentencing code laid down by Parliament, which in turn should be based on the sentencing regimes demanded by the majority of the public. The present system, whereby the public have to endure the harmful consequences of idiosyncratic, inadequate and sometimes perverse sentencing decisions, should not be allowed to continue.

Over the last few years, the public's respect for judges has plummeted. Dissent at their failure to protect us from crime is now more common than even ten years ago. They were once, like surgeons, beyond questioning. However, over the last ten years, business managers, whose role has been to monitor the performance of all hospital staff, have exposed the errors and shortcomings of many senior medical practitioners which previously would have escaped notice. As a result, some have been disgraced and have lost their jobs, and whilst this may seem harsh to some, when measured against the dreadful consequences of their errors for their patients, there was no alternative. Judges should face a similar accountability, as the harm caused to the public resulting from their decisions is beyond measure, as will be discussed in Chapter Thirteen which examines the plight of those victimised by crime.

Chapter 12

Human Rights and Wrongs

The Human Rights Convention – Its Spirit and Intentions

In 1950 the representatives of thirteen nations including the UK met in Rome and signed the Convention for the Protection of Human Rights. Its purpose was to prevent any future government inflicting on its peoples the terrible injustices perpetrated by totalitarian governments such as came to power in Germany and Italy during the 1920s and 1930s, and which resulted in the unimaginable sufferings of millions of people, culminating in profoundly shocking events such as the Holocaust. To achieve this end they defined a list of basic human rights and freedoms which each country, as signature to the convention, agreed to enshrine in law. The UK was slow to enact these principles, but in 1998 it finally passed the Human Rights Act.

It is important to stress that what dominated the minds of those who met in Rome to draw up these principles were images of the dreadful horrors committed by the Nazis and the Fascists against their own and other subject peoples. Thus the *spirit* of the convention could not have been clearer; it was to protect the individual against the abuse of political power by the State, and to prevent it, by legal or illegal means from infringing the freedoms of its citizens.

Human Rights Enshrined in Law

However, what has not been acknowledged by the criminal justice authorities is that when an offender commits a crime against an individual or household that criminal act breaches Part 1 (Article

315

5) of the Human Rights Act, which states, 'Everyone has the right to liberty and security of person', as well as Article 8 which says, 'Everyone has the right to respect for his private and family life, his home and his correspondence'; it also violates Article 1 in Part 2 of the Act which unambiguously lays down that, 'Every natural or legal person is entitled to the *peaceful enjoyment of his possessions*. No one shall be deprived of his possessions except in the public interest...' (my italics).

Furthermore, Article 17 (Part 1) says, 'Nothing in this Convention may be interpreted as implying for any State, group or person the right to engage in any activity or perform any act aimed at the destruction of any of the rights and freedoms set forth in this Act'. Article 17 directly implicates all of those involved in the UK justice system because, by following a sentencing policy which allows thousands of criminals their freedom, it is engaging in an activity which results in the destruction of the human rights of countless millions of its citizens who are victimised by those criminals. Its guilt in this respect is all the more certain because it is able to accurately predict the likelihood of further offending, and so encourages the release of thousands of criminals at the time of their sentence, in the knowledge that it is certain they will carry on offending.

Human Rights: Actions Speak Louder than Words

What is extraordinary is that everyone has ignored these serious violations of the Human Rights Act, brought about by crime and existing sentencing policy. Not one civil liberty group, MP, lawyer or government minister, indeed anyone, has ever called attention to these massive injustices. Does this mean that the Human Rights Act does not apply to those victimised by crime? The answer to this is definitely no. Article 17 of the Act quoted above prevents any such conclusion. Our criminal justice system has no excuse whatever for its flagrant refusal to acknowledge that the concept of human rights must be applied to the public's need to be protected from crime, and particularly to the plight of victims already robbed of their rights which the Act is supposed to guarantee.

Paradoxically, a 1999 ruling by the European Commission of Human Rights established this very principle in relation to the degree of protection children have a right to expect from local councils who are charged with their welfare. The commission ruled that children must be able to pursue compensation against local councils who failed to protect them from abuse and neglect. A previous House of Lords decision had gone against this view, but significantly, the commission ruled that this had breached the children's right not to be subject to inhuman or degrading treatment.[1] It is therefore entirely logical to argue that the public also have a right not to be subject to inhuman and/or degrading treatment at the hands of criminals, and this right (already enshrined in the Human Rights Act) should be recognised and acted upon.

This is all the more so because although crime victims have been ignored as far as the application of the Act is concerned, the UK government, at its highest level, has played lip service to the idea that it applies to *everyone*. In 2001, following the deliberations of the task force set up by the government to help implement the Human Rights Act, the following points were included in the recommendations from the then Acting Permanent Secretary John Warne to Sir Richard Wilson, Head of the Civil Service, and to all permanent secretaries:

> It is clearly right that all public authorities should not act incompatibly with the Convention on Human Rights .. The Act was intended to do more than merely avoid direct violations of human rights. It is a constitutional measure, legislating for basic values which can be shared *by all people* throughout the United Kingdom [my italics] .. There should be a clear and public expression of commitment to the Convention's values and principles at the highest levels of government and public authorities'.[2]

These pious, if vacuous, statements, plus the wording of the Act itself make it abundantly clear that the State has a legal duty to ensure that persistent and unrepentant criminals are not free to victimise the public and so undermine their basic rights and freedoms identified by the convention. However, since the Act came into force it has suited the justice system to ignore its implications for the victims of crime; a sinister blanket of denial has been drawn over this issue, so that no one, not even victim-support groups, have challenged the authorities on this issue.

Human Rights – For Whom?

Not only have the crime-beleaguered public been denied the benefits the Act was intended to provide them, but their situation has been *worsened* because it is the criminals who have benefited most from its application. As a result of the way the Act has been interpreted, they have enjoyed even greater freedom to commit crime due, for example, to the restrictions placed on the investigative methods used by the police, customs and excise and others.

I do not believe that those responsible for drafting the convention had in mind that it should be used to shackle the legitimate forces of law and order beyond the establishment of those restraints commensurate with the maintenance of the rule of law, natural justice and democratic freedom. Yet our Human Rights Act has been used to place severe restrictions on all law enforcement bodies in their legitimate fight against crime, which has made it much harder for them to observe, follow and collect evidence against criminals. These restrictions have been put in place in order to protect the human rights and freedoms of the criminal suspects the police and others are trying to combat. But is this really what the original thirteen nations had in mind when they met in Rome and drew up the convention? I very much doubt it.

Why have our lawyers stretched the meaning of the Act beyond what was obviously intended for it? Why have they not been able to take the view that by successfully bringing criminals to justice the police and other law-enforcing agencies are protecting the human rights and freedoms of the law abiding public? Why have they not championed the idea that any restrictions on their ability to do so results in those human rights being undermined by criminals who are allowed to get away with their crimes?

Few may be aware that when the Human Rights Act came into force on 2 October 2000, it was applied retrospectively. This allowed many convicted criminals and their lawyers to argue that the covert surveillance techniques used by the police to collect evidence against them was an infringement of Article 8 of the Act (which establishes the individual's 'right to privacy'), even though the crime in question took place before the Act became law.[3] But the public, from the point of view of *natural justice*, might ask if a covert listening device provided the unarguable evidence to prove someone was guilty of a crime, how can that person possibly have a defence against it? If the police were found guilty of failing to comply with all of the convention's requirements in the way the device was applied for and used, then surely this is a separate matter, but it does not mean that the defendant is not guilty of the crime.

Similarly, it may not be generally known that on 15 July 2002, the European Court of Human Rights ruled that the disciplinary system used by prison governors in the UK, of adding days to a prison sentence as a form of punishment, violated the prisoner's right to a fair trial.[4] This is a ridiculous interpretation of 'fairness' because under our system a prisoner rarely serves the whole of his sentence. For example, a prisoner sentenced to two years will only serve approximately eight months, which is the effect of 50 per cent remission and the early release scheme on Home Detention Curfew. It follows that any days added on by a governor, as a disciplinary measure, would never result in the prisoner serving *more* than his sentence. It therefore follows that the prisoner's 'rights' have not been infringed in any way and therefore no human rights issue has been involved. I suspect that those responsible for our criminal justice system were more than prepared to agree with the European Court's ruling because they saw it as a way of getting prisoners out of jail; in fact within days of the ruling almost a thousand prisoners were released back into the community.[5] As matters now stand prisoners know they can break prison rules and get away with only minor sanctions such as the loss of part of a week's wages, or the loss of a privileged visiting order (but not a statutory one).

Criminals in other settings have also benefited from the Act. The European Court of Human Rights has, for example, asserted that the way our courts martial operate is unfair.[6] They have ruled that because two serving Armed Forces officers are amongst those sitting in judgment, and because they are subject to army, navy or air force discipline and reports, these courts are not 'impartial' or independent. Therefore they have ruled that military courts cannot continue to operate despite the fact that they are no less fair than they were in 1950.

As argued in one national newspaper, the Armed Forces operate under special conditions. Discipline is of prime importance and the culture of obedience and duty needs to reign, not a culture of 'rights',[7] and when recruits join the forces they knowingly and willingly sign up to these conditions, hence there is no human rights issue at stake here. Once again, I suspect that it is unlikely that those who formulated the convention ever thought that it would be applied in this way, and would regard its principles as having been stretched far beyond what they intended. The UK has, of course, accepted this European ruling, but, significantly perhaps, at least eight other countries, including France and Spain, have refused, and as a result their Armed Forces continue to use the military court system.

Human Rights and Mental Illness

In addition to influencing military justice, human rights considerations have played their part in the closure of large numbers of mental hospitals over recent years. Whilst a full discussion of this subject is beyond the scope of this book, passing reference must be made to the fact that this policy has allowed offenders who are mentally ill to increasingly victimise the public. As with their misguided attitudes towards prisons, the motive of successive governments has been the wish to cut back expenditure on institutions for the mentally unstable and those diagnosed as mentally ill. Whilst it is true that reviews carried out in the early 1960s found that a number of patients in long-stay wards had been incarcerated for quite the wrong reasons, many others who *need* to be kept in institutions for their own and the public's safety have been discharged on the mistaken belief that a policy of 'care in the community' could both look after them and safeguard the public. These policies were encouraged by groundless theories which argued that it was not the individual who was mentally sick but 'society', and therefore it was wrong to hospitalise them.[8]

These absurd policies also represent a massive injustice for the thousands of mentally ill people, whether offenders or not, who have been released onto the streets unable to cope with the normal demands of everyday life. Large numbers of them have been abandoned to lonely, miserable lives, moving from one bedsit to another. Nothing could be more contradictory to their true human rights and needs. Some exhibit unstable and dangerous behaviour and thousands of people have become victims of crimes committed by those who should be being looked after in proper hospital conditions.

The scale of the problem can be gauged by the large numbers of violent crimes perpetrated by mentally ill or psychopathic individuals left free to roam our streets and carry out the most terrifying and often random attacks on defenceless members of the public. For example, on 25 February 2005 John Barrett, a mentally ill man pleaded guilty to stabbing to death a former banker in a London park. As with Christopher Clunis, another ex-mental patient, who had randomly killed a young musician in a London Tube station eleven years previously, his history of violence and paranoia was known to the authorities, but they had failed to properly detain him.

Yet these consequences are ignored by officials who stick by their claims that community provision is more suitable. Those like myself who have had to supervise mentally ill offenders, know first-hand how difficult it is to ensure such patients take their medication. Many do not and often hide this from the authorities. Likewise, many dangerously unstable people are highly skilled at convincing others they do not need medication or that there is nothing wrong with them, and the consequences of such artful deception are often dire. The numbers of killings by mentally unstable people has quadrupled over the last forty years.[9] The sense of injustice and grief born by the victim's family is only made worse, in many cases, by the knowledge that the perpetrator had been released from hospital confinement because officials thought it was safe to do so and that it was in line with the patient's 'human rights'.

Protection of Criminals' Rights

Probation literature in my possession includes leaflets spelling out to criminals what their rights are.[10] Some civil-liberty groups have gone further and made a mockery of justice by arguing that the courts had previously defined these too narrowly, and that a criminal's ability to sue is a *fundamental right* that needs protecting in the courts.[11] For many this bizarre view contradicts any sense of natural justice. We should not be ashamed or inhibited to argue that criminals, by their offending, should forfeit their natural claim to any 'rights' and so leave them with the incentive to earn them back by reforming and committing no more crime. However, such a policy should never be used as a licence for any response other than one based on justice for all concerned. But neither should the status of the criminal be associated with gain or benefit; only loss.

However, our criminal justice establishment looks at this issue, as with all other matters, through the eyes of the criminal, not of the public. The Law Commission, in 2001, issued a consultation paper which questioned the reasons given for depriving criminals of the right to sue.[12] This appeared, on the face of it, to amount to an invitation to Parliament to consider changes in the law to make it easier for criminals to claim damages when they are injured whilst committing crime. To justify their arguments, the commissioners quote Lord Lester of Hern Hill, QC and David Pannick, QC in their book *Human Rights Law and Practice*, who claim that the arbitrary way the law is applied in respect of this issue may be a breach of offenders' human rights as defined by the convention.[13]

After some prevarication, in May 2003 David Blunkett announced the government would respond to this issue. Much later, his successor Charles Clarke announced in a radio discussion on the Radio 4 *Today* programme that the government had made it more difficult for burglars to seek compensation against householders who had injured them.[14] The question remains why they did not remove this right from them completely. Mr Clarke's statement still means that judges will not be able to throw out all cases for compensation simply because they are brought by criminals who are injured whilst committing crime; families of burglars and other criminals shot in the course of their criminality will be encouraged to think that they have been wronged and sue for redress. Thus the public continues to face the fact that if a burglar is injured or worse in a confrontation with a householder whilst the latter is defending himself, his family and his property, the criminal, or those acting for him, may well be able to take legal action for damages against the householder.

Abuse of the Human Rights Law

In fact, although victims' rights have been ignored, lawyers and other organisations frequently bend over backwards to defend the so-called rights of offenders. For example, in 2002 a convicted drug smuggler won £3,000 compensation because he claimed the police had violated his human rights by intercepting his pager messages.[15]

During the 1970s an elderly war veteran was kicked to death in a bout of gratuitous violence. His killer was sentenced to life imprisonment. He was freed on parole in the mid 1980s, and in May 2000 he was found guilty of attempted rape of a teenage girl. In July 2001 he was sentenced to five years for attacking someone with an axe in an Indian restaurant; he was returned to jail and his parole licence was terminated. At the time of the axe attack, he was employed by the council who, following the incident in the restaurant, sacked him for gross misconduct.

From his cell, he launched an appeal for unfair dismissal on the grounds that he was not allowed to challenge the evidence against him at the disciplinary hearing and was not offered an alternative post in line with council procedure. Despite the fact that he had been returned to prison following his conviction for the axe attack and was serving two life sentences and was therefore not in a position to take up alternative employment, the employment tribunal, abandoning common sense, agreed with his application, ruling that 'the correct procedures' had not been followed and awarded him two weeks' wages for breach of contract.[16]

If the Human Rights Act can be invoked for matters such as this, whatever its rights and wrongs, then how much stronger is the case for the victims of crime to sue the authorities for pursuing sentencing policies which allow unrepentant criminals to assault, rob and burgle them, and so deny them their right to 'peaceful enjoyment of their property' as defined in Part 2 of the Convention for the Protection of Human Rights? Our so-called criminal justice elite, so vocal in defending the rights of persistent offenders, ignores the public's torment at the hands of persistent offenders.

This was amply illustrated in May 2003 when it was reported that a married couple had been burgled 192 times over a period of seven years.[17] Despite their desperate effort to seek help, and the wide discussion this case provoked, the issue of the loss of their human rights was never raised. Unlike the case of the asylum seekers mentioned above, no one prompted them to claim that their right to 'live in peace', their 'right to privacy' and their 'right to peaceful enjoyment of their possessions' had been infringed.

Likewise, in June of the same year, the *Today* programme on Radio 4 discussed the results of Home Office research into the effects of burglary on old people.[18] Measured over two years, the research found that the death rate of elderly people who had been burgled was as least twice as high as amongst those who had not been. The Home Office said that they were surprised by this difference; not so the general public, who suffer the brunt of Home Office sentencing policies and are aware of many such tragic instances.

In February 2001, for example, I learned from a former senior probation officer colleague of an elderly person well known to him who had been burgled. This fit, active eighty-year-old widow lived alone in the leafy suburbs of Surrey, spending many days a week in London at theatres, art galleries and dining out. It soon became clear that, as a result of the burglary, not only had she lost many family treasures, but her sense of tranquillity and peace of mind had been damaged beyond repair and her enjoyment of life seriously impaired. Only weeks later, she died without warning, even though she had not been ill.[19] Yet during the *Today* programme discussion not one person made reference to the fact that the violation of the privacy of elderly people due to crime and the loss of their possessions and their peace of mind represented a blatant breach of their human rights, which it was in the government's power to prevent.

The Public's Loss of Freedom

However, our justice system has insulated itself against the public's need for protection. As argued by Civitas, as the criminals have been allowed more freedom to roam at will and commit crime where and when they like, the public has experienced a severe diminution of its freedom to go and do as it pleases. Law-breakers begin by robbing the law-abiding citizens of their tranquillity, property and bodily safety. They end by robbing them and their children of the benefits of a free society.[20]

This encroachment on our liberties due to crime has been relentless and wide-ranging. There is now a very long list of activities and decisions that we cannot contemplate with any degree of safety, and some which are avoided all together. In 2000 research by an insurance company revealed that seven out of ten women motorists steer clear of multistorey town-centre car parks because they are afraid of being attacked. The advice given to women drivers by the insurance company consisted of a list of restrictions which represented serious inroads into their freedom of action. They were urged to park only under a light, to use only the lower floors, to reverse into spaces for a quick getaway and to carry a torch.[21]

In fact, almost all of the advice issued to the public by the Home Office and insurance companies about how to avoid becoming a victim of crime falls into this category. For example, in 1999 a random check of a hundred cars in the north of the country found that one in four had property visible – everything from mobile phones, laptop computers, tapes, compact disks, leather jackets and chequebooks. The police described this as a perfect example of how to become a victim of crime.[22] But why should the public not be free to leave their property where they wish? The question is not why do people leave their possessions visible in their cars, but why does our sentencing policy leave thousands of criminals on the streets knowing they will continue to steal these items?

Security advice given to the public shows that we are not free from the danger of attack and physical harm even in our own homes; that we are not free to leave our home without fear or thought about what might happen to it while we are away; that we are not free to leave our possessions anywhere without fear of them being stolen, even in our own homes; that we are not free to walk in public places without fear of robbery and attack; that we are not free to open our front doors to callers without the need for caution and possible defence; and that we are not free to defend ourselves against marauders, robbers and burglars.

Viewed from the perspective of those human rights that the 1998 Act supposedly guaranteed for *everyone*, the following advice (in italics), taken in the main from booklets issued by the Home Office, make interesting reading.[23]

When out walking

Don't take short cuts through dark alleys or across waste ground.

Walk facing the traffic so no one can pull up behind you.

Don't hitch-hike or take lifts from strangers.

Cover up expensive jewellery.

If you are out late, get a lift or take a taxi.

If you often walk home in the dark get a screech alarm from a DIY store; carry it in your hand to scare off an attacker.

Carry your bag close to you with the opening facing towards you. But if someone grabs it let it go. Keep your house keys in your pocket.

On buses and trains

Stay away from lonely bus stops, especially after dark.

On an empty bus, sit near the driver or the conductor.

On a train, sit with other people. If possible sit in a part of the train where you can get off easily.

When driving

Plan your route carefully and stay on main roads.

Carry a spare petrol can.

Keep change and a phone card (or mobile phone) in case you need to call for help.

Let those you are visiting know what time you hope to arrive.

Don't pick up hitch-hikers. Only get out of your car in an emergency.

Keep doors locked when driving in towns and keep your handbag/briefcase/laptop etc. out of sight, especially if the windows are open.

At night, park in a well-lit place and look around before you get out.

Have your keys ready when you go back to your car. Make sure there is no one in the car.

If you have a problem don't accept lifts from strangers.

When you are attacked

You can use your umbrella, hairspray or keys against your attacker. You must not carry an offensive weapon, like a knife or sharpened comb.

Help for the elderly

Make sure you are safe when you are out by following the above points.

Protect your possessions by making sure your home is safe and mark your property.

Never keep savings in the house. Put them in a bank, post office or savings account.

(But what if the person concerned does not want to do any of these things but prefers to keep his/her money at home?)

Don't let strangers in the door. They may be thieves and robbers disguising themselves as council or gas officials etc.

(We should ask why the courts allow such thieves and robbers to prey on the elderly and vulnerable and indeed on the rest of the community. It is not inevitable and it is within our means to control it.)

Always lock up even if you are just popping out for a few minutes to the corner shop.

Looking After Your Home

One Home Office security advice booklet starts off by saying 'a lot of burglaries can be prevented' because 30 per cent of burglaries occur when a door or a window is left open, thus implying that the burglary is the fault of the householder for not locking their windows or doors.[24] What the booklet does not say is that *almost all* burglaries could be avoided if we passed sentencing laws which kept burglars off the streets. So, in addition, the victims are burdened not just by crime, but by a system that makes them feel responsible. The booklet lists steps the householder must take to reduce the risk of being targeted. All of them represent intrusions into his freedom to live his life as he wants and to arrange his household and property in a manner of his choosing, as opposed to following practices forced upon him by crime.

Gates and Fences

High walls and fences at the back of the house can put off a burglar. But keep them low at the front so a burglar can't work unseen.

Burglar Alarms

Visible burglar alarms make burglars think twice.

(Certain knowledge of a very long prison sentence would give him time to think more than twice and protect the public from him absolutely.)

Small Windows

Even small windows like casement windows, skylights or bathroom fanlights might need locks. A thief can get in through any gap larger than a human head.

Spare Keys

Never leave a spare key in a hiding place like under a doormat or in a flowerpot – a thief will look there first.

Front Door Roof

A thief could reach first-floor windows from this roof – so fit window locks.

Garages

Never leave a garage or a garden shed unlocked, especially if it has a connecting door to the house. Lock tools and ladders away so that a thief cannot use them to break in.

(It is the thief who should be locked away.)

Front and Back Doors

If your doors seem weak, replace them! If your front and back doors are not safe, neither is your home.

328

(It is salutary to read this statement alongside the advice given by Lord Woolf, the Lord Chief Justice, that first- or second-time burglars should not go to jail. This statement condemns Home Office sentencing policy – the reason our homes are not safe is not because of the kind of doors we have but because burglars are deliberately left free to commit crime at will.)

Front Doors

Get a good lock fitted – a deadlock is best.

Windows

Get locks for ground-floor windows and others that can be reached by a thief. When getting new glass think about laminated glass – it is harder to break. Think about security grilles for your windows.

Door Viewers

Check whose calling before you open the door. Ask to see IDs from official callers.

Side Passage

Fix a strong gate to prevent a thief getting to the back of the house where he can work unseen.

When You Are Away from Home

Most burglaries occur when a house or flat is empty.
Use a time switch to bring lights on and off when you are out. This will make it look as if you are at home.

Don't let your TV or video show through a window.

Draw the curtains if you are going out for the evening.

Get a friend or neighbour to look after your home whilst you are away on holiday.

If you go away, cancel milk and newspaper deliveries.

The Home Office advice amounts to telling members of the public they should live behind security grilles, locked and heavily chained doors, tightly secured windows made of unbreakable glass, surrounded by high walls and fences overlooked by security lights, and all backed up with an alarm system. Furthermore, it recommends that unknown visitors should be allowed in only after a strict security regime has been followed involving physical and documentary identification. Thus the justice system's real crime strategy is revealed in all its perversity. It is to persuade the public to lock themselves away behind a battery of security features remarkably similar to those found at a prison, while the criminals are left free to roam at will through our streets untroubled by the prospect of likely capture or the risk of a long prison sentence if they are caught.

Because the law-abiding public are no longer free to roam at will but the criminals are, they are no longer free to enjoy their homes and possessions free of the fear of molestation. Neither, as previously stated, are they free to protect themselves and their homes from criminals and face the real risk of prison if they do. Yet every day the courts grant offenders their freedom, allowing them to continue to victimise individuals, households and businesses, buoyed by the knowledge that if they are injured or otherwise hurt whilst committing crime, the courts may well uphold their 'rights' to sue for compensation and grant them legal aid to do so.

In September 2003 a YouGov survey reported that 14 per cent of people in the UK thought that the introduction of ID cards (believed to be a potent weapon in the fight against crime) would reduce their personal freedom to an unacceptable degree.[25] However, it soon became apparent that far larger numbers supported the notion that crime has already undermined many of their basic freedoms, and that the requirement to carry an ID card would be a small price to pay if, by controlling offenders, it freed the public from the heavy restrictions now placed upon them by crime. Significantly, in April 2004 Home Secretary David Blunkett announced that draft legislation was already being prepared to introduce these cards and in the same month a MORI poll revealed that four out of five Britons were in favour of them being introduced.[26]

Chapter 13

Let the Victims Speak

The Machinery of Injustice

No parallel would be too strong to drive home the truth of what has been allowed to happen to the public over the last forty years in terms of their unnecessary and avoidable suffering at the hands of greedy, relentless criminals without conscience for the harm they do. No other department of government has been allowed to fail the public in such a dramatic way, and survive, as has the criminal justice service. What would we say of government officials who inflicted on the public a transport system that predictably caused most of the public who used it to be seriously injured and some of them killed? Some may protest at what seems an extreme analogy. But that is my point. What is happening in the criminal justice system is beyond reason and the analogy I make is accurate.

I have also stressed that in order to follow such policies those responsible have had to resort to explanations of crime that have ranged from the preposterous to the grotesque, in a constant and sickly recycling of old and discredited anti-prison propaganda. They have, for example, sought to deflect blame from criminals by pointing out that much of property crime arises from what they have called the offenders' 'criminogenic needs' and that much crime is 'spontaneous'. These are grotesque inventions, and their assumption that the impact of the casual brutality often meted out to members of the public by burglars, thieves and robbers can be downgraded on these grounds beggars belief. Even if victims escape serious physical injury, large numbers of them find their lives coarsened and diminished as a result of being targeted by criminals. As eloquently described by one journalist, such experiences represent

331

for many an irreversible loss of innocence, with their peace of mind undermined for ever.[1]

The Size of the Problem

It is impossible to compute accurately how many people fall victim to crime. As discussed in a previous chapter, estimates for the number of crimes committed each year suggest that this could be as high as 60 million, a truly staggering figure. Even if it were only half of this number, it would make the figure for the number of victims astronomical. We know that the British Crime Survey (BCS) figure for 2001/02 of almost 13 million crimes per year is a dramatic understatement of the problem, despite David Blunkett's highly misleading claim that 'The BCS provides the most comprehensive and reliable evidence data on crime, and deserves to be treated as the most important'.[2] But just based on that figure, assuming two victims per crime (there are often far more), at least 26 million people are victimised each year by criminals. The more accurate figure will be much higher than this.

Crime has now leached its way into almost every part of our society. In 1992, for example, it became known that fear of violence was driving hundreds of trained staff out of the National Health Service, with three out of four nurses suffering verbal or physical abuse during their career. The numbers of attacks on nurses had become such a problem that in the same year the Labour MP for Hampstead and Highgate introduced a Bill in the House of Commons to improve hospital security.[3]

In 1998 it was reported that nearly a quarter of the population knew somebody who had been mugged or robbed in that year and one in five knew someone who had been attacked or assaulted.[4] Twelve months later the problem had deteriorated even further, with two out of three people having been either burgled, mugged, assaulted or had something stolen.[5] In 1999 the smuggling of cheap alcohol and cigarettes had reached such levels that small corner shops were losing on average 16 per cent of their income, totalling approximately £1,000 per week for each shop.[6] Even when in prison some criminals have continued to intimidate and harass victims and their families by sending them letters containing lurid details of crimes thinly disguised as protests of their innocence.[7]

Over recent times a greater variety of people have found themselves subject to repeated attacks by criminals. Many robbers have switched from banks and building societies because of their improved security, and targeted petrol stations, off-licences, jeweller's and stores that offer financial services. Shops have likewise suffered increased waves of attacks from criminals who see them as easy targets.[8] In January 2001 and again in July 2002, the Home Office reported soaring rates for mugging, violent robberies, street crimes and other thefts.[9]

As long ago as 1991, it was reported that by halfway through that year there had been a break-in to someone's home every minute of every day, totalling more than a quarter of a million burglaries.[10] By the end of 1998, according to the British Crime Survey, there were at least 1.6 million domestic burglaries *every year*.[11]

Repeat Victimisation

Research has shown that many people are the subject of repeated victimisation, sometimes daily. During the 1980s a newsagent in Yorkshire was burgled sixty-three times in a seven-year period, despite turning his premises into a defended fortress.[12] Respondents to the 1992 BCS indicated half of those who were victimised were repeat victims and suffered 81 per cent of all recorded crime and that those most at risk of being repeatedly victimised were amongst the most vulnerable and disadvantaged members of the community.[13] In December 1999 the large numbers of repeat burglaries on one estate in the south-west meant that victims faced more than a one in three chance of the burglar returning.[14]

Furthermore, a growing body of research carried out from the mid-1990s came to recognise that much of this crime was not reported to the police.[15] It also found that victims are significantly affected by crimes even when these incidents appear trivial to others, and that victims do not get 'used' to crime. This echoed the experience of one particular member of the public, who several years earlier, when interviewed after her fourth experience of burglary said, 'No matter how often it happens, you never come to terms with it'.[16] That she clearly felt she had to is as terrible an indictment as one can find of the failure of government to protect its citizens.

The Impact of Crime

The continued depredations of the persistent offender affect the quality of the lives of their victims and the public in general, to a degree unequalled by any other recent phenomenon. A debilitating loss of confidence, physical or emotional damage, a pervasive anxiety and devastating loss of privacy and sense of safety are but some aspects of the grim legacy of many who are victimised by criminals. As a result, many of them are afraid to walk the streets and become prisoners in their own homes; some endure a life sentence of fear and, in some cases, physical disability. The harmful, intrusive effects of being victimised by criminals cannot be overstated although they often remain hidden to the casual observer. The victim may appear, after a while, to have returned to normal, but the effects may linger on in the form of unspoken anxieties, and in subtle emotional and behavioural symptoms. It is known that a vague sense of shame prompts many victims to pretend they have recovered, and to deny their debilitating loss of confidence and security.

The enormous volume of crime has desensitised many in the justice system to these pervasively destructive effects. During 1990 a young mother was burgled four times.[17] She moved after the first two attacks, but other criminals targeted her and her family in their new home. On one occasion, their kitchen was stripped bare of every moveable item. On another, whilst she was heavily pregnant, a burglar broke in and stole jewellery and their video recorder. The replacement was stolen again in yet another burglary. The despair and anxiety such experiences leave cannot be measured. This victim now dreads coming home for fear of what she may discover. The quality of her life and that of her family has been totally undermined by these criminal acts. Perhaps most telling of all was the comment she made following the last burglary of their home: 'I guess it is just a sign of the times and we must all learn to live with the fear of being victims again and again.' Thus, not only has she suffered repeated burglaries but she had also been victimised by the false belief that there is nothing anyone could do to prevent burglars from striking her at will.

Such a defeated attitude on the part of the public suits the government's purpose because it reduces the chances of victims and members of the public waking up to the fact that they have every right to demand more prisons and stiffer sentences in order to be certain of protection from persistent offenders. For the authorities to allow such despairing beliefs as expressed by this victim to germinate is as heinous as the experience of burglary itself, because the means by which the public *can* be protected from burglary and other crimes are well within our reach, as will be discussed in the final chapter.

In another example, Mrs M. went into shock the night in 1995 that she discovered her stepfather's house had been broken into and much of its contents stolen. He was ill in a nursing home, and his house had been left empty. His stepdaughter found a great deal of damage. The burglars had smashed a window, hacked through locks on the doors, damaged the doorframes and left the house in a terrible mess. Mrs M. made a four-page list of missing items. She said, 'It was like death, you grieve. They took all the things from my past, the things I grew up with. My mother died five years ago and they stole everything that was dear to her.' Four months later she was still coping with the aftermath of the break-in. Insurance claim details were not settled, carpets needed cleaning, cushions recovering. A major nightmare for her was trying to obtain valuations of all the stolen possessions without the help of her stepfather. Everything of value was stolen, which included amongst other items family silver, lamp shades and four large Victorian garden urns. Even the bedclothes had been taken to wrap up the smaller fragile pieces.[18]

In 1997 a survey found that thefts of and from cars were occurring at the rate of one every eight seconds, totalling 1.5 million for that year.[19] They are so common that they are no longer viewed with the seriousness required to match the impact they have on the victims, and although many have called for car thieves to be jailed, their protests have gone unheard as most escape with a non-custodial sentence. In 1996 a young victim known to me had her car stolen from outside of her flat.[20] Her grandparents had saved up and bought her the vehicle because they knew she desperately needed a car to get to work and that she could not afford to buy one herself. To the police, the theft was 'just another car', a statistic that they would not think twice about, and no effort was made to find the vehicle; it was never seen again. The theft involved the victim in weeks of anxiety, inconvenience as well as the loss of her no-claims bonus leaving her increased car insurance premiums that she could ill-afford. But her response to the crime went beyond the financial and practical problems it posed for her. The car was an expression of her grandparents' love and concern, and its loss moved her deeply. The substitute car could not replace their gift that she had cherished, and it was this which above all else caused her tears and distress for weeks afterwards. A middle-aged woman was robbed of her car when the thief rammed a double-barrelled shotgun into her stomach and told her he would kill her if she did not give him the keys. She took *several years* to recover from this experience.[21]

In January 2003 a psychology student was robbed at gunpoint in the street. Before robbing him, one of the two criminals involved beat him, leaving him unconscious and with a gaping head wound.[22] After his discharge from hospital some days later, he felt he could no longer live in the area and gave in his notice to his landlord, but had to stay on for another two months because of the tenancy agreement. Those two months were a living nightmare for him. He was constantly afraid and did not eat or sleep, and it was three weeks before he could get his heartbeat under control; to make matters worse his attackers lived only a few doors away from him. When they were caught one was sentenced to only three years and the other to twelve months. These sentences came nowhere near matching the seriousness of the crime, or the effects they had on the victim, whose life had not only been disrupted by a major relocation to a different area, but was marked by extreme fear and stress for months afterwards.

Undermining the Public's Quality of Life

One of the most serious findings of a MORI poll carried out in 1988 was the extent to which crime was even then transforming our lives. Many respondents spoke about the changes they had seen in the towns and cities where they lived. Where once they felt free to wander, their movements were increasingly restricted because of the appearance of no-go areas, the domains of criminals who would routinely assault and rob the public, unchallenged or opposed by the police. Many, including the elderly, had lost the freedom to walk out after dark. One respondent, an ex-WAAF driver, said that in the war she could go without fear into the roughest parts of Britain's ports, but by the 1980s she was afraid to go out anywhere at night without her husband.[23]

In the summer of 1987 a married couple returned to their home

336

in the north from holiday to find that thieves had broken in through glass panels, cutting themselves in the process. Blood splattered the walls, carpets and furniture. Drawers had been emptied, clothes and bedding ripped, jewellery – all, for sentimental reasons, irreplaceable – stolen.[24] The victims were deeply scarred by the experience and their home never felt the same to them again. In June 2002 the wife of a wealthy businessman was badly beaten and robbed in their home by a burglar wielding a knife, who tied her up before stealing their jewellery and leaving her badly bruised and traumatised. The house they lived in was their dream home, the rewards of years of hard work, but this horrific ordeal left the couple no longer wanting to live there.[25] This appalling legacy of burglary cuts deep into quality of life for the hundreds of thousands of other victims who suffer this fate every year.

In another part of the country, a young woman was punched viciously in the back by a street robber seconds before stealing her purse. It traumatised her so much that for some time afterwards she kept bursting into tears and was filled with dread every time a man passed close by her because she feared he was going to attack and rob her. For weeks and weeks, she could not sleep, rising at 3 or 3 a.m. every morning to stare out of the window or walk round the room. She lost all ability to concentrate and to do her job. For several months she could hardly bear to go out, even in her locality where she knew almost everyone. The robbery changed her personality, from an outgoing confident person to a nervous, timid individual who now has to park as close to her flat as possible and scurry to her front door. She has never felt safe since. On top of all this, she was left to grieve the loss of photos of her father which were in her purse. He had died a year before she was robbed, and she had carried the photos everywhere.[26]

University research carried out in 1994 found that severe psychological reactions were caused by *what* was taken, not *how much*, and by the fear that the burglars would return. These fears and anxieties often lasted for months, with victims lying awake at night frightened by the slightest noise.[27] One victim identified by the research took two showers a day trying to wash away the feelings of violation left by the experience of burglary. She told the researchers that she did not want to live in her home anymore – she had come to hate it. Many others also felt they had to move from a home where they were once happy and settled, but which was now irrevocably associated with a hateful and altogether destructive experience.

Research has clearly identified that victims are frequently deeply distressed over the loss of items with sentimental value because they are usually associated with an individual or member of the family. However, such findings have not influenced Lord Bingham who, when he was Lord Chief Justice, declared such burglaries to be less serious if they were unplanned. His successor, Lord Woolf, also failed to recognise the deeply painful legacy of burglary by recommending that burglars who steal property of little intrinsic value should be given their freedom.

I sometimes wonder what would happen if a criminal justice official turned up at the door of a family traumatised by a burglary, to bring them the good news that the thief who broke into their home, robbed them of their peace of mind, stole items of irreplaceable sentimental value, and left them deeply disturbed and unable to sleep and think straight, had committed the crime on the spur of the moment and had not planned it beforehand. I try to imagine the reaction of the family as the official explained that as none other than the Lord Chief Justice of England had declared such burglaries to be less serious there was therefore no reason for them to feel particularly bad about what happened. After all, it would have been far worse if the burglar had planned it! Wouldn't that make them feel better?

Overall, the research found that the experience of being burgled had a fundamental effect on many individuals and their families, often producing highly dysfunctional reactions which threw family members off balance, and produced skewed psychological behaviour with sometimes devastating results. Some fell into depression, others stopped being able to work and lost the ability to concentrate; others could no longer go on living in the same house. Family members sometimes blamed each other, and sometimes even their dog, for allowing the break-in to happen.[28]

Many victims suffer repeated anxiety attacks and feel guilty believing they should have done more to protect themselves.[29] Many others remain fearful after being burgled and become obsessed with security rituals that prove disruptive to them and those they live with. In November 2003, for example, one woman victim confessed that she had hardly slept since her home had been subject to a break-in, due to fear that a burglar might strike again. From that moment on, she could not leave any windows open so that throughout the summer there was no air in the house. Going to bed became an arduous ritual of locking all the internal doors and making sure all exterior doors were secured.[30]

Many who are robbed, burgled or otherwise victimised often never recover fully from the horror, and the anxieties they are left with, and this undermines any chance of them living a normal life. As long ago as 1995, research by a large insurance company found that thieves were costing Britain £100 million a year in stress alone; that at any one time 6 million people were suffering from crime-induced trauma, and thousands of those victimised by criminals took several days off work, and some several weeks.[31] It also found that at least 50 per cent of victims suffered some form of trauma after a burglary. Seven years later Home Office research found it had increased to 82 per cent,[32] and that almost 80 per cent of victims of violent crime suffered significant emotional effects, with shock, fear, loss of confidence and feeling unsafe all being common experiences.[33] If policies run by hospitals, dentists or any other service providers caused even a fraction of this harm to the public they would be run out of business and in all likelihood prosecuted. Yet criminal justice policy makers survive, insulated from the harm they cause by a scornful indifference to any argument but their own.

Putting Victims at the Heart of the Justice System: A Hollow Promise

For some years now, the Home Secretary and other criminal justice officials have repeatedly claimed that they have put victims 'at the heart of the criminal justice system' and made the protection of the public their first concern. No claim could be more meaningless because the influence of the Home Office and the Probation Service has played a major part in ensuring persistent offenders remain free to predate on the public. For this reason their recent stated concern for the victims of crime appear as crocodile tears.[34] The Probation Service is now tasked to ensure that victim awareness informs their work with offenders, but these are empty gestures. It is not possible to undo the experience of being a victim. No amount of support can alter their frequent experience of loss of irreplaceable family and personal items, or their basic peace of mind and sense of security.

If the authorities were serious in their concern, they would ensure that persistent offenders unmotivated to reform were locked up for increasingly long periods so they could not prey on the public and make victims of them in the first place. As it stands, millions of them are left to cope with their emotional and physical wounds, abandoned by those required to protect them.[35] Paul Boateng, formerly Home Office minister responsible for the Probation Service, also claimed that 'victim work is at the heart of effective practice with offenders. We work to get offenders to recognise the impact of their crimes on victims.'[36] The irony is that it is the Probation Service that fails to recognise the dreadful impact their policies have had in creating more victims, by successfully campaigning for persistent offenders to be kept out of prison.

A recent savage killing of a young woman by a dangerous offender occurred when he was out of touch with the Probation Service responsible for his supervision. Despite knowing of the serious threat he posed to the safety of the public, the supervising officer failed to visit the offender's home address when he did not report as instructed.[37] In another recent example, both the court and probation staff failed to inform the victim that her attacker's bail condition was that he should stay away from her.[38] Examples such as these expose the emptiness of claims by the then director of the National Probation Service that 'victims are uppermost in our priorities'.[39]

Likewise, the courts, the police and the Crown Prosecution Service frequently fail to give the victim the priority they have a right to expect. For example, in 1997 'Mrs D.', the owner of an antique jewellery shop was attacked by a robber who felled her with a vicious blow to the head using a twelve-inch metal cosh. For days afterwards she lapsed in and out of consciousness. She suffered terrible head wounds and could not remember what happened, but the assault had been captured on a CCTV camera. The criminal eventually received ten years in prison, a sentence that in my view came nowhere near matching the seriousness of the crime. After the attack she was unable to work again and had to give up the business that she had funded with her life savings only eighteen months before and which had been her pride and joy. From being outgoing and confident, she became wary and fearful of stepping out of her front door. She had lost her hearing in one ear and could no longer taste or smell and found it necessary to walk with a stick and take powerful anti-convulsive drugs. The attack had left her central nervous system permanently damaged.[40]

In short, her life had been ruined but what followed made a mockery of the government's claim that it was putting victims at the heart of the criminal justice system. Despite her condition, she had to *fight* a benefit tribunal to win a £2 per day disability allowance. Two years later, her Criminal Injuries Compensation claim had still not been settled and her local council threatened her with court action and bailiffs unless she paid the rates on the business she had not been able to run since the assault. Yet worse was to follow. In late 1999 her attacker had his sentence reduced to eight years at an uncontested appeal hearing before three judges in London. The victim knew nothing about this until a local journalist telephoned her. The policeman involved in the case first heard about the hearing on the local news. As reported in the press in October of that year, the Appeal Court had failed to tell the police or the Crown Prosecution Service (CPS) that the appeal, paid for out of the public purse, was going ahead. Even had they known, neither the Crown nor the victim, Mrs D, would have had the right to contest the case.

Unbelievably, the CPS rarely attends such hearings and the victim has no right to be represented before the Appeal Court. Yet is this not the very place where the government had promised to put victims of crime – a pledge made as long ago as 1990 by the then Home Secretary David Waddington?[41] If the 'heart of the criminal justice system' is not to be found in such arenas as the central Appeal Court, then where is it? Yet while the press complain at these injustices, and the public look on with bewildered amazement and the victims are left aghast at the contempt shown to them by the system, *nothing* is done to change the situation, and fourteen years after David Waddington's promise to put the public and victims centre stage of the criminal justice system, it continues to ignore them, often in the most spectacular way.

In 2000 the police refused to tell a newly-wed that her husband was on the sex offenders register, and that he had a violent past which included a conviction for rape and abduction. They kept a close eye on him, but when his wife asked why they kept visiting their home, they claimed they could not tell her because of the data protection act. This dangerous man later took his wife hostage and brutally raped her at knifepoint. She was lucky to escape with her life.[42]

In 2001 a defendant was sent to prison for life for attempted murder and rape of a woman committed whilst he was on parole. He had been sentenced to life imprisonment years before, for the brutal murder of a young woman who, wanting to help him had offered him temporary shelter in her flat. The sister of the murdered girl, 'Miss A.', had been promised that she would be contacted in good time before his release so that she could make her objections known. He was eventually freed after serving fourteen years of his sentence. But Miss A, was telephoned with this news only when his release was imminent, and when she registered her objection she was told it was too late and that it would have no effect on the outcome.[43] The callous and indifferent way she had been treated left her devastated.

A year earlier a policeman was badly beaten up by seven youths whilst on duty, but he only learned of the reduction in the charges at court and other developments in the case by reading about them in the local newspaper.[44]

In 2000, in response to rising public concern, Crown prosecutors were instructed for the first time to take account of the views of victims in deciding whether to prosecute.[45] However, this appears to have had little effect, as the number of offenders being brought to trial continued to fall. Two years later there was still mounting public resentment over the way victims of crime were treated, and in March 2002 the government announced that victims were to have a Bill of Rights as one of a series of ideas designed to restore public confidence in British justice. At the time of writing, no action has been taken on these proposals, but a Bill of Rights will not undo the harm caused to those who are targeted by criminals given their freedom by government sentencing policies.[46]

Justice and Retribution: Looted Concepts

Standard minimum rules have been established to govern the treatment of prisoners, and government machinery exists, in addition to an independent prisoners' 'ombudsman', to ensure they are followed and maintained.[47] The rationale for all of this is, quite rightly, to ensure that prisoners are treated properly. Yet no ombudsman has been appointed or similar system created to ensure courts provide even the minimum standards of justice for victims or protection for the public, who more often than not are ignored and trampled on by an insensitive criminal justice bureaucracy.

It is therefore not surprising that surveys have found thousands of victims (and witnesses) would be reluctant to report further crimes because of the poor treatment they previously received from the courts or other parts of the justice system, and that likewise large sections of the public have lost faith in the courts' willingness to either protect them from criminals or provide proper retribution for the crimes committed against them. Even the police have been criticised by research for their insensitive handling of some victims.[48] However, it was the police from one area of the country who firmly supported a campaign that was launched to stop witness intimidation in courts; and it was the Bar Council who opposed it on the grounds that it was a thinly disguised manoeuvre by the police to increase their chances of gaining a conviction. Many believed this was a cynical dismissal of genuine concern by the police to protect the rights of victims and witnesses, from an organisation overly concerned with protecting the rights of its criminal defendants.[49]

Leaving Persistent Offenders in the Community: The Price Paid by the Elderly

Large numbers of pensioners are targeted by criminals. Some are subject to the most horrific violence, frequently during a burglary. The following are just a few examples taken, in the main from the 1990s, of the thousands of elderly people who every year are forced to endure these experiences.

During the early 1990s 'Mrs S.', a cleaner from the north of England and in her 60s, was burgled four times. The effect on her was devastating. After the fourth break-in (one of 55,000 burglaries committed every year at that time in the police district where she lived) she later saw the youth who had burgled her flat and told the police. He was arrested, and at his trial his lawyer was allowed to question her in an aggressive manner and made Mrs S. feel like a liar.[50]

'Mrs R.', a 90-year-old great-grandmother was robbed of her pension books, electricity and TV saving stamps, a savings book and £50 by a burglar pretending to be a water board worker. The crime left her traumatised and unable to sleep or leave her flat. She

343

was therefore also robbed of her freedom and much of the quality of her life.[51]

In 2003 a 72-year-old grandmother was beaten, robbed and left for dead as she walked to see her grandchild's nativity play. The injuries to her brain were so severe it was thought she might not survive. However, her injuries go far beyond her smashed skull, as she has not been able to remember anything since. The impact on her grown up children has been heavy as they feel they have lost the mother they once knew.[52]

In 2000 a frail pensioner aged eighty-seven was blinded and left for dead by a burglar she disturbed at her home. The thief kicked and repeatedly struck her about the face with a heavy weapon. She suffered multiple fractures to her skull, forehead and left shoulder.[53]

In 1992 a Bath pensioner aged sixty-eight was left in a coma after a hammer attack by an intruder, and a 77-year-old man was battered to the floor with a pickaxe handle by a burglar who burst in through his front door demanding money. The victim was left semi-conscious with a shattered leg as well as a broken nose and cheekbones.[54]

In September of the same year, a 91-year-old widow who lived alone had her skull and jaw smashed by a robber who then robbed her of five pounds,[55] and in the same month a burglar struck an 87-year-old man in the face, frog-marched him into his bedroom and pinned him down while two young accomplices ransacked his home and robbed him of his savings amounting to £400.[56]

Death by Burglary

In 1991 a 94-year-old pensioner from Bristol was found dead forty-five minutes after she entered her home and found it ransacked by a burglar.[57] Her grieving family believed she died from shock and that the burglar was therefore responsible for her death. In the mid-1990s someone posing as an odd-job man murdered an elderly widow in her bed.[58] In 1992 another pensioner died of a heart attack after discovering her home had been burgled. Her last conversation was a telephone call to a relative to say she was being burgled. She was later found dead with the contents of her bedroom drawers tipped out onto the floor.[59]

In the same year, a 59-year-old grandmother from Durham collapsed and died after returning home and finding her terraced house had been broken into and burgled. As far as her family were concerned the burglar had killed their mother.[60] In 1996 a widow of eighty-three killed herself because she was terrified that the burglars who robbed her and ransacked her home would return. Prior to this attack she was in good health, was lively and enjoyed dancing and parties. However, she left a note saying she was too frightened to continue, and walked into the sea and drowned.[61] In 1993 an elderly brother and sister were found dead in their flat in east London. The brother had been bound and had died due to suffocation. His sister had died from heart failure. Their flat was in disarray and had been burgled.[62]

Death by Mugging

In April 1991 an 83-year-old man was mugged. It left him so anxious that he became a prisoner in his own home and refused to go out and after a short interval he hanged himself.[63] A Swindon-based victim suffered constant and severe pain from injuries received as a result of an unprovoked attack. Eventually the pain became too much to bear and he committed suicide.[64]

Victims of 'Envy'

Many crimes are motivated by a vicious malice, motivated by what appears to be a deep sense of envy on the part of the criminals who perpetrate them. For example, in 1992 the son of a well-known MP lost an eye after being assaulted with a broken glass. An associate of the attacker offered the justification that the victim and his friends should not have come into a 'working-class' pub. Such views are typical of an attitude that threatens the quality of life of anyone trying to enjoy the fruits of even modest success. The simplest gesture – wearing smart clothes, enjoying a private garden, driving a smart car, eating at a pavement café – can now be enough to provoke unpredictable and brutal spontaneous attacks.

One married couple returned home to find their house had been subject to wanton destruction by burglars who had scrawled 'rich bastards' on the wall of one room. In another example, a middle-aged man, enjoying a barbecue with his family on the lawn of his home, was attacked when he went to get rid of youths kicking his fence. He died two days later in hospital. A senior academic from Sheffield University's Centre for Criminological and Legal Research links such crimes to envy, pointing out that they do not arise from poverty and hunger, but because the criminals concerned expect society to give them what they see other people possess, such as designer clothes, and commit crime to get them.[65]

A Voice for Victims?

But instead of signalling their concern at the sheer size of the crime problem faced by the public, the government was triumphant in its claim that the 2.3 million vehicle thefts (see Note 1) recorded by the BCS for 2002, represented a 14 per cent fall over the previous year, and the number of burglaries recorded by the police had dropped to just below 900,000 per year.[66] But such statistics offer no comfort to those who are victimised in such breathtaking numbers.

The 2001/02 British Crime Survey showed that there were almost one million incidents of domestic burglary which meant that as many as one in thirty households fell victim to this offence.[67] They should be thought of as casualties in the undeclared war that persistent offenders wage against a largely unprotected public, causing them often serious physical and emotional injuries as well as death. Yet, far from taking steps to provide them with adequate protection, the government's sentencing policy has ensured that no more than 1.5 per cent of all recorded burglaries and 0.3 per cent of all known crime has resulted in a prison sentence.[68]

The chairman of the magistrates in one area of the country said, 'It would be much simpler just to send people to prison. But we don't think like that. We want to help people find their way again,'[69] thus illustrating how many magistrates have become so focused on the offender that they have forgotten that their first duty is to protect the public. Offenders appearing before these JPs were highly likely to receive a non-custodial sentence, yet in November 2003 it became known that criminals they so much wanted to help owed them £3 million in unpaid fines.[70] In 1999 the average prison sentence passed in the magistrates' courts for burglary was only 3.5 months, and in the crown courts, where more serious cases are dealt with, it was

346

still only 22.5 months.[71] By 2001, the average prison sentence given in the crown courts (taking into account all offences) was still only twenty-six months,[72] despite the fact that judges know in practice a two-year sentence means only eight months.

However, locked into these sentencing practices there are a number of other glaring injustices rubbing salt into the wounds of a largely unaware and crime-beleaguered public. First, they have been denied the truth concerning the massive failure of these sentencing policies to protect them from further crime by a torrent of anti-prison propaganda, frequently ideologically motivated. Thus reasonable and effective protest by the public is choked before it can start.

Second, there is at present no publicly recognised avenue by which judges and magistrates are held accountable to the victims who suffer loss, injury or distress as a result of being victimised by those criminals the courts have chosen to place back into the community, rather than send them to prison. In thousands of cases, as shown by the records, they gamble with the safety and well-being of the public by passing community sentences, despite the offenders' frightening history of previous criminality.[73] All too often, as previously noted, the consequences for victims in terms of physical and mental trauma and financial loss at the hands of the criminals given their freedom are unthinkable. This calamitous failure to protect the public from further crime shows beyond doubt that the decisions to trust these offenders with their freedom are frequently wrong. As demonstrated, the scale of the problem is vast, and the culpability of the sentencers is unarguable. Yet, unlike all other professionals and service providers, judges and magistrates are not subject to any meaningful professional standards review, where sentencing decisions which result in harm to the public can be judged against a professional code of requirements underpinning their duty to protect the public.

Third, given that persistent offenders are placed in the community despite it being known that they pose a considerable threat of reoffending, the public has never been asked to say what level of risk of further victimisation by criminals they are prepared to accept. Instead they are used as unconsenting guinea pigs in what amounts to dangerous community-supervision experiments which actually increase the crime rate. Victims of crime have been vulnerable and defenceless for too long. They should be enabled to hold magistrates or judges accountable for allowing an offender to stay in the community when they are victimised by that offender. Sentencers

347

should be subject to a system of professional review and censure by a competent body who can evaluate their sentencing decisions that result in harm to members of the public. In addition, the government should issue objective information to the public informing them of the true picture concerning the results of current sentencing policies. In particular it should explain how the level of risk of further offending presented by offenders is now computable, and what different levels of risk mean in terms of the likely number of offences the offender may commit if given his freedom.

Highly accurate 'risk of reoffending scores' can now be worked out for each offender using a formula constructed over recent years by criminologists. Sentencers should be required to make such risks public at the time of sentence. Information about these as well as other relevant data should be presented to the public in the form of Green and White Papers as the basis for a lengthy period of public consultation. At the end of this discussion period, local MPs would be in no doubt as to the views of their constituents concerning the level of risk of further offending they would be prepared to accept from criminals let loose into the community. Armed with these views, MPs should then be allowed a free vote to decide on the maximum 'risk of reoffending' score of offenders to be allowed into the community at the time of sentence. My instincts tell me that, given the correct information and time to think about it, the vast majority of members of the public would vote for a nil-risk score.

At first sight, the idea of victims holding judges or magistrates accountable may seem unpalatable to many, yet on closer inspection it can be seen to fit in with our expectations of professional behaviour and service provision in every other walk of life. If doctors or dentists, for example, made professional decisions which caused serious harm or distress to the public, there would be an outcry. They would be named and blamed, and subject to the review and judgment by a disciplinary panel relevant to their profession and if the situation warranted it they would lose their licence to practice. They would also be vulnerable to being sued by those hurt or otherwise affected by their professional mistakes. It is an accepted norm that the choice to sue those who have caused harm through professional negligence is an acceptable way to seek redress.

It is extraordinary that judges and magistrates escape similar accountability, given that millions of people are hurt and distressed

348

each year as a result of their sentencing decisions. If drug companies used the public as guinea pigs for products knowing that their previous failure rate was catastrophic, they would be regarded as criminals and treated as such. Whilst some may find this parallel distasteful, it is an exact analogy of present sentencing practices whereby thousands of criminals are sentenced to community supervision programmes despite their known previous failure rates.[74]

A system that monitors the success and failure rates of judges and magistrates to protect the public would be relatively easy to introduce as the information required is readily available. The review panel could score a point against a judge or magistrate whose decision to place a criminal in the community resulted in further crime by that criminal. This could be on a similar basis to the totting-up process involved in monitoring those convicted of driving offences. When the judge or magistrate concerned reached an agreed points ceiling, he or she would be subject to a competency review where decisions could be made concerning their need for further training or, where necessary, removal from office.

The results of these recommendations, if brought into practice, would I believe be dramatic. If it was an established principle that victims could sue the State for its failure to protect them from crime, and magistrates and judges knew that in certain circumstances, this would result in their being held accountable by a professional standards authority, it would significantly focus the minds of all concerned to make certain that sentences passed by judges and magistrates protected the public. They would be far less likely 'to take a chance' with their safety by placing back in the community persistent offenders who showed no motivation to reform. I believe it would also result in judges and magistrates demanding clear and specific information from the Probation Service, concerning offenders' 'risk of reoffending' score, before they passed sentence.[75] (Unbelievably, the Probation Service previously withheld this information from the courts, unless it was specifically requested.) Similarly, the sanction of disciplinary action or worse by a professional review body concerning wrong sentencing decisions, would bring judges and magistrates into line with every other workforce in the country and would go far in ensuring greater justice for the public.

I have no doubt that if the public were properly briefed concerning the injustices inflicted upon them by the present sentencing system, and were given the facts concerning the failure rate of present sentencing policy, they would make it clear to their parliamentary representatives that the courts' duty to protect them from persistent offenders unmotivated to reform is paramount.

These changes if brought about would not affect the independence of the judiciary in their all-important task of establishing guilt and innocence. However, the present lack of accountability to the public in our sentencing procedure, and the lack of objective information available to them concerning the failure of the courts to protect them from crime, represents an injustice that would not be tolerated in any other discipline or walk of life. We now have a vast army of people who have been victimised by criminals,[76] yet they have no influence on those in the criminal justice system who make decisions that frequently backfire mercilessly on them. The case for change is unarguable. Yet instead of introducing much needed policies to protect the public, the government is instead inventing strategies to defuse mounting public anger about its failed crime policies in a bid to ward off what many see as otherwise inevitable major protests and significant social disruption.

Chapter 14

Dampening the Flames of Protest

A Social and Political Time Bomb

It has been said of the United Kingdom that in the latter half of the twentieth century numerous of its citizens developed a mawkish interest in the sufferings and plight of 'victims', evidenced by the arrival of a 'counselling culture' that has burgeoned over the last twenty years. There does appear something excessive in the arrival of armies of stress and grief counsellors at the scene of tragic events whose victims may just want to be left alone and will, in most cases, have the resources to cope.

All this stands out in contrast to the public's response to the victims of crime, which has been strangely muted. The almost free rein our crime policies have given to offenders since the 1950s has, as stated in the previous chapter, resulted in untold millions of UK citizens suffering emotional, practical and financial loss. Yet whilst only two relatively small organisations exist to offer support to those targeted by criminals, there are sound reasons why we *should* take a more active interest in the effects that crime has on members of the public.

Their natural feelings of fear, anger and wish for retribution and justice have either been minimised or ignored. As a result, the mood of the country, even over the last five years has noticeably changed. The courts are no longer as trusted as they were; there is little or no confidence in the forces of law and order, and increasing numbers of the public now feel a sense of alienation from the criminal justice system that only even a few years ago they would not have owned.

We continue to ignore the effects of crime at our peril; the public's sense of injustice is now such that, if not remedied, it will destabilise,

351

I believe, even our long-established political and social system. We should intervene *now* with realistic sentencing policies to avert these potentially dangerous consequences. Otherwise resentment and distrust towards the State at the continued absence of proper retribution will lead to major protests. A complete alienation of the public from the forces of law and order will then be but a short step away, igniting a chain of events whose results we would all live to regret.

Disturbingly, the first signs of this upheaval are already visible. Increasing numbers of otherwise law-abiding people no longer bother to report crime to the police and instead are taking the law into their own hands. Large numbers of the public now realise they are on their own and unprotected in the face of unrelenting crime. Over recent years the public's long-held belief in British justice has been worn away and it has been replaced by a widespread resentment that, at a local level at least, law and order has been allowed to collapse. As long ago as 1993, a senior police officer warned that if the law, Parliament and the courts continued to fail to protect the public and ignore the victims of crime then ordinary people would increasingly administer their own justice.[1] Ten years later, as he predicted, large numbers in the community are defying the law and taking steps to protect themselves, sometimes forcibly.

Victims Fight Back

In 1992 a victim of a burglary stabbed the intruder in the chest with a six-inch knife. The householder had been driven to despair by no fewer than eighteen break-ins to his home in a two-month period. No one, including the police, could rescue him from this torment, and he finally struck out in self-defence.[2] The law generally takes a serious view of such acts, but what exactly was he to do? Whilst the police and the courts are often quick to condemn such vigilante acts, the blame lies with our failed and corrupted judicial system.

It was desperation which caused a villager who had suffered months of torment from teenagers revving their bikes outside of his home to snatch one of the machines and destroy it by dragging it through the streets tied to the back of his car. He had previously tried reasoning with the youths, organised a petition and had sought help from the police, but, to his dismay, their only advice was that he should move house. He was left with no option but to take measures into his own hands. Magistrates made him pay compensation for the bike, but he remained unrepentant. Perhaps most significant of all is that as a result of his actions, the motorbike problem ceased.[3]

In another example, a businessman in the north of the country who was plagued by a series of crimes including arson attacks against his business and damage to his vehicles finally snapped when he saw a gang of youths trying to break into a neighbour's car. A chase ensued; one youth struck out with a bottle, and in the fight which followed he was stabbed to death with a chisel held by his pursuer. In court the businessman said that he had not intended to kill anyone, but armed himself because he saw the criminals had a Rottweiler dog. Most telling of all was his statement that he went after the youths because the police had told him in response to his past requests for help that there was nothing they could do unless he caught the culprits. Here was a blatant example of them admitting they could not catch the criminals, even though it was their job to do so, and in effect, delegating it to a member of the public, who would otherwise not have been in the dock facing a charge of murder.[4]

It was only after months of extreme provocation that a 300-strong force of angry villagers marched on the house of a teenage hoodlum, who had made their lives miserable by robbing them, breaking into their houses and committing over 300 thefts. Throughout this period he had appeared in court time after time only to be let free again to start his crime spree all over again. Having surrounded his house, the crowd refused to leave until the youth was driven away to another location. He did not return, prompting one protester to say, 'This has been a victory for people power and common sense'.[5]

In 1994 an Essex man went to visit his parents' empty house. He was surprised and frightened by a hooded figure of a burglar coming at him from a bedroom. The burglar sprayed CS gas into the victim's eyes, temporarily blinding him. The burglar was also armed with a pickaxe handle, a twelve-inch chisel and a commando knife. The victim struck out with a knife and the attacker dropped to the floor. He died in the ambulance on the way to the hospital. On this occasion, the coroner ruled it a lawful killing.[6]

The increase in the number of booby-traps left for burglars and other thieves is a clear sign of how the mood of the public is changing. Only a relatively short time ago, most people would have been governed by a severe sense of restraint over these matters, but now more and more victims, at their wits' end to know how to stop criminals targeting them and their families, are resorting to violent means of self-defence.

During an interview in 2003 a victim of repeated thefts told me he had been driven to despair because the police could do nothing to stop thieves returning again and again to steal his cars. Each time this occurred, he was put to enormous financial and practical difficulties, and eventually he could cope with it no more. He electrified the driver's seat, and, at his next attempt, the thief was badly burned and needed emergency hospital treatment. The 'victim' was given a two-year suspended prison sentence for grievous bodily harm. When I last checked, my informant had not suffered any more car thefts. Another victim of repeated motorbike thefts finally booby-trapped the petrol tank of his vehicle. When the next thief started the engine in order to steal the machine, it exploded and killed him outright.

A law-abiding householder was driven to distraction by the repeated burglaries of his home. The effects upon his wife and family were traumatic, yet as usual the authorities could do nothing. As with all other victims in a similar position, he was posed with the dreadful question of what he should do. It was, in the circumstances, unreasonable to expect him to do nothing; yet on the other hand he knew it was against the law to leave a trap for the burglar, even though this was in defence of his own property. He was therefore forced to break the law and electrified the windows of his house. Sometime later he found tell-tale signs of an intruder's presence in the back garden, but no break-in had occurred and he has not been burgled since.

Farmers have been increasingly targeted by criminals over the last few years. Even ten years ago the majority of them did not feel the need to lock away all of their machines and other property. But now it is essential, and even then the expensive security systems many have installed do not deter the determined thieves.[7] The criminals know the police are a long way away, and in all likelihood too thin on the ground to respond quickly. So farmers and their equipment have become easy targets. Many have been burgled again and again. Tony Martin, the Norfolk farmer who shot and killed a burglar on his farm, had called for help on numerous occasions but none came. In the end he took his defence into his own hands. At

354

the time of this tragic incident Norfolk had the lowest number of police officers per 100,000 of the population in the country.[8]

In a similar incident the police failed to send officers to a burglary on a Lincolnshire farm in the summer of 2002. The farmer, left to cope alone, intended to fire a warning shot at the burglar but the shotgun went off accidentally and peppered the thief in the stomach. The jury cleared the farmer of grievous bodily harm.[9] In the winter of 2002 an inquest ruled that a grandfather who had killed a burglar had acted within the law. Two armed burglars had burst into the victim's home and assaulted him and his wife. The victim fought back and in the course of a bloody and desperate fight the burglar was stabbed with his own knife.[10]

A Failed Contract

Whilst some people accused of crimes connected with killing or injuring criminals have been found not guilty, the law generally takes a serious view of members of the public who use force to defend themselves against criminals. Many have been prosecuted, amidst widespread protests that such a response is draconian and unjust. What exactly does the law expect a victim to do when he and/or his family and home are threatened by a criminal intent on robbing them and doing them harm? The Tony Martin case gave fresh impetus to this debate, and many MPs argued that householders and individuals should be allowed to defend themselves, and that there should be a presumption in favour of the victim in those cases where a burglar or other criminal is hurt or killed as a result of a confrontation with a member of the public.

The counter argument has always been that if such a ruling were adopted by our courts, this would give free rein to vigilante groups who would administer violence wherever and whenever they liked. However, as demonstrated, the more certain road to anarchy is to leave the public in its present condition without adequate protection and justice. In 2000 a judge sent four men to prison for branding a burglar with a heated coat hanger, saying, 'If society were for one moment to allow this behaviour to rule, then civilised life would slide away like shifting sand'.[11] But we are already witnessing civilised life sliding away from us, as a result of the unfettered activity of criminals against a vulnerable and largely helpless public.

The debate about whether we should be allowed to defend ourselves and, if so, with what degree of force would lose its urgency if all persistent criminals, on further conviction, were locked up for longer and longer periods of time, thus giving the public the protection they have a right to expect. After all, we give the authorities the right to rule us in exchange for their promise to defend us. It is widely recognised, as stated by the then Home Office Minister in a speech in the House of Lords in 1997 that 'the first duty of any government is to protect its citizens by maintaining law and order'.[12] Yet while the public *pays* to be protected, the government fails to keep its part of the contract by refusing to spend the necessary sums of money required to apprehend, convict and lock up thousands of more offenders. Corner shops and other victims plagued by robbers should not have to *bid* for money from the Home Office to help defend themselves against criminals.[13] Whilst this situation lasts, irrespective of what the law says, it will be inevitable that more and more people will take steps to defend themselves against criminals and exact the justice and retribution denied them by the State. It was the government's awareness of this change in public mood, I believe, which prompted them, in early 2005, to announce some limited changes in the way the courts would view acts of aggression by householders against burglars.

The Establishment Starts to Worry

In 1992 the criminal justice establishment once again registered its concern at the rise in vigilante activity against criminals. The Director of Public Prosecutions took the unusual step of publicly admitting that this was the result of the public's loss of faith in the criminal justice system.[14] But the steps she took to rectify the situation were no more than empty gestures. What the public wanted were far more persistent offenders caught, prosecuted and imprisoned, to *prevent* them becoming victims in the first place. Instead she merely ordered that lawyers handle victims more 'sensitively' and in particular instructed them to explain more clearly their decisions when they did not proceed with charges. Her belief this approach would restore confidence in the system is yet one more indicator of how naive and out of touch senior justice officials are with the public's experience of crime.

De-politicising Victims of Crime

Nevertheless, the government had shown that it was aware that the increased willingness of the public to fight back against criminals was directly related to their unrest about its failed crime policies. In addition, research had shown that although the public feared crime, their *anger* about it was far stronger.[15] However, the government's response has been to ignore such findings and instead devise tactics to head off the public's anger in order to *defuse* what it fears could become a threatening political issue. These have included campaigns to make the victims feel that the crime was their fault due to their lack of care; attempts to persuade the public that victims of crime are being given a high priority, and other measures designed to make the victim feel that they have a role to play in the reform of the criminal.

Over recent years the government has published a great deal of propaganda to encourage people to take more care of their property. For example, in the 1980s, the media were used to launch two massive advertising campaigns ostensibly focused on encouraging the public to become more security-conscious,[16] but I believe their real purpose was to make victims feel that if they left their possessions lying around where thieves could get at them and they were stolen then the loss was the victim's fault. Similarly, it is now expected that the public should avoid certain places at particular times in our town centres. This attitude was clearly expressed by a policeman to a female victim of a street robbery when he said, 'What do you expect, this is always happening here on a Friday and Saturday'. His meaning was plain. She shouldn't have been there and so the crime was her fault. Some insurance companies are equally explicit on this issue. They make their customers pay several hundred pounds of any claim if they failed to take the 'proper' security measures.[17]

The government hopes that if the public can be persuaded to believe that it is because of their own carelessness that criminals target them then it is less likely that they will direct their anger at the justice system and demand change. Such a scenario was anticipated in a cult comic strip called *2000 AD*. In a 1989 issue two prisoners are discussing their fate. One complains he was given sixty days for a mugging. The other replies that he was lucky to get such a light sentence. 'But,' says his comrade, 'I was the victim!'[18]

Other initiatives are dressed up as providing for the needs of victims, or as putting them at the 'heart of the criminal justice system'. They are all phoney; their real purpose is to rob victims of their natural and justified feelings of anger and protest at what has happened to them. At the same time, the government grants paid to charities concerned with victims and to the Neighbourhood Watch movement serve to muffle these organisations as possible sources of criticism of their crime sentencing policies.

Claims by the Probation Service that its work is now 'victim-centred' are largely meaningless because they continue to campaign for the release into the community of thousands of persistent offenders who pose major threats to the safety of the public. Its promise to provide information to victims about the release of those who have robbed or attacked them does nothing to undo their experience of trauma, stress and fear. These feeble gestures are no more than attempts to give the appearance of concern for those affected by crime. A recent report by the Probation Inspectorate focused on the need to 'value the victim'.[19] Such outpourings are all too late. It is not possible to undo the effects of a burglary or robbery. It would be more to the point if the probation inspectorate valued the safety of the public and encouraged policies that prevented individuals falling foul of crime in the first place.

Some of the most blatant methods used by the government to neutralise victims' feelings of protest are to be found in the 'restorative justice' schemes. This system purports to encourage offenders to reform and at the same time bring resolution for victims' hurt and angry feelings. During 2003, the restorative justice was pushed hard by the government as its latest panacea and many naive observers have been taken in by it. As a cynical mechanism for 'protest control' it has few equals. Wild claims have been made for its success which when examined are found to be bogus.

Restorative Justice

Restorative justice has been defined as a problem-solving approach to crime which involves the criminal, the victim and the community. It is said to be concerned with restoration: restoration of the victim and of the offender to a law-abiding life.[20]

It was first used, in the late 1970s, as a term to describe the principles arising out of early experiments in America using mediation between victims and offenders. It has been modified several times over the years, but now rests on a number of highly dubious assumptions: that the public makes demands for severe punishments and that this is counter-productive; that the needs of the victims, the offenders and the community are not independent, and that justice agencies should actively engage with all three in order to make any impact.[21]

These ideas are pure inventions, and they are as far removed from reality and the public's experience of crime as it is possible to be. The public have nothing in common with those who rob, assault and burgle them, and want nothing more than to be left in peace; it is wrong to explain criminal behaviour as an expression of the offender's 'needs'. 'Severe punishments' in the form of long prison sentences, far from being counter-productive, are shown by the evidence to be more effective at persuading criminals to reform and at protecting the public than any other disposal. Far from demanding vengeance, the British public are and have been noticeably long-suffering in the face of a torrent of non-stop victimisation at the hands of criminals who strike them at will and almost invariably escape.

The restorative justice programmes which have been run in this country since the 1980s have taken various forms and have largely involved juvenile offenders, though not exclusively. They focus on a conference involving the offender, local justice figures, sometimes representatives of the local community and, where they agree to attend, the victim. Their purpose is to establish the type of reparation to be made by the offender for his crimes, and, where the victim is present, this will invariably involve the offender 'apologising' to his victim. These so-called 'mediation' meetings take place as part of a police caution, and therefore they are a *substitute* for formal court action

Does it Work?

Research results from a number of these projects have sometimes claimed small, positive effects on recidivism.[22] However, these 'effects' are theoretical and do not represent real benefits for the public. A sample of seventy-three offenders (all aged 17 and over), dealt with by the Leeds Victim Offender Unit during 1993–4, showed a reconviction over two years of 46.6 per cent compared with the theoretical expected rate of 54.2 per cent,[23] while another programme for shoplifters failed to find even these differences.[24] Similarly, research from the US has shown statistical effects for some cases and not for others.

But as explained in earlier chapters, such comparisons are a red herring. The only meaningful question from the point of view of protecting the public is how many offences have been committed by those on restorative-justice schemes – irrespective of how they compare with the theoretical predicted rate. Viewed in this way, it is seen that restorative justice, like all other community offender programmes, not only fails to protect the public from persistent criminals, but exposes it to great risk.

Pathways to Injustice

A number of these problems are to be found in a recent Home Office study, carried out between 1998 and 2001, of a large sample of offenders from the Thames Valley area. This reported a 24 per cent reconviction rate measured over two years, for 15,000 of he 19,000 adult offenders who had been referred to a restorative-justice conference as part of their police caution.[25] Despite the fact that almost all of them were 'first' offenders, and presumably regarded as good risks, at least a quarter of them (3,750) were known to have been reconvicted at least once during the two-year period following their apology to their victim. If we assume only a quarter of the remaining 4,000 (for whom reconviction data was not available) were also reconvicted during the same period then we must add another 1,000 to those known to have victimised the public.

However, the 4,750 known offenders who were reconvicted would have, in the majority of cases, committed several offences. If we assume a very modest five offences each for the two-year period, then based on the known reconvictions only, 23,750 offences were committed against the public by offenders following their referral to a restorative-justice scheme. But the real picture is far worse, because these results are based on just those offenders who were caught. As previously noted the detection rate (offences cleared up) is 5.5 per cent, and so the number of actual offences committed against the public by offenders on this scheme will have reached into the hundreds of thousands.

But this calculation will not be presented to the public, who will be told that the scheme is a successful way of dealing with offenders who otherwise would have been sent to a more 'expensive' court system and dealt with less 'effectively'. Past performance suggests that the government will, having claimed the scheme a success, go on to legislate for its wider use. This will mean that thousands of criminals will avoid going to court and be referred instead to these pseudo-mediation sessions with local criminal justice officials and/or their victims and 'apologise' for their crimes.

But the scheme contains yet more traps for the unwary public. I am sure the government will, after a period of time, extend these schemes to include persistent offenders, and the floodgates will then be open for untold numbers of them to be diverted from the courts, and the possibility of prison, altogether. Thus the government's true aim of reducing both court and prison costs will have been met, but the victims will once again have been robbed of any sense of justice and the criminals provided with yet more encouragement to carry on as before.

Manipulation and Blackmail

Although meetings between victim and offender supposedly only take place with the agreement of both parties, it is quite wrong to make the victim feel that he or she is part of the offender's reform process. That is entirely the responsibility of the offender. Whilst the evidence from some restorative-justice programmes shows that many victims refuse to attend,[26] it is almost certain that some attempt will be made to persuade the victims that their attendance will be of benefit to the criminal and to themselves. This pressure will make it difficult for many to say no because they will not want to be seen as unhelpful or difficult. Hence I am sure many take part under a subtle form of duress, and some have said that they found the confrontation with the offender a worse experience than going to court.[27]

From any humane standpoint it is simply unacceptable that victims should be used in this way and be encouraged to confront the person who has robbed, burgled and/or terrified them. They should be encouraged to forget their assailant. True 'restorative justice' for the victim is achieved not by meeting the offender, but by the knowledge

361

that he has been suitably punished, that justice has been done, and that they are safe from further victimisation. This is what enables the victim to 'move on', not conferences that exploit the vulnerability of the public.

It is said that in facing their victims criminals are made to 'face up to the consequences of their offending', an experience many naive commentators seem to imbue with almost magically reforming powers. However, the reconviction rates referred to above leave no doubt that this is a forlorn hope. Far from making the criminals face up to their crimes, such encounters allow them to escape the consequences of their offending because they are a *substitute* for prosecution and punishment. They are the ultimate soft option, and former Home Secretary Jack Straw's hope, expressed in 1998 that they would turn offenders away from crime has proved to be tragically misjudged.[28]

Restorative justice practices are manipulative in other ways. Victim–offender meetings are dressed up as opportunities to help the victim achieve what Home Office ministers have referred to as 'closure' or a resolution of the victim's angry feelings towards the offender. But why should he or she not feel angry about being victimised – do they not have every right to feel this way? Victim–offender mediation sessions are an attempt to disarm the victim and deflect their wholly appropriate feelings of anger and protest away from the criminal justice system that has failed them. Victims should be encouraged to express their protest, not to the criminal but to those who allowed him the freedom to go on committing crime.

The criminal justice establishment must be anxiously aware that if the millions who are victimised every year took to the streets in serious protest about the lack of protection afforded them by a government concerned only to keep prison numbers down, they would be presented with a serious problem, and restorative-justice schemes are being used to dampen down the flames of this protest before they take hold.

Sweet Words and Bitter Deeds

In the summer of 2002 a major article appeared in a well-known broadsheet arguing for the so-called benefits that follow when the victim of a crime confronts the perpetrator.[29] It cited cases where the victims had reported that, before they met the criminal, they were angry and wanted him punished, but afterwards they felt differently because the criminal had talked to them in a decent way and seemed a nice person. Likewise, a magistrate involved in running victim–offenders mediation sessions recently told me that a judge with severe doubts about the value of restorative-justice schemes had been completely won over after attending a meeting between a victim and a criminal. He had been impressed with how normal and decent the criminal had seemed, and the conciliatory manner he showed.

This is naivety on a breathtaking scale. The fact that criminals can also be 'nice' and impress as being 'decent' does nothing to stop them being criminals, and to mistake their pleasant manner and conversation as evidence they had reformed is utterly foolish. Many of the offenders I met in the probation office were very impressive to listen to; they had a sense of humour and could come over as thoroughly decent; but none of this touched their willingness and ability to commit crime and cause distress and havoc in the lives of others. Many of them were psychopathic and dangerously skilled at charming and manipulating others, traits which have been identified as core personality characteristics associated with psychopathy by experts in this field.[30]

Their special ability, and I saw it in action thousands of times, was to convince even the most hardened and experienced magistrates and judges that they were being absolutely sincere when they promised not to commit any more crime. In such situations, my heart sank as the offender walked free from the court, usually having been made the subject of a probation order. They almost always failed to keep its conditions and frequently disappeared, and were only ever seen again as a result of an arrest for yet more offences.

The government hopes that restorative-justice schemes and its other palliatives will quell the public's resentment at being left to the mercy of unscrupulous criminals. They are more likely to fuel the public's already growing alienation from the forces of law and order that is taking us to the brink of a social and political abyss.

Chapter 15

Stepping Back from the Brink

The Slippery Path to Political Extremism

The route charted by those responsible for our sentencing policy has led us to the brink of serious social and political upheaval. For over forty years, criminal justice legislation has favoured the criminal and seriously imperilled the public, leading to mounting resentment over the alarming level of lawlessness and anarchy now prevalent on our streets. The public has watched helplessly as their police forces have all but given up any attempts to maintain local law and order, so overwhelmed are they by the sheer volume and variety of crime.

The previous chapters have revealed that many people now feel alone and unprotected in the face of a non-stop torrent of criminality. They have also pointed to the evidence of their increased willingness to strike back at criminals in an effort to defend themselves and their property, sometimes injuring or even killing the criminals who targeted them. We have seen how large numbers who have acted in this way have been arrested and put before the courts by a police force and Crown Prosecution Service still motivated to stamp out these acts of self defence. But what happens when these occurrences become so numerous that the police cannot respond to them all? What happens when not hundreds, but thousands of vigilante actions are perpetrated each year? What view will the authorities take at the prospect of *thousands* of members of the public being sentenced to prison for violent acts of self-defence against offenders?

The most likely outcome is that the police and other justice authorities will simply give up trying to combat the problem, in the same way that there is now no longer any serious policing of local crime. Our communities will then become dominated by groups and individuals hired by local communities seeking protection against criminals. Occurrences of vigilante acts carried out supposedly on behalf of a frightened public will increase; anarchy and discord will reign. Fear will dominate our communities above all else, and in such an atmosphere we will become vulnerable to extremists offering their brand of political leadership and hope for a safer future.

We should not be tempted to think such a scenario is far-fetched. Wide recognition is now given to the real threat that crime poses to our civil liberties; if we want to keep them and remain a stable, moderate and well-ordered society, we must step back from the abyss that will surely be our fate if current sentencing policies are allowed to continue.

Far from being unreal or exaggerated the ingredients of this scenario, namely lawlessness, fear and public resentment, are already with us. Take, for example, the newspaper report which gave a snapshot of just a few of the offences committed over Christmas and New Year in 2001/02. It revealed that ten children between ten and thirteen years old, emerging from a cinema were robbed in the street, a teenage girl was shot in the head in east London during the street robbery of her mobile telephone, a man was murdered after a car theft in Yorkshire, a ten-year-old boy was forced to hand over his £25 Christmas money at gunpoint. In Essex, a landowner was arrested by the police he had summoned to evict people having a 'rave' on his property: he had unplugged the sound system so he was taken into custody 'for his own safety'.[1]

The numbers of people shot dead in England and Wales has increased by two-thirds in the last twenty years. The number of people killed with a knife has risen by 20 per cent for the same period, and the number of all homicides among young men has likewise increased by 50 per cent.[2] Behind the statistics for gun crime, car jacking, robberies, drug crimes, there are millions of other property crimes. It is therefore not surprising that the public view the police as having lost not only the control of the streets but also the will to enforce the law.

I have heard reports that as many as 700,000 people have left Britain over the last fifteen years largely because they no longer felt safe, including many with talents we can ill-afford to lose. A London estate agent, no doubt meaning to be helpful, told an American visitor to this country that, if mugged, he should 'give

366

them what they want', making him sound like a victim-in-training.[3] The atmosphere in London and in many other British cities – of simmering public anger in the face of unchallenged crime – is now reported to be identical to that in New York before Rudolph Giuliani took over as mayor and initiated his now famous and successful anti-crime programme.[4] The everyday concerns of increasing numbers of people in this country, which were once focused on such matters as house prices, holidays, politics and children's schools are now dominated by crime – which friend has been burgled, which mugged, whose children robbed, how to avoid being assaulted on the street, and so on.

The public have watched helplessly as the justice system has become more and more ineffective, and in June 2002 the Audit Commission report confirmed their fears with a report which showed how few criminals are ever caught;[5] no one can be surprised that the public's faith in the justice system has dwindled alarmingly; and that they now fail to report most of the crime committed against them.[6] Their loss of trust in the ability of the police to protect them was graphically illustrated by the results of an NOP poll commissioned in 2002. It revealed that thousands of people in Britain sleep with a gun by the side of their bed because of the fear of burglary. The guns featured alongside an even bigger arsenal of bats, hammers, golf clubs or similar items, which almost half of the respondents admitted were kept as weapons to be used against criminals.[7] Nothing could make clearer the change in the public's mood; their alienation from the forces of law and order that many predicted is now a reality. That so many in our nation have felt it necessary to arm themselves in this way is a development that twenty-five years ago most would have thought unimaginable.

The peace and orderliness of our communities is now being undermined by the failure of the authorities to deliver basic justice and retribution in the face of soaring crime. As previously reported, increasing numbers of individuals and groups have taken the law into their own hands in response to non-stop burglaries and other criminal acts. This has led to violent conflicts between local police and vigilante groups acting on behalf of local neighbourhoods, and in some cases this has resulted in the police suffering serious injuries.[8]

These scenes should be taken as a warning that our hitherto peaceful and orderly communities are under severe strain, and that, unless radical action is taken to remove the burden of crime carried

367

by the public, they will only get worse. Only ten years ago the police objected to residents hiring private street patrols to keep their districts safe. Yet it is a measure of how serious this problem has become that today this practice is widespread and that not only are such schemes frequently set up in consultation with the police,[9] but a government report has been forced to acknowledge the role they now play.[10]

However, these private patrols can be hired only by residents who can afford them. Most cannot, and for them self-help is their only option. The possibility for severe unrest on our streets is building rapidly; the potential for conflict between private guards defending wealthy areas and vigilantes from poorer districts stalking criminals the police cannot deal with should be seriously considered. Factionalised communities living in fear and suspicion of each other will provide the perfect breeding ground for extremist politics. This, I believe, is what Mrs Thatcher, the then Prime Minister, meant when she said in 1989 that crime was 'a challenge to our civilisation'.[11]

The Route to Safety, Order and Peace

Yet none of this is inevitable. The means by which we can reverse this process and make our communities safe from criminals are well within our reach. Furthermore, we do not have to resort to extreme measures to bring about these changes. What *is* extreme is the government's insistence on its present sentencing policy, which results in at least 26 million victims of crime every year. We should develop an intolerance to *anyone* becoming a victim of crime. If there were only *one* crime a year, it would still be an abrogation of the State's duty to protect the person targeted. We need to take a number of bold steps to unravel the effects of more than forty years of criminal justice misrule, but the first, and probably the most difficult, is for the nation to shake off the effects of the propaganda which for years has successfully persuaded many that prisons do not work and that the majority of persistent offenders should stay in the community. In other words, we have to learn to think differently about crime and our response to it.

Figure 15.1: Proportion of offenders found guilty or cautioned – by indictable offence (2000)

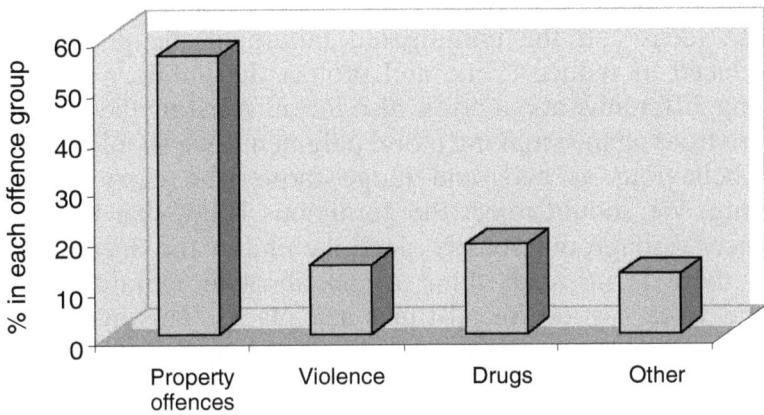

Source: Home Office, *Criminal Statistics England & Wales, 2000*

Changing the Way We Think About Crime

We must reject the government message that only serious sex and violent offenders need to go to jail. The public have a right to be protected from persistent property crime just as much as from any other offence. As illustrated in Figure 15.1, the majority of crimes are against property, and because of their large numbers they cause the most misery to the most people.

Society Is Not to Blame for Crime

Over the decades, crime has been pathologised by social scientists using a bewildering array of social and psychological diagnoses, and this has prevented many from taking account of the large amount of high-quality research that has been carried out in recent years demonstrating beyond question that genetic predisposition plays an important part in producing criminal activity. However, this is not to deny the role of environmental factors with which it interacts. Heredity does not claim to explain everything, but if we are to think differently about crime we must reject the message of those sociologists who for too long have preached an almost fanatical belief in social forces alone being responsible for crime. Although

369

these beliefs have governed government thinking for the last forty years, we must, if we want a different and more effective criminal justice system, open our eyes to the obvious connection between these false ideas and the unmitigated failure of the policies they have produced to reduce crime and protect the public.[12]

Thinking differently about crime also means resisting the politically correct strictures against making moral judgments; we should condemn criminal behaviour as bad, and judge those who carry it out as undeserving. We should reject the pernicious belief that has spread like a cancer through our society since the end of the Second World War that there is no such thing as an absolute morality – fixed virtues and vices – good for all times and places. This evil doctrine teaches that morality is relative and the moral norms of society are created not by what *should* happen but what actually *does* happen. Its disciples argue, therefore, that, because a wide range of crimes are common and widespread, they can be interpreted as a 'normal' way of life for large groups of people.[13]

It is imperative to understand that we are deliberately targeted with propaganda whose express purpose is to make us feel guilty about punishing criminals. In some courts more drivers are now imprisoned than burglars.[14] We must wake up to the fact that we have been tricked into tolerating criminality and social disorder together with a penal establishment motivated to label as few people as possible as criminals, whatever their guilt. Such policies have hidden the powerful truth that law and order, good authority and respect for the private ownership of property, are fundamental to a healthy democratic society.[15]

The Protection of the Public – The First Priority

There must be a sea change in the way judges and magistrates approach the sentencing of offenders. Their first concern should be, not what can they do in the interests of the criminal, but what sentence should they pass to *ensure* the safety of the public. The present practice of placing offenders back into the community who are *known* to have a high risk of further offending must stop; currently, for most of them, it is greater than 20 per cent, and almost a third have a measured risk score of over 70 per cent. This *ensures* that millions of people will be victimised by their continued offending.[16] If doctors in hospitals knew that a particular medicine made patients ill but continued to administer it, the world would regard them as insane. Issues related to the reform of the persistent offender are important, but they must be held as secondary to the question of public safety. It is right that sentencing should take account of remedial schemes for offenders, such as drug and work programmes designed to encourage them to reform, but these should be carried out in circumstances which do not involve any risk of further crime against the public. Where there is any doubt about the offender's ability or motivation to stop offending he should be sent to prison.

However, for this change to come about, we need to revamp the present system of training and selection for judges and radically change the make-up of those who sit as magistrates. In addition, both judges and magistrates need to follow a sentencing code laid down by Parliament, which in turn expresses the majority will of the British people.

A Revamped Judiciary

One of the powerful lessons I learned whilst working as a probation officer in a variety of magistrates' courts, both in Inner London and the provinces was that our system of lay justices needs to be scrapped. Most are inefficient, take far too long to decide what to do about even straightforward issues, are too often swayed by the latest fashionable ideas and often lack the confidence to resist questionable lines of defence or mitigation. In my experience, their much-vaunted advantage of delivering 'lay justice' in their own community was rarely achieved as most of them were overly influenced in their sentencing decisions by the acting skills and game playing of defence lawyers. Many senior police officers and lawyers have likewise long felt that large numbers of lay magistrates are incapable of dealing with legal issues, and that they should be removed from the justice system altogether.[17]

Magistrates should be replaced by what were once called 'stipendiary magistrates', but who are now known as 'district judges'. The stipendiaries I worked with were all professionally trained lawyers with an expert and confident grip on the workings and purposes of the magistrates' court. During the 1960s in one court known to me it was common for just one of these magistrates to deal with half a dozen 'matrimonial' applications (women seeking redress against their husbands for neglect and/or violence), and up to twenty-five cases of 'drunk and disorderly', all before 10 a.m., when the main court list started. Between 10 a.m. and 1 p.m. they then worked through a long list of fresh criminal charges and held summary trials on those who pleaded not guilty; all were dealt with fairly and justly. Meanwhile, next door in the lay justice's court they would still be struggling to finish a court list only a fraction of the size.

These reforms are well overdue and the public should ask why such a system, in which lay justices are frequently bemused and sometimes intimidated by the clever tricks and antics of defence lawyers, is tolerated. Although district judges would have to be paid and lay justices are not, reform along these lines would save significant amounts of money in the long run because the work of the courts would be so much more efficient.

There is similarly a need to revamp the training and selection of judges. At present, too many of them emerge from a background which has kept them apart from mainstream society. Many will have attended a private preparatory school until the age of eight or nine, followed by several years at a public school, and then university (often Oxford or Cambridge), after which, if they or their families can afford it, they will go straight into a legal firm as a probationer barrister to await selection to a chambers. After several years as a barrister, they may be 'selected' by a less than transparent system to sit as a judge. Some judges are known for their skill and high levels of professionalism and they richly deserve the support and praise of the community. Too many others, as evidenced by their decisions, forget that their first duty is to protect the public and fail to provide the victims or the community with either retribution or justice. Scores of trials are stopped on a 'technicality', allowing persistent criminals to go free, and hundreds of thousands of people are victimised by criminals that judges (and magistrates) have chosen to release back into the community.

There needs to be a recognised professional course of study followed by a period of postgraduate training for those wishing to work as a judge, as there is with other professional occupations. The training should emphasise the role of the judge in steering the court process away from the worst aspects of our adversarial system, which are designed to profit those skilled in debate and obfuscation rather than getting to the truth. Those choosing this career can become qualified by means of their ability, divorced from the question of their wealth and social standing. France, for example, has a system similar to this where relatively young people make this a career choice.

A New Sentencing Code

Put bluntly, our judiciary has failed the nation. Although there are always exceptions, judges and magistrates can no longer be trusted to put the interests of the public before those of the criminals they sentence. Whilst they should retain some discretion when dealing with offenders who are at the beginning of their criminal careers (capital offences apart), prison should be mandatory for persistent offenders in order to remove any opportunity for the courts to pass overly lenient and idiosyncratic sentences that fail to protect the public. The courts' record in this respect is dire. To provide just one more example, the proportion of offenders sentenced to community supervision for indictable offences of *violence* almost doubled between 1990 and 2000. So much for the government's rhetoric about making the courts get tough with violent and dangerous offenders.[18]

The minimum sentence for persistent offending against people and property should be sufficiently severe to ensure that the benefits of the crimes are completely outweighed by the punishment. At present almost all of the millions of pounds spent on catching criminals is wasted because they are almost always given their freedom or a meaningless prison sentence of a few weeks or months.[19] Likewise, increasing the size of the police force will make no difference to our crime problem unless the time served for the crime becomes more meaningful.

In general, prison sentences for persistent offending against people or property should, once an offender has passed a certain threshold, be automatic, without mitigation and increasingly severe. Just how severe would need to be worked out by Parliament after a period of consultation between MPs and their local constituents; Parliament could then establish which offences (for example, burglary, mugging, theft and assault) were to be dealt with in this way and the mandatory

373

sentence attached to each of them. I would suggest the following general approach. Juveniles (those under 17) should be given three chances, which is generous. During this period the courts would, as described, have a measure of discretion in the way the offender was dealt with, but it would provide an opportunity for the offender to be supervised in the community and offered help and encouragement to go straight. Where appropriate, the courts could order offenders to be electronically tagged, but this would operate for the full twenty-four hours and not the maximum of twelve as at present, and offenders would be automatically returned to court on the first violation and be given a mandatory prison sentence. In addition, educational, psychological and behavioural programmes could be made available to them, but whatever their circumstances, if they continued to offend after their third court appearance the protection of the public would become paramount and they would be sent to prison for a minimum of one year. Thereafter, any future property offences or crimes against a person would result in a prison sentence at least twice as long as the previous one and possibly much longer if large numbers of offences have been committed.

If we think about this objectively, it can be seen that this is not draconian but sensible if the public is to be protected. What *is* draconian is to allow millions of members of the public to be victimised by criminals who are rarely if ever brought to justice. Additional time could be added to the sentence in those cases where there were multiple offences. For example, a sixteen-year-old appearing in court for the fifth time for theft would receive two years plus an additional term if, for example, he had committed ten or more offences. The threshold for additional time and the amount to be added could be established by Parliament, in line with its objectives of providing the public with substantial protection and retribution. (A separate sentencing tariff would operate for crimes such as bank robberies, arson, abduction, rape and other sex crimes of a serious nature, drug offences, and violent crimes such as grievous bodily harm and killing.)

Allowing juveniles three bites of the apple before they are sent to prison would mean that they would have more than sufficient opportunity to demonstrate their willingness to go straight. In practice, few of them would serve prison sentences of any length, given that generally it takes time to accumulate three court appearances. For example, a fourteen-year-old making his first appearance might well

374

be sixteen or seventeen by the time he was standing before the court for a third time. But, for example, a prolific fifteen-year-old offender who was caught a fourth time would serve at least one year in prison. If, when he came out as a sixteen-year-old he continued to commit crime and was apprehended again, he would receive at least two years and not be released until he was eighteen or more. Thus the community would gain enormous benefit from the years during which he was unable to burgle their homes or victimise them in some other way.

An adult should be allowed two bites of the apple (assuming he had not offended as a juvenile) before receiving a mandatory prison sentence of at least one year on his third court appearance. Thereafter he would receive prison sentences which increased each time in multiples of three, thus he would receive at least one year in prison for the third court appearance (as with juveniles there would be additional time added to the sentence depending on the number of offences he had committed), at least three years for the next appearance, at least six for the next and so on. A juvenile who continued his offending beyond the age of eighteen would receive a first prison sentence as an adult of three years.

Time for the Crime

There is no point in sentencing an offender to four years in jail if it is intended he should serve only considerably less than half of this time, which is what happens at present under the remission and Home Detention Curfew arrangements. Cancelling out most of the offender's punishment in this way even before he has started it gives him the message that we do not take his crimes seriously. The principle behind these new sentencing proposals is that he should be given the opposite message, and that the public must be provided with the maximum protection from unrepentant offenders determined to carry on with a life of crime. Under a reformed sentencing scheme, therefore, all early-release schemes would be scrapped.

It is the public's right to be protected from criminals which should be the driving force for these arrangements, rather than the needs of the offender. Prisoners must not be allowed to think that early release is their right. They must be made to realise that their victims are given no remission from the legacy of crimes committed against them, and that if they commit an offence which Parliament has deemed attracts a four-year sentence then four years they will serve. The remedy is in their hands; all they have to do to avoid spending time in prison is stop committing crime. Under these new proposals the prisoner's reward for good behaviour would be that he would serve no more than the sentence he was given. Offences committed against prison rules would be dealt with by draconian additions to their sentence, to mark society's total rejection of their continued anti-social behaviour.

Prisoners should be treated in accordance with their self-elected status – as criminals who have terrorised society. They should be kept in humane and decent conditions, and treated fairly. Every effort should be made to ensure their well-being, and to guard them against any form of abuse. No efforts should be spared to encourage them, by whatever means, to give up crime, but no one should forget that ultimately whether they reform or not is up to them.

But criminals in prison should not be allowed to harbour expectations beyond being kept safe, healthy and secure. In 2003 the Chief Inspector of Prisons submitted a report to the government in which prisoners complained that when they summoned prison staff the majority of them had to wait more than five minutes for someone to arrive.[20] We do not encourage offenders to reform by allowing them to believe they have a right to make demands that are more in keeping with wealthy guests at a five-star hotel, and it was irresponsible of the Chief Inspector to encourage them to think they did. Criminals should be made to feel the disapprobation of society for what they have done, and made to realise that it is for them to win back its approbation and the rights and rewards that go with it, by leading a law-abiding life. If such approbation means nothing to them and they prefer to remain outlaws, then they should be treated as such.

Accepting a Rising Prison Population

Sending persistent offenders to prison for longer and longer means that we must accept far higher numbers in custody than we are used to. For years anti-prison propaganda has encouraged us to believe that prisons are entirely negative and are to be avoided except for the most serious violent and sex crimes. We must shake off this mindset and view prison as our most effective weapon in the fight not just against sex and violent offences but crime generally. The reason the government is keen to tell us that prison does not work for the majority of property offenders, for example, is that there are so many of them and it baulks at the prospect of funding prison places in sufficient numbers to house them.

There is nothing intrinsically wrong with having large numbers of convicted offenders in prison. We must learn not to lament such a prospect, but to be pleased that the offenders concerned are not on the streets causing misery and mayhem to people's lives. But government is a long way from seeing the problem in this light. For example, in 2004 even the Home Secretary's announcement of modest plans to build only two more prisons provoked a sense of crisis from the Treasury, who, as usual, showed great reluctance to agree to release the funds required.[21] The public must signal its refusal to accept the present state of affairs whereby the state tolerates at least 24 million people falling victims to crime every year, but shows reluctance to pay for relatively small additions to the equally small number of 45,000 convicted mainly property offenders at present in jail.

In order for the public to be properly protected from crime, we need to be prepared to accept a prison population of at least 200,000 convicted offenders. The majority of the 155,000 at present under supervision to the Probation Service are persistent offenders, as evidenced by their known reconviction rates, and therefore they should be serving custodial sentences. This number added to the approximate 45,000 convicted persistent offenders currently serving time in our jails brings the total to 200,000. To this we must add the numbers currently on remand, foreign prisoners (who now total one in seven of those in jail) and those serving life sentences, which brings the overall *minimum* prison population required to ensure the safety of the public to 225,000 – three times the current number.

We should not be intimidated by scare stories from the anti-prison organisations that such a sentencing policy is beyond our means, or that it would result in 'too many' offenders in jail. 'Too many' in this context is a concept without meaning. Critics often question how such an expansion in the prison population could be funded, given the competing demands on the government's purse. But these costs should be the *first call* on the exchequers funds because the protection of society is the government's *first duty*. If we can afford £60 billion per year, which is the current cost of crime, we can cope with a prison bill three times the present figure of approximately £2.7 billion. But financial costs should not, in any case, be the overriding issue; what should predominate is the overriding need to prevent the human misery caused by crime which is beyond calculation. We would make immediate inroads into this problem if we stopped wasting large sums of money on non-custodial sentences such as fines, probation supervision and community programmes and courses for repeat offenders, as their reconviction rates, as well as separate research evidence, show that these sentencing options are treated by them as a licence to offend.[22]

However, if we followed such a sentencing policy the majority of persistent offenders, particularly property offenders, would start to think twice about whether further offending was worth it. The absolute *certainty* of a six- or twelve-year prison sentence the next time they were caught, without remission or any other form of early release, plus much increased odds in favour of them being caught, would cause many of them to reform themselves with an ease not previously thought possible. (During my probation career I knew many hardened offenders who had eventually become *fearful* of another prison sentence, and who gave up crime because they were haunted by the prospect of spending more time behind bars.) For this reason I doubt we would get to the point of locking up 225,000. There would be an initial surge in prison numbers while the criminal fraternity tested out our resolve, but if this remained firm most would give up crime as a bad deal. Those that did not would have to be locked up for increasingly long periods at each new conviction.

The Revival of the Police

Such reformed sentencing policies would also transform police morale, as the time and energy they spent tracking down and catching criminals would not be wasted, as it is at present. Their job satisfaction would increase and such a revitalised law and order strategy would, I am certain, result in the police abandoning the many 'pseudo-policing' practices on which they have wasted so much time over the last two decades.

But to achieve this there needs to be a substantial increase in the size of the police force, well beyond the numbers at present countenanced by the Home Secretary, who, for example, in 2001 promised to increase the police force to 128,000 by 2003, and eventually to 130,000 by the end of that Parliament.[23] (In fact, by April 2004 police numbers had reached a record level of 138,000.[24]) However, we have already seen from the analysis in Chapter Nine that for our policing effort to be meaningful in the face of present *reported* crime levels, it needs to be *at least* three times this size, but between four and ten times larger to cope anywhere successfully with *actual present* crime levels.

What this analysis reveals is that the number of crimes committed each year has been allowed to rise to a point that is totally beyond the capacity of the current police force to combat. Even if it were increased to ten times its present size (currently 138,000 officers) it would still leave, given the estimate of sixty million crimes per year, forty-four crimes per year per police officer, or three times the ratio in 1971.

However, if the sentencing policy argued for in this chapter was adopted and persistent offenders were locked up at each new conviction for increasingly long periods, it would make the job of the police far more manageable as they would, over time, have fewer and fewer persistent criminals to look out for and many others would be deterred due to fear of the consequences if they were caught. So, although there would need to be a serious injection of manpower into the police force in order to kick start this process, the effect of a significantly increased prison population serving much longer prison sentences than at present, would be to steadily diminish the need for further increases in police strength well before it reached the estimate outlined above because the crime rate would plummet. The forces of law and order would then be in the ascendancy and not the criminals, as should be the case in a civilised well-ordered society. There would be extra costs involved, but they would be more than compensated for because the massive costs incurred by crime would be cut and the general standard of life for millions of people in Britain would significantly improve.

Not only do the police need sufficient increases in manpower to combat the huge crime problem which faces them, but they need to be supported, rather than undermined, by other criminal justice organisations that supposedly work with them. In this regard, the Crown Prosecution Service must be abolished because its objective of keeping as many offenders in the community as possible is directly in conflict with those of the constabulary. We must revert to a system which allows the police to prosecute their own cases with the help of specialist lawyers. There can be no place in a reformed criminal justice service for any organisation which is not bent on prosecuting as many offenders as possible and providing the public with maximum protection from persistent offenders. Likewise, the heavy paperwork burden carried by the police must be reduced and rationalised. There can be little doubt that their enthusiasm for chasing criminals is severely dampened by the excessively large number of forms the police must complete every time they make an arrest (see Chapter Nine, Note 1, for a description of the police paper trail).

The Public Decides

The last forty years have demonstrated beyond argument that mandatory prison sentences for persistent offenders are the only way to provide the public with adequate protection from persistent criminals. Therefore, if we are to have a system which gives offenders a number of chances before they qualify for a mandatory prison sentence, the public needs to be consulted, as argued in the previous chapter, about how long this should be and the level of risk they are prepared to accept from criminals left in the community. We should reject the present practice in which criminal justice officials make this decision without reference to the public who suffer grievously as a result. My proposals for a reformed sentencing code which allows juveniles three court appearances before they are jailed, and adult offenders two court appearances, may be too severe or too lenient for the majority of the public, but this needs to be *genuinely* tested and MPs need to be reminded that they are in Parliament to represent the views of their constituents on these matters, whatever their own ideas may be.

In January 2004 listeners to the BBC Radio 4's *Today* programme were asked to suggest a piece of legislation to improve life in Britain, with the promise that an MP would then attempt to get it on the statute book. Significantly, the winning proposal, voted for by thousands, was to allow homeowners 'to use any means to defend their home from intruders'. The MP chosen to support the proposal in Parliament let it be known he was appalled at the public's choice and could not have been more patronising in his response. He arrogantly referred to the voters as 'bastards', and despite the earlier promise, he made it clear that he would do nothing to ensure their wishes were acted upon.[25] His response encapsulates an attitude found too often among some MPs and others in the criminal justice system who are prepared to treat the public's wishes with disdain when they clash with their 'elitist' views. He was either ignorant of or did not care that it is the liberal sentencing policy currently supported by Parliament that has allowed burglars and other criminals to cut ever wider swathes through our communities, and that Radio 4 listeners, along with everyone else, want it stopped.

The MP should have seen the vote as an indicator of how fiercely many of the public now reject current sentencing practices. Was he unaware that over the last few years the Crown Prosecution Service has *refused* to prosecute hundreds of thousands of criminals, and that as a result of this and chronic undermanning the police have all but given up any attempt to combat local crime? Rather than call the voters 'bastards', it was an opportunity for him to seize the moment and proclaim that the vote indicated how alone and unprotected the public now feel in the face of crime. He could have argued that it is in accordance with natural justice that those who are victimised by criminals be allowed to defend themselves, their families and their property without fear of misplaced retribution from the State which blatantly fails to protect them.

Telling the Public the Truth

Consultation with the public to help them decide on the level of risk they are prepared to accept from criminals allowed to stay in the community requires that they be given accurate information about what different levels of risk mean in terms of the number of offences likely to be committed against them. As described in Chapter Thirteen, reliable risk predictors now exist which can compute for each offender his or her risk of further offending. This and other information required should be given to the public in easily understood formats, so they can decide just what risk levels they are prepared to accept from offenders before they are sent to prison. There should be no spin or deception in the information given to the public to help them make up their minds, and that whatever the majority does decide should be acted upon, whether it falls in with the views of our criminal justice elite or not.

Just as Parliament should genuinely listen to the public and take seriously their demands to be protected from crime, so there needs to be a shift in the balance of power away from the executive and back to the elected representatives of the people. Parliament should reassert its authority over ministers, who should remember that in the final analysis they are servants of the people. They should report the truth to Parliament concerning the failure of present sentencing policies. Ministers in turn should be told the truth about these matters by their civil servants.

As matters stand at present, because of the prevailing anti-prison ideology, civil servants are reluctant to tell their superiors that government sentencing policies are failing. No one wants to risk their careers by rocking the boat. Preferment is more likely if they tell their department heads what they want to hear. By this process ministers are frequently deceived into believing that community-based supervision for offenders offers an effective alternative to prison for the majority of offenders; ministers in turn pass on this lie to the public. But because this policy is based on a lie, it will eventually implode, causing grave social and political upheaval with all the dangers this represents.

In 1993 one Home Office minister, David Maclean, did try to speak out against this deception but was ruthlessly silenced by senior members of the government more concerned about their political advancement than telling the truth.[26] Likewise, in Frank Snepp's account of his work as a CIA intelligence analyst during the Vietnam War, he tells how intelligence reports reflected what military commanders in the field wanted Washington to hear.[27] The truth – that their military policies were failing to have any impact on the enemy and that eventual defeat was highly likely – was avoided. In 1974 the US military policy in Vietnam imploded, and thirty years later the social and political scars left by that event have still not healed. We should be in no doubt that our sentencing policy is being run on a similar basis and, unless it is changed, it will eventually collapse causing our communities dangerous levels of conflict and upheaval.

Monitoring the System

The government frequently uses league tables to disseminate its criminal justice propaganda. In 2003 the Lord Chancellor announced plans to publish tables which graded the forty-two police and prosecution areas in terms of their promptness in dealing with magistrates' and crown court cases.[28] Similarly, the government has in the past published lists of the worst prisons in terms of neglect, staff shortages and impoverished regimes.[29] Likewise, we are all now used to reading league tables showing the performance of our schools. It would not be a radical departure therefore for similar league tables to be published on a regular basis which told the public how successful or otherwise were the non-custodial sentences used by the courts for offenders during their 'grace' period when they are allowed to stay in the community.

It is imperative that such data is also provided to MPs without the spin and obfuscation which characterises so much of the information on crime and sentencing currently provided by officials. In Chapter Six I detailed a number of the deception techniques used by the criminal justice system to keep the public in the dark concerning the failure of present sentencing policies. Whilst it is true the Home Office provides a welter of information on this subject both in published report form and on their web site, the massive size of this database makes it impossible for MPs or the public to identify the salient facts of relevance to their safety. In short, its very size and complexity hides the truth of the government's stark failure to protect them from crime.

Currently, almost all government statistics concerning crime present a minefield for the public. Take, for example, the figure for the number of convictions for burglary each year. This is never presented with the caveat that the true number would be *even larger* if the Crown Prosecution Service did not downgrade thousands of burglary offences each year to the lesser charge of handling stolen goods. The table contained in the Home Office Report 217[30] which tabulates the costs of crime fails to mention the total number of crimes committed, leaving the impression that the Home Office wants to prevent the total of at least 60 million crimes per year impacting on the public's awareness. This is presumably because it is in such obvious conflict with the British Crime Survey figure of 13 million, which they would prefer us to believe.

As part of the review machinery for the proposed new sentencing code, all judges and magistrates would know that if they made sentencing decisions outside of the limits provided by Parliament, and as a result the public was harmed by the criminals they put back into the community, then the victims could sue the State for failing to protect them and that they as judges and magistrates would be held accountable by a competent professional review body. Likewise, the public should be enabled to take court actions against the police who caution an offender who later commits more crime; against the Crown Prosecution Service, where they fail to prosecute an offender who goes on to victimise further members of the public; and against the Probation Service, where their recommendations for leniency are followed and result in more harm to the public at the hands of the criminal concerned. There are a great many possibilities, such as these, for the public to seek redress, all of which can be taken to Europe should they fail in the English courts. The principle behind these proposals is different from that underlying the system of compensation currently available, and has two sources. First, the new principle would be based on the recognition that it is the State's *duty* to protect its citizens from crime. Second, we should take seriously the Human Rights Act whose provisions state that everyone has the right to live in peace free of molestation and to the peaceful enjoyment of their possessions. Therefore victims of crime should be enabled to seek redress from the State should it fail to protect these rights.

Lighting the Political Fuse

These changes, which I have argued must occur to ensure higher levels of safety in our communities, need a catalyst. Nothing will happen until the population finds a way of impressing upon MPs and government the urgent need for reform. As things are at the moment, I believe that many MPs simply have not grasped the seriousness of the problem posed to us by crime, and others, perhaps due to inertia, laziness or lack of interest, remain unmotivated to make it the political issue it should become. Many others remain ideologically opposed to the imprisonment of offenders and sneer at what they call 'populist' demands for protection from criminals. They must be reminded that we live in a democracy, which means

384

the will of the people should prevail. As already noted, financial grants paid out of public funds to at least one victim-support group as well as to the Neighbourhood Watch Organisation have muzzled them as potential critics of sentencing policy. This has denied the public the well-informed arguments they could have otherwise produced, leading to a campaign for change.

But this tells us that the government is fearful of the victims of crime becoming an organised political force. We should learn from this. If the millions of people who fall victim to crime each year could be organised into a political lobby, supported by millions of others who wanted to *avoid* becoming victims, then Parliament, the criminal justice establishment and ultimately the government would be faced with demands they could not refuse. In this sense, our fate is in our own hands. It is far better we bring pressure to bear on the government for change by peaceful, political means than for us to fall into the abyss of anarchy characterised by lynch mob mentality and a widespread disregard for the rule of law. If our democracy means anything, it should be open to us to change our sentencing policy by legitimate political means, and not have to resort to shooting burglars to protect ourselves and our property.

Although what follows are some of my ideas about how this might be done, the purpose of this book is to stimulate wide public debate about these issues, in the hope that those with the necessary political skills will become motivated to find ways of bringing these changes about. One way of doing this would be to form committees in every city, town and village with the express purpose of planning a campaign to persuade the government to respond to the public's demands for adequate protection from criminals. These committees could then elect regional committees. They, in turn, could establish a national body representing untold millions of people. Conferences could be organised to draw up an agenda for change to our sentencing laws.

Such a movement could have a powerful political effect. Its huge membership would give it several options. It could, for example, put up representatives for Parliament, and MPs of other parties who wanted to keep their seats would have to decide where their interests lay. In addition, the prospect of millions of people marching in peaceful demonstrations or making their protests felt in other ways would make deep inroads into government thinking. It will be remembered that the government held out against the protests over the poll tax until the day came, over a decade ago, when hundreds of thousands of people, many not normally associated with civil action, took to the streets. Soon after, it was abolished.

Out of the Shadow of Crime

The criminal justice system no longer deserves its name as it fails to provide justice or protection for the millions predated upon by criminals. Not only has it lost almost all of its authority and support of the public but has become so self-serving and ineffective that it can rightly be described as corrupt. Many now believe that crime is an inevitable part of our lives, but whilst it can never be eradicated completely it can be reduced to a fraction of what it is now. This does not have to be achieved, as some doom-laden left-wing criminologists would have us believe, by creating an oppressed, fear-ridden society. If current crime policies were reversed, law-abiding citizens would enjoy greater freedom and an enhanced standard of life unshackled from the oppression and fear that crime brings.

None of the changes argued for in this book are beyond our reach or our means. Nor are they extreme. They amount to no more than common sense if we want to prevent our country being a land fit for criminals, and instead make it a land where the law-abiding can live in peace and prosperity.

Epilogue

The most pressing need of the British people today is to be protected from persistent offenders unmotivated to reform. Yet, far from protecting us, faceless civil servants unashamedly promote and support weak sentencing policies which allow criminals the freedom to victimise us at will. These bureaucrats are as anonymous as the offenders they protect, and they need to be identified and held to account for the havoc their ideology has wreaked on our communities. These unknown civil servants and their political masters are equally culpable for allowing crime to thrive like a cancer on the life of our communities. But they share a nightmare. It is that one day the British people will shake off the mindset induced by decades of anti-prison propaganda and realise what needs to be done to free them from the tyranny imposed by unrepentant criminals, and re-gain the levels of peace and security experienced, for example, by the British people in the 1950s. If today we imprisoned the same ratio of offenders relative to the number of offences, as we did then, our prison population would be nearer 300,000. Our communities will never be besmirched by an enlarged prison estate, but they will decay and rot under the influence of unchecked criminality.

Notes

Chapter 1

Note 1

The 1959 government report *Penal Practice in a Changing Society* gives the number of persons found guilty of indictable offences in 1957 as 340 per 100,000 of the population. Home Office Digest 2 (1993), *Information on the Criminal Justice System in England and Wales* gives the number of persons found guilty of indictable offences in 1991 as 1.4 per 100 of the population. To compare the two figures, the 1991 figure of 1.4 has been multiplied by 1,000 to make 1,400 per 100,000 of the population.

Chapter 2

Note 1

The Home Office *Introductory Guide to the Crime and Disorder Act 1998* found on the Government web site, states as follows:

Bail

Sections 54 and 55 make various changes to the legislation relating to the grant of bail aimed at reducing court delays.

Section 54 introduces two new powers relating to the conditions which may be attached to a grant of bail:

a) the powers of the police and the courts to require a person to give a security before being released on bail are increased, removing the restrictions allowing them to do so only if there is reason to believe that the person is unlikely to remain in Great Britain; and

b) the court is able to require a defendant, as a condition of bail, to attend an interview with a legal representative before the next court appearance.

Section 55 amends Section 120 of the Magistrates' Courts Act 1980 to require the court to declare the immediate and automatic forfeiture of a recognizance where a defendant fails to answer to bail. After declaring the recognizance to be forfeited, the court must issue a summons to the surety to appear before the court to explain why he or she should not pay the sum, whereupon the court exercises its discretion to decide whether all, part or none of the sum should be paid. If the surety fails to answer the summons, the court can proceed in his or her absence provided that it is satisfied that the summons has been correctly served. The new provisions apply to magistrates' courts only, but the procedure will be replicated in the higher courts by means of amendments to the rules of court which govern the procedures there.

Chapter 5

Note 1

Offenders sentenced to custody and community sentences, 1995–2000

Custody	Thousands	% change over previous year	Community	Thousands	% change over previous year
1995	79.5		1995	129.9	
1996	85.3	7.0	1996	132.7	2.0
1997	93.8	10.0	1997	140.0	6.0
1998	100.5	7.0	1998	149.5	7.0
1999	105.4	5.0	1999	151.8	1.5
2000	106.6	1.0	2000	156.1	3.0

Source: Home Office Statistics (2000)

Chapter 6

Note 1

Reconviction rates of offenders under supervision to the Probation Service – percentage reconvicted within 2 years of discharge from prison or commencement of a Probation Order, Community Service Order (CSO), or Combination Order (Com. Order; probation combined with community service) during 1996.

Age category	None	Number of previous convictions 1 or 2	3–6	7–10	11 or more	Total
under 21 years						
Probation	52	69	84	92	95	73
CSO	42	72	85	93	95	65
Com. Order	59	76	86	99	95	77
All	47	72	85	94	95	70
Custody	39	69	85	93	94	76
21–24 years						
Probation	39	56	70	82	89	68
CSO	32	43	72	82	92	56
Com. Order	34	54	64	83	90	65
All	34	51	70	82	90	63
Custody	22	48	65	81	92	66
25–29 years						
Probation	21	43	57	72	85	62
CSO	20	37	51	66	78	48
Com. Order	28	38	50	67	79	54
All	22	39	54	70	82	55
Custody	14	32	46	76	84	57
30 years and above						
Probation	15	28	43	51	72	46
CSO	13	23	36	49	70	35
Com. Order	13	22	41	55	65	40
All	14	25	40	51	70	41
Custody	8	18	28	45	70	41

Source: Home Office, *Prison Statistics, England & Wales, 1999*, 2000; reproduced with the permission of the Controller of Her Majesty's Stationery Office

Note 2

Data provided in W.A. Elkin, *The English Penal System* (Penguin Books, 1957), shows the results of a survey made in 1948 by the Department of Criminal Science at Cambridge University. This revealed that the proportion of juvenile probationers with previous convictions was 27.3 per cent, and the corresponding figure for adult probationers was 31.9 per cent.

Data compiled by Coad and Fraser in *Community Sentences: A National Disaster* (June 1999) and extracted from *Prison Statistics, England and Wales 1997*, shows that the proportion of probationers under the age of twenty-one years who were placed on probation in 1994 with no previous convictions was 20 per cent, that is, 80 per cent *did* have previous convictions. The corresponding figure for adult probationers was 13 per cent; that is, 87 per cent had previous convictions

Note 3

Tim Workman, Metropolitan Stipendiary Magistrate, giving evidence to the All Party Home Affairs Select Committee inquiry into Alternatives to Prison on 3 March 1998, said, 'Community service is usually limited to seven hours a week' (see House of Commons Minutes of Evidence, Home Affairs Committee, Tuesday 3 March 1998, p. 28).

Chapter 7

Note 1

Two Home Office reports provide data covering the results of the second year trials for curfew orders: Home Office Research and Statistics Directorate, Research Findings No. 66, *Electronic Monitoring of Curfew Orders: The Second Year of the Trials*; and Home Office Research and Statistics Directorate, Research Findings No. 141, *Electronic Monitoring and Offending Behaviour: Reconviction Results for the Second Year of Trials of Curfew Orders*. Both reported that the average length of curfew order was 3.3 months and that the 374 offenders who were placed on curfew orders in the second year of the research had a reconviction rate of 73 per cent within two years of being sentenced. Therefore, based on these *known* convictions and an assumed low offending rate of five offences per week, we can compute that 273 offenders committed between them at least 1,365 offences each week during the currency of the curfew order, totalling 17,745 offences. However, only 5.5 per cent of offences are detected, which means that the actual reoffending rate of those placed on curfew orders was nearer 100 per cent. Yet the government declared themselves satisfied with these results and they were legislated for in the Powers of Criminal Courts (Sentencing) Act 2000.

Chapter 8

Note 1

The information that there are at least 20,000 outstanding arrest warrants in some counties was given in evidence to the All Party Home Affairs Select Committee Inquiry into Alternatives to Prison on 3 March 1998, by Mrs Gaynor Houghton-Jones, Clerk to the Justices, Horseferry Road Magistrates' Court. She described outstanding arrest warrants for breach of community supervision orders as a 'horrendous problem' (see House of Commons Minutes of Evidence, Home Affairs Committee, Tuesday 3 March 1998, p. 31).

Chapter 9

Note 1

It was reported in the *Independent* on 28 March 2000 that Scotland Yard had admitted that the police typically have to fill out *seventeen* forms in relation to a single offence.

After the suspect is first arrested and taken into custody, (**1**) 'Booking in' documentation has to be completed. This includes the offender's name, address, occupation and other personal details, which will later be filled out another sixteen times, although a computer does this automatically. The police will then interview the suspect, during which (**2**) details of how the interview is conducted are taken under the Police and Criminal Evidence Act, together with (**3**) the suspect's statement. Officers may also take (**4**) fingerprints from the suspect and (**5**) possibly a sample of DNA. Details are also logged of the (**6**) suspect's possessions. Where necessary, (**7**) doctors, (**8**) interpreters or, in the case of child offenders, (**9**) appropriate adults may have to be contacted and informed. Statements must be taken from (**10**) witnesses. The suspect may be (**11**) released on bail or kept in custody. Police then must provide (**12**) details of the case to the Crown Prosecution lawyers who will decide whether there is sufficient evidence to prosecute. If charges are brought, the officer has to transfer in long-hand all the information from the custody file onto a case preparation file. If necessary, (**13**) charge forms must then be filled out and details of any (**14**) previous cases must be researched. At a remand hearing in court, police may produce (**15**) further documentation recommending that bail is opposed. After the first court appearance, the CPS may ask the police to produce (**16**) further evidence. If the defendant pleads not guilty, the police must (**17**) let prosecution witnesses know they are required to give evidence in court.

Chapter 10

Note 1

Details of the evidence given by the representatives of the Association of Chief Officers of Probation (ACOP) to the All Party Committee can be found in *Home Affairs Committee, Third Report, Alternatives to Prison Sentences, Volume 2, Minutes of Evidence (1997–1998).* The detail of the evidence they gave is revealing. At one point (p. 4), they told the committee that the failure rate for offenders under community supervision to the Probation Service was about 52 per cent. This was in itself misleading. The reconviction rate for the majority of those under probation supervision is nearer 60 per cent.

However, later on in the discussion a committee member asked the ACOP representatives how many of the orders were completed successfully (p. 9). The answer they gave was: 'The year-on-year figures show an average for the probation order of around 72%' (p. 9).

In their written evidence to the committee (p. 166), they stated that, 'About 72% of probation orders ran their full course with only 4% being breached for failure to comply with requirements.' What is interesting is that the committee never challenged the obvious disparity between ACOP's claim of a 52 per cent failure rate and its 72 per cent success rate for probation orders. Also, the committee were prepared to accept the ambiguity in the phrase 'orders which ran their full course', which is equally highly misleading, because ACOP did not explain (and the committee not ask), that offenders commit numerous offences whilst on probation and the courts deal with them by allowing the order to continue. Thus the phrase 'orders which ran their full course' is meaningless and deliberate obfuscation, which must have been apparent to the committee members, as they had been told by other witnesses what the true failure rates were for offenders on supervision. However, they kept their counsel because, I believe, they had been told what they wanted to hear.

Chapter 11

Note 1

Lord Chief Justices 1980 to the present:

Lord Lane, 1980–1992

Lord Taylor of Gosforth, 1992–1996

Lord Bingham, 1996–2000

Lord Woolf, 2000 until the present

Chapter 13

Note 1

'Vehicle thefts' defined as thefts of motor vehicles, thefts from motor vehicles and attempted thefts. (Source: Home Office Bulletin 1/03, *Crime in England & Wales 2001/2002*)

References

Chapter 1

1. C. Murray, 'Does Prison Work?', *Choice in Welfare*, 38, 1997
2. 'Crime has gone up ... or rather it's gone down', *Observer*, 11 January 1998
3. Home Office Research Study 179, *Attitudes to Punishment: Findings from the British Crime Survey*, 1998
4. 'Three out of four drivers fall victim to car crime', *Independent*, 1 February 2001
5. '18 million crimes', *Daily Mirror*, 22 March 1995
6. 'Street Crime', issue of *Which? Magazine*, November 1990
7. 'Lessons for the criminal classes', *Sunday Telegraph*, 31 March 1991
8. See, for example, 'Official: more muggings in England than in the US', *Sunday Times*, 11 October 1998 and 'English crime rates overtake America', *Daily Telegraph*, 12 October 1998
9. Home Office, *Penal Practice in a Changing Society*, February 1959
10. Home Office Digest 2, *Information on the Criminal Justice System in England & Wales*, 1993
11. 'England & Wales head crime league of Western nations', *The Times*, 27 May 1997
12. 'Crime Wave', *Daily Mail*, 27 May 1997
13. 'Young are committing 13 crimes each minute', *The Times*, 26 July 1997
14. 'Shop owners demand "zero tolerance" crime policy', *Independent*, 6 July 2002

15. Home Office Statistical Bulletin, Issue 21/98, *The 1998 British Crime Survey, England & Wales*
16. Home Office Research & Statistics Department Digest 4, *Information on the Criminal Justice System in England & Wales*, 1999
17. *NNWA News*, Spring, 2000
18. 'One step closer to real security', *Bristol Observer*, 22 May 1992
19. 'Funeral parlour coffins stolen', *Independent*, 23 January 2002
20. HTV TV news item, 8 July 02
21. Interview with Lee Kuan Yew in *End of Empire*, BBC Radio 4, 9 September 2002
22. 'Blame crime on the economy – Straw', *Metro*, 27 August 1999
23. T.S. Ashton (1961), *The Industrial Revolution 1760–1830*, Oxford University Press
24. Singapore Government Crime Statistics (2002), *Intelligence and Security Committee Annual Report, 1999–2000*

Chapter 2

1. 'More protection is urged after PC is battered with an iron bar', *Independent*, 4 January 1996
2. 'Labour leaves the thin blue line thinner', *Metro*, 28 March 2000
3. 'Cost drives bobbies off the beat', *The Times*, 3 August 1998
4. 'Britain's part-time police stations', *Independent*, 14 January 2001
5. 'Village wants to buy its own beat bobby', *Evening Standard*, 5 January 2001
6. In support of this common-sense argument, see 'We cannot cope without more officers say police', *Daily Telegraph*, 14 May 2001
7. See, for example, 'New York crime plunge wins over the sceptics', *Sunday Times*, 6 April 1997 and 'The Bronx used to be a killing field', *Daily Mail*, 22 July 1998
8. Radio 4 news item, 29 October 2003
9. 'We cannot cope...', *Daily Telegraph*
10. 'House burglary total is up by 13%', *Bristol Evening Post*, 17 September 2002

11. Home Office *Criminal Statistics, England & Wales, 2000*
12. 'Street crime soars as stop-and-search falls', *Daily Mail*, 28 February 2000
13. 'We cannot cope...', *Daily Telegraph*
14. 'Terror suspects in suburbia – but what was the target?' *Independent*, 31 March 2004
15. 'Widdecombe clashes with Tory rival on police pledge', *Guardian*, 27 January 2000
16. 'We have taken back New York block by block', *Independent*, 4 January 1996
17. 'France to increase gendarme force by 18,000', *Daily Telegraph*, 11 July 2002
18. 'Wardens scheme expands into city', *Bristol Evening Post*, 26 September 2002
19. See C. Maslach and S.E. Jackson, 'Burned-out Cops and Their Families', *Psychology Today*, 12:12 (1979), pp. 59–62; C. Maslach and S.E. Jackson, 'The Measurement of Experienced Burnout', *Journal of Occupational Behavior*, 2 (1981), pp. 99–113; and W.B. Bradley, 'Community-based treatment for young offenders', *Crime and Delinquency*, 15:3 (1969), pp. 359–370
20. 'Counting criminals instead of catching them', *Daily Mail*, 26 August 1999
21. R. Kerridge, 'Saying the Unsayable', *The Salisbury Review*, 20:3 (Spring 2002)
22. 'The police paper trail', *Independent*, 28 March 2000
23. 'The shaming of justice, *Daily Mail*, 23 January 2003
24. H. Jones, *Crime in a Changing Society*, Penguin, Middlesex, 1965
25. Home Office 20/01, *Cautions, Court Proceedings and Sentencing, England & Wales, 2000*
26. '*Diverting Young Offenders from Prosecution*, NACRO, 1992
27. Home Office *Criminal Statistics, England & Wales, 2000*
28. Home Office Digest 2, *Information on the Criminal Justice System in England & Wales, 1993*
29. 'Audit Commission urges forces to introduce caution plus scheme', *Police Review*, 5 June 1998
30. 'Don't charge so many crooks, police ordered', *Daily Mail*, 8 April 1991
31. Home Office 20/21, *Cautions, Court Proceedings and Sentencing*
32. 'Home Office, *The Offenders Index*, Janus Studies 4th edn, July 1994

33. Home Office *Criminal Statistics England & Wales 2000*
34. Home Office *Criminal Statistics England & Wales 2000*; 'Can the thin blue line stop street criminals?', *Daily Telegraph*, 14 May 2001
35. Reported in 'Youth Justice Explained', *Guardian*, 29 May 2002
36. 'Police cautions no longer mean a criminal record', *The Times*, 8 February 2001
37. B. Lawrence, *They Call It Justice*, Lewes, The Book Guild, 1998
39. 'CPS director faces dissent from lawyers', *Independent*, 12 November 1993
40. 'Evidence failed vital test', *The Times*, 6 December 1993
41. 'CPS goes on trial as convictions plunge by a third', *Daily Mail*, 13 June 1997
42. For example, 'The jury's out on the lady from the DPP', *Sunday Times*, 31 October 1993; 'Mills rides out storm of protest', *The Times*, 6 December 1993; and 'You are soft on crime, law chief tells CPS', *Daily Mail*, 30 May 1997
43. 'This damning case against the prosecution', *Daily Mail*, 21 October 1993
44. 'You are soft on crime...', *Daily Mail*
45. Speech by the Home Secretary Michael Howard to the 1995 Conservative Party Conference, Blackpool
46. Interview with crown court victim-support worker, 2001
47. *Ibid.*
48. 'Customs fiasco costs £100 million', *Telegraph*, 22 January 2003
49. Reported on the *Today* programme, BBC Radio 4, 6 August 2003
50. 'Intimidation causes 30,000 court cases a year to collapse', *Telegraph*, 10 March 2002
51. Radio 4 news, January 2003
52. Home Office Research Study 167, *Offenders on Probation*, 1997
53. *Ibid.*
54. 'I get such a buzz from stealing', *Daily Mail*, 10 December 1993
55. 'Transcription of pre-sentence summing up by crown court judge in July 2000
56. 'Weekly Digest', *Justice of the Peace*, 165, 8 December 2001
57. Crown court documents providing example of a concurrent offence for a persistent offender, February 1998

58. Home Office, *Probation Statistics, England & Wales, 1998*
59. BBC Radio 4, 27 January 2002
60. Home Office Statistical Bulletin, Issue 19/99, *Reconvictions of Offenders Sentenced or Discharged from Prison in 1995, England & Wales*
61. Home Office Research & Statistics Department Digest 4
62. Interview with crown court victim-support worker, July 2001
63. 'Tagging order for boy driver', *Bristol Evening Post*, 9 July 2001
64. 'Burglar escapes jail term', *Bristol Evening Post*, 12 May 2001
65. 'Executives jailed for biggest timeshare swindle', *Independent*, 30 June 2000
66. 'In the courts', *Bristol Evening Post*, 30 June 2000
67. 'Fire attack woman slams boy's adventure-camp remand', *Daily Mirror*, 25 February 1993
68. See Home Office *Criminal Statistics England & Wales 2000*; and Home Office 20/21, *Cautions, Court Proceedings and Sentencing*
69. Home Office press release on the Sentencing Advisory Panel, October 1999
70. Speech given by the Home Secretary, Michael Howard, to the House of Commons on 18 November 1994. Reported in *Nacro Criminal Justice Digest, 83*, January 1995
71. Home Office, *Probation Statistics England & Wales 1998*
72. *Ibid.*
73. Crime and Disorder Act 1998
74. Home Office, *Probation Statistics England & Wales 1998*
75. 'The killer next door', *Independent*, 23 July 2002
76. 'How can a police killer be free in 6 years?', *Daily Mail*, 16 November 1999
77. Home Office 20/01, *Cautions, Court Proceedings and Sentencing*
78. 'Bail-crime link contradicted by London study', *The Times*, July 1991
79. 'New law urged to beat the bail bandits', *Western Daily Press*, 20 July 1991
80. 'Bandits on bail', *Daily Telegraph*, 20 July 1991
81. 'Bail offenders run amok', *Justice of the Peace*, 10 August 1991
82. 'Weekly Digest', *Justice of the Peace*, 165, 8 December 2001
83. 'Bandits on bail', *Daily Telegraph*
84. *Ibid.*
85. 'Bail offenders run amok', *Justice of the Peace*

86. Home Office 20/01, *Cautions, Court Proceedings and Sentencing*
87. *Action Against Crime: The Government's Strategy on Law & Order*, April 1995
88. Home Office Research Directorate, Research Findings No. 72, *Offending on Bail and Police Use of Conditional Bail*, 1998
89. Ibid.; see, too, 'One in four offends again while on bail', *Daily Mail*, 15 May 1998
90. *Action Against Crime*
91. 'Tearaways aged 12 warned: We'll lock you up before trial', *Daily Mail*, 16 October 1997
92. 'Notes on juvenile bail – based on verbal evidence from Clerk of the Court for Juvenile Panel, North East London, August 2002
93. Home Office (Janus Studies), *The Offender's Tale*, version 2, August 1992
94. Home Office 20/01, *Cautions, Court Proceedings and Sentencing*
95. Home Office, *The Offender's Tale* and *The Offender's Index*, 4th edn, July 1994
96. 'Tackling persistent offenders is the key to improving effectiveness of the criminal justice system', Home Office press release, 31 January 2001
97. 'To bail or not to bail', *Police*, August 1991
98. See, for example, a letter to *The Times*, from His Honour Judge Michael Mott, Worcester Crown Court, 10 September 1991

Chapter 3

1. S. Brittan, *The Treasury under the Tories, 1951–1964*, Penguin Books Ltd, 1964
2. 'Professor Leslie Wilkins', *The Times*, 2 June 2000
3. L.T. Wilkins, *Delinquent Generations*, London, HMSO, 1961
4. I. Taylor, et al., *The New Criminology: For a Social Theory of Deviance*, London, RKP, 1973
5. V. Packard, *The Hidden Persuaders*, Middlesex, Penguin Books, 1957
6. B. Sheppard, *A War of Nerves, Soldiers and Psychiatrists, 1914–1994*, London, Jonathan Cape, 2000
7. Packard, *The Hidden Persuaders*
8. *Ibid.*, p. 29

9. Home Office, *Penal Practice in a Changing Society*, 1959
10. T.R. Fyvel, *The Insecure Offenders*, Middlesex, Penguin Books, 1963; H. Jones, *Crime in a Changing Society*, Middlesex, Penguin Books, 1965; D. Miller, *The Age Between*, London, Cornmarket Hutchinson, 1969; H. Wilson, *Delinquency and Child Neglect*, London, Allen & Unwin, 1962; A. Cohen, *Delinquent Boys*, London, Routledge and Kegan Paul, 1956; D.J. West, *The Habitual Prisoner*, London, Macmillan, 1963; T.C.N. Gibbens, *Psychiatric Studies of Borstal Lads*, Oxford University Press, 1963; R.A. Cloward and L.E. Ohlin, *Delinquency and Opportunity*, London, Routledge and Kegan Paul, 1961; J.B. Mays, *Crime and the Social Structure*, London, Faber and Faber, 1963
11. Fyvel, *The Insecure Offenders*, p. 111
12. Jones, *Crime in a Changing Society*, p. 99
13. Fyvel, *The Insecure Offenders*, p. 13
14. Judge Crowther, 'The Criminal Justice Act 1991: A Charter for Criminals', *Justice of the Peace*, 18 January 1992
15. Thirty years later similar programmes are still being run. A report from the University of Sheffield in 1999 acknowledged that millions of pounds was being spent on hang-gliding, horse-riding and other activity courses for offenders without any evidence that they prevent reoffending. See P. Taylor, *Demanding Physical Activity Programmes*, Sheffield University, 1999
16. B. Lawrence, *They Call it Justice*, Lewes, The Book Guild, 1998
17. See, for example, Lord Mackenzie, 'Tough Justice', *Police Review*, 5 February 1999 and 'Income-related fines scrapped', *Independent*, 14 May 1993
18. D. Faulkner, *In Defence of the Criminal Justice Act 1991*, Prison Report, Autumn 1991
19. 'Bring the Outs In', *Independent*, 12 March 1997
20. *Ibid.*
21. The Auld Report, *Justice for All*, CM 5563, HMSO, July 2002
22. G. Sheehy, *Gorbachev*, Heinemann Ltd, 1991
23. A. Sampson, *The Changing Anatomy of Britain*, Book Club Associates, London, 2003
24. 'At the heart of the Hutton Inquiry is Blair's corruption of the Civil Service', *Independent*, 19 August 2003
25. N. Jones, *The Control Freaks: How New Labour Gets Its Own Way*, London, Politico's, 2001

26. 'At the heart of the Hutton Inquiry is Blair's corruption of the Civil Service', *Independent*, 19 August 2003
27. 'Blair's spin is the porn of politics, says Major', *Telegraph*, 24 October 2003
28. *Time Out Film Guide*, London, British Film Institute/Penguin, 2003
29. V. Stern, 'Reducing Crime by Resettling Offenders', *The Magistrate*, 49:5, June 1993
30. The web site of the Howard League for Penal Reform – www.howardleague.org
31. See, for example, Penal Affairs Consortium, *A Joint Manifesto for Penal Reform*, 2000
32. *Repeat Burglars*, NACRO's response to the minimum three-year sentence, reported in the *Justice of the Peace*, 163, 4 December 1999
33. Web site of the Howard League
34. 'Prison does not work. We know that', *Guardian* 2 January 2001
35. 'Closure of Eastwood Park Prison', HM Prison internal memorandum, August 1990
36. See, for example, 'Why our prisons are not working', *Independent*, 20 March 1998 and 'Prison under pressure', *Guardian*, 2 February 2001
37. 'Why our prisons are not working', *Independent*
38. 'Prison under pressure', *Guardian*
39. For example, 'We were victims too', *Observer*, 7 July 2002
40. 'When punishment becomes a crime', *Independent*, 28 November 2001
41. 'When to punish is to betray', *Independent*, 27 October 2000
42. 'Suicide rears for teen victims of Blunkett's get tough rules', *Observer*, 7 July 2002

Chapter 4

1. See W.A. Elkin, *The English Penal System*, Middlesex, Penguin, 1957 and Home Office, *Penal Practice in a Changing Society*, February 1959; see also T. Fyvel, *The Insecure Offenders*, Penguin Books, p. 64, 1963
2. A. Sampson, *The Changing Anatomy of Britain*, London, Book Club Associates, 1982

3. T.R. Fyvel, *The Insecure Offenders*, Middlesex, Penguin Books Ltd, 1963
4. D. Marsland, 'The ology that's crippling Britain', *Daily Mail*, 1 April 1994
5. *Statewatch Bulletin*, 'Prison Population Statistics', November-December 2002, found on www.statewatch.org
6. 'Prison crisis as foreign inmates soar', *Independent*, 6 August 2003
7. 'Prisoners fail to curb their inner man', *The Times*, 18 November 2003
8. 'Straw ditches tough stance on burglars', *Sunday Telegraph*, 20 July 1997
9. 'Prison riots warning', *Daily Mail*, 26 July 1997
10. *Ibid.*
11. 'Blair warns police chiefs over crime', *Independent*, 8 June 1998
12. 'Blunkett and Brown argue over cash for prisons', *Independent*, 16 September 2002
13. 'Hurd call for fewer jail sentences', *Independent*, 16 January 1988
14. 'Crisis looms as British prisons declared full', *Independent*, 2 March 2002
15. 'Increases in numbers of offenders released on parole. Information supplied by the Parole Board, 2003
16. 'Courts blamed as prison population reaches new high', *Independent*, 21 February 1987
17. 'Soft on crime? No, courts are jailing more villains', *Daily Mail*, 18 September 1998
18. 'Sentencing policy means jails will be full in the new year', *Independent*, 16 January 2002
19. 'Prison riots warning', *Daily Mail*
20. 'Make prisons work', *The Times*, 1 February 2001
21. 'Jail sentences must be cut to ease overcrowding, Woolf says', *The Times*, 30 October 2002
22. 'Hundreds of offenders to be freed early', *The Times*, 30 October 2002
23. 'Sharp fall in offenders to face courts', *Independent*, 18 October 2002
24. 'Audit Commission Report, June 2002
25. '90% of crimes go unpunished', *Daily Mirror*, 20 January 2003
26. 'Despair of the crown court lawyers', *Daily Mail*, 30 November 1993

27. 'The basis of justice is right, its administration is appalling', *Independent*, 8 March 2002

28. 'Sentence for drug dealer is criticised', *Bristol Evening Post*, 10 September 2002

29. Home Office, *Crime Statistics England & Wales 2000*

30. C. Murray, *Does Prison Work?*, Choice in Welfare No. 38, London, 1997

31. 'Overflowing cells are reasons for policy change', *Daily Telegraph*, 21 December 2002

32. 'Soften the Labour line on crime, Straw told', *Daily Mail*, 2 June 1997

33. J. McGuire, ed., *What Works: Reducing Offending: Guidelines from Research and Practice*, Chichester, Wiley, 1995

34. R. Lewis, 'Will Probation Survive Social Work?' *Justice of the Peace*, 7 October 1989

35. 'Letwin says society creates criminals', *Sunday Telegraph*, 6 January 2002

36. J. Graham, *What Works In Preventing Criminality*, Home Office Research Study 187, 1998

37. 'Criminal', *Daily Mail*, 12 October 1998

38. 'Hague is right to confront the liberal establishment', *Sunday Telegraph*, 21 May 2002

39. J. Young, *The Exclusive Society: Social Exclusion, Crime and Difference in Late Modernity*, London, Sage, 1999

40. 'Serious crime by the young doubles in 7 years', *Sunday Telegraph*, 6 January 2002

41. 'Home Secretary says that proposals on criminal punishment are not aimed at cutting jail population', *Independent*, 10 November 1990

42. 'Straw attacks liberal lawyers on young thugs', *Mail on Sunday*, 12 September 1999

43. 'Straw told plans to name lenient JPs is utter nonsense', *Independent*, 13 July 2000

44. 'Britain's part time police stations', *Independent on Sunday*, 14 January 2001

45. *Ibid.*

46. Home Office Research Study No. 187, *Reducing Offending: An Assessment of Research Evidence on Ways of Dealing with Offending Behaviour*, 1998

47. 'Cost drives bobbies off the beat', *The Times*, 3 August 1998

48. 'The bargain bobbies', *Daily Mail*, 14 March 2000
49. 'Police blame statistics for 10% leap in violent attacks', *Independent*, 24 April 2003
50. 'Street crime soars as stop-and-search falls', *Daily Mail*, 28 February 2000
51. See, for example, 'Wardens scheme expands into city', *Bristol Evening Post*, 26 September 2002 and *Home Office Crime Prevention News*, p. 19, 2000
52. See, for example, 'Wardens scheme expands into city', *Bristol Evening Post*; 'Straw vows to beat crime with bobbies', *Daily Mail*, 27 May 1997; and 'Labour plans more street cops to tackle shock rise in offences', *Mirror*, 27 May 1997
53. Home Office, *Probation Statistics England & Wales* 2000

Chapter 5

1. Home Office Research & Statistics Department *Digest 4: Information on the Criminal Justice System in England & Wales*, 1999
2. 'Boss's fears over street crime', *Bristol Evening Post*, 5 November 2002
3. 'Send fewer to jail, judges told', *Daily Telegraph*, 5 November 2002
4. Home Office 20/01, *Cautions, Court Proceedings and Sentencing, England & Wales 2000*, 2001
5. *Ibid.*; Home Office, *Probation Statistics England & Wales 1998*; Home Office Research & Statistics Department, *Digest 4: Information on the Criminal Justice System in England & Wales*, 1999
6. Home Office Findings 154, *Prison Population in 2000: A Statistical Review*; Home Office, *The Prison Population, March 2002*
7. For the sharp rise in foreign inmates in British prisons, see 'Prison crisis as foreign inmates soar', *Independent*, 6 August 2003
8. Home Office, *Probation Statistics England & Wales 2000*
9. Home Office Criminal Statistics England and Wales 1999, *Homicide, 1946–1999*; *A Century of Change: Trends in UK Statistics Since 1900*, House of Commons Research Paper 99/111, 21 December 1999

10. M. Gosling, 'Managing Life Sentence Prisoners – Where are we now?' *Justice of the Peace*, 165, p. 575, 28 July 2001
11. Home Office, *Probation Statistics England & Wales 2000*, 'Prison Population Brief – England and Wales, October 1999', *The Magistrate*, 56:2, p. 37, February 2000; Home Office, *The Prison Population*, March 2002
13. 'Drugs and robbery behind record rise in women jailed', *Daily Mail*, 5 June1999
14. K. Pease, 'Cross-national Imprisonment Rates', *British Journal of Criminology*, 34, Special Issue, 1994
15. C. Murray, *Does Prison Work?*, Choice in Welfare Series, No. 38, in association with *The Sunday Times*, 1997
16. *Ibid.*
17. J. Young, 'The Dilemmas of a Libertarian', in C. Murray, *Does Prison Work?* Choice in Welfare Series, No. 38, in association with *The Sunday Times*, 1997
18. S.D. Levitt, 'The Effect of Prison Population Size on Crime Rates: Evidence from Prison Over-crowding Litigation', *Quarterly Journal of Economics*, 3, pp. 319–52, 1996
19. T.B. Marvell and C.E. Moody, Jr., 'Prison Population Growth and Crime Reduction', *Journal of Quantitative Criminology*, 10:2, p. 136, 1994
20. P.A. Langan, 'Between Prison and Probation: Intermediate Sanctions', *Science*, 264, p. 791, 1994
21. P. Coad et al., *Criminal Justice: Fact and Fiction*, 2nd edn, briefing document of Criminal Justice Association, 2000
22. Home Office, *Prison Statistics England & Wales 1999*
23. Department of Health, *National Treatment Outcome Research Study*, 1996
24. Home Office, *Probation Statistics England & Wales 2000*
25. Home Office Statistical Bulletin, Issue 5/97, *Reconvictions of Prisoners Discharged from Prison in 1993*, 24 March 1977; Home Office, *Prison Statistics England & Wales 1997*
26. 'The figures that show prison is working', *Daily Mail*, 25 March 1997
27. P. Coad and D. Fraser, 'Reducing Re-offending by the Penal Affairs Consortium: A Critical Analysis', Paper presented to the All Party Home Affairs Committee investigating alternatives to imprisonment, 1997
28. Home Office, *Prison Statistics England & Wales 1996*

29. Home Office Research Findings R154, *Prison Statistics England & Wales 2000*

30. 'The Prison Reform Trust & HM Prison Service, *The Prisoners' Information Book*, 1995

31. *British Crime Survey, 1998*; Home Office Research & Statistics Department, *Digest 4*

32. P. Coad, et al., *Criminal Justice*; 'Crime costs nation £60 billion a year', *The Times*, 23 December 2000

33. Paper submitted to the Police Suprintendents' Annual Conference, 1998

34. 'Cost of youth crime would provide 100 new hospitals a year', *Daily Mail*, 26 July 1997

35. P. Coad, et al., *Criminal Justice*

36. 'Longer prison sentences are the cheapest way to cut crime', *Daily Telegraph*, 28 December 1988

37. Home Office, *The Economic and Social Costs of Crime*, 2000

38. 'Audit Commission, *Safety in Numbers: Promoting Community Safety*, 1998

39. Home Office 20/01, *Cautions, Court Proceedings and Sentencing*

40. Home Office, *Prison Population Brief England & Wales*, 2001

41. 'Correspondence between Brian Lawrence, former Clerk of the Court, and the General Synod of the Church of England, 12 November 1999

42. 'Jail mobile phone thieves, says law chief', *Independent*, 30 January 2002

43. 'Road killers to face up to 14 years in jail', *Independent*, 12 May 2003

44. 'Jail burglars for at least nine months, court told', *Telegraph*, 11 May 2002; Home Office press release on the Sentencing Advisory Panel, October 1999

45. 'The good thing about prison is that it protects innocent people from villains such as you', *Daily Mail*, 4 March 1997

46. V. Stern, 'Harsh Words on Prison Sentences', *Independent*, 17 March 1989

47. 'Church condemns jails as deeply damaging', *Telegraph*, 10 November 1999

48. Correspondence between Lawrence and the General Synod, 12 November 1999

49. 'Speech by Baroness Faithfull to the Conference on Government Proposals for Young Offenders, 1994

50. 'Prisons are unhappy places that make people worse', *The Times*, March 28 1997
51. S. Shaw, Criminal Justice Matters, ISTD, 1998, quoted in J. Braggins, J., 'Twelve Months of Labour', *Prison Service Journal*, Issue No. 117, May 1998
52. J. Halliday, *Making Punishments Work: Report of a Review of the Sentencing Framework for England and Wales*, 2001

Chapter 6

1. Reported in 'Interpretation of statistics allows for deception', *Police Review*, 31 March 2000
2. Home Office, *Prison Statistics England & Wales 1999*, 2000
3. W.A. Elkin, *The English Penal System*, Middlesex, Penguin Books Ltd, 1957
4. Home Office, *Prison Statistics England & Wales 1999*
5. '*Think First, Offence Focused Problem Solving Group*, Information for Sentencers, Avon and Somerset Probation paper, 2000
6. 'Keep probation for worst cases, review says', *Guardian*, 8 August 2003
7. Home Office, *Probation Statistics England & Wales 2000*; Home Office, *Digest 4: Information on the Criminal Justice System in England & Wales*, 1999
8. Home Office, *Cautions, Court Proceedings and Sentencing 20/01, England and Wales*, 2000
9. Home Office, *Probation Statistics England & Wales 1998*, 2000
10. Home Office, *Probation Statistics England & Wales 1993*
11. Home Office Statistical Bulletin, Issue 5/97, *Reconvictions of Prisoners Discharged from Prison in 1993*
12. Avon Probation Service, Annual Report 1993/4, *Serving the Courts and the Public*
13. Home Office Statistical Bulletin, Issue 6/97, *Reconvictions of Those Commencing Community Penalties in 1993, England & Wales*
14. T. Chapman and M. Hough, *Evidence Based Practice*, London, Home Office, 1998
15. 'Avon Probation Service, *Communications and Marketing Strategy, 1996–1999*
16. 'Empty jargon is put to the sword by Bullfighter', *Telegraph*, 25 June 2003

17. 'Probation in the Eighties Exhibition', Victoria Rooms, Clifton, Bristol, 30–31 March 1982; Avon Probation Service, *Commmunications and Marketing Strategy, 1996–1997*
18. Home Office, *Restorative Justice: An Overview*, 1999
19. Avon Probation Service, Annual Report 1999/2000
20. Home Office, Research Study No. 187 was commented on, for example, in 'Straw fights crime war on a new front', *Daily Mail*, 22 July 1998 and C. Nuttall, 'Reducing Offending', newsletter for the Criminal Justice Consultative Council, 1998
21. Home Office, Research Study No. 187, *Reducing Offending: An Assessment of Research Evidence on Ways of Dealing with Offending Behaviour*, pp. 56–58, 65, 1998
22. See, for example, 'The Bronx used to be a killing field', *Daily Mail*, 22 July 1998 and 'New York crime plunge wins over the sceptics', *Sunday Times*, 6 April, 1997
23. Home Office, Research Study No. 187, pp. 65–66
24. D. Green, Forces of Law and Order have lost Control, Civitas, 2002
25. 'Crime overwhelms police', *Telegraph*, 7 April 2003
26. 'Police get 1200 more wardens', *The Times*, 3 May 2003
27. 'Crime overwhelms police', *Telegraph*
28. Home Office, Research Study No. 187, p. 30; 'Straw in the wind', *Telegraph*, 23 July 1998
29. Home Office, Research Study No. 187, p. 129
30. *Targeting Prolific Offenders*, An Avon & Somerset Probation briefing paper, 9 June 2003
31. *Evaluating the Effectiveness of Operation ARC (Addressing Repeat Criminality)*, University of Exeter, p. 3, 2001
32. *Ibid.*, p. 3
33. Eighteen Months Later: Evaluating the Effectiveness of Project ARC in the Medium Term, University of Exeter, p. 50, November 2002
34. *Evaluating the Effectiveness of Operation ARC (Addressing Repeat Criminality)*, University of Exeter, p. 75, 2001
35. Home Office, *National Standards for the Supervison of Offenders in the Community*, p. 2, section D13, 2000; see also Home Office, *Required Levels of Contact, Achieving Compliance and Ensuring Enforcement*, National Standards for the Probation Service, 2000; 'Young Offender Referral Order Pilot Sites, *The*

411

Magistrate, p. 36, February 2000; and P. Coad, *The Probation Service 1996: A Personal Perspective*, Criminal Justice Association briefing paper, 1996

36. 'Minutes of evidence taken before the House of Commons All Party Home Affairs Committee, alternatives to imprisonment, Tuesday 3 March 1998
37. 'Throwing away the key', *Independent Magazine*, 17 October 1992
38. M. Bryant, *Doing Time for the Community: The Sentence of Tomorrow in Action Today*, Berkshire Probation Service, January 1997
39. P. Coad, *Society and the Persistent Offender*, a Criminal Justice Association briefing paper, 1995
40. Reported in T. Dalrymple, 'Stalinist Statistics', *Spectator*, 17 March 2003
41. 'Young are committing 13 crimes each minute', *The Times*, 26 July 1997
42. 'Survey shows extent of youth crime', *Police Review*, 9 January 1998
43. 'Serious crime by the young doubles in 7 years', *Sunday Telegraph*, 6 January 2002
44. 'Schools in high-crime areas will get their own police stations', *Daily Mail*, 9 April 2002
45. Reported in T. Dalrymple, 'Stalinist Statistics', *Spectator*, 17 March 2003
46. 'Youth crime soars as sentences drop', *Bristol Evening Post*, 4 April 2002
47. C. Murray, ed., *Does Prison Work?*, Choice in Welfare Series No. 38, London, Civitas, 1997
48. Home Office, *Young People and Crime*, 1997
49. 'Teenage crime on the rise as peak age for offending drops', *Independent*, 10 October 2002
50. Home Office, *Three Year Plan for the Probation Service, 1995–1998*; Home Office, *The Offender's Index: A User's Guide*, 1996; Home Office, *Prison Statistics England & Wales 1997*; Home Office, *Programmes for Offenders: Guidance for Evaluators*, Crime Reduction Programme, 1999
51. Correspondence between Peter Coad, Director of the Criminal Justice Association, and the Home Office concerning 'pseudo convictions', 3 September 1998

52. *A Review of the Avon Probation & After Care Service from 1974 to 1981*
53. 'Probation reduces re-offending rates', *Independent*, 24 January 1995
54. 'Letter from Cumbria Chief Probation Officer, *Justice of the Peace*, 26 August 1995
55. 'Probation Service rises to challenging times', *Guardian*, 4 February 1994
56. '80% success rate a myth, declares Home Office Minister David Maclean', *Independent*, 10 February 1995
57. 'Outrage as violent criminals escape justice', *Daily Express*, 21 January 2001
58. House of Commons All Party Home Affairs Committee, Tuesday 3 March 1998
59. Home Office, *Three Year Plan for the Probation Service, 1996–1999*
60. The Auld Report, *Justice for All*, CM 5563
61. 'Prison Licence, Community Order Breaches and the Prison Population', *NAPO News*, Issue 149, May 2003
62. Home Office Probation Circular 42/03, *Parole, Licence and Recall Arrangements*
63. *Justice for All*, CM 5566, Foreword, 2002
64. *Justice for All*, CM 5566, p. 131, 2002
65. *Justice for All*, Summary, p. 4, 2002
66. *Justice for All*, Summary, p. 7, 2002
67. *Justice for All*, Summary, p. 7, 2002
68. *Justice for All*, CM 5566, p. 26, 2002
69. *Justice for All*, Summary, pp. 2–3, 2002
70. *Justice for All*, Summary, p. 8, 2002
71. *Justice for All*, Responses to the Auld and Halliday Reports, p. 4, 2002
72. *Justice for All*, Responses to the Auld and Halliday Reports, p. 4, 2002
73. *Justice for All*, Responses to the Auld and Halliday Reports, p. 5, 2002
74. *Justice for All*, Responses to the Auld and Halliday Reports, p. 5, 2002
75. *Justice for All*, Responses to the Auld and Halliday Reports, p. 3, 2002
76. *Justice for All*, CM 5566, p. 106, 2002

77. *Justice for All*, CM 5566, p. 71, 2002
78. Compare 'Justice Bill deludes the public, says Labour QC', *Telegraph*, 18 November 2002 with 'Far reaching changes go to the heart of the justice system', *Independent*, 22 November 2002
79. 'Justice Bill deludes the public...', *Telegraph*
80. 'Criminal Justice Bill', *Prison Service Journal*, Issue 146, April 2003
81. 'Jail terms of a year or less are useless says Chief Justice', *Independent*, 16 April 2003
82. *Ibid.*
83. See, for example, 'Longer jail terms will not reduce crime', *Evening Standard*, 7 August 2003 and 'Keep probation for worst cases...', *Guardian*
84. 'Longer jail terms will not reduce crime', *Evening Standard*
85. D. Green, *Crime Is Falling Because Prison Works*, Briefing paper by Civitas, 2003
86. 'England & Wales top crime league', *Guardian*, 26 May 1997
87. Home Office, *Probation Statistics England & Wales 2000*

Chapter 7

1. 'Scientists to investigate misleading research', *The Times*, 12 August 2003
2. 'Patients put at risk by medical research fraud', *Independent*, 5 May 1998
3. Department of Health, *National Treatment Outcome Research Study*, 1998
4. Home Office Research Findings 176, *Evaluation of Drug Testing in the Criminal Justice System in Three Pilot Areas*, 2002
5. Home Office Research Findings 120, *Impact of Methadone Treatment on Drug Misuse and Crime*, 2000
6. 'Prisons failing to help two thirds of addict inmates', *Telegraph*, 8 September 2003
7. Home Office Research Findings 148, *Drug Use and Offending: Summary Results from the First Year of the NEW-ADAM drug programme*, 2001
8. R. Matthews, and J. Trickey, *Drugs and Crime: A Study Amongst Young People in Leicester*, University of Leicester, Centre for

the Study of Public Order, in association with Middlesex University, 1996

9. 'Jailing addicts fails to make them quit drugs', *Independent*, 19 October 1999
10. 'Jail for attempted theft', *Bristol Evening News*, 20 February 2003
11. Home Office Research Findings 128, *Drug Testing and Treatment Orders: The 18 Month Evaluation*, 2000; Home Office, *Cautions, Court Proceedings and Sentencing 20/01, England & Wales 2000*, 2001
12. Home Office Research Findings 128; Home Office Research Study No. 212, *Drug Treatment and Testing Orders: Final Evaluation Report*, 2000
13. Home Office Research Study No. 212, pp. vii–viii
14. '50% drop out rate in drug addict test plan,' *Independent*, 8 November 1999
15. E. Wallis, *National Probation Service Performance Report 7*, April 2003
16. Results of an informal police survey of the DTTO scheme in a major force in the South West. Supplied anonymously by a serving police officer
17. 'Blair orders probe into why cop killer was free', *Daily Express*, 12 December 2003
18. Results of an informal police survey of the DTTO scheme in a major force in the South West. Supplied anonymously by a serving police officer
19. 'Blunkett says legal system is 200 years out of date', *Independent*, 7 June 2003
20. 'Be inspired by my burglar and keep drug addict out of prison', *Independent*, 27 March 2004
21. Results of an informal police survey of the DTTO scheme in a major force in the South West. Supplied, anonymously by a serving police officer
22. Home Office Research Study 218, *Employment and Crime: 'Working their Way Out of Offending'*, 2001
23. 'Avon Probation Service Bulletin No. 7, *Summary of the Bristol Wheels Project*, 15 February 1995
24. G. McIvor and M. Barry, University of Sterling, Crime & Criminal Justice Research Findings No. 50, *Social Work and Criminal Justice: The Longer-Term Impact of Supervision*, 2000

25. *Ibid.*, pp. 2–3
26. *Ibid.*, p. 3
27. *Ibid.*, pp. 2–3
28. D. Lobley and D. Smith, *Working with Persistent Juvenile Offenders: An Evaluation of the Apex Cue Ten Project*, Crime & Criminal Justice Research Findings No. 31, p. 3, 1999
29. 'Thousands of prisoners to be tagged and set free', *Sunday Telegraph*, 29 November 1998
30. '30,000 tagged prisoners to go free', *Independent*, 19 January 1999
31. 'Name swap', *Mail on Sunday*, 4 July 1999
32. *Ibid.*
33. 'Tagging is a success', *Police Review*, 23 July 1999
34. Home Office news bulletin, 'Tagging has been a success', BBC News, 30 November 2001
35. Home Office Findings 139, *Electronic Monitoring of Released Prisoners: An Evaluation of the Home Detention Curfew Scheme*, 2001
36. 'Details provided by the press officer of one of the private contractors supervising HDC prisoners, March 1999; Home Office, *Assessing Prisoners for Home Detention Curfew: A Guide for Practitioners*, 1999
37. 'Tagging crime wave,' *Daily Mail*, 15 November 2000
38. *Ibid.*; Home Office Research Findings No. 110, *Home Detention Curfew: The First Year of Operation*, 2000
39. 'Prisoners freed with tags go on the run', *The Times*, 4 March 2000
40. 'Information supplied anonymously by prison staff involved in the operation and administration of the Home Detention Curfew scheme, 2003
41. 'Faith in tags has grown as fears of re-offending fades', *Independent*, 22 March 2002
42. 'Jails free extra 5,000 offenders to cut crowding', *Independent*, 4 April 2003
43. Home Office Research Study 222, *Home Detention Curfew*, 2001
44. 'Tagging crime wave,' *Daily Mail*
45. Information supplied anonymously by prison probation staff involved in the operation and administration of the Home Detention Curfew scheme, June 2003

46. Home Office Research Study 222
47. 'The perspective of one police area on the working of the Home Detention Curfew scheme: details supplied anonymously by a police officer, 2003
48. 'Example of Home Detention Curfew conditions ignored by offender and the court given in interview with serving probation officer, February 2004
49. Home Office Bulletin 15/04, Prison Service Instruction 31/2003
50. Home Office, *Probation Statistics England & Wales 2000*
51. Home Office, *Home Detention Curfew*, 2003
52. Home Office Research Findings 141, *Electronic Monitoring and Offending Behaviour: Reconviction Results for the Second Year of Trials of Curfew Orders*, 2001
53. Home Office Research Findings 66, *Electronic Monitoring of Curfew Orders: The Second Year of the Trials*, 1998
54. Home Office Research Study 177, *Electronic Monitoring in Practice: Second Year of Trials of Curfew Orders*, 1997
55. Home Office Research Findings 141
56. 'Police attack Blunkett scheme to tag muggers', *Independent*, 27 February 2002
57. Home Office Research Findings 140, *A Year on the Tag: Interviews with Criminal Justice Practitioners and Electronic Monitoring Staff about Curfew Orders*, 2001
58. Home Office Research Findings 141
59. Home Office Research Study 177
60. Home Office Research Findings 66
61. G.V. Glass, B. McGaw and M.L. Smith, *Meta-analysis in Social Research*, Beverley Hills, CA, Sage, 1981
62. These include: C.J. Garrett, Effects of Residential Treatment on Adjudicated Delinquencies: A Meta-analysis, *Journal of Research in Crime & Delinquency*, 22, pp. 287–308, 1985; W.S. Davison et al., *Interventions with Juvenile Delinquents: A Meta-analysis of Treatment Efficacy*, Washington, DC, National Institute of Juvenile Justice and Delinquency Prevention, 1984; R. Gottschalk et al., 'Community based interventions', in H.C. Quay, ed., *Handbook of Juvenile Delinquency*, New York, Wiley, 1984; J.P. Mayer et al., 'Social Learning Treatment within Juvenile Justice: A Meta-analysis of Impact in the Natural Environment', in S. Apter and A. Goldstein, eds, *Youth Violence: Program and Prospects*, New York, Pergamon, 1986

417

63. J. McGuire, ed., *What Works: Reducing Offending: Guidelines from Research and Practice*, Wiley, 1995
64. J. McGuire, 'Plenary Sessions: Researching "What Works": Some Implications for the Use of Imprisonment', *Inside Psychology*, Vol. 3, 1, 1997
65. C.J. Garrett et al., 'Effects of Residential Treatment...'; J. McGuire, ed. *What Works*
66. For example, P. Raynor and M. Vanstone, *STOP Programme for Offenders: Third Interim Evaluation Report*, Glamorgan Probation Service, 1994; M. Oldfield, *Kent Reconviction Survey*, Kent Probation Service, 1996; J. Wilkinson, and D. Morgan, *The Impact of Ilderton Motor Project on Motor Vehicle Crime & Offending*, Inner London Probation Service, 1995; J. Roberts, *Discovering What Works*, Hereford & Worcester Probation Service Young Offender Project 1984–9, 1994; Inner London Probation Service, 'A Cognitive Therapy Programme', *Probation*, Issue no. 20, November 1997; Home Office Research Findings No. 81, *Motor Projects in England & Wales: An Evaluation*, 1988
67. Inner London Probation Service, 'A Cognitive Therapy Programme'
68. Home Office Research Findings No. 81
69. Roberts, *Discovering What Works*
70. Raynor and Vanstone, *STOP Programme for Offenders*
71. J. McGuire, ed., *What Works: Reducing Offending: Guidelines from Research and Practice*, Chichester, Wiley, 1995
72. J. McGuire, *Problem-solving Training and Offence Behaviour Manual: Introduction and User Guide*, p. 13, 1997; see also McGuire, 'Plenary Sessions'
73. A. Underdown and T. Ellis, *What Works Project: 'Strategies for Effective Offender Supervision'*, HM Inspectorate of Probation Report, 1998
74. K. Pease, House of Commons Home Affairs Select Committee, *Third Report on Alternatives to Prison*, vol. 2, pp. 209–10, 28 July 1998
75. For example, Underdown and Ellis, *What Works Project* and M.J. Furniss, *A Guide to Effective Evidence-based Practice*, HM Inspectorate of Probation, 1998
76. Furniss, *A Guide to Effective Evidence-based Practice*, p. viii
77. A. Underdown and T. Ellis, *What Works Project: 'Strategies*

for Effective Offender Supervision', HM Inspectorate of Probation Report

78. Home Office Probation Circular 35/1998, *Effective Practice Initiative: A National Implementation Plan for the Effective Supervision of Offenders*

79. Home Office Probation Circular 35/1998; Home Office, *What Works: First Report from the Joint Prison/Probation Accreditation Panel, 1999–2000*; Home Office, *Probation Pathfinder Circular 35/1999*

80. National Probation Service, 'A Comprehensive Guide to Vacancies Throughout the Probation Service', *Probation Bulletin*, Issue No. 4, 25 February 2002; advert for group work officer, *NAPO Bulletin*, 2001

81. 'Speech by Home Office minister Joyce Quin to the HMIP conference, 'What Works', 25 February 1998

82. '"What Works": Significant Progress', *NAPO News*, 1999

83. 'Strategy for Reducing Offending', *Justice of the Peace*, 31 May 1997

84. Home Office Probation Circular 35/1998

85. 'Correspondence with Home Office minister Paul Boateng and his advisor Mark Slater, Home Office, October 2001; see also a speech by Home Office minister Paul Boateng to the 'What Works' Conference, Manchester, 20 September 2000

86. 'Letter to the chairman of 'Probation 2000', an 'International Conference on the Future of Crime and Punishment, at the Queen Elizabeth II Conference Centre, 26–28 January

87. 'Correspondence with Avon & Somerset Probation Service concerning 'what works' community programmes for offenders

88. C. Strachan, 'Partners against Crime', *Police Review*, p. 25, 19 May 2000

89. 'Welcome note from Eithne Wallis, Director of the National Probation Service, issued to all staff, March 2001; 'Meet the new director: Eithne Wallis shares her plans and aspirations', *The Probation Manager*, July 2001

90. Home Office, *Programme for Offenders: Guidance for Evaluators*, Crime Reduction Programme – guidance note 2, 1999

91. *Ibid.*

92. 'Correspondence with the Research, Development and Statistics

Directorate, Offenders and Corrections Unit, Home Office, January 2001

93. Welcome note from Eithne Wallis
94. S. Merrington and S. Stanley, 'Doubts about the What Works Initiative', *Probation Journal* 47:4, December 2000
95. See note 89
96. 'Accredited Programmes', *NAPO News*, Issue No. 150, p. 2, June 2000
97. *Probation Training*, National Probation Service Training Document for 'What Works' programmes, 2000
98. J. McGuire, 'Plenary Sessions: Researching "What Works": Some Implications for the Use of Imprisonment, *Inside Psychology*, 3:1, 1997
99. Home Office Circular 63/1996, *Guidance for Use of OGRS, Prediction of Reoffending Scale*; Home Office, *Interpreting OGRS Scores*, 2000; Avon Probation Service, *Think First: Offence Focused Problem Solving Group*, Information for Sentencers, 2001; Avon Probation Service Plan, 2000/2001; example of Probation Service documentation, *Monitoring of Service Plan Objectives*, November 2000; Home Office Probation Circular 60/2000, *What Works Strategy for the Probation Service*
100. Home Office Probation Circular 96/2000, *What Works: Implementation of Accredited programmes, 2*
101. 'Pathfinders and the Core Curriculum, At Your Service', an internal Avon Probation Service document, Vol. 1, Issue 2, November 1999
102. Home Office Research Findings 177, *Introducing Pathfinder Programmes into the Probation Service*, 2002
103. 'National Probation Service, 'Reasoning and Rehabilitation Programme', internal document, 2002
104. 'Some observations on 'what works' programmes provided anonymously by a serving probation officer, 2000
105. Home Office briefing on progress of 'What Works' Pathfinder Programme reported in: '"What Works": Significant Progress', *NAPO News*, 1999
106. Home Office, *Correctional Services Accreditation Panel*, a joint National Probation Service and HM Prison Service document, 2002
107. 'Information on the methods used for selecting prisoners for 'What Works' programmes run in prisons, provided

anonymously by serving probation staff based in a UK prison, 2003

108. *Ibid.*
109. 'Accredited Programmes', *NAPO News*, Issue 150, June 2000
110. 'Prisoners fail to curb their inner man', *The Times*, 18 November 2003
111. 'Jail thinking courses show you can't teach an old lag new tricks', *The Times*, 7 August 2003
112. 'Release me from this paperwork', *The Times*, 5 August 2003
113. 'Accredited Programmes', *NAPO News*, Issue No. 157, March 2004
114. S. Merrington and S. Stanley, ' "What Works": Revisiting the Evidence in England and Wales', *Probation Journal*, 5:1, pp. 7–20, 2004
115. Underdown and Ellis, *What Works Project*, p. 111
116. *New Choreography: The Strategic Framework for the National Probation Service, 2001–2002*
117. Home Office, *The Probation Service: Working to Reduce Crime and Protect the Public*, 1996
118. Information supplied by Stevane Hill, Psychotherapist, LLB, Dip.Psych., Dip.REBT, 2001
119. 'Prisoners fail to curb their inner man', *The Times*
120. 'Criminals who offer an apology may escape prosecution', *Telegraph*, 23 July 2003
121. 'An Interview with Martin Narey, Commissioner, Correctional Services, England and Wales', *NAPO News*, Issue No. 152, September 2003
122. 'Keep probation for worst cases, review says', *Guardian*, 8 August 2003
123. *The Bigger Picture*, Annual Report of the Association of Chief Officers of Probation, 1998/99
124. 'Release me from this paperwork', *The Times*, 5 August 2003

Chapter 8

1. 'Criminals identifiable at age 8', *Guardian*, 4 March 1998
2. 'Crime linked to unemployment, *The Times*, 5 December 1995
3. P. Coad, *Criminal Justice in Need of Reform*, Criminal Justice Association briefing paper, 1997

4. R. Lewis, 'The Poverty of the Treatment Philosophy', *The Justice of the Peace*, 1975
5. *Ibid.*, p. 3
6. 'The great myth of poverty and crime', *Daily Mail*, 2 January 1997
7. Home Office Statistical Findings, Issue 1/94, *A Study of the Relationship Between Unemployment and Crime*, 1994
8. T.R. Fyvel, *The Insecure Offenders*, Middlesex, Penguin Books, 1963
9. P. Coad, *Crime and Unemployment*, a Criminal Justice Association briefing paper, 1994
10. 'The Boomerang Boy', *Telegraph*, 11 February 1999
11. 'They're teenagers working in gangs of 10 or more, they've graduated from stealing designer clothes, now they rob banks', *Evening Standard*, 31 August 1999
12. 'Jail thinking courses show you can't teach an old lag new tricks', *The Times*, 7 August 2003
13. 'Out of the blue, into the black, under the cosh', *Guardian*, 8 August 1998
14. R. Graef, *Living Dangerously*, London, HarperCollins, 1993, see also 'Prison does not work. We know that', *Guardian*, 2 January 2001
15. 'Speech by the Prime Minister, Tony Blair, on criminal justice, August 2002
16. 'Knife robbers tripped up by their Prada shoes', *Telegraph*, 18 November 2003
17. 'Young steal to order in inner-city crime wave', *Independent*, 5 January 1998
18. 'Going Straight, *The Police Review*, April 2000
19. 'He's black, 16, inside for robbery and when he gets out he'll do it again', *Evening Standard*, 31 August 1999
20. 'I get such a buzz from stealing', *Daily Mail*, 10 December 1993
21. '£1m an addict', *Bristol Evening Post*, 2 October 2003
22. 'Lord Woolf to clarify burglary ruling again', *Telegraph*, 14 January 2003
23. 'Why the thugs have turned to carjacking', *Daily Mail*, 1 February 2002
24. 'Jail staff tell of misery inflicted by children', *The Times*, 13 November 1998

25. 'The Home Secretary's review of sentencing', *Observer*, 2 September 2002
26. 'People with high self-esteem pose a greater risk to society', *Independent*, 28 November 2001
27. 'Young steal to order in inner-city crime wave', *Independent*
28. 'Elderly lose £40 million in distraction burglaries', *Telegraph*, 28 December 2001
29. Home Office Research Bulletin Special Edition, *Prisons and Prisoners*, No. 36, 1994
30. Home Office Research Findings No. 26, *Crime Against Retail Premises in 1993*, 1995
31. 'Artful dodgers revel in daylight robbery', *The Times*, 26 January 1998
32. 'Home raider addict jailed', *Bristol Evening Post*, 11 August 2001
33. 'Despicable muggers jailed', *Bristol Evening Post*, 10 October 2002
34. 'Burglars turn Christmas into the season of taking', *Telegraph*, 27 December 1997
35. B. Lawrence, *They call It Justice*, Lewes, The Book Guild Ltd, 1998
36. 'Basis of plea malpractice: information obtained in interview with serving probation officer, January 2004
37. 'Chief trouble maker leaves the nick', *Independent*, 27 May 1995
38. 'Boycott call over rise in attacks on probation hostel staff', *Independent*, 14 January 1992
39. 'Letter from a chief probation officer to the author, 1988
40. 'Information obtained from the organiser of the Woodlands Scheme in Basingstoke, established by the Rainer Foundation as an alternative to prison, 27 November 1987
41. 'Discussion on gang rape, *Today*, BBC Radio 4, 15 January 2004
42. Home Office, *Criminal Statistics England & Wales 2000*
43. 'In the courts', *Bristol Evening Post*, 29 September 2001
44. 'Probation cheats who mock the law', *Daily Mail*, 11 September 1998
45. House of Commons, Minutes of evidence taken before the All Party Home Affairs Committee, alternatives to imprisonment, Tuesday 3 March 1998

46. R. Lewis, 'It's All Our Fault', *Justice of the Peace*, 14 July 1990
47. 'Management errors blamed for prison riots', *Independent*, 19 January 1995
48. 'Prisons failing to help two-thirds of addict inmates', *Telegraph*, 8 September 2004
49. See, for example, 'Prison is not the answer to cutting crime', *Independent*, 1 February 2002; 'Truants targeted in drive against juvenile crime', *Telegraph*, 3 January 1998; 'Truant pupils blamed for wave of street crime', *Guardian*, 2 January 1998
50. 'Crime rates higher for expelled pupils', *Guardian*, 25 August 1998
51. 'Letter to Graham Smith, Chief Probation Inspector, from John Patten, Home Office Minister, December 1989
52. *'Probation Works – and Everyone Benefits*, Paper produced by the Association of Chief Officers of Probation, 1994
53. 'Teenage crime on the rise as peak age for offending drops', *Independent*, 10 October 2002
54. See, for example, 'Truants targeted in drive against juvenile crime', *Telegraph*; 'Truant pupils blamed for wave of street crime', *Guardian*; 'Straw to combat crime-breeding excuse culture', *Guardian*, 26 September 1997
55. 'Truants targeted in drive against juvenile crime', *Telegraph*
56. 'We'll jail your child gang leaders, says Widdecombe, touring crime hot estate', *Independent*, 30 December 2000
57. 'Children to be locked up in crime blitz', *Independent*, 4 February 2002
58. 'Number of boys held on remand doubles', *Guardian*, 2 January 2001
59. Cited in 'Don't dice with death in our community', *Express on Sunday*, 13 July 1997

Chapter 9

1. Home Office, *Probation Statistics England & Wales 2000*
2. 'Boycott call over rise in attacks on probation hostel staff', *Independent*, 14 January 1992
3. D. Fraser, 'A Study of Stress and Burnout in a Sample of UK Probation Staff', Unpublished M.Phil thesis, University of Bristol, 1996

4. R. Lewis, 1990, 'Probation: A Philosophical Perception', *Justice of the Peace*, 24 February
5. Kent Probation Board, *Annual Report 2001–2002*
6. 'Probation staff to get health checks to cut sick leave', Report from the West Midlands Probation Board, 2003
7. *Report from the Gwent Probation Board*, 2001–02
8. *Absence Management Report for 2002–3*, Avon and Somerset Probation Board
9. '2001 … A Probation Odyssey', Avon Probation Service Staff Conference, May 1997
10. 'Work with youngsters released from prison – 94% success', *Probation News*, Issue No. 1, summer 1997
11. P. Raynor, 'Reading Probation Statistics: A Critical Comment', *Vista: The Journal of the Association of Chief Officers of Probation*, 3:3, p. 184, Spring 1998
12. *New Choreography: The Strategic Framework for the National Probation Service 2001–2002*, Paper circulated to all staff by the director, September 2001
13. 'A Comprehensive Guide to Vacancies Throughout The Probation Service, *Probation Bulletin*, Issue No. 8, 2 February 1992
14. *High Tariff Group Management Team Vision*, Internal Probation Service document, 1992
15. Avon & Somerset Probation Service, 'The future shape of probation', *Probation News*, Issue No. 4, Summer 1999; Avon Probation Service, 'Work with youngsters released from prison – 94% success'
16. 'Release me from this paperwork', *The Times*, 5 August 2003
17. Devon Probation Service official slogan: 'Tackling Offending'
18. Glamorgan Probation Service official slogan: 'Confronts Offending'
19. Avon and Somerset Probation Service official slogan: 'Enforcement, Rehabilitation and Public Protection'
20. 'Justice system unfair to the black population', *Bristol Evening Post*, 17 August 1990
21. 'Information on amounts spent by probation management on gender awareness training provided anonymously by a serving probation officer, 2001
22. 'Probation officers wrap up pair of naked angels', *Telegraph*, 27 October 1990; 'Naked angels go under cover in sexist storm', *Western Daily Press*, 27 October 1990

23. 'Bridlington bristles at race snub', *Telegraph*, 9 October 1993
24. 'Drug dealer is offered pay out', *Sunday Times*, 22 May 1994
25. P. Coad, *NAPO and Political Correctness: Criminal Justice Fact & Fiction*, Briefing document by the Criminal Justice Association, June 2001
26. 'Magistrate criticises advisory role for thief', *Telegraph*, 1 January 1997
27. 'Why do we need a public relations officer?' Internal Probation Service document, 2 December 1996
28. 'Information on drug use in probation hostels provided anonymously by a serving probation officer, July 2002
29. Association of Chief Probation Officers (ACOP), 'Campaign "set to ignore social aspects"', *Probation Matters*, February 1992
30. 'Blunkett crime blitz will swamp prisons', *The Times*, 2 July 2001
31. 'Good Practice Standards in Report Writing', Internal Probation Service document, 1990
32. 'Custody Codes/Dual Sentencing process', Internal Probation Service document, 1989
33. 'Court documentation providing (anonymous) example of lenient recommendation for dangerous offender, March 1996
34. 'The wheels of justice', *Daily Mail*, 1 January 1998
35. 'The Probation Order in ACOP Policy', Internal document by the Association of Chief Officers of Probation, 26 June 1987
36. H. Kemshall, 'Quality in Probation: Getting it Right First Time?', Vista: *Perspectives in Probation, 2:1, May 1996*
37. *Offender Assessment and Supervision Planning: Helping to Achieve Effective Intervention with Offenders*, Report by HM Inspector of Probation, 1999
38. 'The battle Labour's still losing', *Daily Mail*, 13 October 1999; 'The probation fiasco', *Daily Mail*, 29 September 1999; 'Probation cheats who mock the law', *Daily Mail*, 11 September 1998
39. 'Probation is too soft, says Straw', *The Times*, 23 July 1999
40. 'Straw plans to privatise probation', *Independent*, 13 September 1999
41. 'Probation failure as thousands flout orders', *Daily Mail*, 12 April 2000

42. *Ibid.*
43. 'Middle classes failed by the law', *Daily Mail*, 11 January 2001
44. 'Chief constable snubs Blunkett's crime-cutting targets', *Independent*, 3 March 2003
45. 'Crime detection rates fall as burglary and car crime rise', *Independent*, 22 October 2003
46. 'One million attacks a year as violence rises again', *Independent*, 5 April 2003
47. 'Not enough is being done to protect us', *Sunday Mirror*, 28 September 2003
48. 'Armed police operations in city up by a third over last year', *Bristol Evening Post*, 3 February 2004
49. 'Gun crime has doubled since Labour took office', *Telegraph*, 17 October 2003
50. 'Mourners witness the cost of gun crime', *The Times*, 6 October 2003
51. 'Street crime: police give in', *Daily Express*, 22 April 2002
52. D. Green, *Forces of Law and Order Have Lost Control*, London, Civitas, 2002
53. D. Green, *Reducing Crime: Does Prison Work?*, London, Civitas, 2003
54. *The 1998 British Crime Survey, England & Wales*, Home Office Statistical Bulletin, Issue 21/98
55. Information obtained during interview with victim of house burglary, Summer 1999
56. 'The police paper trail', *Independent*, 28 March 2000
57. D. Green, *Forces of Law and Order Have Lost Control*
58. N. Dennis, G. Erdos and D. Robinson, *The Failure of Britain's Police Force: London and New York Compared*, London, Civitas, 2002
59. Home Office Research Paper 217, *The Economic and Social Costs of Crime*, 2000; Home Office Digest 4, *Information on the Criminal Justice System in England & Wales*, 1999
60. 'No sign of police to help catch thief', *Bristol Evening Post*, 21 February 2003
61. 'Straw focuses on repeat offenders', *Financial Times*, 1 February 2001
62. 'We are overrun by gun crime, says police chief', *Telegraph*, 10 October 2003
63. Information obtained from an interview with member of Bristol

University staff, concerning the police response to the robbery of a student, 12 December 2002

64. 'Yobs banned for terror reign', *Sunday Mirror*, 28 September 2003
65. 'Street crime: police give in', *Daily Express*
66. 'No wonder the police are sickened by society's ills', *Mail on Sunday*, 21 December 1997
67. *Ibid.*
68. 'Internal probation service memo concerning the secondment of police officer to local criminal justice scheme, April 2001
69. *Evaluating the Effectiveness of Operation ARC (Addressing Repeat Criminality)*, Report prepared for the Avon and Somerset Constabulary, Exeter University, February 2001
70. 'Thieves told don't bother with city car parks', *Bristol Evening Post*, 4 November 2002
71. 'Police start round up of city's suspects', *Bristol Evening Post*, 11 March 2003
72. 'Police Notice – Crime Crackdown', note issued by Avon and Somerset Constabulary to local Neighbourhood Watch organisers, February 2000
73. 'Scheme aims to reduce number of muggings and break-ins', *Bristol Evening Post*, 2 October 2003, and 'Operation Relentless' – details contained in a letter from a chief constable, June 2005
74. 'Persistent offenders are facing crackdown', *Bristol Evening Post*, 17 October 2002
75. 'Police need to get priorities right – and fast', *Bristol Evening Post*, 1 April 2003
76. 'Traffic police given monthly fine targets', *Sunday Times*, 11 May 2003
77. 'Drivers shell out £4 million in speed camera fines', *Bristol Evening Post*, 2 October 2003
78. 'Police chiefs reject Tory tough line', *Sunday Times*, 28 July 1996
79. 'Cost of youth crime would provide 100 new hospitals a year', *Daily Mail*, 26 July 1997
80. 'Police leader casts doubt on zero tolerance', *Sunday Telegraph*, 19 October 1997
81. 'Police chiefs back plea for social improvements', *Independent*, 13 May 1995
82. 'Police chiefs reject Tory tough line', *Sunday Times*

83. *Ibid.*
84. *Ibid.*
85. 'Less politics, more policing', says chief, *Telegraph*, 9 June 2000
86. 'Criminal', *Daily Mail*, 12 October 1998
87. 'Less politics, more policing, says chief', *Telegraph*, 9 June 2000
88. 'Prison chiefs and police in jail split', *Guardian*, 10 March 1998
89. 'Devon and Cornwall Police hand out welcome packs to convicted criminals', *Plymouth Herald*, 13 October 2003
90. 'The criminal justice system should not be politicised', *Independent*, 9 October 2003
91. 'Internal probation documents relating to New Adult Cautioning Policy introduced by Avon and Somerset Police, November 1989
92. 'Give addicts free heroin, says chief constable', *Independent*, 4 February 2002
93. See, for example, 'Police crime figures pure rubbish', *The Times*, 26 January 2000; 'Crime cover up', *Bristol Observer*, 12 November 1993; 'Police launch inquiry into clear-up rates', *Independent*, 4 December 2002
94. 'Assaults on police up by 10%', *Bristol Evening Post*, 17 October 2002
95. *Comparison of BCS Crime Figures with Crimes Recorded by the Police, 1999–2000*, Intelligence and Security Committee Annual Report
96. D. Green, *Crime Is Falling Because Prison Works*, London, Civitas, 2003
97. 'The Government says crime has fallen. Why doesn't it feel like that'? *Independent on Sunday*, 20 July 2003
98. D. Green, *Do the Official Crime Figures Tell the Full Story?* Background Briefing Paper, Civitas, Institute for the Study of Civil Society, 2003
99. For example, 'Crime levels lower than much of UK', *Cornish Guardian*, 25 September 2003; 'Crime report', *Sunday Mirror*, 28 September 2003
100. *'Victim Survey Covering 12–16 year olds*, NOP research carried out for Victim Support and Direct Line Home Insurance, February 2003

101. D. Green, *Do the Official Crime Figures Tell the Full Story?*
102. *Ibid.*
103. *Horizons*, official publication of the Office for National Statistics, September 2002
104. 'Violent crime rises by 20%', *Bristol Evening Post*, 17 July 2003
105. 'Boss's fears over street crime', *Bristol Evening Post*, 5 November 2002
106. 'Crime detection rates fall as burglary and car crime rise', *Independent*
107. Home Office Research Paper 217
108. 'I bet I'll offend again', *The Times*, 16 November 1998
109. 'Drugs scheme slashed crime, says research', *Guardian*, 16 March 1998
110. Home Office (Janus Studies), *The Offender's Tale*, Version 2, August 1992; Home Office (Janus Studies), *The Offenders' Index*, 4th edn, July 1994
111. 'Tackling persistent offenders is the key to improving effectiveness of the criminal justice system', Home Office Press Release, January 2001; 'Now the liberal elite wants criminals on our streets', *Telegraph*, 1 February 2001
112. '25 per cent of youths are revealed to be criminals', reported in the *Telegraph*, 26 January 2005
113. Home Office Research Paper 217, 2000
114. 'Town's anti-crime strategy leads way', *Telegraph*, 17 February 1995
115. 'Probation case notes (anonymous) illustrating time and money wasting in court procedures dealing with persistent offenders 2001/2, provided anonymously by serving probation officer
116. 'Cost of youth crime would provide 100 new hospitals a year', *Daily Mail*
117. 'British Bench struggles to keep up with crime wave', *The Times*, 16 February 2001
118. 'Discontent that may force many JPs to quit', *Telegraph*, 14 July 2000
119. 'Why our JP system is a jewel of democracy', *The Times*, 9 January 2001
120. 'Meet the young offender, soon to be burgling a house near you', *Telegraph*, 5 March 2002

Chapter 10

1. T. Keneally, *The Playmaker*, London, Hodder & Stoughton, 1987
2. 'Curfew options cheaper than prison', *Sunday Telegraph*, 18 May 1997
3. 'Carey attacks prison revenge', *Telegraph*, 10 May 1996
4. 'Crunch the crooks, say the poor', *Sunday People*, 18 October 1998
5. Discussion on the restoration of peace and justice in Bosnia, following the wars between the former states of Yugoslavia, *Today*, Radio 4, 17 May 2003
6. D. Faulkner, 'A Welcome Attempt at Penal Reform But Watch the Small Print', *The Magistrate*, p. 237, September 2001
7. Home Office Statistical Bulletin, Issue 21/98, *The 1998 British Crime Survey, England & Wales*
8. 'Blunkett crime blitz will swamp prisons', *The Times*, 2 July 2002
9. Response of the Association of Chief Officers of Probation to the Crime Sentences Bill 1997, 6 February 1997
10. 'Court attacked for bailing man who went on to murder', *Independent*, 11 June 1992
11. 'Conman jailed for 600 raids in just 18 months', *The Times*, 8 February 2003
12. 'The good thing about prison is that it protects innocent people from villains like you', *Daily Mail*, 12 July 1997
13. 'Assault and Affray', *Justice of the Peace*, vol. 165, p. 550, 14 July 2001
14. 'Café boss looks for justice', *Bristol Observer*, 11 December 1992
15. 'Letter to the *Telegraph*, from Peter Coad, director of the Criminal Justice Association, 3 March 1997
16. 'Boy 11 freed over death of granny, 93', *Daily Mirror*, 2 December 1992
17. 'Judges are told to spare the muggers', *Daily Mail*, 10 April 2003
18. 'Correspondence with William Waldegrave, MP, from local constituent writing about burglary in their area and of their home, 8 April 1991
19. 'My 200 raids in six months', *Bristol Evening Post*, 20 November 1991

20. 'Martin stays in jail', *Daily Express*, 17 January 2003; 'Tony Martin denied parole because of public support', *Sunday Telegraph*, 26 January 2003
21. 'The final insult', *Daily Mail*, 14 May 2003
22. Home Office Bulletin 1/03, *Crime in England & Wales, 2001/2002*
23. 'Justice system is failing victims of crime, says public', *The Times*, 10 January 2003
24. 'Yard chief: justice system is appalling', *Independent*, 7 March 2002
25. 'A day in the life of British justice: witness too scared to testify and a violent man walks free', *Independent*, 8 March 2002
26. 'Sharp fall in offenders to face courts', *Independent*, 18 October 2002
27. Home Office, *Prison Statistics England & Wales 2000*
28. Avon and Somerset Constabulary Annual Report, 1989
29. 'Yard chief: justice system is appalling', *Independent*
30. 'Crime: is anyone safe out there?' *Independent*, 21 June 1995
31. Home Office Statistical Bulletin, Issue 21/98
32. 'More criminals than ever don't go to jail', *Mail on Sunday*, 13 July 1997
33. 'Report predicts 40% increase in property crime', *The Times*, 7 June 1999
34. 'Judges go direct to jail in rehabilitation drive', *Independent*, 13 October 2001
35. 'Custody is for the convicted', *Telegraph*, 27 December 2001; 'Reporting from inside Parliament', *Prophecy Today*, 12:13, May 1996
36. 'Going straight isn't as easy as it sounds', *Independent*, 2 July 2002; 'Give ex-prisoners more money, says No. 10 poverty unit', *Independent*, 3 July 2002
37. Undercover investigation into Anti-Social Behaviour Orders, BBC 1, 5 November 2003 and 'ASBOOM', *Daily Mirror*, 2 March 2005
38. Home Office, *National Standards for the Probation Service: Required Levels of Contact, Achieving Compliance and Ensuring Enforcement*, 2003
39. 'Correspondence with MP from a local constituent complaining about crime 30 August 1991
40. 'The fear on our streets', *Daily Mail*, 1 March 1988
41. 'Crime hits record level as burglaries increase by 21%', *Independent*, 28 March 1991

42. 'Crime: the battle Britain is losing', *Daily Mirror*, 23 January 1992
43. 'It's a crime', *Bristol West Challenger*, Winter 1993; 'We cannot cope without more officers, say police', *Telegraph*, 14 May 2001; 'Can the thin blue line stop street criminals?' *Telegraph*, 14 May 2001
44. 'Most crime is now worse here than in America', *The Mail on Sunday*, 11 October 1998
45. 'Attacker sentenced', *Bristol Evening Post*, 30 October 2001
46. 'Keep non-contact burglars out of jail, say LibDems', *Daily Mail*, 23 September 2003
47. B. Lawrence, *They Call It Justice*, Lewes, The Book Guild Ltd, 1998
48. *Ibid.*
49. Radio 4 news item, 27 November 2002
50. 'Jail inmates call for a chance to preserve family life', *Independent*, 25 May 1991
51. 'Blunders by the CPS let one in ten go free', *Financial Times*, 16 September 1999
52. 'One home in Britain is burgled every 37 seconds', Neighbourhood Watch Leaflet, 2003
53. Home Office, *Criminal Statistics England and Wales, 2000/01*
54. '90% of crimes go unpunished', *Daily Mirror*, 20 January 2003
55. 'Prison does not work. We know that', *Guardian*, 2 January 2001
56. 'Families of Holly and Jessica entitled to just £11,000 damages', *Independent*, 2 February 2004; 'Just £11,000 each for the lives of Holly and Jessica', *Daily Mail*, 2 February 2004
57. *Ibid.*
58. *Ibid.*
59. 'Victims losing out', *Daily Star*, 19 October 1998
60. Interview with victim of attempted car theft, 24 December 2003
61. Information obtained from Southmead Police Station (Bristol) identifying the areas covered by them, January 2004
62. *Population by Age for Wards in Bristol*, 2001 Census Key Statistics
63. 'War on crime is taking off', *Bristol Evening Post*, 28 January 2004
64. 'Blair fails to convince public that he is tough on crime', *Daily Telegraph*, 11 January 2003

65. 'Shelters smashed' and 'Police in raids on fake DVD factory', *Bristol Evening Post*, 28 January 2004
66. 'Anarchy taking over the streets', *Daily Mirror*, 16 May 2000
67. Home Office, *Criminal Statistics England & Wales 2000/01*
68. 'The Dumbing Down of the Lord Chief Justice', Paper by the Criminal Justice Association, January 2002
69. *Ibid.*
70. C. Murray, *Does Prison Work?*, Choice in Welfare Series No. 38, IEA Health & Welfare Unit, p. 22, 1997
71. 'Bring the outs in', *Independent Tabloid*, 12 March 1997
72. 'House of Commons Home Affairs Select Committee, *Report on Alternatives to Prison* (minutes of evidence and appendices), Vol. 2, 28 July 1998
73. *Ibid.*, pp. 86–7
74. *Ibid.*, p. 94
75. *Ibid.*, p. 87
76. *Ibid.*, p. 166
77. *Ibid.*, p. 9
78. *Ibid.*, p. 4
79. *Ibid.*, p. 250
80. Home Office, *Prison Statistics England & Wales 1999*, 2000
81. 'Letter from Chief Inspector of Probation to the All Party Home Affairs Committee investigating non-custodial sentences, 23 January 1998
82. 'Evaluation by Professor Ken Pease of Andrew Underdown's report, *Strategies for Effective Offender Supervision*, 20 April 1998 (correspondence); 'House of Commons Home Affairs Select Committee, *Report on Alternatives to Prison*, Vol. 2, p. 210
83. 'House of Commons Home Affairs Select Committee, *Report on Alternatives to Prison*, Vol. 2, p. 205
84. *Ibid.*, p. 205; 'Prison not working as cure for crime, say MPs', *Telegraph*, 11 September 1998
85. House of Commons Home Affairs Select Committee, *Third Report on Alternatives to Prison*, Vol. 1, pp. 210–212, 28 July 1998
86. *Alternatives to Prison*, Government reply to the Third Report from the Home Affairs Committee session, HC486, p. 24, 1997–8
87. P. Coad, ' "They Got it Wrong": A Critique of the Home Affairs Committee Report on Alternatives to Prison', Criminal Justice Association paper, 1998

88. 'To imprison or not to imprison', *Independent*, 18 September 1998
89. 'The quest for rigorous alternatives to prison', an interview with Home Affairs Committee Chairman Chris Mullin, *Social Services Parliamentary Monitor*, 26 May 1998
90. P. Coad, 'Analysis of the Report of the Home Affairs Select Committee Considering Alternatives To Prison Sentences', Paper by the director of the Criminal Justice Association, December 1998
91. Letter to Peter Coad, Director of the Criminal Justice Association, from Robin Corbett MP, member of the All Party Home Affairs Committee reporting on alternatives to prison, 3 November 1998
92. Debate in the House of Commons on the report of the All Party Home Affairs Committee on alternatives to prison', Hansard, p. 504, 10 December 1998

Chapter 11

1. 'Judge rues giving burglar a chance', *Telegraph*, 7 November 1998
2. 'A burglary every 30 minutes', *Bristol Evening Post*, 9 February 1993
3. Home Office, *Prison Statistics England & Wales 2000*; P. Coad, 'Rising Crime', Unpublished research paper by the Criminal Justice Association, June 2002
4. Lord Derwent, 'Justice in mandatory sentences', letter to *The Times*, 18 February 1997
5. *Ibid.*
6. P. Coad, 'Mandatory sentences', 2nd edn, Research paper by the Criminal Justice Association, 2000
7. P. Coad, 'Mandatory Sentences: Putting the Record Straight', Research Paper by the Criminal Justice Association, July 1997
8. *Ibid.*
9. Lord Derwent, 'Justice in mandatory sentences'
10. Coad, 'Rising Crime'
11. *Ibid.*
12. Lord Derwent, 'Justice in mandatory sentences'; Coad, 'Mandatory Sentences'

13. 'The Lords aren't soft on crime, just sensible', *The Times*, 17 February 1997
14. P. Coad, 'Mandatory Sentences', Letter to *The Times*, 17 February 1997
15. 'Public opinion on criminal justice', *The Times*, 19 February 1997
16. 'Three strikes and you are out (of jail, that is)', *Daily Mirror*, 2 February 2003; 'Burglars who still laugh at the law', *Daily Mail*, 28 December 2000
17. Home Office, *Cautions, Court Proceedings and Sentencing 20/01, England & Wales 2000*, 2001
18. Coad, 'Rising Crime'
19. 'Burglars who still laugh at the law', *Daily Mail*
20. 'Three strikes rule fails to jail a single burglar', *Mail on Sunday*, 2 June 2002
21. 'Judges thwart policy on persistent burglars', *Independent*, 31 January 2001
22. Home Office *Prison Statistics England & Wales 2000*
23. L. James, 'Justice Without Retribution', *Justice of the Peace*, 161, pp. 502–3, 24 May 1997
24. Details provided by serving probation officer, 2000
25. Crown court documentation
26. 'Bingham in plea over murder sentences', *Independent*, 14 March 1998; 'Murder shouldn't always mean life says Bingham', *Daily Mail*, 14 March 1998
27. 'Howard's way won't do, warns top judge', *Daily Express*, 11 November 1996
28. 'Bingham attacks politically driven justice reforms', *The Times*, 15 March 1997
29. 'Custody is for the convicted', *Telegraph*, 27 December 2001; 'Reporting from Inside Parliament', *Prophecy Today*, 12:13, May 1996
30. 'Taylor renews attack against sentence plans', *Independent*, 13 April 1996
31. 'Reporting from Inside Parliament', *Prophecy Today*
32. 'Referee kicked unconscious by player after showing him red card', *The Times*, 17 February 1999
33. P. Coad, 'Mandatory Sentences: Putting the Record Straight'
34. 'Courts get guidance on prison sentences', *Telegraph*, 10 August 1998

35. P. Coad, An Analysis of Lord Bingham's Guidelines on Sentencing, Criminal Justice Association paper, p. 1, 1998
36. 'Courts get guidance on prison sentences', *Telegraph*, 10 August 1998
37. 'Chief Justice attacks prison as Straw plans to jail more', *Telegraph*, 1 February 2001
38. *Ibid.*
39. 'Lord Woolf is right to set James Bulger's killers free', *Independent*, 27 October 2000
40. 'Letter to Rt. Hon. Gerald Howarth MP from Stevanne Hill, LLB, Dip.Psych., Dip.REBT
41. 'Probation for teenager after horrific assault', *Independent*, 1 April 1994
42. 'Burglar's poetry defended by judge', *The Times*, 8 February 2003
43. An interview with the judge who sentenced Roy Whiting, the killer of Sarah Payne, *Today*, BBC Radio 4, 16 December 2001
44. '25 years for drug dealer who shot police', *Independent*, 10 February 1995
45. Cited in H. Phillips, *The Constitutional Law of Great Britain and the Commonwealth*, London, Sweet & Maxwell, 1952
46. 'Probation Works – and Everyone Benefits', Paper produced by the Association of Chief Officers of Probation, 1994
47. 'An interview with Britain's most senior judge', *Daily Mail*, 1 August 2002
48. 'Jail mobile phone thieves, says law chief', *Independent*, 30 January 2002
49. 'Woolf denies his guidelines were burglar's charter', *Telegraph*, 15 January 2003
50. 'Keep the criminals out of prison', *Daily Mail*, 11 July 1997
51. Quoted in 'Drug care order meets Appeal Court guidelines', *Telegraph*, 4 January 2003
52. *Ibid.*
53. 'Lord Woolf to clarify burglary ruling again', *Telegraph*, 14 January 2003; 'Try telling a New Yorker that burglary doesn't matter', *Telegraph*, 22 January 2003
54. 'Woolf denies his guidelines were burglar's charter', *Telegraph*
55. Statement by Lord Irwin, Radio 4, 6 January 2003
56. 'Why many criminals should be spared jail, Lord Woolf', *Daily Mail*, 17 April 2003

57. 'Woolf denies his guidelines were burglar's charter', *Telegraph*
58. *Ibid.*
59. 'Public is endangered by judicial leniency', *Telegraph*, 13 January 2003
60. Quoted in 'Drug Care Orders meets Appeal Court guidelines', *Telegraph*, 4 January 2003
61. 'Are the scales of justice weighted in favour of the burglars?' *Bristol Evening Post*, 5 February 2003
62. 'Serial burglar is spared jail by new ruling', *Telegraph*, 4 January 2003
63. 'Downfall of the Mayfair burglar', *Telegraph*, 7 February 2003
64. 'Are the scales of justice weighted in favour of the burglars?' *Bristol Evening Post*
65. 'Custody for the convicted', *Telegraph*
66. 'Jail mobile phone thieves, says law chief', *Independent*
67. 'We still fail our prisons', *The Times*, 1 February 2001
68. 'Jail more criminals Straw tells judges', *Daily Mail*, 1 February 2001
69. 'Public's harsh sentence on judges', *Guardian*, 6 January 1998
70. 'PR men to give soft judges an image booster', *Daily Mail*, 6 January 1998
71. 'Judge frees offender who admits: I might attack again', *Express*, 31 March 1999
72. Information supplied by a serving probation officer, October 1999
73. 'Jailed Iraqi to get payout for blunder', *Telegraph*, 16 January 2004
74. 'An interview with Britain's most senior judge', *Daily Mail*
75. P. Coad, 'The Dumbing Down of the Lord Chief Justice', Criminal Justice Association paper, January 2002

Chapter 12

1. 'Child-abuse victims can sue councils, says EU', *Independent*, 6 November 1999
2. *Human Rights Act: Building the Culture of Rights and Responsibilities*, Letter from acting Permanent Secretary John Warne to Sir Richard Wilson KCB (Secretary of the Cabinet and Head of the Home Civil Service) and all permanent Secretaries, 9 April 2001

3. 'When is a human right not a human right?' *The Times*, 25 January 2000
4. 'Prisoners given extra days in jail to go free', *Independent*, 27 July 2002
5. *Ibid.*
6. 'Justice under fire', *Telegraph*, 12 October 2000
7. *Ibid.*
8. S. Eysenck, *'Mentally Disordered Individuals in the Prison System'*, *Justice of the Peace*, pp. 265–6, 25 April 1987
9. 'Growing murder toll of mentally unstable monsters in our midst', *Sunday Express*, 12 September 2004
10. *Your Rights: Information for Programme Participants*, Probation Service literature explaining the rights of offenders attending community supervision programmes, 2000
11. 'Criminal's right to sue fundamental say reform groups', *Independent*, 29 June 2001
12. 'Correspondence with the Law Commission concerning criminals' right to sue, 9 December 2003
13. 'Lord Lester of Herne Hill and D. Pannick, *Human Rights Law and Practice*, London and Croydon, Butterworths Tolley, March 2000
14. *Today*, Radio 4, 13 January 2005
15. 'Human rights gone mad', *Bristol Evening Post*, 4 February 2003
16. 'The killer who won his case of unfair dismissal', *Daily Mail*, 3 April 2003
17. 'Burgled 192 times', *Daily Express*, 20 May 2003
18. *Today*, BBC Radio 4, 25 June 2003
19. Letter from Ron Lewis, former senior probation officer, 15 February 2000
20. D. Green, 'Forces of Law and Order Have Lost Control', London, Civitas, 2002
21. 'Car park horror stories haunt women motorists', *Bristol Evening Post*, 10 June 1997
22. 'Drive to cut car crime with lessons for motorists', *Glasgow Herald*, 8 September 1999
23. Home Office and Central Office of Information, *Practical Ways to Crack Crime: The Family Guide*, 2nd edn, 1991; *Let's Close the Door on Burglary Boom*, Survey by the Woolwich Building Society, 1995; *A Checklist of Suspicious Incidents*, Pamphlet

issued by Neighbourhood Watch; Home Office Communications Directorate, *Steer Clear of Crime: Security Tips for Motorists*, 1995; *Your Guide to a Safer Home*, Home security booklet issued by British Gas

24. Home Office, 'Practical Ways to Crack Crime: The Family Guide', 2nd edn, p. 16, 1991
25. 'ID Cards may be Blair's plastic poll tax', *Telegraph*, 8 September 2003
26. 'The MORI poll on ID Cards, commissioned by Detica, April 2004

Chapter 13

1. 'The victims of crime', *Evening Standard*, 23 September 1998
2. Home Office, *British Crime Survey 2001/2*
3. 'Attacks on nurses awful dimension', *Telegraph*, 8 July 1992; 'Don't be a nurse, it's too dangerous', *Daily Mail*, 8 May 1991
4. 'Low-level crime creates climate for violence', *Independent*, 20 October 1998
5. 'Nearly everyone thinks they will be a victim of crime', *Daily Mirror*, 4 June 1999
6. 'Shops lose £1,000 a week to smugglers', *Sun*, 24 September 1999
7. 'Action needed to prevent prisoners writing to victims', *Police Review*, p. 16, 29 May 1998
8. 'Shop staff suffer as robbers seek easier targets', *The Times*, 19 February 1998
9. 'Alarm in huge rise in street crime and thefts', *Independent*, 12 July 2002; 'New figures reveal big jump in street robberies', *Sunday Times*, 14 January 2001
10. 'Burglary every minute: crooks soak the poor: average crook aged 15', *Daily Mirror*, 30 August 1991
11. *The 1998 British Crime Survey, England & Wales*, Home Office Statistical Bulletin, Issue 21/98
12. 'Burgled sixty-three times in seven years', *Daily Mirror*, 27 November 1991
13. 'Repeat Victimisation: Implications for the Probation Service', *Vista*, Perspectives on Probation, p. 31, May 1995
14. '£90,000 to tackle repeat burglaries', *Bristol Advertiser*, 3 December 1999

15. For example, M.K. Shaw, 'Fear of Crime in Greater Manchester: The Relative Importance of Repeat Victimisation and Gender', Unpublished Ph.D thesis, Manchester University, Department of Geography, 1997; M. Shaw, 'The Bereavement Process and Repeated Crime Victimisation', in G. Farrell and K. Pease, eds, *Repeat Victimisation*, New York, Willow Tree Press, 2000; J. Ditton et al., 'Afraid or Angry? Re-calibrating the Fear of Crime', *International Review of Victimology*, 1999; G. Farrell and K. Pease, 'Repeat Victim Support', *British Journal of Social Work*, 27, pp. 101–13, 1997
16. 'Violence, hatred and theft', *Daily Mirror*, 15 April 1991
17. 'Victims who live in terror', *Daily Mirror*, 28 November 1990
18. 'You've been burgled. You a) panic, b) call the police. Now you can c) call in your personal incident manager', *Independent*, 10 June 1995
19. 'Car thieves strike every eight seconds', *Express*, 29 September 1997
20. 'An interview by the author with a victim of car theft, 1999
21. 'The gunman caused my mother years of upset', *Bristol Evening Post*, 30 December 2003
22. 'Justice system is failing victims of crime, says public', *The Times*, 10 January 2003
23. 'Britain: A Society in Fear of Criminals', *Readers Digest*, Vol. 132, April 1988
24. *Ibid.*
25. '£20,000 to catch thief', *Daily Mirror*, 23 June 2002
26. 'I looked up and my blood ran cold', *Independent*, 6 July 1992
27. 'Insensitive police add to stress of burglary', *Independent*, 25 February 1994
28. *Ibid.*
29. 'Victims count on us', *Bristol Evening Post*, 7 October 2002
30. 'Victims are scarred for ever', *Bristol Observer*, 7 November 2002
31. 'You've been burgled...', *Independent*
32. P. Coad, 'Rising Crime', Criminal Justice Association briefing paper, 2002
33. Home Office Bulletin 1/03, *Crime in England & Wales, 2001/2002*
34. Paul Boateng's speech to the 'What Works' Conference, Manchester, 20 September 2000; 'Victims to be consulted before prosecution', *Guardian*, 12 October 2000; 'Courts launch

crackdown on offending', *The Times*, 12 October 2000; *New Choreography: The Strategic Framework for the National Probation Service, 2001–2002*, Paper issued to all staff by the Director of the National Probation Service, September 2001

35. *The 1998 British Crime Survey, England & Wales*
36. Paul Boateng's speech to the 'What Works' Conference, 2000
37. Criminal Justice Association correspondence giving details of the failure of probation supervision in relation to Paul Beart, 13 November 2001
38. An example provided anonymously by a probation officer of probation and court staff ignoring a victim, November 2001
39. 'Director of the National Probation Service, Eithne Wallis, shares her plans and aspirations', *The Probation Manager*, July 2001
40. 'My mother has been mugged by the system', *Telegraph*, 23 October 1999
41. 'Priority pledge to crime victims by David Waddington', *Bristol Evening Post*, 4 March 1990
42. 'Nobody told me my husband was a convicted rapist', *The Mirror Magazine*, 22 June 2002
43. 'Courts attacker had been jailed for murder', *Independent*, 23 January 2002
44. 'Is the system unfriendly to victims?', *Police*, 31:4, April 1999
45. 'Victims to be consulted before prosecution', *Guardian*
46. 'More support for victims is promised', *Independent*, 22 March 2002
47. 'Ombuds and Upwards', *Prison Service News*, 18:188, May 2000; United Nations, Department of Public Information, *Standard Minimum Rules for the Treatment of Prisoners, and Procedures for the Effective Implementation of the Rules*, New York, 1984
48. 'Law fails victims of crime', *The Times*, 25 February 2000; 'Insensitive police add stress to burglary', *Independent*
49. 'Courts must be safer for crime victims', *Telegraph*, 14 January 2002
50. 'Violence, hatred and theft', *Daily Mirror*
51. *Ibid.*
52. 'Kathleen's stand', *Bristol Evening Post*, 15 May 2003
53. 'This is what a burglar did to Edith, aged 87', *Telegraph*, 5 September 2000

54. 'Cowardly criminals single out vulnerable victims', *Western Daily Press*, 12 December 1991
55. 'It could be your gran next', *Daily Star*, 24 September 1992
56. 'Thugs in school caps', *Bristol Evening Post*, 4 September 1992
57. 'Cowardly criminals single out vulnerable victims', *Western Daily Press*
58. *Ibid.*
59. 'Burglary provoked fatal heart attack', *Bristol Observer*, 21 February 1992
60. 'Boy 11 freed over death of granny, 93', *Daily Mirror*, 2 December 1992
61. 'Burglars left widow so afraid she killed herself', *Telegraph*, 30 May 1996
62. 'Burglar blamed for elderly pair's death', *Independent*, 25 August 1993
63. 'Mugging victim hanged himself', *Telegraph*, 25 April 1991
64. 'Tragedy of a crime victim', *Western Daily Press*, 17 October 1992
65. 'Crimes of envy that do not stop short of death', *Sunday Telegraph*, 24 May 1992; H. Schoeck, *A Theory of Social Behaviour*, Harcourt, 1970
66. Home Office Bulletin 1/03, *Crime in England & Wales, 2001/2002*; 'Tories say Government has gone soft on crime', *Bristol Evening Post*, 12 February 2004; 'Alarm in huge rise in street crime and thefts', *Independent*
67. Home Office Bulletin 1/03, *Crime in England & Wales, 2001/2002*; Home Office, *British Crime Survey 2001/2*
68. *The 1998 British Crime Survey, England & Wales*; 'Tories say Government has gone soft on crime', *Bristol Evening Post*
69. 'Lenient JPs want to help', *Bristol Evening Post*, 8 August 2001
70. 'Crooks owe £3 million in fines', *Bristol Evening Post*, 6 November 2003
71. 'Sentencing Advisory Panel, Sentencing for Domestic Burglary: A Consultation Document', *Justice of the Peace*, Vol. 165, pp. 236–43, 31 March 2001; Home Office, *Cautions, Court Proceedings and Sentencing 20/01, England & Wales 2000*, 2001
72. 'Prison works, so build more prisons', *Telegraph*, 23 February 2004
73. *The 1998 British Crime Survey, England & Wales*
74. Home Office Statistical Bulletin, Issue 19/99, *Reconvictions of*

Offenders Sentenced or Discharged from Prison in 1995, England & Wales 25/10/99; P. Raynor and M. Vanstone, *STOP Programme for Offenders, Third Interim Evaluation Report*, Glamorgan Probation Service, 1994; J. Roberts, *Discovering What Works*, Hereford & Worcester Probation Service, Young Offender Project (1984–9), 1994; J. Wilkinson and D. Morgan, *The Impact of Ilderton Motor Project on Motor Vehicle Crime & Offending*, Inner London & Probation Service, April 1995; 'A Cognitive Therapy Programme Run by the Inner London Probation Service', *Probation*, Issue No. 20, November 1997; G. McIvor and M. Barry, Crime & Criminal Justice Research Findings No. 50, *Social Work and Criminal Justice: The Longer-term Impact of Supervision*, University of Sterling, 2000; Home Office Research Study 218, *Employment and Crime: Working Their Way Out of Offending*, 2001; A.E. Bottoms, *Intensive Community Supervision for Young Offenders: Outcomes, Process & Cost*, Cambridge, Institute of Criminology Publications, 1995

75. Home Office Circular 63/1996, *Guidance for Use of OGRS, Prediction of Re-offending Scale*
76. Home Office Digest 4, *Information on the Criminal Justice System in England & Wales*, 1999; Home Office Research Paper 217, *The Economic and Social Costs of Crime*, 2000

Chapter 14

1. 'Top cop calls for Victims Charter to stamp out mob rule on our streets', *Daily Mirror*, 19 February 1993
2. 'Man stabbed intruder after 18 break-ins', *Telegraph*, 31 July 1992
3. 'Villager pays for revenge on bikers', *Telegraph*, 17 July 1992
4. 'Business man is cleared of killing suspected vandal', *Independent*, 17 December 1992
5. 'Village vigilantes drive out tearaway teenager', *Daily Mirror*, 7 May 1992
6. 'You were quite right to kill a burglar', 16 June 1994
7. 'Criminals move in as the village bobbies move out', *Sunday Telegraph*, 29 August 1999
8. 'Police are abandoning villages to criminals', *Daily Mail*, 30 August 1999

9. 'Farmer cleared of shooting intruder outside his home, *Independent*, 1 July 2002
10. 'Within the law', *Daily Mail*, 7 December 2002
11. 'Burglar branded with coat hanger in revenge attack', *Telegraph*, 6 January 2001
12. 'Parliamentary Debates (Hansard) House of Lords Official Report, 577:44, Monday 27 January 1997
13. 'Shop owners demand zero tolerance crime policy', *Independent*, 6 July 2002
14. 'Law chief seeks to let victims down gently', *Sunday Telegraph*, 21 June 1992; 'Soaring crime gives rise to urban vigilantes', *Sunday Telegraph*, 14 June 1992
15. *Afraid or Angry? Recalibrating the Fear of Crime*, Research paper from University of Sheffield, 1999
16. 'Fear of crime can cripple lives', *Independent*, 13 March 1989
17. 'Make burglars feel the pinch', *Daily Mirror*, 12 September 1990
18. *2000 AD*, Fleetway Publications, 25 March 1989
19. 'National Probation Service Bulletin and HMIP, *Victims Report*, 113/03
20. Home Office, *Restorative Justice: An Overview*, 1999
21. *Ibid.*; K. Roach, 'Changing Punishment at the Turn of the Century: Restorative Justice on the Rise', *Canadian Journal of Criminology*, pp. 249–80, July 2000
22. J. Dignan, *Repairing the Damage*, University of Sheffield, 1992; S. Warner, *Making Amends*, Aldershot, Avebury, 1993; J. Braithwaite, 'Restorative Justice: Assessing Optimistic and Pessimistic Accounts', *Crime and Justice: A Review of Research*, Vol. 25, Chicago, IL, University of Chicago Press, 1999
23. Home Office, *Restorative Justice*
24. H. McCulloch, *Shop Theft: Improving the Police Response*, Home Office, Police Research Group, Paper 76, 1997
25. Home Office, *Reconviction Study of Thames Valley Restorative Justice Schemes, 1998–2001*
26. 'Face values', *Guardian*, 5 February 1997
27. 'Criminals who offer an apology may escape prosecution', *Telegraph*, 23 July 2003
28. 'No more soft options for young criminals', *Express*, 1 August 1998
29. 'Let's face it', *Guardian*, 17 July 2002
30. 'Sadistic snakes in suits in the office identified by new psychological test', *Independent*, 12 January 2004

Chapter 15

1. 'Lawless Britain', *Telegraph*, 5 January 2002
2. 'Stabbing deaths rise by 20% in 20 years', *The Times*, 4 August 1999
3. 'Crime drives out the talent that Britain needs', *Sunday Times*, 24 March 2002
4. *Ibid.*
5. Audit Commission Report, June 2002
6. 'Fifty per cent of crime not reported', *Police Review*, 15 August 1997
7. 'Cause for Alarm', *NNWA News*, Summer 2002
8. 'Soaring crime gives rise to urban vigilantes', *Sunday Telegraph*, 14 June 1992
9. 'The streets where peace and safety come at a price', *Sunday Telegraph*, 3 February 2002
10. Home Office, *Criminal Justice: The Way Ahead*, 2001
11. 'Crime challenge to civilisation', *Telegraph*, 3 March 1989
12. Professor H.J. Eysenck, 'Causes of, and cures for, criminal behaviour', *Independent*, 24 February 1993
13. 'Britain's yob culture', *Daily Mail*, 22 April 1995
14. 'Getting away with it?' *Bristol Evening Post*, 22 January 2004
15. 'Retribution or Deterrence?', *Justice of the Peace*, Vol. 165, 30 June 2001
16. Home Office, *Offenders' Careers: Risk Profiles of Sentenced Offenders*, 2001
17. J. Morton, 'Lay Down the Law', *Police Review*, p. 25, 7 May 1999; 'Flawed judgment', *Police Review*, p. 16, 30 April 1999
18. Home Office, *Criminal Statistics England & Wales 2000*
19. 'Cash Grants for local crime initiatives', Home Office press release, 26 March 2002
20. 'Prisoners complain about poor service', *Telegraph*, 7 October 2003
21. 'Blunkett thinks big as prison population soars', *Telegraph*, 5 January 2004
22. P. Taylor, *Demanding Physical Activity Programmes*, Sheffield University, 1999
23. 'Blunkett pledges biggest rise in police numbers', *The Times*, 28 June 2001
24. 'Blunkett and Brown clash over policing', *Independent*, 14 April 2004

25. 'MP calls Radio 4 listeners "bastards" over vote', *Independent*, 2 January 2004
26. 'How a minister was muzzled', *Independent*, 19 September 1993
27. F. Snepp, *Decent Interval*, Harmondsworth, Penguin, 1977
28. 'League tables will show where justice is not being done', *Telegraph*, 30 June 2003
29. 'The nine worst prisons are named', *Independent*, 16 September 1997
30. Home Office Research Paper 217, *The Economic and Social Costs of Crime*, 2000

Index

457

Lightning Source UK Ltd.
Milton Keynes UK
UKHW020344260422
402021UK00005B/133